# MICROSOFT POWER PLATFORM SOLUTION ARCHITECT

MASTER THE EXAM (PL-600): 10 PRACTICE TESTS, 500 RIGOROUS QUESTIONS, 475+ EXAM FOCUSED TIPS, 480+ CAUTION ALERTS AND CONCISE EXPLANATIONS.

**ANAND M**
AMEENA PUBLICATIONS

Copyright © 2024 ANAND M
All rights reserved.
ISBN: 9798329416473

# DEDICATION

**To the Visionaries in My Professional Odyssey**

*This book is dedicated to the mentors and leaders who guided me through triumph and adversity in my professional universe. Your guidance has illuminated the path to success and taught me to seize opportunities and surmount obstacles. Thank you for imparting the advice to those who taught me the value of strategic thinking and the significance of innovation to transform obstacles into stepping stones. Your visionary leadership has inspired my creativity and motivated me to forge new paths.*

*Thank you for sharing the best and worst of your experiences with me, kind and severe employers. As I present this book to the world, I am aware that you have been my inspiration. All of your roles as mentors, advisors, and even occasional adversaries have helped me become a better professional and storyteller.*

*This dedication is a tribute to your impact on my journey, a narrative woven with threads of gratitude, introspection, and profound gratitude for the lessons you've inscribed into my story.*

*With deep gratitude and enduring respect,*
**Anand M**

# FROM TECH TO LIFE SKILLS – MY EBOOKS COLLECTION

Dive into my rich collection of eBooks, curated meticulously across diverse and essential domains.

  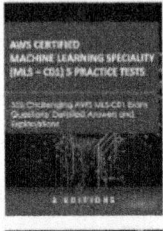 

**Pro Tips and Tricks Series**: Empower yourself with life-enhancing skills and professional essentials with our well-crafted guides.

**Hot IT Certifications and Tech Series**: Stay ahead in the tech game. Whether you're eyeing certifications in AWS, PMP, or prompt engineering, harnessing the power of ChatGPT with tools like Excel, PowerPoint, Word, and more!, we've got you covered!

**Essential Life Skills**: Embark on a journey within. From yoga to holistic well-being, Master the art of culinary, baking, and more delve deep and rediscover yourself.

**Stay Updated & Engaged**
For an entire world of my knowledge, tips, and treasures, follow me on Amazon
**https://www.amazon.com/author/anandm**

**Your Feedback Matters!**
Your support, feedback, and ratings are the wind beneath my wings. It drives me to curate content that brings immense value to every aspect of life. Please take a moment to share your thoughts and rate the books. Together, let's keep the flame of knowledge burning bright!

*Best Regards,*

**ANAND M**

# INTRODUCTION

Welcome to **"MICROSOFT POWER PLATFORM SOLUTION ARCHITECT, MASTER THE EXAM (PL-600): 10 PRACTICE TESTS, 500 RIGOROUS QUESTIONS, 475+ EXAM FOCUSED TIPS, 480+ CAUTION ALERTS, CONCISE EXPLANATIONS."** This eBook is your definitive guide to mastering the PL-600 certification, a crucial milestone for individuals aiming to excel within the sophisticated ecosystem of Microsoft Power Platform.

In the digital era, the Microsoft Power Platform is an essential suite of technologies enabling organizations to analyze data, automate workflows, and develop complex applications with ease. The PL-600 certification denotes a deep understanding of Power Platform solutions and their real-world applications.

Our guide is meticulously structured to enhance your understanding of the Microsoft Power Platform. It covers a wide range of topics, from basic concepts to advanced applications and strategies vital for leveraging Power Platform services effectively. Within these pages, you will find 500 challenging questions designed to test your knowledge and sharpen your problem-solving skills. Detailed explanations accompany each question, providing deep insights into each topic, ensuring you grasp not only the correct answers but also the rationale behind them.

As organizations increasingly rely on Power Platform to propel their digital transformation, expertise in this domain is more crucial than ever. The PL-600 certification prepares professionals like you to excel in roles that optimize business processes, innovate solutions, and perform data analysis within the Power Platform environment.

Here's a brief overview of what the PL-600 exam entails:

**Duration:** The examination lasts 180 minutes, offering an in-depth assessment of your Power Platform knowledge.
**Enrollment Cost:** The exam fee is $165, subject to regional tax variations.
**Exam Format:** The test includes a variety of detailed multiple-choice and multiple-response questions, administered in a professional testing environment.
**Prerequisites:** While prior knowledge of Power Platform fundamentals is beneficial, it is not mandatory. This foundational knowledge can greatly enhance your comprehension of the more advanced concepts covered in the PL-600 exam.

This guide is more than a preparation tool; it is your ally on the journey to becoming a Microsoft Power Platform Solution Architect expert. Crafted to provide strategic insights, comprehensive knowledge, and the confidence needed to excel, it is the ultimate companion for your certification journey.

Embark on your path to becoming a Microsoft Power Platform Solution Architect expert. Let this eBook guide every step of your preparation, helping you achieve your ultimate goal - mastering the PL-600 exam

# ADVANTAGES OF CERTIFICATION

*As you prepare to achieve the Microsoft Power Platform Solution Architect (PL-600) Certification, it's important to understand the significant benefits this credential can offer for your professional growth. Here are the key advantages of earning the PL-600 certification:*

**Established Expertise in Power Platform:** *In today's digital-centric environment, the PL-600 certification sets you apart as an expert in Microsoft Power Platform. This certification is more than a qualification; it's a testament to your deep understanding and skill in leveraging Power Platform to enhance business innovation and efficiency. It showcases your ability to develop solutions that transform and automate business operations.*

**Expanded Career Prospects:** *Earning the PL-600 certification opens up numerous career opportunities in business analysis, solution architecture, and digital strategy. It prepares you for key roles in deploying and managing Power Platform solutions across various business contexts. Professionals with this certification often see significant career progression, moving into more strategic and rewarding positions.*

**Potential for Higher Earnings:** *Certifications generally correlate with higher earning potential. By obtaining the PL-600 certification, you affirm your specialized skills, making you more appealing to employers. Companies actively search for experts in Microsoft Power Platform, positioning you as a sought-after candidate, which can lead to better job offers and salary increases.*

**Elevated Professional Standing:** *In the competitive field of technology, distinguishing yourself is crucial. The PL-600 certification enhances your professional image, making you a prime candidate for both current and future employers. It's not merely about securing a job; it's about setting your career on a trajectory aligned with your long-term goals in business solution architecture and automation.*

**Robust Skill Set:** *Securing the PL-600 certification confirms that you have a comprehensive understanding of the Microsoft Power Platform, encompassing both theoretical knowledge and practical application. This equips you to effectively innovate and optimize business processes, giving you an edge over peers without this specialized certification.*

*In conclusion, the Microsoft Power Platform Solution Architect (PL-600) certification acts as a crucial catalyst for your career in business process automation and solution architecture. It reinforces your standing in the competitive tech landscape and facilitates ongoing professional development and success in leveraging the Power Platform to overcome business challenges.*

# EXAM OBJECTIVE

*Welcome to your guide for the Microsoft PL-600 exam! This certification tests your skills in envisioning, architecting, and implementing solutions using Microsoft Power Platform. Here's a concise overview of the syllabus.*

| Exam Section | Weightage |
|---|---|
| *Perform Solution Envisioning and Requirement Analyses* | *35-40%* |
| *Architect a Solution* | *40-45%* |
| *Implement the Solution* | *15-20%* |

### Perform Solution Envisioning and Requirement Analyses (35-40%)

*In this section, you'll demonstrate your ability to kick start solution planning by evaluating business requirements and identifying the necessary solution components. This includes assessing existing apps and third-party tools, as well as estimating migration efforts. You'll also need to understand organizational risk factors and document current business processes. Your task is to refine requirements to ensure they meet organizational goals and perform fit/gap analyses to ensure the proposed solutions are viable and comprehensive.*

### Architect a Solution (40-45%)

*This is where your design skills come into play. You'll lead the design process by creating the overall solution topology and customizing existing applications. You'll need to design robust data models, define data relationships, and determine effective integration strategies with existing systems while adhering to security standards. This involves crafting strategies for data visualization, automating processes using Power Automate, and managing the application lifecycle. Your goal is to ensure that the solution is not only effective but also sustainable in the long term.*

### Implement the Solution (15-20%)

*Finally, you'll focus on bringing your design to life. This involves validating the solution design to ensure it meets all security standards and API limits. You'll need to resolve any conflicts related to automation and integration and support the go-live process by addressing performance issues and troubleshooting data migration problems. Ensuring smooth execution of deployment plans and resolving any go-live readiness issues is crucial for the successful implementation of your solution.*

*By mastering these areas, you will be well-prepared to lead successful implementations of Power Platform solutions, addressing both business and technical needs effectively. Good luck with your exam preparation!*

# QUESTION BANK AND EXAM OBJECTIVE MAP

*This Question Bank extensively maps to the exam syllabus, ensuring a comprehensive coverage with industry-relevant use cases. Each question has been meticulously crafted to present real-life challenges that a Microsoft Power Platform Solution Architect might face. To foster a deep understanding, the majority of questions are framed around compelling business scenarios, highlighting specific challenges or constraints, and often require selecting multiple answers. This approach is designed to prepare you thoroughly for the exam by enhancing your ability to quickly grasp concepts, bridge knowledge gaps, and apply the correct understanding.*

*Additionally, each question is accompanied by exam-focused tips and cautionary alerts in the answer section to boost your chances of success. Below is a table that aligns each question to detailed business use cases according to the exam syllabus, ensuring that your preparation is both targeted and effective.*

### EXAM TOPIC 1 - ARCHITECT A SOLUTION (40-45%)
*Note: P indicates Practice Test and Q indicate Question*

| Business Use cases | Mapped Questions |
|---|---|
| AI and Cognitive Services Integration | P2Q12, P3Q16, P7Q24, P3Q32, P8Q32, P2Q36, P4Q36, P5Q36, P3Q40 |
| Advanced Analytics and Data Insights | P6Q30, P8Q30, P9Q30, P10Q30, P4Q44 |
| Advanced Customization Techniques | P6Q33, P7Q33, P8Q33, P9Q33, P10Q33 |
| Advanced Reporting and Data Analysis | P9Q35 |
| Application Lifecycle Management | P2Q16, P4Q16 |
| Application Lifecycle Management (ALM) | P1Q23, P2Q23, P3Q23, P4Q23, P5Q23, P1Q49 |
| Automation and Workflow Optimization | P6Q4, P7Q4, P3Q12, P7Q12, P10Q12 |
| Business Intelligence and Analytics | P8Q4, P10Q4, P8Q16, P7Q30, P6Q43 |
| Cloud-Native Architecture | P1Q41, P3Q41 |
| Collaboration and Team Dynamics | P4Q37 |
| Cost Analysis and Optimization | P5Q9 |
| Cross-Functional Integration | P1Q37 |
| Customer Loyalty Program | P1Q5 |
| Customer Relationship Management | P1Q1, P6Q1 |
| Data Governance and Stewardship | P3Q37, P5Q37 |
| Data Modeling and Management | P1Q20, P3Q20, P5Q20, P6Q20, P7Q20, P8Q20, P9Q20, P10Q20, P6Q22, P8Q22, P10Q22, P1Q24, P2Q24, P3Q24, P4Q24, P5Q24 |
| Data Privacy and Ethical Considerations | P8Q9, P3Q44 |
| Disaster Recovery and Business Continuity Planning | P6Q27, P7Q27, P8Q27, P9Q27, P10Q27, P5Q28, P6Q39, P7Q39, P8Q39, P9Q39 |
| Enterprise Architecture Integration | P1Q21, P2Q21, P3Q21, P4Q21, P5Q21 |
| Global Deployment and Multi-Region | P6Q37, P7Q37, P8Q37, P9Q37, P10Q37, P7Q41 |

| | |
|---|---|
| Considerations | |
| Governance and Policy Management | P7Q22, P9Q22 |
| Integration Strategies | P1Q12, P5Q12, P6Q12, P1Q16, P10Q16, P10Q24, P1Q32, P2Q32, P4Q32, P7Q32, P10Q32, P4Q34, P9Q34, P2Q37, P4Q41 |
| Integration Strategy and Planning | P2Q22, P4Q22 |
| Inventory Management | P3Q1, P8Q1 |
| IoT Solutions Integration | P10Q28, P1Q31, P2Q31, P3Q31, P4Q31, P5Q31, P5Q32, P6Q32, P9Q36, P4Q39 |
| IoT-based Monitoring | P4Q5 |
| Loan Processing | P3Q3 |
| Microservices Architecture | P2Q41, P5Q41 |
| Order Processing | P1Q3 |
| Performance and Scalability | P2Q9, P2Q44 |
| Sales Data Analysis | P6Q3 |
| Scalability and Load Management | P6Q35, P7Q35, P8Q35 |
| Scalability and Performance | P1Q9, P6Q41, P8Q41, P10Q41 |
| Security and Compliance Architecture | P9Q4, P7Q9, P9Q9, P2Q39, P3Q39, P5Q39, P10Q39, P9Q41, P1Q44 |
| Security and Privacy Planning | P6Q9, P1Q22, P3Q22, P5Q22 |
| Solution Deployment and Management | P4Q12, P8Q12, P9Q12, P5Q16, P9Q24 |
| Solution Design | P5Q2, P6Q2, P7Q2, P8Q2, P9Q2, P10Q2 |
| Solution Scaling and Expansion Strategies | P4Q9 |
| Sustainability and Eco-Friendly Practices | P1Q33, P2Q33, P3Q33, P4Q33, P5Q33 |
| Technology Trends and Future Readiness | P1Q13 |

## EXAM TOPIC 1 - IMPLEMENT THE SOLUTION (15-20%)
*Note: P indicates Practice Test and Q indicate Question*

| Business Use cases | Mapped Questions |
|---|---|
| Agile Methodology and Iterative Development | P6Q13, P7Q13, P8Q13, P9Q13, P10Q13 |
| Automation and Workflow Optimization | P1Q28, P8Q28, P1Q40 |
| Automation of Business Processes | P2Q1, P7Q1 |
| Compliance and Regulatory Adherence | P2Q17, P4Q17 |
| Custom Application Development | P5Q40 |
| Customer Data Management | P6Q5 |
| Customer Feedback System | P10Q5 |
| Customer Loyalty Program | P5Q6 |
| Customer Relationship Management | P10Q6 |
| Customization and Configuration Management | P9Q16, P7Q49 |
| Data Integration | P4Q28 |
| Data Management and Integration | P10Q40 |
| Data Migration Techniques | P1Q4, P3Q4, P4Q4, P5Q4, P7Q16, P1Q34, P3Q34, P5Q34, P6Q34, P8Q34, P10Q34, P6Q44, P9Q44 |
| Data Validation | P7Q28 |
| Deployment Strategies and Challenges | P1Q14, P2Q14, P3Q14, P4Q14, P5Q14 |
| Education Management | P5Q1, P10Q1, P5Q3 |
| Integration Implementation | P2Q4, P6Q16, P2Q20, P4Q20, P6Q24, P6Q28, P9Q32, |

| | |
|---|---|
| | P2Q34, P7Q34, P1Q36, P3Q36, P6Q36, P7Q36, P8Q36, P10Q36, P2Q40, P4Q40, P6Q40, P7Q40, P8Q40, P9Q40, P5Q44, P6Q48, P8Q48 |
| Inventory Management System | P6Q6 |
| Inventory Tracking | P8Q5 |
| Investment Analysis | P8Q3, P3Q5 |
| IoT-based Monitoring | P4Q3 |
| IoT-based Monitoring System | P3Q6 |
| Issue Resolution and Troubleshooting | P7Q44, P1Q50, P3Q50, P4Q50 |
| Learning Management System | P9Q6 |
| Loan Management System | P1Q6 |
| Long-term Sustainability Planning | P3Q17 |
| Monitoring and Analytics | P6Q42, P7Q42, P8Q42, P9Q42, P10Q42, P6Q47, P7Q47, P8Q47, P9Q47, P10Q47, P10Q50 |
| Operational Efficiency | P4Q1, P9Q1 |
| Patient Management | P2Q3, P7Q3, P2Q5, P7Q5 |
| Patient Management System | P2Q6, P7Q6 |
| Performance Tuning and Optimization | P1Q2, P2Q2, P3Q2, P4Q2, P10Q35, P10Q44, P6Q46, P7Q46, P8Q46, P9Q46, P10Q46, P5Q47, P1Q48, P2Q48, P3Q48, P4Q48, P10Q48, P2Q50, P5Q50 |
| Process Automation | P1Q26, P2Q26, P3Q26, P4Q26, P5Q26 |
| Production Data Analysis | P9Q3 |
| Quality Assurance and Testing | P1Q47, P2Q47, P3Q47, P2Q49 |
| Security Implementation | P8Q24, P9Q28, P1Q46, P2Q46, P3Q46, P4Q46, P5Q46, P4Q47, P5Q48, P7Q48, P9Q48 |
| Security and Compliance | P2Q28 |
| Solution Maintenance and Updates | P8Q44, P3Q49, P4Q49, P5Q49 |
| Student Information System | P5Q5, P9Q5, P4Q6 |
| Student Performance Analysis | P10Q3 |
| Supply Chain Management System | P8Q6 |
| Sustainability and Eco-friendly Practices | P1Q17, P5Q17 |
| User Experience Design Principles | P3Q28 |

## EXAM TOPIC 1 - PERFORM SOLUTION ENVISIONING AND REQUIREMENT ANALYSIS (35-40%)

Note: P indicates Practice Test and Q indicate Question

| Business Use cases | Mapped Questions |
|---|---|
| AI and Cognitive Services Integration | P6Q26, P7Q26, P8Q26, P9Q26, P10Q26 |
| Business Intelligence and Analytics | P6Q25, P7Q25, P8Q25, P9Q25, P10Q25 |
| CRM System | P5Q7 |
| Change Management Strategies | P5Q10, P6Q31, P8Q31, P10Q31 |
| Citizen Service Portal | P9Q7 |
| Collaboration and Team Dynamics | P1Q15, P2Q15, P3Q15, P4Q15, P5Q15, P2Q35 |
| Communicating Change Effectively | P5Q8 |
| Compliance and Regulatory Considerations | P9Q49 |
| Cost Estimation and Budgeting | P1Q29, P2Q29, P4Q29, P5Q29 |
| Customer and User Insights Gathering | P8Q38 |
| Customization vs Configuration Decisions | P6Q15, P7Q15, P8Q15, P9Q15, P10Q15, P10Q38, P6Q49, P8Q49, P10Q49 |
| Data Analysis and Interpretation | P7Q43, P9Q43, P10Q43 |

| | |
|---|---|
| Data Governance and Stewardship | P6Q14, P7Q14, P8Q14, P9Q14, P10Q14 |
| Data Migration | P1Q45, P2Q45, P3Q45, P4Q45, P5Q45 |
| Data Security and Ethical Handling | P2Q42, P5Q42 |
| Documentation and Knowledge Management | P1Q35, P4Q35, P5Q35 |
| Global and Cultural Considerations | P4Q42 |
| Governance and Policy Compliance | P6Q17, P7Q17, P8Q17, P9Q17, P10Q17 |
| Governance and Policy Management | P1Q27, P4Q27 |
| Innovation and Emerging Trends | P2Q13, P3Q13, P4Q13, P5Q13, P6Q18, P7Q18, P8Q18, P9Q18, P10Q18, P3Q38 |
| Integration Architecture Design | P7Q8 |
| Integration Challenges | P8Q8 |
| Integration Strategy and Planning | P1Q43, P2Q43, P3Q43, P4Q43, P5Q43 |
| Integration Tools and Technologies | P10Q8 |
| Inventory Management System | P8Q7 |
| Loan Approval System | P7Q7 |
| Managing Resistance to Change | P2Q8 |
| Measuring Change Impact | P3Q8 |
| Mobile and Cross-Platform Solutions | P1Q25, P2Q25, P3Q25, P4Q25, P5Q25 |
| Organizational Change Planning | P1Q8 |
| Project Planning and Scheduling | P1Q7 |
| Prototyping and Proof of Concept | P6Q7 |
| Quality Assurance Planning | P6Q10, P7Q10, P8Q10, P9Q10, P10Q10 |
| Quality Control System | P3Q7 |
| Regulatory and Compliance Considerations | P10Q9, P3Q18, P6Q21, P7Q21, P8Q21, P9Q21, P10Q21, P2Q27, P3Q27, P5Q27, P6Q29, P7Q29, P8Q29, P9Q29, P10Q29, P5Q38, P1Q42, P3Q42, P8Q43 |
| Resource Allocation and Management | P2Q7 |
| Scalability and Performance Considerations | P3Q9, P1Q18, P4Q18, P5Q18, P3Q29, P2Q38 |
| Security and Privacy Planning | P6Q19, P7Q19, P8Q19, P9Q19, P10Q19, P1Q39 |
| Solution Flexibility and Adaptability | P2Q18 |
| Solution Lifecycle Management | P6Q11, P7Q11, P8Q11, P9Q11, P10Q11 |
| Solution Prototyping and Proof of Concept | P1Q38 |
| Stakeholder Identification and Analysis | P2Q10, P4Q10 |
| Stakeholder Involvement | P4Q8 |
| Student Information System | P10Q7 |
| Sustainability and Eco-Friendliness | P6Q50, P7Q50, P8Q50, P9Q50 |
| System and Data Integration Planning | P6Q8 |
| Technology Trends and Future Readiness | P4Q38 |
| Testing and Validating Integrations | P9Q8 |
| Timeline Estimation and Scheduling | P4Q7 |
| Training and Skill Development | P7Q31, P9Q31, P3Q35 |
| User Experience Design Principles | P3Q19, P5Q19, P6Q23, P7Q23, P8Q23, P9Q23, P10Q23, P6Q38, P7Q38, P9Q38 |
| User Training and Support | P6Q45, P7Q45, P8Q45, P9Q45, P10Q45 |
| User and Stakeholder Communication | P1Q10, P3Q10, P1Q19, P2Q19, P4Q19 |
| Vendor and Technology Evaluation | P1Q11, P2Q11, P3Q11, P4Q11, P5Q11, P1Q30, P2Q30, P3Q30, P4Q30, P5Q30 |

# CONTENTS

PRACTICE TEST 1 - QUESTIONS ONLY .............................. 13
PRACTICE TEST 1 - ANSWERS ONLY ................................ 29
PRACTICE TEST 2 - QUESTIONS ONLY .............................. 47
PRACTICE TEST 2 - ANSWERS ONLY ................................ 63
PRACTICE TEST 3 - QUESTIONS ONLY .............................. 81
PRACTICE TEST 3 - ANSWERS ONLY ................................ 97
PRACTICE TEST 4 - QUESTIONS ONLY .............................. 114
PRACTICE TEST 4 - ANSWERS ONLY ................................ 130
PRACTICE TEST 5 - QUESTIONS ONLY .............................. 148
PRACTICE TEST 5 - ANSWERS ONLY ................................ 164
PRACTICE TEST 6 - QUESTIONS ONLY .............................. 181
PRACTICE TEST 6 - ANSWERS ONLY ................................ 197
PRACTICE TEST 7 - QUESTIONS ONLY .............................. 215
PRACTICE TEST 7 - ANSWERS ONLY ................................ 230
PRACTICE TEST 8 - QUESTIONS ONLY .............................. 248
PRACTICE TEST 8 - ANSWERS ONLY ................................ 263
PRACTICE TEST 9 - QUESTIONS ONLY .............................. 281
PRACTICE TEST 9 - ANSWERS ONLY ................................ 297
PRACTICE TEST 10 - QUESTIONS ONLY ............................. 315
PRACTICE TEST 10 - ANSWERS ONLY ............................... 331
ABOUT THE AUTHOR ............................................... 349

# PRACTICE TEST 1 - QUESTIONS ONLY

## QUESTION 1

Your client, a global retail chain, wants to enhance their customer relationship management system using Microsoft Power Platform. The key business objectives are to improve customer engagement, increase sales, and streamline marketing efforts. You are tasked with aligning the solution with their business goals. The specific challenges are:
• Current CRM lacks integration with social media channels.
• Marketing campaigns are not personalized.
• Customer data is fragmented across systems.
What solutions would you implement to align the solution with business goals and measure its impact on business outcomes? Select two correct answers.

A) Use Power Automate to integrate CRM with social media APIs.
B) Implement AI Builder to personalize marketing campaigns.
C) Consolidate customer data in Dataverse.
D) Develop a Power BI dashboard to track customer engagement metrics.
E) Implement a custom model-driven app for marketing management.

## QUESTION 2

As part of a healthcare provider's initiative to use Power Apps for patient management, users in remote locations report slow app performance. You are tasked with identifying and mitigating the root causes of these performance issues.
• Identify root causes of slow performance.
• Mitigate performance issues for users in remote locations.
What two areas should you focus on to improve the app's performance for all users, regardless of location?

A) Network congestion
B) Content delivery network implementation
C) Microsoft Dataverse log capacity
D) Network latency
E) Application code optimization

## QUESTION 3

A global retail company wants to enhance its order processing system using Microsoft Power Platform. They need to analyze existing business processes and identify areas for improvement. The specific challenges are:
• Current manual processes are causing delays and errors.
• Lack of integration between order management and inventory systems.
• Difficulty in tracking order status in real-time.
What solutions would you recommend to address these challenges? Select two correct answers.

A) Use Power Automate to automate order processing workflows.
B) Implement Dataverse to integrate order management and inventory systems.

C) Develop a model-driven app to track order status in real-time.
D) Use Power BI to analyze order processing data.
E) Implement a custom API for order management integration.

## QUESTION 4

You are reviewing JavaScript code that a developer wrote for a Microsoft Power Platform project. The developer is using RetrieveMultiple calls to retrieve a single row from a Microsoft Dataverse table. The code retrieves data using a secondary key from an external system.
- The solution must simplify the code and improve performance.
- It should leverage built-in Dataverse capabilities.

Which components should you recommend the developer use? Select two answers.

A) Alternate keys
B) OData $filter query
C) OData $expand query
D) FetchXML query
E) Business rules

## QUESTION 5

A retail company wants to implement a new customer loyalty program using Microsoft Power Platform. They need to evaluate available technologies and match them with solution requirements. The specific challenges are:
- Ensuring seamless integration with existing CRM systems.
- Minimizing costs while maximizing benefits.
- Future-proofing the technology choices to accommodate potential business growth.

What actions would you take to address these challenges? Select two correct answers.

A) Use Dataverse to store and manage customer loyalty data.
B) Implement Power Automate to integrate with existing CRM systems.
C) Conduct a cost-benefit analysis to evaluate different technologies.
D) Use Azure Logic Apps for custom integration.
E) Apply ALM practices to manage changes.

## QUESTION 6

A financial services company is implementing a new loan management system using Microsoft Power Platform. The project requires identifying potential risks and developing strategies for risk mitigation. The specific challenges are:
- Identifying security risks in data handling.
- Ensuring system scalability for future growth.
- Preparing for potential system downtimes.

What actions would you take to address these challenges? Select two correct answers.

A) Use Dataverse to securely store loan data.
B) Implement RBAC to control access to sensitive data.
C) Use Power Automate to automate backup processes.
D) Develop a contingency plan for system downtimes.

E) Conduct a scalability assessment using Power BI.

## QUESTION 7

A financial services company is implementing a new client onboarding system using Microsoft Power Platform. The project requires effective project planning and scheduling. The specific challenges are:
- Estimating the timeline for system development.
- Allocating resources efficiently.
- Setting milestones to track project progress.

What actions would you take to address these challenges? Select two correct answers.

A) Use Azure DevOps to manage project tasks and timelines.
B) Implement Dataverse to store onboarding data.
C) Use Power Automate to automate resource allocation.
D) Develop a Gantt chart for project milestones using Power BI.
E) Conduct regular progress reviews.

## QUESTION 8

A manufacturing company is implementing a new workflow automation system using Microsoft Power Platform. The project requires planning for organizational change. The specific challenges are:
- Ensuring smooth transition to the new system.
- Communicating the changes effectively to all employees.
- Involving key stakeholders in the change process.

What actions would you take to address these challenges? Select two correct answers.

A) Use Power Automate to design the new workflows.
B) Create a comprehensive change management plan.
C) Develop a communication strategy using Microsoft Teams.
D) Use Power BI to monitor workflow performance.
E) Implement Azure DevOps for project tracking.

## QUESTION 9

A large retail organization is expanding its online sales platform using Microsoft Power Platform. The project requires designing for scalability to handle increased user traffic. The specific challenges are:
- Ensuring the system can scale to meet peak demand.
- Maintaining performance under load.
- Balancing performance with cost.

What actions would you take to address these challenges? Select two correct answers.

A) Use Azure Functions for serverless computing.
B) Implement Dataverse for data storage.
C) Use Power BI for real-time monitoring.
D) Implement load balancing using Azure Traffic Manager.
E) Use Power Automate for automating data processing.

## QUESTION 10

A manufacturing company is implementing a new inventory management system using Microsoft Power Platform. The project requires effective communication methods with stakeholders. The specific challenges are:
- Ensuring all stakeholders are kept informed of progress.
- Managing stakeholder expectations.
- Gathering feedback for improvements.

What steps would you take to address these challenges? Select three correct answers.

A) Use Microsoft Teams for regular status updates.
B) Implement Power BI dashboards for real-time reporting.
C) Use Power Automate for workflow automation.
D) Schedule weekly meetings with stakeholders.
E) Use Power Virtual Agents for stakeholder queries.

## QUESTION 11

A healthcare organization is implementing a new patient management system using Dynamics 365 and Microsoft Power Platform. The specific challenges are:
- Evaluating vendors based on their API integration capabilities with existing EHR systems.
- Ensuring compliance with HIPAA regulations.
- Negotiating service-level agreements (SLAs) that include data privacy terms.

What steps would you take to address these challenges? Select three correct answers.

A) Develop an evaluation matrix focusing on API integration capabilities and compliance.
B) Use Azure API Management to facilitate vendor API testing.
C) Implement Power Automate for automated data privacy audits.
D) Conduct on-site visits to assess vendor capabilities.
E) Compare vendor SLAs focusing on data privacy and HIPAA compliance.

## QUESTION 12

A global organization wants to implement a Dynamics 365 Sales solution. They require a seamless integration with their existing ERP system and need to ensure minimal downtime during data migration.
- The ERP system is hosted on-premises.
- The organization operates in multiple regions and needs to ensure data compliance with regional regulations.

What would be the best approach to integrate and migrate data while ensuring compliance?

A) Use Azure Data Factory for data migration, implement Power Automate for ongoing integration, and set up regional instances of Dynamics 365 Sales
B) Use Import Data Wizard for initial migration, implement Power Apps for integration, and centralize Dynamics 365 Sales instance
C) Use Azure Logic Apps for data migration and integration, and implement a single global instance of Dynamics 365 Sales
D) Use Microsoft Power BI for data migration, implement Power Automate for integration, and set up regional instances of Dynamics 365 Sales
E) Use Data Migration Assistant for initial migration, implement Azure Functions for integration, and

centralize Dynamics 365 Sales instance

**QUESTION 13**

A retail company is looking to stay competitive by adopting new technologies. As a solution architect, you need to ensure the solution addresses the following challenges:
- Staying current with industry trends.
- Evaluating and adopting new technologies.
- Balancing innovation with practicality.

Which technologies should you recommend to address these challenges? Select three correct answers.

A) Integrate AI Builder for predictive analytics.
B) Use Power Automate for process automation.
C) Implement Power BI for real-time reporting.
D) Use Dynamics 365 for CRM capabilities.
E) Implement Azure IoT for smart inventory management.

**QUESTION 14**

You are leading the deployment of a new customer engagement platform using the Microsoft Power Platform for a large retail company. The challenges include:
- Planning deployment phases.
- Handling deployment challenges.
- Managing user transition during deployment.

Which strategies should you adopt to ensure a successful deployment? Select three correct answers.

A) Implement Azure DevOps for continuous integration and continuous deployment (CI/CD).
B) Use Power Virtual Agents for user training and support.
C) Conduct a pilot deployment with a small user group.
D) Develop a rollback plan to handle deployment failures.
E) Utilize Power BI for monitoring deployment progress and performance.

**QUESTION 15**

You are leading a project team using Microsoft Power Platform to build a solution for a retail company. The challenges include:
- Building an effective project team.
- Enhancing collaboration and teamwork.
- Using tools and techniques for team communication.

Which steps should you take to address these challenges? Select three correct answers.

A) Implement Microsoft Teams for team collaboration.
B) Use Power Automate to streamline communication workflows.
C) Develop a team charter outlining roles and responsibilities.
D) Use Power BI to monitor team performance.
E) Assign specific roles using Dynamics 365.

## QUESTION 16

A company is developing a Power Platform solution to streamline its sales process. The solution must integrate with Dynamics 365 Sales and automate data synchronization with a third-party ERP system.
• The integration should support real-time data updates.
• It should ensure data security and compliance with industry standards.
Which tool should you use to implement the integration?

A) Azure Logic Apps
B) Power Automate
C) Data Export Service
D) Azure Data Factory
E) Azure Functions

## QUESTION 17

You are leading a project to implement Microsoft Power Platform for a logistics company. The challenges include:
• Assessing environmental impact of solutions.
• Designing for sustainability.
• Implementing eco-friendly practices.
Which strategies should you adopt to address these challenges? Select three correct answers.

A) Use Power BI to create sustainability dashboards and track environmental impact.
B) Implement Power Automate to streamline processes and reduce energy consumption.
C) Develop custom APIs to integrate with environmental monitoring systems.
D) Utilize AI Builder to analyze data and optimize resource usage.
E) Use Dataverse to centralize environmental data and ensure consistency.

## QUESTION 18

A financial services company is implementing a new customer management system using Microsoft Power Platform. The solution must:
• Be flexible and adaptable to future changes in regulations.
• Scale easily with the growing number of customers.
• Maintain stability while adapting to new business needs.
You need to choose two actions to ensure the solution meets these requirements. Which two actions should you take? (Select two)

A) Use Dataverse for data storage to ensure scalability.
B) Develop custom connectors for future integrations.
C) Implement role-based security to handle varying access needs.
D) Use Power Automate for workflows and process automation.
E) Develop a single, large canvas app to handle all functions.

## QUESTION 19

A financial services company is redesigning its customer portal using Microsoft Power Platform. The solution must:

- Gather comprehensive customer insights.
- Utilize feedback effectively in the solution design.
- Develop user personas to guide the design process.

Which three actions should you take to achieve these requirements? (Select three)

A) Conduct user interviews and surveys.
B) Use Power BI to analyze customer data.
C) Implement AI Builder to predict customer behavior.
D) Develop model-driven apps for customer interactions.
E) Create user personas based on customer feedback.

## QUESTION 20

You are designing the data model for a Microsoft Dataverse solution. You need to identify the tables that form part of the Common Data Model.
Which three tables should you identify? Each correct answer presents part of the solution. Select three answers.

A) Account
B) Business
C) Grant
D) Marketing List
E) Program
F) Task

## QUESTION 21

A global retail company is looking to align their Power Platform solutions with their enterprise architecture. The solution must:
- Align with enterprise architecture.
- Integrate with existing IT infrastructure.
- Follow architectural standards and best practices.

Which three actions should you take to meet these requirements? (Select three)

A) Use Power Automate to connect to existing legacy systems.
B) Implement Dataverse for centralized data management.
C) Develop a custom API for integration.
D) Utilize Azure Logic Apps for workflow orchestration.
E) Adopt a modular design approach using Canvas Apps.

## QUESTION 22

A multinational corporation is planning to implement a cloud-based Power Platform solution integrated with Azure. The solution must:
- Ensure high availability and disaster recovery.
- Securely manage sensitive customer data.
- Optimize cost and performance.

Which two actions should you recommend? (Select two)

A) Use Azure SQL Database with Geo-Replication for high availability.
B) Implement Azure Policy for cost management.
C) Use Dataverse for data storage and management.
D) Enable Multi-Factor Authentication (MFA) using Azure AD.
E) Use Power BI for real-time data analytics.

## QUESTION 23

A global manufacturing company is implementing an ALM strategy for their Power Platform solutions. They need to ensure best practices are followed to manage version control, deployment, and testing effectively. The solution must:
• Implement CI/CD pipelines.
• Automate deployment processes.
• Ensure version control of Power Apps.
Which two tools should you recommend? (Select two)

A) Azure DevOps
B) Power Apps Solution Checker
C) GitHub Actions
D) Power Automate
E) Dataverse

## QUESTION 24

A retail company wants to build a new inventory management system using Microsoft Dataverse. They need to ensure that related records in the inventory table are automatically deleted when a product is deleted.
• The solution must enforce referential integrity.
• It should automate the deletion of related records.
Which type of relationship behavior should you configure? Select two answers.

A) Referential
B) Custom
C) Parental
D) Referential, Restrict Delete
E) Delete Cascade

## QUESTION 25

A logistics company wants to develop a mobile application using Power Apps to track and manage deliveries. The solution must:
• Be cross-platform compatible to work on both iOS and Android devices.
• Ensure offline capabilities for areas with poor connectivity.
• Synchronize data efficiently once online.
What three strategies should you implement? (Select three)

A) Use Canvas Apps for custom UI design.
B) Implement Azure API Management for secure API handling.
C) Use Power Automate for data synchronization.

D) Implement local caching for offline capabilities.
E) Utilize Dataverse as the backend database.

**QUESTION 26**

A logistics company wants to automate their order processing system using Power Automate. The solution must:
- Automatically trigger workflows when a new order is placed.
- Validate order details using AI.
- Send notifications to the logistics team for any discrepancies.

What three components should you implement? (Select three)

A) Power Automate Cloud Flow for triggering workflows.
B) AI Builder for order validation.
C) Power BI for order tracking.
D) Power Automate approvals for sending notifications.
E) Azure Logic Apps for integrating with external systems.

**QUESTION 27**

A global enterprise is deploying Power Platform solutions and needs to establish a governance framework to ensure compliance and data security. The solution must:
- Define clear policies for data access and usage.
- Enforce compliance with industry regulations.
- Provide auditing and reporting capabilities.

Which components and practices should be included in the governance framework? (Select three)

A) Dataverse for data storage and policy enforcement.
B) Azure Policy for compliance monitoring.
C) Power Automate for workflow automation.
D) Role-Based Access Control (RBAC) for managing user permissions.
E) Power BI for auditing and reporting.

**QUESTION 28**

A consulting firm uses Microsoft Power Platform to manage their client projects. They want to automate the process of generating project status reports and sending them to clients weekly. Which solution should they implement to achieve this automation?

A) Power BI Dashboards
B) Power Automate Flows
C) Power Apps Canvas Apps
D) Dynamics 365 Marketing
E) Azure Logic Apps

**QUESTION 29**

You are a Microsoft Power Platform Solution Architect working on a project to optimize costs for a client. The client has a limited budget and needs to ensure that their solution is cost-effective. They have

expressed concerns about the Total Cost of Ownership (TCO) and want to identify cost-saving opportunities.
1. Estimating the overall cost of implementing Power Platform solutions.
2. Managing and optimizing resource utilization to stay within budget.
3. Implementing best practices for cost savings without compromising on performance.
What steps should you take to address the client's concerns and optimize costs for the Power Platform solution? Select two answers.

A) Use Azure Cost Management and Billing to monitor and manage costs associated with Power Platform components.
B) Implement Power Platform ALM best practices to streamline development and reduce redundant resources.
C) Use Power Automate to automate manual processes and reduce operational costs.
D) Implement high-cost custom connectors without evaluating out-of-the-box alternatives.
E) Use AI Builder to predict and manage future costs accurately.

## QUESTION 30

You are a Microsoft Power Platform Solution Architect working for a client in the retail industry. The client needs help evaluating and selecting vendors for a new Power Platform implementation.
1. Assessing vendor capabilities to integrate with existing Power Platform solutions.
2. Managing vendor relationships to ensure successful project outcomes.
3. Negotiating contracts to include favorable terms for both parties.
What steps would you recommend to effectively evaluate and select vendors for the project? Select two answers.

A) Use Power BI to create vendor performance dashboards.
B) Evaluate vendors based on their experience with Power Platform and similar projects.
C) Select vendors solely based on cost.
D) Conduct comprehensive vendor assessments including technical capabilities and past performance.
E) Negotiate contracts focusing only on short-term gains.

## QUESTION 31

A manufacturing client wants to implement an IoT solution using Microsoft Power Platform to monitor their equipment in real-time. They need a solution that ensures scalability and performance while processing real-time data.
1. Integrating IoT devices with Power Platform for real-time data processing.
2. Ensuring scalability and performance of the IoT system.
3. Managing and securing IoT devices.
What measures would you recommend to achieve these objectives? Select two answers.

A) Use Azure IoT Hub to connect and manage IoT devices.
B) Implement Power BI to visualize real-time data from IoT devices.
C) Store all IoT data in a local SQL database.
D) Use Azure Stream Analytics for real-time data processing.
E) Develop custom applications for IoT device management.

## QUESTION 32

A manufacturing company uses Microsoft Power Platform and Dynamics 365 Supply Chain Management to manage inventory and production processes. They need to integrate an external inventory management system that is not aware of the GUIDs of the rows in Microsoft Dataverse. The integration must minimize the number of requests and ensure real-time data updates. Which capability should you select to achieve this integration?

A) Webhooks
B) Azure Functions
C) Alternative Keys
D) Batch API
E) Microsoft Graph API

## QUESTION 33

You are a Microsoft Power Platform Solution Architect working with a client who wants to implement eco-friendly solutions using Power Platform. They need to design solutions that reduce environmental impact and comply with green standards.
1. Designing eco-friendly solutions.
2. Reducing environmental impact through technology selection.
3. Ensuring compliance with green standards.
What steps would you recommend to achieve these objectives? Select two answers.

A) Use Power BI to monitor and analyze the environmental impact of business processes.
B) Implement Azure IoT to monitor energy consumption and optimize usage.
C) Ignore green standards to focus on functionality.
D) Use Power Automate to streamline eco-friendly workflows.
E) Select energy-efficient cloud services and hardware.

## QUESTION 34

Your company is integrating a legacy CRM system with Dynamics 365. You need to ensure that the data migration process minimizes disruption to ongoing operations. The project team must:
• Maintain data integrity and consistency.
• Ensure minimal downtime during migration.
• Address potential data quality issues pre-migration. What are the best approaches to achieve these objectives? (Select 2 answers)

A) Perform a big bang migration over a weekend.
B) Use an ETL tool to incrementally migrate data during off-peak hours.
C) Export data to CSV files and manually import them into Dynamics 365.
D) Develop custom scripts to migrate data in real-time.
E) Use Azure Data Factory for orchestrating and automating data migration.

## QUESTION 35

Your company is documenting the integration of Dynamics 365 with an existing ERP system. The team must ensure comprehensive documentation for future maintenance and knowledge transfer. The

documentation must:
• Include detailed architecture diagrams.
• Provide step-by-step configuration guides.
• Be easily accessible and regularly updated. What are the best practices to achieve this? (Select 3 answers)

A) Use a shared document repository like SharePoint.
B) Conduct regular review meetings to update documentation.
C) Create video tutorials for complex configurations.
D) Implement version control for documentation using Azure DevOps.
E) Use a wiki for collaborative documentation.

## QUESTION 36

An e-commerce company uses Dynamics 365 Commerce to manage their online store. They need to integrate their order management system with a third-party shipping provider to automate shipping label generation and tracking updates. The solution must ensure real-time data synchronization and reliability. What integration method should they choose?

A) Use Azure Functions
B) Implement a Custom Connector
C) Use Power Automate with an HTTP request action
D) Use Dynamics 365 Customer Insights
E) Use Azure Data Factory

## QUESTION 37

Your organization needs to integrate Power Platform with several business functions, including sales, finance, and HR. The integration must:
• Ensure data consistency across departments.
• Facilitate seamless cross-functional workflows.
• Maintain data integrity and security. What strategies should you adopt? (Select 3 answers)

A) Use Dataverse as the central data store for all integrated systems.
B) Implement Power Automate for cross-functional workflows.
C) Use separate data stores for each department.
D) Employ Azure API Management for secure data access.
E) Develop custom connectors for each department's systems.

## QUESTION 38

Your organization wants to explore the use of AI Builder to enhance customer service operations. The solution must:
• Leverage AI to automate routine tasks.
• Ensure the technology can scale with business growth.
• Assess the impact on current workflows. What strategies should you implement? (Select 2 answers)

A) Integrate AI Builder with Power Automate for automated workflows.
B) Use AI Builder for sentiment analysis in customer feedback.

C) Deploy AI Builder without evaluating current workflows.
D) Conduct a pilot project to assess the impact on workflows.
E) Scale AI Builder implementations manually as the business grows.

## QUESTION 39

You are designing a Power Platform solution for a healthcare organization. The solution must:
- Ensure secure communication and data transmission.
- Implement advanced security frameworks.
- Regularly evaluate and update security measures. What steps should you take? (Select 2 answers)

A) Use Dataverse with encryption at rest and in transit.
B) Implement Azure API Management to secure APIs.
C) Conduct regular security audits and penetration testing.
D) Use HTTP for data transmission.
E) Apply a single security policy for all users regardless of their roles.

## QUESTION 40

A pharmaceutical company uses Dynamics 365 Sales to manage their sales pipeline. They want to implement a process where sales representatives can submit proposals for discount approvals through a canvas app. The proposals must be reviewed and approved by the sales manager automatically based on predefined criteria. What solution should they use to automate the approval process?

A) Create a Power Automate flow using the "Request manager approval for a selected item" template.
B) Implement a business rule on the proposal table that enforces approval criteria.
C) Develop a custom plug-in to handle the approval logic.
D) Use a model-driven app with an embedded approval workflow.
E) Integrate an external approval system using Azure Logic Apps.

## QUESTION 41

A logistics company wants to leverage cloud-native architecture to modernize their shipment tracking system. The solution must:
- Utilize serverless architecture for scalability.
- Ensure secure communication of shipment data.
- Use containerization for deployment consistency. What steps should you take? (Select 2 answers)

A) Use Azure Functions for implementing serverless components.
B) Use Azure Kubernetes Service (AKS) for container orchestration.
C) Use Power Automate to manage container deployment.
D) Use Azure Logic Apps for secure communication.
E) Use Power BI for shipment tracking.

## QUESTION 42

A healthcare organization is implementing a Power Platform solution to manage patient data. They need to ensure data privacy and compliance with health regulations. The solution must:
- Implement privacy by design principles.

- Handle sensitive and personal data securely.
- Balance data utility with privacy concerns. What strategies should be implemented? (Select 3 answers)

A) Use Dataverse with role-based access control (RBAC) to restrict access to sensitive data.
B) Implement Azure Security Center for continuous monitoring and compliance.
C) Use Power Automate to anonymize patient data before processing.
D) Store all patient data in a local database to avoid cloud storage.
E) Use Azure Key Vault to manage encryption keys and secure data access.

## QUESTION 43

A healthcare organization needs to integrate a third-party patient management system with their existing Power Platform solution. They must:
- Ensure secure data transfer between systems.
- Maintain compliance with healthcare regulations.
- Implement reliable and maintainable integration. What actions should they take? (Select 3 answers)

A) Use Azure Logic Apps to create workflows for data integration.
B) Implement SSL/TLS for secure data transfer.
C) Store patient data in an unencrypted format for easy access.
D) Use Azure API Management to manage and secure API calls.
E) Perform manual data transfers using Excel exports and imports.

## QUESTION 44

As a solution architect, you are tasked with designing a Microsoft Power Platform application for a healthcare provider that must comply with HIPAA. The application will manage patient records and must ensure data is not only secure but also quickly accessible by authorized personnel.
- Compliance with HIPAA.
- Secure and rapid access to patient records.

Which combination of Power Platform features should you utilize to meet these requirements?

A) Power Apps with Azure SQL
B) Power Automate with data policies
C) Power BI with Row-Level Security
D) Power Apps with Common Data Service
E) Power Virtual Agents with Azure Bot Service

## QUESTION 45

A logistics company is migrating data from their legacy system to Dynamics 365 using Power Platform. They need to ensure:
- Data integrity and quality during migration.
- Handling of large datasets efficiently.
- Post-migration validation and troubleshooting. What strategies should they employ? (Select 2 answers)

A) Use Azure Data Factory for data migration.
B) Manually validate data for quality checks.
C) Use Dataverse for storing and managing data.

D) Implement automated data validation rules during migration.
E) Skip data quality checks to speed up migration.

## QUESTION 46

You are tasked with implementing a security protocol for a new Dynamics 365 deployment. The key requirements are:
- Ensure role-based access control (RBAC).
- Implement data protection measures.
- Validate security compliance. What steps should you take to meet these requirements?

A) Use Azure AD for RBAC.
B) Implement data encryption at rest and in transit.
C) Conduct security compliance audits using Power BI.
D) Use manual role assignments.
E) Skip compliance validation.

## QUESTION 47

A financial services company is implementing a new Power Apps application. To ensure quality, they must:
- Plan and execute a quality assurance strategy.
- Conduct both automated and manual testing.
- Perform User Acceptance Testing (UAT). What should they include in their QA plan?
Select 2 answers.

A) Use Power Apps Test Studio for automated testing.
B) Conduct manual testing by end-users.
C) Skip UAT and move directly to production.
D) Implement performance testing using Azure Monitor.
E) Include security testing using Microsoft Defender for Cloud.

## QUESTION 48

A financial services firm uses a complex Power Apps application to track client interactions. The app is slow to load and navigate due to extensive data connections. You are tasked with improving the app's performance.
- Optimize app load times.
- Improve navigation speed.
What two improvements should you implement to meet these performance requirements?

A) Optimize data sources
B) Use the Concurrent function
C) Reduce screen complexity
D) Implement data pagination
E) Add more data connectors

## QUESTION 49

Your organization uses Power Apps and Power Automate for critical business processes. As a solution architect, you need to ensure the long-term sustainability of these solutions. The key requirements are:
• Implementing routine maintenance procedures.
• Managing and applying updates efficiently.
• Ensuring version control and rollback capabilities.
What actions should you take to meet these requirements? (Select 3 answers)

A) Use Azure DevOps for version control and CI/CD pipelines.
B) Schedule regular maintenance windows to apply updates.
C) Utilize Power Platform's Solution Checker to identify and fix issues.
D) Implement automated testing using Power Automate Test Framework.
E) Store solution backups in Dataverse for easy rollback.

## QUESTION 50

Your organization has implemented a Power Platform solution that integrates Power Apps, Power Automate, and Dataverse. Users report that some automated workflows are failing intermittently. As a solution architect, you need to troubleshoot and resolve these issues. The key requirements are:
• Identifying the root cause of workflow failures.
• Implementing a solution to prevent future occurrences.
• Ensuring minimal disruption to users.
What steps should you take? (Select 3 answers)

A) Use the Power Automate flow checker to identify issues in the workflows.
B) Review the Dataverse audit logs for any related errors.
C) Implement retry logic in Power Automate flows.
D) Create a monitoring dashboard in Power BI to track workflow performance.
E) Use Azure DevOps to automate the deployment of workflow updates.

# PRACTICE TEST 1 - ANSWERS ONLY

## QUESTION 1

Answer – B), C)

Option A – Integrating CRM with social media is useful but does not address personalized marketing or data consolidation.
Option B – AI Builder can analyze data and personalize marketing campaigns, aligning with business goals.
Option C – Consolidating customer data in Dataverse will improve data management, addressing one of the key challenges.
Option D – Power BI dashboards help measure impact but do not enhance engagement or sales directly.
Option E – A custom app for marketing management can streamline efforts but does not directly personalize campaigns.

| 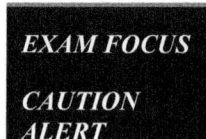 | |
|---|---|
| EXAM FOCUS | *Remember, personalizing campaigns with AI Builder and consolidating data in Dataverse are key to enhancing CRM effectiveness.* |
| CAUTION ALERT | *Stay cautious, focusing on solutions that directly address integration and personalization challenges for CRM improvements.* |

## QUESTION 2

Answer – B), D)

Option A – Incorrect. Network congestion could be a factor, but focusing on it may not provide a comprehensive solution for remote users.
Option B – Correct. Implementing a content delivery network (CDN) can greatly enhance app performance by distributing load and reducing latency, which is beneficial for users in remote locations.
Option C – Incorrect. Dataverse log capacity affects database performance internally but is less likely to impact end-user experience directly.
Option D – Correct. Addressing network latency issues by optimizing routes or using acceleration services can significantly improve performance, especially critical for remote users.
Option E – Incorrect. While optimizing application code is generally beneficial, it does not address the specific issue of location-based performance discrepancies.

| EXAM FOCUS | *"Implement a CDN and optimize for network latency to enhance app performance for remote users."* |
|---|---|
| CAUTION ALERT | *"Don't overlook network latency; it's critical for remote performance."* |

## QUESTION 3

Answer – A), B)

Option A – Power Automate can automate order processing workflows, reducing delays and errors.
Option B – Dataverse can integrate order management and inventory systems, addressing the lack of integration.
Option C – A model-driven app helps track order status but does not address process automation or integration.

Page | 29

Option D – Power BI is useful for analysis but does not directly improve processes.

Option E – A custom API might help integration but is more complex and less suitable than Dataverse for this scenario.

| | |
|---|---|
| **EXAM FOCUS** | *You should automate order processing with Power Automate and integrate systems with Dataverse to reduce delays and errors.* |
| **CAUTION ALERT** | *Stay cautious, focusing solely on tracking order status won't address the root cause of delays and integration issues.* |

## QUESTION 4

Answer – A), B)

Option A – Correct choice as Alternate keys simplify data retrieval by providing a unique identifier other than the primary key.

Option B – Correct choice as OData $filter query can retrieve specific records more efficiently than RetrieveMultiple.

Option C – OData $expand query is used to retrieve related entity data, which is not required in this scenario.

Option D – FetchXML query can retrieve data but is more complex than using alternate keys.

Option E – Business rules enforce validation rules but do not simplify data retrieval in JavaScript.

| | |
|---|---|
| **EXAM FOCUS** | *"Remember, using Alternate keys simplifies data retrieval by providing a unique identifier other than the primary key."* |
| **CAUTION ALERT** | *"You should stay cautious, relying on multiple RetrieveMultiple calls can severely impact performance."* |

## QUESTION 5

Answer – B), C)

Option A – Dataverse is useful for managing data but does not address integration with CRM.

Option B – Power Automate can integrate with existing CRM systems, ensuring seamless operation.

Option C – Conducting a cost-benefit analysis helps in evaluating and selecting the most suitable technologies.

Option D – Azure Logic Apps are useful for custom integration but might increase complexity and cost.

Option E – ALM practices are essential but do not directly address the specific challenges listed.

| | |
|---|---|
| **EXAM FOCUS** | *You should use Power Automate for CRM integration and conduct a cost-benefit analysis to choose the best technology.* |
| **CAUTION ALERT** | *Stay cautious, focusing on custom integration solutions may increase complexity and costs unnecessarily.* |

## QUESTION 6

Answer – B), D)

Option A – Dataverse provides secure data storage but does not address access control or contingency planning.

Option B – RBAC controls access to sensitive data, mitigating security risks.
Option C – Power Automate is useful for backup processes but does not directly address risk mitigation.
Option D – Developing a contingency plan ensures preparedness for potential system downtimes.
Option E – Power BI is useful for data analysis but does not directly address scalability assessment.

| EXAM FOCUS | You should implement RBAC for data security and develop a contingency plan for system downtimes to mitigate risks. |
|---|---|
| CAUTION ALERT | Stay cautious, Dataverse alone won't address access control or system downtime preparedness effectively. |

## QUESTION 7

Answer – A), D)

Option A – Azure DevOps can be used to manage project tasks and timelines effectively.
Option B – Dataverse is useful for data storage but does not directly address project planning or scheduling.
Option C – Power Automate is useful for automating tasks but not specifically for resource allocation.
Option D – Developing a Gantt chart for project milestones using Power BI helps track progress.
Option E – Regular progress reviews are important but do not directly address initial planning and scheduling.

| EXAM FOCUS | You should use Azure DevOps for task management and Power BI for milestone tracking to ensure effective project planning. |
|---|---|
| CAUTION ALERT | Remember, Dataverse is great for data storage but won't help with project planning or scheduling directly. |

## QUESTION 8

Answer – B), C)

Option A – Power Automate is useful for designing workflows but not directly related to change management planning.
Option B – Creating a comprehensive change management plan helps ensure smooth transition.
Option C – Developing a communication strategy using Microsoft Teams ensures effective communication of changes.
Option D – Power BI is useful for monitoring performance but not directly related to change management.
Option E – Azure DevOps is useful for project tracking but not directly related to change management.

| EXAM FOCUS | Develop a change management plan and communication strategy using Microsoft Teams to ensure a smooth transition. |
|---|---|
| CAUTION ALERT | Remember, Power Automate is for workflow design, not change management. |

## QUESTION 9

Answer – A), D)

Option A – Azure Functions provide serverless computing that scales automatically.
Option B – Dataverse is useful for data storage but not directly related to scalability.
Option C – Power BI is useful for monitoring but not directly related to designing for scalability.
Option D – Implementing load balancing using Azure Traffic Manager helps distribute traffic and maintain performance.
Option E – Power Automate is useful for automating processes but not directly related to scalability.

| | |
|---|---|
| **EXAM FOCUS** | *Use Azure Functions and Azure Traffic Manager to ensure scalability and performance during peak demands.* |
| **CAUTION ALERT** | *Remember, Power Automate is useful for automation, not for handling scalability directly.* |

## QUESTION 10

Answer – A), B), D)

Option A – Using Microsoft Teams ensures regular communication and status updates.
Option B – Implementing Power BI dashboards provides real-time reporting to stakeholders.
Option C – Power Automate is useful for workflow automation but not directly related to communication with stakeholders.
Option D – Scheduling weekly meetings ensures continuous engagement and feedback.
Option E – Power Virtual Agents is useful for queries but not directly related to effective communication methods with stakeholders.

| | |
|---|---|
| **EXAM FOCUS** | *Use Microsoft Teams and Power BI for consistent stakeholder communication and real-time reporting.* |
| **CAUTION ALERT** | *Remember, Power Automate is useful for workflow automation, not for direct communication with stakeholders.* |

## QUESTION 11

Answer – A), B), E)

Option A – Developing an evaluation matrix ensures all critical factors are considered.
Option B – Using Azure API Management helps in testing vendor API integration.
Option C – Power Automate can automate audits but is not directly used for initial evaluation.
Option D – On-site visits can be beneficial but are not always feasible.
Option E – Comparing vendor SLAs with a focus on data privacy ensures compliance with HIPAA.

| | |
|---|---|
| **EXAM FOCUS** | *Develop an evaluation matrix and compare SLAs to ensure vendors meet integration and compliance needs.* |
| **CAUTION ALERT** | *Remember, Power Automate is useful for automating processes but not for initial vendor evaluation.* |

## QUESTION 12

Answer – A)

Option A – Correct choice as Azure Data Factory handles complex migrations, Power Automate provides robust integration, and regional instances ensure compliance.

Option B – Import Data Wizard is too basic for this scenario.
Option C – Azure Logic Apps can handle migration but doesn't address compliance as effectively.
Option D – Power BI is not suitable for data migration.
Option E – Data Migration Assistant is more suitable for database migrations rather than complex ERP integrations.

| EXAM FOCUS | *"Use Azure Data Factory and Power Automate for efficient migration and integration."* |
|---|---|
| CAUTION ALERT | *"Avoid using Import Data Wizard for complex migrations; it's too basic."* |

## QUESTION 13

Answer – A), C), E)

Option A – AI Builder for predictive analytics helps stay current with trends and adopting new technologies.
Option B – Power Automate is useful but more for process automation.
Option C – Power BI for real-time reporting is essential for staying current with industry trends.
Option D – Dynamics 365 is useful but not directly related to innovation and emerging trends.
Option E – Azure IoT for smart inventory management addresses the challenge of adopting new technologies.

| EXAM FOCUS | *You should integrate AI Builder and Azure IoT for innovative and practical solutions in retail technology.* |
|---|---|
| CAUTION ALERT | *Stay cautious, focusing too much on automation like Power Automate might miss broader innovation opportunities.* |

## QUESTION 14

Answer – A), C), D)

Option A – Azure DevOps is essential for CI/CD, ensuring smooth deployment phases.
Option B – Power Virtual Agents are useful for user training but not directly related to deployment challenges.
Option C – A pilot deployment helps identify and handle deployment challenges early.
Option D – A rollback plan is crucial for handling deployment failures.
Option E – Power BI is useful for monitoring but not directly for handling deployment challenges.

| EXAM FOCUS | *Remember, a pilot deployment helps identify potential issues early and ensures a smoother main rollout.* |
|---|---|
| CAUTION ALERT | *Please keep in mind, skipping a rollback plan can lead to significant disruptions if deployment fails.* |

## QUESTION 15

Answer – A), B), C)

Option A – Microsoft Teams is essential for enhancing collaboration and communication within the team.

Option B – Power Automate can streamline communication workflows, ensuring efficient information sharing.
Option C – Developing a team charter helps in defining roles and responsibilities, which is crucial for building an effective project team.
Option D – Power BI is useful for monitoring performance but less critical for building collaboration and teamwork.
Option E – Dynamics 365 can assign roles but is less focused on team communication and collaboration tools.

| EXAM FOCUS | *Remember, using Microsoft Teams enhances collaboration and communication within the team effectively.* |
|---|---|
| CAUTION ALERT | *Stay cautious, neglecting a team charter can lead to role confusion and reduced team efficiency.* |

## QUESTION 16

Answer – B)

Option A – Azure Logic Apps is a good choice, but Power Automate provides more seamless integration within the Power Platform ecosystem.
Option B – Correct choice as Power Automate supports real-time data updates and integrates well with Dynamics 365.
Option C – Data Export Service is more suited for exporting data rather than real-time integration.
Option D – Azure Data Factory is more appropriate for batch data processing.
Option E – Azure Functions can be used but requires more custom development.

| EXAM FOCUS | "Use Power Automate for seamless real-time data updates and integration within Power Platform." |
|---|---|
| CAUTION ALERT | "Avoid using tools like Data Export Service for real-time integrations; it's more suited for exporting data." |

## QUESTION 17

Answer – A), B), E)

Option A – Using Power BI to create sustainability dashboards helps in assessing environmental impact.
Option B – Implementing Power Automate streamlines processes and reduces energy consumption.
Option C – Developing custom APIs adds complexity and should be avoided unless necessary.
Option D – Utilizing AI Builder can be beneficial, but it does not directly address environmental impact and sustainability.
Option E – Using Dataverse to centralize environmental data ensures consistency and aids in sustainability planning.

| EXAM FOCUS | *Use Power BI for sustainability dashboards, Power Automate to reduce energy use, and Dataverse for data consistency.* |
|---|---|
| CAUTION ALERT | *Avoid custom APIs unless necessary; they add complexity without directly addressing sustainability.* |

## QUESTION 18

Answer – A), D)

Option A – Using Dataverse ensures scalable data storage.
Option B – Developing custom connectors allows future integrations but might add unnecessary complexity.
Option C – Role-based security handles varying access needs but does not directly address flexibility and adaptability.
Option D – Using Power Automate for workflows ensures automation and adaptability to changing processes.
Option E – Developing a single, large canvas app can hinder flexibility and scalability.

| EXAM FOCUS | *Use Dataverse for scalable data storage; Power Automate ensures flexible workflows adapting to business changes.* |
|---|---|
| CAUTION ALERT | *Avoid large canvas apps; they hinder flexibility and scalability.* |

## QUESTION 19

Answer – A), B), E)

Option A – Conducting user interviews and surveys gathers comprehensive customer insights.
Option B – Using Power BI to analyze customer data helps utilize feedback effectively in the solution design.
Option C – Implementing AI Builder predicts customer behavior but might not directly gather insights or utilize feedback.
Option D – Developing model-driven apps supports customer interactions but might not gather insights or utilize feedback effectively.
Option E – Creating user personas based on customer feedback guides the design process.

| EXAM FOCUS | *Use Power BI to analyze customer data and create personas based on feedback for a user-centric design.* |
|---|---|
| CAUTION ALERT | *Avoid over-relying on AI Builder for insights without thorough initial data gathering.* |

## QUESTION 20

Answer – A), D), F)

Option A – Correct choice as Account is part of the Common Data Model.
Option B – Business is not a standard table in the Common Data Model.
Option C – Grant is not a standard table in the Common Data Model.
Option D – Correct choice as Marketing List is part of the Common Data Model.
Option E – Program is not a standard table in the Common Data Model.
Option F – Correct choice as Task is part of the Common Data Model.

| EXAM FOCUS | *"Utilize standard tables like Account, Marketing List, and Task for Common Data Model compatibility."* |
|---|---|

| CAUTION ALERT | *"Ensure you select tables part of the Common Data Model; avoid non-standard tables like Business or Grant."* |

## QUESTION 21

Answer – A), B), D)

Option A – Power Automate can connect to existing legacy systems, facilitating integration.
Option B – Dataverse provides centralized data management, aligning with enterprise architecture.
Option C – Custom API integration is an option, but not always necessary for alignment.
Option D – Azure Logic Apps helps orchestrate workflows across the IT infrastructure.
Option E – Modular design with Canvas Apps helps, but is not directly related to alignment with enterprise architecture.

| EXAM FOCUS | *Use Power Automate and Azure Logic Apps for integration; Dataverse for data management.* |
| CAUTION ALERT | *Avoid overlooking the importance of aligning solutions with enterprise architecture.* |

## QUESTION 22

Answer – A), D)

Option A – Azure SQL Database with Geo-Replication ensures high availability and disaster recovery.
Option B – Azure Policy is useful for cost management but not directly for high availability or disaster recovery.
Option C – Dataverse is suitable for data storage but not specifically for high availability and disaster recovery.
Option D – MFA using Azure AD enhances security for managing sensitive customer data.
Option E – Power BI helps with data analytics but does not address high availability or disaster recovery.

| EXAM FOCUS | *Remember, Azure SQL Database with Geo-Replication and MFA using Azure AD are key for high availability and secure data management.* |
| CAUTION ALERT | *You should stay cautious about options that do not directly address high availability or disaster recovery, like Power BI.* |

## QUESTION 23

Answer – A), C)

Option A – Azure DevOps supports CI/CD pipelines and version control for Power Apps.
Option B – Power Apps Solution Checker helps in maintaining solution quality but does not manage version control or deployment processes.
Option C – GitHub Actions provides CI/CD pipeline capabilities and automates deployments.
Option D – Power Automate helps with workflows and automation but not directly with CI/CD pipelines or version control.
Option E – Dataverse is used for data storage and management, not for CI/CD or version control.

| EXAM FOCUS | *Remember, Azure DevOps and GitHub Actions streamline CI/CD pipelines and version control for ALM in Power Platform.* |

| CAUTION ALERT | Stay cautious about choosing tools like Power Automate, which don't directly manage CI/CD or version control. |

## QUESTION 24

Answer – C), E)

Option A – Referential relationships enforce referential integrity but do not automatically delete related records.
Option B – Custom relationships can be configured for specific behaviors but are more complex.
Option C – Correct choice as Parental relationships automatically delete related records.
Option D – Referential, Restrict Delete prevents deletion if there are related records, but does not automate deletion.
Option E – Correct choice as Delete Cascade will automatically delete related records.

| EXAM FOCUS | "Use Parental and Delete Cascade relationships to ensure automatic deletion of related records." |
| CAUTION ALERT | "Referential and Restrict Delete settings do not automate related record deletion." |

## QUESTION 25

Answer – A), D), E)

Option A – Canvas Apps are ideal for creating custom, cross-platform mobile applications.
Option B – Azure API Management is useful but not directly related to offline capabilities and data synchronization.
Option C – Power Automate helps with data synchronization but may not be sufficient alone.
Option D – Implementing local caching ensures offline capabilities and efficient data synchronization once online.
Option E – Dataverse provides a robust backend database for managing and synchronizing data.

| EXAM FOCUS | Use Canvas Apps, local caching, and Dataverse to ensure cross-platform compatibility, offline access, and efficient data sync. |
| CAUTION ALERT | Stay cautious about relying solely on Power Automate for data synchronization; it may need supplementary tools. |

## QUESTION 26

Answer – A), B), D)

Option A – Power Automate Cloud Flow can automatically trigger workflows when a new order is placed.
Option B – AI Builder can be used for validating order details using AI.
Option C – Power BI is primarily for data visualization and tracking, not workflow automation.
Option D – Power Automate approvals can be used to send notifications to the logistics team for discrepancies.
Option E – Azure Logic Apps is useful for integration but not necessarily required for the described workflow automation.

| EXAM FOCUS | Use Power Automate Cloud Flow, AI Builder, and approvals for automated workflows, AI validation, |

| CAUTION ALERT | *and notifications.*<br>*Be cautious about relying on Power BI for automation; it's primarily for data visualization.* |
|---|---|

## QUESTION 27

Answer – A), B), D)

Option A – Dataverse can be used for data storage and policy enforcement.
Option B – Azure Policy helps in compliance monitoring.
Option C – Power Automate is useful for workflow automation but not directly for governance framework.
Option D – RBAC is essential for managing user permissions.
Option E – Power BI can be used for reporting but not directly for enforcing policies.

| EXAM FOCUS | *Implement Dataverse, Azure Policy, and RBAC to ensure compliance, data security, and user access management.* |
|---|---|
| CAUTION ALERT | *Be cautious about relying solely on Power Automate for governance; it focuses on workflow automation, not policy enforcement.* |

## QUESTION 28

Answer – B)

Option A – Power BI Dashboards are used for data visualization but do not automate report generation and distribution.
Option B – Power Automate Flows can be used to automate the process of generating and sending reports on a scheduled basis.
Option C – Power Apps Canvas Apps are used for building custom applications but not for automating report generation.
Option D – Dynamics 365 Marketing is focused on marketing automation, not project status reporting.
Option E – Azure Logic Apps is a viable option but more complex compared to Power Automate for this scenario.

| EXAM FOCUS | *"Use Power Automate Flows to automate report generation and distribution effectively."* |
|---|---|
| CAUTION ALERT | *"Power BI Dashboards are for visualization, not automation."* |

## QUESTION 29

Answer – A), B)

Option A – Correct. Azure Cost Management and Billing is essential for tracking and optimizing costs.
Option B – Correct. ALM best practices help reduce resource redundancy and improve efficiency.
Option C – Incorrect. While automation can reduce operational costs, it is not as directly related to the initial cost estimation and management.
Option D – Incorrect. Custom connectors can be costly, and evaluating out-of-the-box alternatives is more cost-effective.
Option E – Incorrect. AI Builder can help with predictions, but it is not as directly impactful on

immediate cost management.

| EXAM FOCUS | Use Azure Cost Management and ALM best practices to track and optimize costs effectively. |
| CAUTION ALERT | Stay cautious about using high-cost custom connectors without evaluating out-of-the-box alternatives. |

## QUESTION 30

Answer – B), D)

Option A – Incorrect. Power BI can help with performance tracking but is not the first step in vendor evaluation.
Option B – Correct. Evaluating vendors based on relevant experience ensures they are capable.
Option C – Incorrect. Cost should not be the sole criterion for selection.
Option D – Correct. Comprehensive assessments ensure a thorough evaluation of capabilities.
Option E – Incorrect. Contracts should consider long-term partnership and benefits.

| EXAM FOCUS | Evaluate vendors based on relevant experience and conduct comprehensive assessments. |
| CAUTION ALERT | Don't select vendors solely based on cost; consider capabilities and past performance. |

## QUESTION 31

Answer – A), D)

Option A – Correct. Azure IoT Hub is designed to connect and manage IoT devices effectively.
Option B – Incorrect. While Power BI is useful for visualization, it is not primarily for managing IoT devices.
Option C – Incorrect. Storing data locally limits scalability and real-time processing.
Option D – Correct. Azure Stream Analytics is ideal for real-time data processing.
Option E – Incorrect. Custom applications can increase complexity and are not necessary with Azure IoT solutions.

| EXAM FOCUS | Use Azure IoT Hub and Stream Analytics for scalable, real-time data processing. |
| CAUTION ALERT | Avoid storing IoT data locally; it limits scalability and real-time processing. |

## QUESTION 32

Answer – C)

Option A – Webhooks are useful for event-driven integrations but do not address the issue of identifying rows without GUIDs.
Option B – Azure Functions can process data but do not minimize the number of requests as efficiently as alternative keys.
Option C – Alternative Keys allow the integration to identify and update rows based on a unique attribute, minimizing the number of requests.
Option D – Batch API can help minimize requests but does not address the identification of rows without GUIDs.
Option E – Microsoft Graph API is not specific to Dataverse and does not address the problem of missing

GUIDs.

| EXAM FOCUS | *"Use Alternative Keys to integrate external systems without relying on GUIDs."* |
| CAUTION ALERT | *"Webhooks and Batch API do not solve row identification without GUIDs."* |

## QUESTION 33

Answer – B), E)

Option A – Incorrect. Power BI is useful for monitoring but not primarily for reducing environmental impact.
Option B – Correct. Azure IoT helps monitor and optimize energy consumption.
Option C – Incorrect. Ignoring green standards can lead to non-compliance and increased environmental impact.
Option D – Incorrect. Power Automate can streamline workflows but is not the primary tool for eco-friendly practices.
Option E – Correct. Selecting energy-efficient cloud services and hardware reduces environmental impact.

| EXAM FOCUS | *Use Azure IoT and energy-efficient services to meet eco-friendly goals and comply with green standards.* |
| CAUTION ALERT | *Ignoring green standards can lead to non-compliance and increased environmental impact.* |

## QUESTION 34

Answer – B), E)

Option A – A big bang migration risks high downtime and data integrity issues.
Option B – Using an ETL tool for incremental migration minimizes downtime and maintains data integrity.
Option C – Manual CSV import is error-prone and inefficient for large datasets.
Option D – Custom scripts are complex and may not ensure data consistency.
Option E – Azure Data Factory is useful for orchestrating and automating the migration process.

| EXAM FOCUS | *Remember, you should use an ETL tool during off-peak hours to ensure minimal downtime and maintain data integrity.* |
| CAUTION ALERT | *Avoid big bang migrations; they can lead to high downtime and significant data integrity issues.* |

## QUESTION 35

Answer – A), D), E)

Option A – SharePoint provides a centralized and accessible document repository.
Option B – Regular review meetings are useful but may not ensure documentation is updated in real-time.
Option C – Video tutorials are helpful but should complement written documentation.

Option D – Azure DevOps allows version control for maintaining up-to-date documentation.
Option E – Wikis are effective for collaborative documentation and easy updates.

| EXAM FOCUS | Use SharePoint for centralized documentation and Azure DevOps for version control to keep documents updated and accessible. |
|---|---|
| CAUTION ALERT | Avoid relying solely on meetings for updates; documentation must be updated in real-time for accuracy. |

## QUESTION 36

Answer – C)

Option A – Azure Functions require custom code and are not as straightforward for real-time synchronization.
Option B – A Custom Connector can work but might be more complex to develop and maintain for this use case.
Option C – Power Automate with an HTTP request action is ideal for real-time integration and automates the process effectively.
Option D – Dynamics 365 Customer Insights is for customer data analysis and not for order management and shipping integration.
Option E – Azure Data Factory is used for ETL processes, not real-time data synchronization.

| EXAM FOCUS | "Use Power Automate HTTP action for real-time integration and automated shipping updates." |
|---|---|
| CAUTION ALERT | "Azure Functions require custom code and are not ideal for simple real-time synchronization." |

## QUESTION 37

Answer – A), B), D)

Option A – Dataverse as a central data store ensures data consistency.
Option B – Power Automate facilitates cross-functional workflows.
Option C – Separate data stores can lead to data inconsistencies.
Option D – Azure API Management ensures secure data access across departments.
Option E – Custom connectors can be useful but may increase complexity and maintenance efforts.

| EXAM FOCUS | Use Dataverse and Power Automate to ensure data consistency and secure workflows across departments. |
|---|---|
| CAUTION ALERT | Avoid separate data stores; they lead to data inconsistencies and management challenges. |

## QUESTION 38

Answer – A), D)

Option A – Integrating AI Builder with Power Automate automates routine tasks efficiently.
Option B – Sentiment analysis is useful but does not address automation of routine tasks.
Option C – Deploying AI Builder without evaluating workflows can disrupt current operations.
Option D – A pilot project helps assess the impact on workflows.

Option E – Manual scaling is inefficient compared to automated scaling approaches.

| EXAM FOCUS | Integrate AI Builder with Power Automate and conduct a pilot project to assess workflow impacts. |
|---|---|
| CAUTION ALERT | Avoid deploying AI Builder without evaluating current workflows; it can disrupt operations. |

## QUESTION 39

Answer – A), C)

Option A – Dataverse with encryption ensures secure data transmission.
Option B – Azure API Management secures APIs but does not directly address the need for regular security evaluations.
Option C – Regular security audits and penetration testing help in evaluating and updating security measures.
Option D – HTTP is not secure for data transmission; HTTPS should be used.
Option E – Applying a single security policy does not account for role-specific security needs.

| EXAM FOCUS | Use Dataverse with encryption and conduct regular security audits to ensure secure data transmission and updates. |
|---|---|
| CAUTION ALERT | Avoid using HTTP for data transmission; always use HTTPS to ensure data security. |

## QUESTION 40

Answer – A)

Option A – Power Automate provides templates for manager approval workflows, allowing easy automation of the approval process.
Option B – Business rules enforce data validation and logic but do not handle complex approval workflows.
Option C – Custom plug-ins require more development effort and are not as easily maintained.
Option D – Model-driven apps are more data-centric and less flexible for custom approval processes compared to Power Automate.
Option E – Azure Logic Apps can handle workflows but are more complex and less integrated with Dynamics 365 compared to Power Automate.

| EXAM FOCUS | "Use Power Automate templates to quickly automate approval workflows." |
|---|---|
| CAUTION ALERT | "Custom plug-ins require more effort and are harder to maintain than Power Automate flows." |

## QUESTION 41

Answer – A), B)

Option A – Azure Functions is a serverless compute service that allows for scalable and efficient processing, which aligns with the requirement for serverless architecture.
Option B – Azure Kubernetes Service (AKS) is ideal for container orchestration, providing deployment consistency and scalability.
Option C – Power Automate is not suitable for managing container deployment; it is primarily used for

workflow automation.

Option D – Azure Logic Apps can handle secure communication, but it is not a serverless compute option.

Option E – Power BI is used for data visualization and reporting, not for implementing serverless architecture or containerization.

| EXAM FOCUS | Use Azure Functions and AKS for scalable serverless architecture and container orchestration. |
|---|---|
| CAUTION ALERT | Avoid using Power Automate for managing container deployment; it is primarily for workflows. |

## QUESTION 42

Answer – A), B), E)

Option A – Dataverse with RBAC ensures that only authorized personnel can access sensitive patient data, supporting data privacy by design principles.

Option B – Azure Security Center provides continuous monitoring and helps maintain compliance with health regulations.

Option C – While anonymizing data is useful, Power Automate is not the best tool for this purpose, and anonymization alone may not be sufficient.

Option D – Storing data locally does not leverage the benefits of cloud security and compliance tools available in Azure.

Option E – Azure Key Vault manages encryption keys securely, ensuring that sensitive data is protected and access is controlled.

| EXAM FOCUS | Use Dataverse with RBAC and Azure Security Center for compliance and monitoring. |
|---|---|
| CAUTION ALERT | Avoid storing sensitive data locally; use cloud security features. |

## QUESTION 43

Answer – A), B), D)

Option A – Azure Logic Apps is ideal for creating workflows that facilitate reliable data integration between systems.

Option B – Implementing SSL/TLS ensures that data transfers are secure and compliant with healthcare regulations.

Option C – Storing patient data in an unencrypted format compromises security and violates compliance requirements.

Option D – Azure API Management provides robust tools for managing and securing API calls, ensuring reliable and secure integration.

Option E – Manual data transfers are error-prone and do not ensure reliability or maintainability.

| EXAM FOCUS | Use Azure Logic Apps for workflows and SSL/TLS for secure transfers. |
|---|---|
| CAUTION ALERT | Avoid unencrypted data storage; it violates compliance requirements. |

## QUESTION 44

Answer – D)

Option A – Incorrect. Power Apps with Azure SQL can provide secure data storage but does not inherently offer the specific controls needed for HIPAA compliance.
Option B – Incorrect. Power Automate with data policies can streamline processes but alone isn't enough for the required security and compliance.
Option C – Incorrect. Power BI with Row-Level Security provides data analysis security but does not handle record management or compliance.
Option D – Correct. Power Apps combined with Common Data Service ensures secure data management and accessibility, which are crucial for managing patient records under HIPAA.
Option E – Incorrect. Power Virtual Agents with Azure Bot Service focuses on automated interactions and does not address secure data management or HIPAA compliance.

| | |
|---|---|
| **EXAM FOCUS** | *"You should prioritize Power Apps with Common Data Service for secure, compliant healthcare solutions."* |
| **CAUTION ALERT** | *"Remember, Power Automate alone isn't enough for security and compliance; use Common Data Service."* |

## QUESTION 45

Answer – A), D)

Option A – Azure Data Factory is a robust tool for handling large datasets efficiently during migration.
Option B – Manual validation is time-consuming and prone to errors.
Option C – Dataverse is useful for managing data but not specifically for migration.
Option D – Automated data validation rules ensure data integrity and quality during migration.
Option E – Skipping data quality checks can lead to inaccurate data post-migration.

| | |
|---|---|
| **EXAM FOCUS** | *Use Azure Data Factory for efficient handling of large datasets during migration.* |
| **CAUTION ALERT** | *Avoid skipping data quality checks; it can lead to inaccurate data post-migration.* |

## QUESTION 46

Answer – A), B), C)

Option A – Using Azure AD for RBAC ensures centralized and effective management of user roles and permissions.
Option B – Implementing data encryption at rest and in transit protects data from unauthorized access and breaches.
Option C – Conducting security compliance audits using Power BI helps ensure the solution meets regulatory standards.
Option D – Manual role assignments can be error-prone and inefficient.
Option E – Skipping compliance validation is not acceptable as it can lead to regulatory violations and data breaches.

| | |
|---|---|
| **EXAM FOCUS** | *"Use Azure AD for centralized RBAC management and Power BI for security compliance audits."* |
| **CAUTION ALERT** | *"Avoid manual role assignments; they are error-prone and inefficient."* |

## QUESTION 47

Answer – A), B)

Option A – Using Power Apps Test Studio allows for automated testing of app functionalities.
Option B – Manual testing by end-users ensures the app meets real-world usability standards.
Option C – Skipping UAT is not advisable as it misses critical end-user feedback and validation.
Option D – Implementing performance testing using Azure Monitor helps identify and address performance issues before production.
Option E – Including security testing with Microsoft Defender for Cloud ensures the app is secure against potential threats.

| EXAM FOCUS | *"You should use Power Apps Test Studio for automated testing to ensure robust application functionality."* |
|---|---|
| CAUTION ALERT | *"Remember, skipping UAT can lead to missed critical end-user feedback and validation."* |

## QUESTION 48

Answer – A), C)

Option A – Correct. Optimizing data sources by minimizing the amount of data initially loaded can significantly improve app load times and performance.
Option B – Incorrect. While using the Concurrent function does help execute multiple operations at once, it is more effective when optimizing specific functions rather than overall navigation and load.
Option C – Correct. Reducing screen complexity by minimizing the number of controls and simplifying user interface elements can enhance navigation speed.
Option D – Incorrect. Implementing data pagination is helpful but does not directly increase load times unless combined with other optimizations.
Option E – Incorrect. Adding more data connectors would likely worsen performance, not improve it.

| EXAM FOCUS | *"Optimize data sources and reduce screen complexity to significantly improve Power Apps performance."* |
|---|---|
| CAUTION ALERT | *"Remember, adding more data connectors often worsens performance instead of improving it."* |

## QUESTION 49

Answer – A), B), C)

Option A – Correct. Azure DevOps provides version control and continuous integration/continuous deployment (CI/CD) pipelines, essential for managing updates and ensuring rollback capabilities.
Option B – Correct. Scheduling regular maintenance windows ensures that updates are applied systematically without disrupting business processes.
Option C – Correct. Power Platform's Solution Checker helps identify and resolve issues, ensuring the solution remains sustainable.
Option D – Incorrect. While automated testing is useful, the Power Automate Test Framework is not a direct solution for routine maintenance or version control.
Option E – Incorrect. Storing backups in Dataverse is not a standard practice for version control or rollback; Azure DevOps or a similar tool would be more appropriate.

| EXAM FOCUS | "You should use Azure DevOps for version control and CI/CD pipelines to ensure efficient update management." |
| CAUTION ALERT | "Remember, skipping regular maintenance can lead to unexpected issues and downtime." |

## QUESTION 50

Answer – A), B), C)

Option A – Correct. The Power Automate flow checker helps identify issues in the workflows.

Option B – Correct. Reviewing Dataverse audit logs can help identify related errors and pinpoint the root cause.

Option C – Correct. Implementing retry logic in Power Automate flows can help prevent future workflow failures.

Option D – Incorrect. While useful for monitoring, it does not directly address troubleshooting or preventing workflow failures.

Option E – Incorrect. Azure DevOps is more suited for deployment automation, not direct issue resolution in this context.

| EXAM FOCUS | "Use the Power Automate flow checker to identify issues quickly and efficiently." |
| CAUTION ALERT | "Remember, overlooking Dataverse audit logs can lead to missing critical error details." |

# PRACTICE TEST 2 - QUESTIONS ONLY

## QUESTION 1

A financial services company wants to optimize their loan approval process using Microsoft Power Platform. Their business goals include reducing processing time, ensuring regulatory compliance, and improving customer satisfaction. Specific challenges include:
- Manual data entry causing delays.
- Inconsistent compliance checks.
- Lack of real-time application status updates.

What solutions would best address these challenges while aligning with the company's business goals? Select two correct answers.

A) Use Power Automate to automate data entry from application forms.
B) Implement compliance workflows using Power Automate.
C) Develop a customer portal with Power Apps for real-time updates.
D) Create a Power BI report for regulatory compliance.
E) Integrate AI Builder for automatic data validation.

## QUESTION 2

In a consulting firm, the Power Apps portal used by international clients for project tracking is experiencing slow load times, particularly during multi-regional meetings. You need to determine what could be causing these slowdowns.
- Determine causes of slow load times.
- Optimize app for use during multi-regional meetings.

Which two factors should you consider when diagnosing and resolving the app's performance issues for a better user experience?

A) Network bandwidth
B) Service-level agreement (SLA)
C) Data model optimization
D) Network latency
E) Server scaling options

## QUESTION 3

A healthcare organization wants to improve its patient appointment system using Microsoft Power Platform. They need to analyze current processes and integrate with existing workflows. The specific challenges include:
- Manual scheduling leading to overbooking and missed appointments.
- Lack of integration with patient records.
- Difficulty in managing appointment reminders.

What actions would you take to integrate and improve the appointment system? Select two correct answers.

A) Implement a Power Apps solution for appointment scheduling.
B) Use Power Automate to send automated appointment reminders.

C) Integrate patient records with Dataverse.
D) Develop a Power BI dashboard to track appointment metrics.
E) Implement AI Builder for predictive appointment scheduling.

## QUESTION 4

A financial institution is developing a Power Platform solution to manage customer transactions. The developer's code uses multiple RetrieveMultiple calls to fetch transaction records based on various criteria, which impacts performance.
• The solution must optimize data retrieval performance.
• It should streamline the code.
What should you recommend the developer use to achieve this? Select two answers.

A) FetchXML query
B) Alternate keys
C) OData $filter query
D) Business process flow
E) OData $expand query

## QUESTION 5

A healthcare organization is planning to adopt a new patient management system using Microsoft Power Platform. The project requires selecting the right technologies to meet their specific requirements. The specific challenges include:
• Ensuring compliance with healthcare data regulations.
• Integrating with existing electronic health record (EHR) systems.
• Evaluating the long-term costs and benefits of different technologies.
What actions would you take to address these challenges? Select three correct answers.

A) Implement Dataverse to securely store patient data.
B) Use Azure API Management to integrate with existing EHR systems.
C) Conduct a future-proofing analysis to evaluate long-term costs and benefits.
D) Develop a Power Apps solution for patient data entry.
E) Implement DLP policies to ensure data compliance.

## QUESTION 6

A healthcare organization is implementing a new patient management system using Microsoft Power Platform. The project requires strategies for risk mitigation and impact analysis. The specific challenges include:
• Ensuring data privacy and compliance with HIPAA.
• Analyzing the impact of system changes on patient care.
• Continuous monitoring of system performance.
What actions would you take to mitigate these risks? Select three correct answers.

A) Implement Dataverse to store patient data securely.
B) Use Power BI to monitor system performance.
C) Apply DLP policies to ensure data privacy.
D) Conduct an impact analysis before implementing system changes.

E) Develop a continuous monitoring plan using Azure Monitor.

## QUESTION 7

A healthcare organization is planning to implement a new electronic health record (EHR) system using Microsoft Power Platform. The project requires effective resource allocation and management. The specific challenges include:
- Allocating resources to critical tasks.
- Scheduling training sessions for staff.
- Ensuring project milestones are met.

What actions would you take to address these challenges? Select three correct answers.

A) Use Azure DevOps to assign resources to tasks.
B) Implement Dataverse to manage health records.
C) Use Power Automate to schedule training sessions.
D) Develop a project timeline with milestones using Power BI.
E) Conduct regular resource reviews.

## QUESTION 8

A financial institution is undergoing a digital transformation by implementing a new CRM system using Microsoft Power Platform. The project involves managing resistance to change. The specific challenges are:
- Addressing employee concerns about the new system.
- Encouraging adoption of the new system.
- Providing adequate training.

What actions would you take to address these challenges? Select two correct answers.

A) Use Power Apps to develop a user-friendly CRM interface.
B) Conduct training sessions using Microsoft Teams.
C) Use Power BI to analyze adoption rates.
D) Develop a change management plan that includes employee feedback sessions.
E) Implement Azure Functions for automation.

## QUESTION 9

A financial services company is implementing a new customer relationship management (CRM) system using Microsoft Power Platform. The project requires setting performance benchmarks. The specific challenges are:
- Defining performance requirements.
- Establishing benchmarks for system performance.
- Ensuring the system meets performance standards.

What actions would you take to address these challenges? Select two correct answers.

A) Use Power Automate to automate performance testing.
B) Implement performance testing using Azure DevOps.
C) Use Power BI to create performance dashboards.
D) Develop performance benchmarks using industry standards.
E) Implement Dataverse for data management.

## QUESTION 10

A financial institution is upgrading its customer relationship management system using Dynamics 365. The project requires managing stakeholder expectations. The specific challenges are:
- Aligning stakeholder expectations with project deliverables.
- Addressing stakeholder concerns promptly.
- Ensuring stakeholder satisfaction.

What steps would you take to address these challenges? Select two correct answers.

A) Create a detailed project plan with timelines.
B) Use Power Automate for automated notifications.
C) Conduct regular feedback sessions with stakeholders.
D) Use Azure DevOps for continuous integration.
E) Implement Power BI for performance tracking.

## QUESTION 11

A financial services firm needs to integrate its CRM system with a third-party financial data provider using Microsoft Power Platform. The specific challenges are:
- Assessing vendor data integration capabilities.
- Ensuring secure data transfer and compliance with GDPR.
- Negotiating favorable pricing and support terms.

What steps would you take to address these challenges? Select two correct answers.

A) Conduct a thorough assessment of vendor data integration capabilities, focusing on API and ETL processes.
B) Use Power Apps to create a secure data input form for vendor evaluation.
C) Implement Azure Logic Apps for secure data transfer testing.
D) Use Power Automate to automate contract negotiation workflows.
E) Compare vendor pricing models and support terms.

## QUESTION 12

A healthcare provider is implementing a patient engagement solution using Microsoft Power Platform. The solution needs to integrate with their existing EHR system and ensure patient data is secure.
- The solution must comply with HIPAA regulations.
- It should provide analytics and reporting to improve patient outcomes.

Which combination of tools would best meet these requirements?

A) Power Apps, Power Automate, Power BI, Azure API Management
B) Power Apps, Power Automate, Power BI, Azure Logic Apps
C) Power Apps, Power Automate, Power BI, Microsoft Dataverse
D) Power Apps, Power Automate, Power BI, Azure Synapse Analytics
E) Power Apps, Power Automate, Power Virtual Agents, Azure API Management

## QUESTION 13

A healthcare provider wants to foster an innovative mindset among its IT team while ensuring practical implementation. The challenges include:

- Encouraging innovation.
- Balancing innovation with practicality.
- Predicting and preparing for future changes.

What steps should you take to address these challenges? Select three correct answers.

A) Conduct regular innovation workshops.
B) Implement a sandbox environment for experimentation.
C) Use Power BI to track innovation metrics.
D) Develop a strategic roadmap for technology adoption.
E) Schedule quarterly reviews for innovation initiatives.

## QUESTION 14

A financial services company is deploying a new compliance management system using the Microsoft Power Platform. The challenges include:
- Planning deployment phases.
- Strategies for successful rollouts.
- Post-deployment monitoring and support.

What strategies should you adopt to ensure a smooth deployment and successful rollout? Select three correct answers.

A) Schedule regular post-deployment review meetings.
B) Use Azure Logic Apps to automate deployment processes.
C) Develop comprehensive user documentation and training materials.
D) Implement Power Automate for automated monitoring and alerts.
E) Establish a dedicated support team for post-deployment issues.

## QUESTION 15

A financial services firm is using Microsoft Power Platform to implement a new solution. The team faces challenges such as:
- Enhancing collaboration and teamwork.
- Resolving team conflicts and challenges.
- Managing remote and distributed team members.

Which strategies should you adopt to address these challenges? Select three correct answers.

A) Conduct regular virtual meetings using Microsoft Teams.
B) Implement Dynamics 365 for conflict resolution tracking.
C) Use Power Virtual Agents for team training.
D) Develop conflict resolution protocols.
E) Use Azure DevOps for project management and collaboration.

## QUESTION 16

A financial institution is deploying a new Dynamics 365 Finance and Operations system and needs to ensure proper application lifecycle management (ALM). The institution wants to automate deployments across environments and ensure that the solution is scalable and maintainable.
- The ALM process must support continuous integration and continuous deployment (CI/CD).
- It should minimize manual intervention and ensure traceability of changes.

Which tools should be used for ALM in this scenario? Select all that apply.

A) ALM Accelerator
B) Azure Pipelines in Azure DevOps
C) Manual ALM
D) Microsoft Power Platform Pipelines
E) Scripts that run on an Azure VM

## QUESTION 17

A manufacturing company is planning to deploy a new production management system using Microsoft Power Platform. The team faces challenges such as:
• Assessing environmental impact of solutions.
• Implementing eco-friendly practices.
• Compliance with environmental standards.
What steps should you take to address these challenges? Select three correct answers.

A) Conduct workshops with key stakeholders to gather environmental requirements and feedback.
B) Use Power BI to create detailed environmental impact reports.
C) Implement a phased rollout strategy to manage compliance effectively.
D) Develop custom connectors to integrate with legacy environmental monitoring systems.
E) Utilize Azure Functions for cost-effective, scalable computing.

## QUESTION 18

An e-commerce company is transitioning to a new ERP system using Microsoft Power Platform. The solution must:
• Be flexible enough to integrate with future third-party systems.
• Adapt to evolving business processes and user requirements.
• Maintain relevance and functionality over time.
You need to select three actions to design a solution that meets these requirements. Which three actions should you take? (Select three)

A) Use Power Apps component framework (PCF) to develop reusable components.
B) Implement ALM practices using Azure DevOps.
C) Utilize Dataverse for data management and integration.
D) Develop multiple canvas apps for different functions.
E) Use Azure Functions to handle complex business logic.

## QUESTION 19

An e-commerce company is implementing a new customer engagement solution using Microsoft Power Platform. The solution must:
• Understand user behavior and preferences.
• Incorporate user-centric design principles.
• Utilize feedback loops for continuous improvement.
Which two strategies should you employ to meet these objectives? (Select two)

A) Use Power Apps to create a feedback form for users.

B) Implement Dataverse to store customer preferences.
C) Use Power Virtual Agents to interact with customers.
D) Analyze feedback using Power BI dashboards.
E) Conduct A/B testing with different user interface designs.

## QUESTION 20

A financial institution is implementing a model-driven app using Microsoft Dataverse. They need to ensure the app integrates seamlessly with their existing CRM system and maintains data integrity.
• The solution must ensure data accuracy and consistency.
• It should automate data synchronization between Dataverse and the CRM system.
Which components should you use to achieve this? Select two answers.

A) Business rule
B) Power Automate
C) Duplicate detection rules
D) Virtual tables
E) Dataflows

## QUESTION 21

A financial institution aims to integrate their Power Platform solutions with their existing IT infrastructure while ensuring long-term architectural strategy. The solution must:
• Integrate with existing IT infrastructure.
• Balance innovation with existing systems.
• Ensure long-term architectural strategy.
Which two actions should you take? (Select two)

A) Use Azure API Management to manage and secure APIs.
B) Implement Power Virtual Agents for customer support.
C) Utilize Azure Service Bus for message queuing.
D) Conduct regular architectural reviews and updates.
E) Use AI Builder to add intelligence to applications.

## QUESTION 22

A retail company needs a hybrid Power Platform solution integrated with their on-premises ERP system. The solution must:
• Enable seamless data synchronization.
• Ensure data security during transmission.
• Maintain system performance.
Which two components should you use? (Select two)

A) Use Azure Logic Apps for data integration.
B) Implement Azure Service Bus for messaging.
C) Use Power Virtual Agents for customer support.
D) Use Azure Functions for data processing.
E) Implement Azure API Management for API gateway and security.

## QUESTION 23

A financial services company needs to implement an ALM strategy to manage their Power Platform environments. They want to ensure environments and releases are managed efficiently while maintaining high-quality standards. The solution must:
- Use automated testing.
- Manage multiple environments.
- Ensure controlled releases.

Which two actions should you take? (Select two)

A) Use Azure DevOps for pipeline management.
B) Implement Power Platform Build Tools.
C) Use manual testing for quality assurance.
D) Use Dataverse for environment management.
E) Use Dynamics 365 for release management.

## QUESTION 24

An educational institution is using Microsoft Dataverse to manage student enrollments and course information. They need to ensure that student records are automatically deleted when the corresponding enrollment record is deleted.
- The solution must automate the deletion of dependent records.
- It should enforce data integrity rules.

Which type of relationship behavior should you configure? Select two answers.

A) Custom
B) Parental
C) Referential
D) Referential, Restrict Delete
E) Cascade Delete

## QUESTION 25

An insurance company is developing a cross-platform mobile app using Power Apps to allow customers to file claims. The solution must:
- Ensure high performance and fast load times.
- Be optimized for different form factors.
- Implement robust security measures for sensitive data.

Which three practices should you follow? (Select three)

A) Use responsive design principles.
B) Implement Azure Functions for backend processing.
C) Use Power Automate for process automation.
D) Enable multi-factor authentication (MFA).
E) Implement Data Loss Prevention (DLP) policies.

## QUESTION 26

A healthcare organization wants to optimize their patient admission process using Power Automate. The

solution must:
- Automatically update patient records in Dataverse.
- Trigger alerts for missing information.
- Provide real-time data synchronization across multiple systems.

Which three strategies should you implement? (Select three)

A) Power Automate Cloud Flow for updating patient records.
B) Azure Functions for custom logic and alerts.
C) Dataverse Connector for data integration.
D) Power BI for real-time data visualization.
E) Power Automate Desktop for local automation.

## QUESTION 27

A financial institution needs to ensure that its Power Platform solutions comply with GDPR regulations. The solution must:
- Implement data loss prevention (DLP) policies.
- Provide detailed audit logs.
- Restrict access based on user roles.

Which components should be configured to meet these requirements? (Select three)

A) Power Platform Admin Center for DLP policies.
B) Azure Log Analytics for audit logs.
C) Azure AD for user role management.
D) Power BI for data visualization.
E) Azure Key Vault for data encryption.

## QUESTION 28

An educational institution uses Dynamics 365 to manage student records and academic activities. They want to ensure that all changes to student records are audited and that audit logs are maintained for compliance purposes. Which feature of Dynamics 365 should they use to implement this requirement?

A) Business Rules
B) Audit Logs
C) Security Roles
D) Data Import Wizard
E) Workflows

## QUESTION 29

As a Power Platform Solution Architect, you need to help a client with budgeting and financial planning for a new Power Platform implementation. The client is concerned about over-budgeting and seeks strategies to stay within their financial limits.
1. Identifying and managing potential cost overruns.
2. Creating a detailed budget that aligns with business goals.
3. Ensuring efficient use of resources without sacrificing quality.

What strategies would you recommend to the client to manage their budget effectively? Select three answers.

A) Develop a comprehensive budget plan that includes all anticipated costs and contingencies.
B) Regularly review and adjust the budget based on project progress and changes.
C) Use Power BI to create dashboards that track budget performance and resource utilization.
D) Ignore small overages as they will not impact the overall budget significantly.
E) Use Azure DevOps to manage project tasks and resource allocation efficiently.

## QUESTION 30

A client in the healthcare sector is looking to integrate third-party solutions with their existing Power Platform setup. They need assistance in managing vendor relationships and ensuring compliance with industry regulations.
1. Ensuring the third-party solutions comply with healthcare regulations.
2. Managing and monitoring vendor performance and Service Level Agreements (SLAs).
3. Integrating solutions seamlessly with minimal disruption.
What measures should you implement to manage vendor relationships effectively? Select three answers.

A) Use Dynamics 365 to manage vendor contracts and performance.
B) Implement regular performance reviews and compliance audits.
C) Select vendors based on their ability to provide low-cost solutions.
D) Ensure SLAs include specific compliance and performance metrics.
E) Integrate third-party solutions using Azure API Management.

## QUESTION 31

A retail client wants to implement an IoT solution to monitor their inventory in real-time and generate actionable insights to optimize stock levels. They need a solution that integrates external data sources and ensures data security and privacy.
1. Integrating IoT devices with Power Platform for real-time inventory monitoring.
2. Ensuring data security and privacy.
3. Generating actionable insights to optimize stock levels.
What actions would you take to meet these objectives? Select three answers.

A) Use Azure IoT Hub to connect and secure IoT devices.
B) Implement Power Automate to automate inventory alerts.
C) Use Dataverse to store inventory data securely.
D) Apply AI Builder to develop models predicting inventory needs.
E) Use Azure Functions for real-time data processing.

## QUESTION 32

A financial institution uses Dynamics 365 Finance to manage their financial operations. They need to ensure compliance with international financial regulations by regularly updating their financial data from a third-party regulatory system. The integration must handle high volumes of data efficiently and ensure data accuracy. What approach should they use to integrate the third-party system with Dynamics 365 Finance?

A) Use Azure Logic Apps
B) Implement Dual-write

C) Use Power Automate with an on-premises data gateway
D) Use Custom Connectors
E) Implement Data Export Service

## QUESTION 33

A client in the manufacturing sector is adopting Microsoft Power Platform to enhance their operations. They want to ensure their solutions are sustainable and promote eco-friendly practices.
1. Designing solutions that minimize environmental impact.
2. Promoting sustainable practices in technology use.
3. Ensuring compliance with eco-friendly regulations.
What actions would you take to meet these objectives? Select three answers.

A) Use Power Apps to develop applications that reduce paper usage.
B) Implement AI Builder to optimize resource usage and minimize waste.
C) Select cloud services with low carbon footprints.
D) Focus solely on operational efficiency without considering environmental impact.
E) Use Power BI to track compliance with eco-friendly regulations.

## QUESTION 34

A manufacturing company is using an on-premises ERP system and wants to integrate it with Power Apps for improved workflow automation. The project requirements are:
• Securely connect to the ERP system from Power Apps.
• Ensure real-time data synchronization.
• Minimize custom development efforts. What are the best approaches to meet these requirements? (Select 2 answers)

A) Use Azure API Management to expose ERP data as APIs and connect them to Power Apps.
B) Develop custom connectors in Power Apps to integrate with the ERP system.
C) Use Power Automate to create workflows that synchronize data between ERP and Power Apps in real-time.
D) Implement Azure Logic Apps for integration and automation.
E) Export ERP data to Dataverse and access it through Power Apps.

## QUESTION 35

A distributed team is working on a Power Apps project and requires efficient knowledge transfer and up-to-date documentation. The documentation should:
• Facilitate remote collaboration.
• Be accessible to all team members.
• Include a change history for traceability. What tools and techniques should the team use? (Select 2 answers)

A) Use Microsoft Teams for collaboration and document sharing.
B) Maintain documentation in a centralized SharePoint library.
C) Use email for sharing updates and documents.
D) Implement a documentation management system with version control in Azure DevOps.
E) Print and distribute hard copies of documentation to all team members.

## QUESTION 36

A healthcare organization uses Power Platform to manage patient records. They want to implement an AI solution to predict patient readmission rates using historical data stored in Dataverse. The solution must be easy to deploy and manage without extensive AI expertise. What tool should they use?

A) Power BI
B) Azure Machine Learning
C) AI Builder
D) Power Automate
E) Dynamics 365 Customer Service

## QUESTION 37

A manufacturing company wants to integrate Power Platform solutions with their existing ERP and CRM systems. The integration must:
- Bridge technology gaps between departments.
- Ensure real-time data synchronization.
- Maintain high performance and scalability. What approaches should you consider? (Select 2 answers)

A) Use Power Automate for real-time data synchronization.
B) Implement Dataverse for data storage and integration.
C) Use manual data entry to bridge technology gaps.
D) Implement Azure Service Bus for reliable messaging.
E) Use Power BI for real-time data visualization.

## QUESTION 38

A company is considering implementing IoT solutions integrated with Power Platform to improve operational efficiency. The solution must:
- Utilize real-time data from IoT devices.
- Provide actionable insights through Power BI.
- Ensure scalability for future expansion. What components and approaches should be used? (Select 3 answers)

A) Use Azure IoT Hub to collect and manage IoT data.
B) Integrate IoT data with Power BI for visualization.
C) Use Azure Functions to process IoT data in real-time.
D) Store IoT data in local databases for quick access.
E) Implement Power Automate to trigger workflows based on IoT data.

## QUESTION 39

A financial services firm is implementing a Power Platform solution that requires robust security. The solution must:
- Mitigate potential security threats.
- Ensure secure communication between services.
- Follow best practices for security design. What strategies should you implement? (Select 3 answers)

A) Use Azure Key Vault to manage and secure sensitive information.

B) Implement role-based access control (RBAC) in Dataverse.
C) Use public endpoints for API communication.
D) Conduct threat modeling during the design phase.
E) Use rotating encryption keys for all data.

## QUESTION 40

A university uses Dynamics 365 to manage student admissions. They need to automate the process of sending follow-up emails to applicants after they submit their application forms through a Power Apps portal. The follow-up email should include a personalized acknowledgment and further instructions. What tool should they use to automate this process?

A) Use Power Automate with the "When a record is created in Dataverse" trigger.
B) Develop a custom Azure Function to send emails.
C) Implement a business rule to trigger email notifications.
D) Use Dynamics 365 Customer Insights to manage email campaigns.
E) Create a flow in Power BI to send emails.

## QUESTION 41

A financial services firm is developing a new application using cloud-native principles. The solution must:
- Implement microservices architecture.
- Ensure data security and compliance.
- Provide high availability and performance. What strategies should you adopt? (Select 3 answers)

A) Use Azure API Management for managing microservices APIs.
B) Implement RBAC to secure access to services.
C) Use Azure SQL Database for data storage.
D) Deploy Azure Functions for executing microservices.
E) Utilize Azure Traffic Manager for load balancing across regions.

## QUESTION 42

An e-commerce platform is integrating Power Platform solutions to handle customer data. They need to address data privacy and ethical considerations. The solution must:
- Ensure customer data privacy.
- Implement ethical data handling practices.
- Manage sensitive personal information. What components should be used? (Select 3 answers)

A) Use Power BI to visualize customer data without anonymization.
B) Implement GDPR compliance measures using Dataverse.
C) Use Azure Active Directory for single sign-on (SSO) to secure user access.
D) Utilize Azure Data Lake for centralized storage of sensitive data.
E) Implement Azure Policy to enforce data handling standards.

## QUESTION 43

A financial services company is looking to integrate their CRM system with a third-party fraud detection service. They must:

- Ensure data privacy and security.
- Achieve real-time data processing.
- Maintain compliance with financial regulations. What solutions should they implement? (Select 3 answers)

A) Use Power Automate to trigger real-time data flows.
B) Store sensitive data in an unencrypted format for faster access.
C) Implement data encryption at rest and in transit.
D) Use Azure API Management to handle API integrations.
E) Conduct quarterly manual audits to ensure compliance.

## QUESTION 44

You are designing a Power Platform solution for a retail chain that wants to enhance customer experience by integrating real-time inventory updates across all channels. The solution must be scalable and support high transaction volumes during peak retail periods.
- Scalability for high transaction volumes.
- Real-time inventory updates.

Which Power Platform tool should be the primary focus to ensure the effectiveness of this solution?

A) Power BI
B) Power Apps Canvas
C) Power Automate
D) Common Data Service
E) Power Virtual Agents

## QUESTION 45

A financial institution is planning a data migration from their CRM system to Dynamics 365. They must:
- Ensure data integrity and consistency.
- Handle sensitive financial data securely.
- Validate the migrated data accurately. What best practices should they follow? (Select 3 answers)

A) Encrypt data during migration to protect sensitive information.
B) Use Power Automate for data migration.
C) Implement data quality rules in Dataverse.
D) Conduct a pilot migration to validate the process.
E) Use Excel for data migration to ensure simplicity.

## QUESTION 46

A retail company is implementing a new CRM system with Power Platform. They need to:
- Ensure data privacy and protection.
- Implement role-based access controls.
- Conduct security testing and validation. How should they achieve these goals?

A) Use Data Loss Prevention (DLP) policies.
B) Implement RBAC using Azure AD.
C) Perform regular security testing using Azure Security Center.

D) Rely on default security settings.
E) Conduct security validation once a year.

**QUESTION 47**

A retail company is migrating to Dynamics 365 and needs to ensure high-quality performance and security. They must:
• Implement automated testing strategies.
• Perform performance and security testing.
• Continuously monitor quality. What steps should they take?
Select 3 answers.

A) Use Azure DevOps for continuous integration and automated testing.
B) Conduct load testing using Azure Load Testing.
C) Implement manual security checks only.
D) Use Microsoft Defender for Identity for security testing.
E) Skip continuous quality monitoring.

**QUESTION 48**

As part of an educational institution, you are asked to optimize a Power Apps application used for course registration that has become sluggish. The application integrates with several external systems and has numerous features on each screen.
• Streamline app operations.
• Enhance user experience.
Which two measures should you prioritize to boost the application's speed and efficiency?

A) Simplify user interface
B) Utilize local collections
C) Apply a control dependency
D) Enhance formula efficiency
E) Add non-delegable queries

**QUESTION 49**

A manufacturing company relies on a custom Power Apps application integrated with Dynamics 365 and Azure services. The company is experiencing issues with deprecated features and needs to ensure their solutions are up to date. The key requirements are:
• Identifying and addressing deprecated features.
• Managing updates and version control.
• Ensuring long-term sustainability.
What measures should you implement? (Select 3 answers)

A) Regularly review Microsoft's release notes for deprecated features.
B) Use Azure DevOps for version control and managing updates.
C) Implement Azure Service Health to monitor service status and issues.
D) Utilize the Power Platform Admin Center to manage and apply updates.
E) Schedule regular code reviews and refactoring sessions.

## QUESTION 50

A Dynamics 365 Customer Engagement solution is experiencing performance issues, with users reporting slow response times. As a solution architect, you need to identify and resolve these performance issues. The key requirements are:
- Analyzing system performance metrics.
- Identifying bottlenecks in the system.
- Implementing changes to improve performance.

What actions should you take? (Select 3 answers)

A) Use Dynamics 365 Performance Insights to analyze system performance.
B) Review and optimize custom plugins and workflows.
C) Implement Azure Application Insights for detailed monitoring.
D) Use Power BI to create performance monitoring dashboards.
E) Increase the capacity of the underlying infrastructure using Azure.

# PRACTICE TEST 2 - ANSWERS ONLY

## QUESTION 1

Answer – A), E)

Option A – Automating data entry helps reduce delays, addressing one of the key challenges.
Option B – Compliance workflows ensure consistency but do not address data entry or real-time updates.
Option C – A customer portal improves satisfaction but does not address data entry or compliance.
Option D – Power BI reports help track compliance but do not optimize the process.
Option E – AI Builder can automate data validation, ensuring faster processing and compliance, aligning with business goals.

| | |
|---|---|
| **EXAM FOCUS** | *You should automate data entry and use AI Builder for validation to reduce processing time and ensure compliance.* |
| **CAUTION ALERT** | *Please keep in mind that real-time updates and compliance workflows alone won't address manual data entry delays.* |

## QUESTION 2

Answer – A), D)

Option A – Correct. Checking network bandwidth is essential as insufficient bandwidth can lead to slow load times, particularly when multiple regions access the app simultaneously during meetings.
Option B – Incorrect. The SLA might provide guidelines on performance but does not directly help diagnose or resolve the issue.
Option C – Incorrect. Data model optimization is crucial for overall performance but less so for issues specific to multi-regional use.
Option D – Correct. Network latency, especially in a multi-regional setup, can significantly impact performance, and addressing it can improve user experience.
Option E – Incorrect. Server scaling might help handle more load, but without addressing network issues, performance may still lag during peak times.

| | |
|---|---|
| **EXAM FOCUS** | "Check network bandwidth and latency for better load times during multi-regional meetings." |
| **CAUTION ALERT** | "SLAs won't resolve performance issues; focus on network factors instead." |

## QUESTION 3

Answer – A), B)

Option A – A Power Apps solution can streamline appointment scheduling and reduce overbooking.
Option B – Power Automate can send automated reminders, reducing missed appointments.
Option C – Integrating patient records with Dataverse is important but does not directly improve scheduling.
Option D – A Power BI dashboard is useful for tracking but does not improve the scheduling process.
Option E – AI Builder for predictive scheduling is advanced but might be overkill for this scenario.

| EXAM FOCUS | Use Power Apps for scheduling and Power Automate for reminders to streamline and automate appointment processes. |
|---|---|
| CAUTION ALERT | Please keep in mind, integration with patient records is important but doesn't directly fix scheduling issues. |

## QUESTION 4

Answer – A), C)

Option A – Correct choice as FetchXML query can retrieve multiple records based on complex criteria efficiently.
Option B – Alternate keys are useful for unique identifier-based retrieval, but not for complex criteria.
Option C – Correct choice as OData $filter query can improve performance by retrieving only necessary records.
Option D – Business process flow guides users through processes but does not optimize data retrieval.
Option E – OData $expand query retrieves related data, which may not be necessary for improving performance in this scenario.

| EXAM FOCUS | "Use OData $filter query to retrieve specific records efficiently, improving performance." |
|---|---|
| CAUTION ALERT | "Please keep in mind, Alternate keys are for unique identifiers, not complex criteria retrieval." |

## QUESTION 5

Answer – A), B), C)

Option A – Dataverse provides secure storage for patient data, ensuring compliance.
Option B – Azure API Management allows for seamless integration with existing EHR systems.
Option C – Conducting a future-proofing analysis helps in evaluating the long-term viability and costs of the selected technologies.
Option D – A Power Apps solution is useful for data entry but does not address integration or compliance directly.
Option E – DLP policies ensure compliance but do not address integration or cost-benefit analysis.

| EXAM FOCUS | Implement Dataverse for secure data storage and Azure API Management for seamless EHR integration. |
|---|---|
| CAUTION ALERT | Remember, DLP policies are critical for compliance but won't address integration challenges directly. |

## QUESTION 6

Answer – A), C), E)

Option A – Dataverse provides secure storage for patient data, ensuring compliance with HIPAA.
Option B – Power BI is useful for monitoring performance but does not directly address data privacy or impact analysis.
Option C – DLP policies ensure data privacy and compliance with HIPAA.
Option D – Conducting an impact analysis is essential before system changes.
Option E – Developing a continuous monitoring plan ensures ongoing assessment of system

performance.

| EXAM FOCUS | Implement Dataverse for secure storage, DLP policies for privacy, and continuous monitoring with Azure Monitor for compliance. |
| --- | --- |
| CAUTION ALERT | Remember, Power BI alone won't ensure data privacy or perform impact analysis comprehensively. |

## QUESTION 7

Answer – A), C), D)

Option A – Azure DevOps can be used to assign resources to specific tasks.
Option B – Dataverse is useful for managing health records but does not address resource allocation or scheduling.
Option C – Power Automate can be used to schedule training sessions.
Option D – Developing a project timeline with milestones using Power BI helps ensure milestones are met.
Option E – Regular resource reviews are important but do not address initial allocation and scheduling.

| EXAM FOCUS | Allocate resources with Azure DevOps and schedule training with Power Automate for efficient project management. |
| --- | --- |
| CAUTION ALERT | Please keep in mind, Dataverse won't help with resource allocation or milestone scheduling directly. |

## QUESTION 8

Answer – B), D)

Option A – Power Apps can be used to develop the CRM interface but not directly related to managing resistance to change.
Option B – Conducting training sessions using Microsoft Teams helps provide adequate training.
Option C – Power BI is useful for analyzing adoption rates but not directly related to managing resistance.
Option D – Developing a change management plan that includes employee feedback sessions addresses concerns and encourages adoption.
Option E – Azure Functions is useful for automation but not directly related to managing resistance to change.

| EXAM FOCUS | Conduct training with Microsoft Teams and develop a change management plan including feedback sessions. |
| --- | --- |
| CAUTION ALERT | Please keep in mind, Power Apps alone won't address resistance to change. |

## QUESTION 9

Answer – B), D)

Option A – Power Automate can be used to automate tasks but is not ideal for performance testing.
Option B – Implementing performance testing using Azure DevOps provides a structured approach to

testing.
Option C – Power BI is useful for creating dashboards but not directly related to establishing benchmarks.
Option D – Developing performance benchmarks using industry standards ensures the system meets accepted performance criteria.
Option E – Dataverse is useful for data management but not directly related to performance benchmarks.

| EXAM FOCUS | *Use Azure DevOps for performance testing and develop benchmarks using industry standards to ensure system meets requirements.* |
|---|---|
| CAUTION ALERT | *Please keep in mind, Power Automate is not ideal for performance testing.* |

## QUESTION 10

Answer – A), C)

Option A – Creating a detailed project plan helps in aligning stakeholder expectations.
Option B – Power Automate is useful for notifications but not directly related to managing expectations.
Option C – Conducting regular feedback sessions ensures concerns are addressed promptly.
Option D – Azure DevOps is useful for continuous integration but not directly related to managing expectations.
Option E – Power BI is useful for performance tracking but not directly related to managing stakeholder expectations.

| EXAM FOCUS | *Create detailed project plans and conduct regular feedback sessions to manage stakeholder expectations effectively.* |
|---|---|
| CAUTION ALERT | *Please keep in mind, Power Automate for notifications does not directly manage expectations.* |

## QUESTION 11

Answer – A), E)

Option A – Conducting a thorough assessment focusing on API and ETL processes ensures proper data integration.
Option B – Power Apps can create secure forms but is not directly related to integration assessment.
Option C – Azure Logic Apps can test data transfer but is not used for initial vendor assessment.
Option D – Power Automate is useful for workflow automation but not critical for evaluation.
Option E – Comparing pricing models and support terms addresses cost and support considerations.

| EXAM FOCUS | *Thoroughly assess vendor integration capabilities and compare pricing models to ensure cost-effectiveness.* |
|---|---|
| CAUTION ALERT | *Please keep in mind, Power Apps forms are not directly related to integration assessment.* |

## QUESTION 12

Answer – A)

Option A – Correct choice as it includes secure integration (Azure API Management), automated workflows (Power Automate), and analytics (Power BI).
Option B – Azure Logic Apps is useful but Azure API Management is better for secure API handling.
Option C – Microsoft Dataverse is good but not essential for this specific scenario.
Option D – Azure Synapse Analytics is overkill for patient management and reporting.
Option E – Power Virtual Agents is not necessary for this scenario.

| | |
|---|---|
| **EXAM FOCUS** | *"Ensure compliance with HIPAA using Azure API Management for secure API handling."* |
| **CAUTION ALERT** | *"Azure Logic Apps alone might not provide the necessary security for HIPAA compliance."* |

## QUESTION 13

Answer – A), B), D)

Option A – Regular innovation workshops encourage innovation.
Option B – A sandbox environment allows for experimentation while balancing innovation with practicality.
Option C – Power BI is useful but more for tracking metrics rather than fostering innovation.
Option D – A strategic roadmap for technology adoption helps in predicting and preparing for future changes.
Option E – Quarterly reviews are useful but secondary to the primary steps.

| | |
|---|---|
| **EXAM FOCUS** | *Remember, regular innovation workshops and a sandbox environment foster an innovative mindset.* |
| **CAUTION ALERT** | *You should avoid relying solely on tracking metrics without fostering actual innovation initiatives.* |

## QUESTION 14

Answer – A), C), E)

Option A – Regular post-deployment review meetings ensure continuous monitoring and support.
Option B – Azure Logic Apps can automate processes but are less critical than other options for deployment strategies.
Option C – Comprehensive user documentation and training materials are essential for successful rollouts.
Option D – Power Automate is useful for monitoring but not as critical as other options for deployment strategies.
Option E – A dedicated support team is crucial for handling post-deployment issues.

| | |
|---|---|
| **EXAM FOCUS** | *You should develop comprehensive user documentation and establish a dedicated support team for post-deployment issues.* |
| **CAUTION ALERT** | *Stay cautious, automating everything without detailed planning can overlook critical deployment aspects.* |

## QUESTION 15

Answer – A), D), E)

Option A – Regular virtual meetings using Microsoft Teams can enhance collaboration and teamwork, especially for remote and distributed teams.
Option B – Dynamics 365 is useful for conflict resolution tracking but less critical for enhancing collaboration and teamwork.
Option C – Power Virtual Agents is more relevant for training than team management.
Option D – Developing conflict resolution protocols is crucial for resolving team conflicts and challenges.
Option E – Azure DevOps provides robust project management and collaboration features, essential for managing remote and distributed team members.

| EXAM FOCUS | *You should conduct regular virtual meetings with Microsoft Teams to enhance remote collaboration.* |
|---|---|
| CAUTION ALERT | *Remember, using Dynamics 365 only for conflict resolution tracking is less effective than direct team interaction.* |

## QUESTION 16

Answer – A), B), D)

Option A – Correct choice as ALM Accelerator supports CI/CD in Power Platform.
Option B – Correct choice as Azure Pipelines in Azure DevOps provides robust CI/CD capabilities.
Option C – Manual ALM does not align with the requirement for automated and scalable ALM.
Option D – Correct choice as Power Platform Pipelines provide a native solution for deploying Power Platform components.
Option E – Scripts on an Azure VM could be used but are not as streamlined or recommended as the other options.

| EXAM FOCUS | *"Azure Pipelines and ALM Accelerator ensure robust CI/CD for Power Platform solutions."* |
|---|---|
| CAUTION ALERT | *"Manual ALM processes do not meet the requirements for automated, scalable, and traceable ALM."* |

## QUESTION 17

Answer – A), B), C)

Option A – Conducting workshops with key stakeholders helps gather environmental requirements and feedback.
Option B – Using Power BI to create detailed environmental impact reports aids in compliance and eco-friendly practices.
Option C – Implementing a phased rollout strategy helps manage compliance effectively.
Option D – Developing custom connectors adds complexity and should be avoided unless necessary.
Option E – Utilizing Azure Functions can be beneficial but does not directly address environmental impact and compliance.

| EXAM FOCUS | *Conduct stakeholder workshops, use Power BI for environmental impact reports, and plan a phased rollout.* |
|---|---|
| CAUTION ALERT | *Custom connectors add complexity; avoid unless necessary for environmental monitoring integration.* |

## QUESTION 18

Answer – A), B), C)

Option A – Using Power Apps component framework (PCF) allows development of reusable components for future adaptability.
Option B – Implementing ALM practices using Azure DevOps ensures continuous improvement and relevance.
Option C – Utilizing Dataverse provides robust data management and integration capabilities.
Option D – Developing multiple canvas apps can create maintenance challenges.
Option E – Azure Functions are useful for complex logic but do not directly address flexibility and adaptability.

| EXAM FOCUS | *Implement Power Apps component framework for reusable components; ALM with Azure DevOps ensures continuous improvement.* |
|---|---|
| CAUTION ALERT | *Developing multiple canvas apps can create maintenance challenges.* |

## QUESTION 19

Answer – A), D)

Option A – Using Power Apps to create a feedback form allows for gathering user behavior and preferences.
Option B – Implementing Dataverse stores customer preferences but might not directly understand behavior or incorporate user-centric design principles.
Option C – Using Power Virtual Agents interacts with customers but might not gather detailed behavior and preferences.
Option D – Analyzing feedback using Power BI dashboards utilizes feedback loops for continuous improvement.
Option E – Conducting A/B testing supports user-centric design but might not directly gather insights or utilize feedback loops effectively.

| EXAM FOCUS | *Use Power Apps for feedback forms and Power BI for analyzing feedback to improve user-centric design.* |
|---|---|
| CAUTION ALERT | *Don't neglect direct customer interactions for understanding behavior and preferences.* |

## QUESTION 20

Answer – B), E)

Option A – Business rule enforces validation rules but doesn't handle data synchronization.
Option B – Correct choice as Power Automate can automate data synchronization.
Option C – Duplicate detection rules help with data integrity but don't automate synchronization.
Option D – Virtual tables integrate external data but don't handle synchronization.
Option E – Correct choice as Dataflows can ensure data consistency between Dataverse and CRM.

| EXAM FOCUS | "Use Power Automate and Dataflows to ensure seamless data synchronization and integrity between systems." |
|---|---|
| CAUTION ALERT | "Avoid using Business rules or Duplicate detection rules for data synchronization tasks." |

## QUESTION 21

Answer – A), D)

Option A – Azure API Management is essential for managing and securing APIs, facilitating integration.
Option B – Power Virtual Agents help in customer support but do not directly integrate with IT infrastructure.
Option C – Azure Service Bus helps with message queuing but is not a primary factor in architectural strategy.
Option D – Regular architectural reviews ensure alignment and long-term strategy.
Option E – AI Builder adds intelligence but does not directly address integration or long-term strategy.

| EXAM FOCUS | Implement Azure API Management and conduct regular architectural reviews. |
|---|---|
| CAUTION ALERT | Balancing innovation with existing systems is crucial; don't neglect legacy systems. |

## QUESTION 22

Answer – A), E)

Option A – Azure Logic Apps enable seamless data synchronization between cloud and on-premises systems.
Option B – Azure Service Bus is useful for messaging but not directly for data synchronization or security.
Option C – Power Virtual Agents are useful for customer support but not for data synchronization or security.
Option D – Azure Functions are useful for data processing but do not directly address data synchronization or security.
Option E – Azure API Management provides an API gateway and security, ensuring data security during transmission.

| EXAM FOCUS | Use Azure Logic Apps and Azure API Management for seamless integration and secure data transmission in hybrid solutions. |
|---|---|
| CAUTION ALERT | Avoid components like Power Virtual Agents that don't contribute to data synchronization or security. |

## QUESTION 23

Answer – A), B)

Option A – Azure DevOps allows for efficient management of pipelines, automated testing, and controlled releases.
Option B – Power Platform Build Tools provide capabilities for managing multiple environments and ensuring controlled releases.
Option C – Manual testing is not efficient for automated ALM strategies.

Option D – Dataverse is for data management, not specifically for environment or release management.
Option E – Dynamics 365 is not specifically used for ALM or release management in the context of Power Platform.

| | |
|---|---|
| *EXAM FOCUS* | *You should use Azure DevOps and Power Platform Build Tools for efficient pipeline management and controlled releases.* |
| *CAUTION ALERT* | *Avoid manual testing for ALM strategies; it does not align with automated testing best practices.* |

## QUESTION 24

Answer – B), E)

Option A – Custom relationships can be configured for specific behaviors but are more complex.
Option B – Correct choice as Parental relationships automatically delete related records, enforcing data integrity.
Option C – Referential relationships enforce referential integrity but do not automatically delete related records.
Option D – Referential, Restrict Delete prevents deletion if there are related records, but does not automate deletion.
Option E – Correct choice as Cascade Delete will automatically delete related records.

| | |
|---|---|
| *EXAM FOCUS* | *"Configure Parental and Cascade Delete relationships for automated dependent record deletion."* |
| *CAUTION ALERT* | *"Custom and Referential relationships won't automatically delete related records."* |

## QUESTION 25

Answer – A), D), E)

Option A – Responsive design ensures the app is optimized for different form factors.
Option B – Azure Functions help with backend processing but are not directly related to high performance and fast load times.
Option C – Power Automate is useful for process automation but not directly related to performance optimization.
Option D – Enabling MFA provides robust security measures for sensitive data.
Option E – Implementing DLP policies ensures the protection of sensitive data and compliance with security standards.

| | |
|---|---|
| *EXAM FOCUS* | *Implement responsive design, MFA, and DLP policies to ensure high performance, security, and optimization for different form factors.* |
| *CAUTION ALERT* | *Remember, Azure Functions help with backend processing but are not directly related to high performance and fast load times.* |

## QUESTION 26

Answer – A), B), C)

Option A – Power Automate Cloud Flow can update patient records in Dataverse automatically.

Option B – Azure Functions can be used to implement custom logic and trigger alerts for missing information.
Option C – Dataverse Connector facilitates data integration and real-time synchronization across systems.
Option D – Power BI is useful for data visualization but not directly related to real-time synchronization.
Option E – Power Automate Desktop is for local automation and may not be required for real-time synchronization across multiple systems.

| EXAM FOCUS | Implement Power Automate Cloud Flow, Azure Functions, and Dataverse Connector for automatic updates, custom alerts, and real-time sync. |
| --- | --- |
| CAUTION ALERT | Avoid using Power Automate Desktop for real-time sync; it's designed for local automation. |

## QUESTION 27

Answer – A), B), C)

Option A – Power Platform Admin Center allows configuration of DLP policies.
Option B – Azure Log Analytics can provide detailed audit logs.
Option C – Azure AD can manage user roles and access.
Option D – Power BI is for visualization and does not directly handle DLP or role management.
Option E – Azure Key Vault is for encryption but not directly for these specific requirements.

| EXAM FOCUS | Use Power Platform Admin Center, Azure Log Analytics, and Azure AD for DLP, audit logs, and user role management. |
| --- | --- |
| CAUTION ALERT | Avoid using Power BI for compliance tasks like DLP or role management; it's for data visualization. |

## QUESTION 28

Answer – B)

Option A – Business Rules are used for enforcing business logic, not for auditing changes.
Option B – Audit Logs track changes to records and maintain logs for compliance, meeting the requirement for auditing student records.
Option C – Security Roles control access to data but do not track changes for auditing purposes.
Option D – Data Import Wizard is used for importing data, not for auditing changes.
Option E – Workflows automate processes but do not specifically provide auditing capabilities.

| EXAM FOCUS | "Use Audit Logs in Dynamics 365 to track and maintain changes for compliance." |
| --- | --- |
| CAUTION ALERT | "Business Rules and Workflows do not provide audit logging capabilities." |

## QUESTION 29

Answer – A), B), C)

Option A – Correct. A comprehensive budget plan helps in tracking all costs and preparing for contingencies.

Option B – Correct. Regular budget reviews and adjustments ensure alignment with project progress and financial limits.
Option C – Correct. Power BI dashboards provide real-time insights into budget performance and resource utilization.
Option D – Incorrect. Ignoring small overages can lead to significant budget issues.
Option E – Incorrect. While Azure DevOps is useful for project management, it does not directly address budgeting concerns.

| EXAM FOCUS | *Develop a comprehensive budget plan and use Power BI for real-time budget tracking.* |
|---|---|
| CAUTION ALERT | *Ignoring small overages can lead to significant budget issues.* |

## QUESTION 30

Answer – A), B), D)

Option A – Correct. Dynamics 365 can help manage contracts and performance effectively.
Option B – Correct. Regular reviews and audits ensure compliance and performance.
Option C – Incorrect. Cost should not be the sole criterion.
Option D – Correct. SLAs with specific metrics ensure accountability.
Option E – Incorrect. Azure API Management is useful but not directly related to vendor management.

| EXAM FOCUS | *Use Dynamics 365 for managing vendor contracts and performance reviews.* |
|---|---|
| CAUTION ALERT | *Cost should not be the sole criterion; focus on compliance and performance metrics.* |

## QUESTION 31

Answer – A), C), E)

Option A – Correct. Azure IoT Hub provides secure connection and management of IoT devices.
Option B – Incorrect. Power Automate is useful for automation but not primarily for real-time data processing.
Option C – Correct. Dataverse securely stores inventory data.
Option D – Incorrect. AI Builder is useful but may not be necessary for this scenario.
Option E – Correct. Azure Functions can handle real-time data processing effectively.

| EXAM FOCUS | *Use Azure IoT Hub for secure connections and Dataverse for secure data storage.* |
|---|---|
| CAUTION ALERT | *Power Automate alone cannot handle real-time data processing.* |

## QUESTION 32

Answer – B)

Option A – Azure Logic Apps can integrate systems but may not handle high data volumes as efficiently as Dual-write.
Option B – Dual-write provides seamless, real-time, bi-directional data integration between Dynamics 365 and third-party systems, ensuring data accuracy and compliance.
Option C – Power Automate is useful for workflows but may not handle high data volumes as efficiently

as Dual-write.
Option D – Custom Connectors require significant development and maintenance efforts and may not be as efficient.
Option E – Data Export Service is primarily used for exporting data to Azure SQL Database, not for real-time bi-directional integration.

| EXAM FOCUS | "Implement Dual-write for seamless, real-time integration ensuring data accuracy." |
|---|---|
| CAUTION ALERT | "Power Automate may not handle high data volumes as efficiently as Dual-write." |

## QUESTION 33

Answer – A), C), E)

Option A – Correct. Power Apps can develop applications that reduce paper usage, promoting eco-friendly practices.
Option B – Incorrect. AI Builder is useful but not the primary tool for minimizing waste.
Option C – Correct. Selecting cloud services with low carbon footprints reduces environmental impact.
Option D – Incorrect. Ignoring environmental impact can lead to unsustainable practices.
Option E – Correct. Power BI helps track compliance with eco-friendly regulations effectively.

| EXAM FOCUS | Use Power Apps to reduce paper usage and select low carbon footprint cloud services for sustainability. |
|---|---|
| CAUTION ALERT | Ignoring environmental impact can lead to unsustainable practices and non-compliance. |

## QUESTION 34

Answer – A), C)

Option A – Using Azure API Management allows secure API exposure and easy integration.
Option B – Custom connectors require more development effort.
Option C – Power Automate can synchronize data in real-time with minimal custom development.
Option D – Azure Logic Apps are useful but may require more configuration.
Option E – Exporting data to Dataverse may not ensure real-time synchronization.

| EXAM FOCUS | Use Azure API Management for secure connections and Power Automate for real-time data synchronization with minimal custom development. |
|---|---|
| CAUTION ALERT | Stay cautious of custom connectors; they require more development effort and can complicate integration. |

## QUESTION 35

Answer – A), D)

Option A – Microsoft Teams facilitates remote collaboration and document sharing.
Option B – SharePoint is useful but lacks change history and traceability.
Option C – Email is inefficient for sharing updates and managing documentation.
Option D – Azure DevOps with version control ensures documentation is up-to-date and traceable.

Option E – Hard copies are impractical for distributed teams and do not support updates.

| EXAM FOCUS | *Leverage Microsoft Teams and Azure DevOps for efficient collaboration and traceable documentation with version control.* |
|---|---|
| CAUTION ALERT | *Avoid using email for document updates; it is inefficient and lacks version control.* |

## QUESTION 36

Answer – C)

Option A – Power BI is used for data visualization and analysis, not for deploying AI models.
Option B – Azure Machine Learning is powerful but requires more AI expertise and setup.
Option C – AI Builder allows for easy deployment and management of AI models directly within the Power Platform, suitable for users without extensive AI expertise.
Option D – Power Automate is used for workflow automation, not for AI predictions.
Option E – Dynamics 365 Customer Service is for managing customer interactions, not for implementing AI solutions.

| EXAM FOCUS | *"AI Builder is ideal for deploying and managing AI models without extensive expertise."* |
|---|---|
| CAUTION ALERT | *"Azure Machine Learning requires more setup and AI expertise compared to AI Builder."* |

## QUESTION 37

Answer – A), D)

Option A – Power Automate enables real-time data synchronization across systems.
Option B – Dataverse is useful for data storage but not directly for real-time synchronization.
Option C – Manual data entry is inefficient and error-prone.
Option D – Azure Service Bus provides reliable messaging for high performance and scalability.
Option E – Power BI is useful for visualization but not for integration and synchronization.

| EXAM FOCUS | *Use Power Automate for real-time synchronization and Azure Service Bus for reliable messaging.* |
|---|---|
| CAUTION ALERT | *Manual data entry is error-prone and inefficient for integrations.* |

## QUESTION 38

Answer – A), B), E)

Option A – Azure IoT Hub effectively collects and manages IoT data.
Option B – Integrating IoT data with Power BI provides actionable insights.
Option C – Azure Functions are useful but may not ensure scalability as well as other integrated solutions.
Option D – Local databases are less scalable compared to cloud solutions.
Option E – Power Automate triggers workflows based on IoT data, improving operational efficiency.

| EXAM FOCUS | *Use Azure IoT Hub for data collection and Power Automate to trigger workflows based on IoT data.* |
|---|---|
| CAUTION ALERT | *Avoid using local databases for IoT data; they lack scalability and real-time access.* |

## QUESTION 39

Answer – A), D), E)

Option A – Azure Key Vault secures sensitive information effectively.
Option B – RBAC is essential but may not directly address communication security.
Option C – Public endpoints are less secure compared to private endpoints.
Option D – Threat modeling helps identify and mitigate potential security threats during the design phase.
Option E – Rotating encryption keys are more secure than static keys.

| EXAM FOCUS | *Implement Azure Key Vault and rotating encryption keys to manage and secure sensitive information effectively.* |
|---|---|
| CAUTION ALERT | *Avoid using public endpoints for API communication; they are less secure compared to private endpoints.* |

## QUESTION 40

Answer – A)

Option A – Power Automate with the Dataverse trigger can automate the sending of personalized emails based on application submissions.
Option B – Azure Functions can send emails but require more development effort and complexity.
Option C – Business rules do not handle sending emails; they are used for data validation and logic.
Option D – Dynamics 365 Customer Insights is used for customer data analysis, not for simple email automation.
Option E – Power BI is for data visualization and analysis, not for automating email workflows.

| EXAM FOCUS | *"Power Automate with Dataverse trigger is ideal for automating follow-up emails after form submissions."* |
|---|---|
| CAUTION ALERT | *"Business rules don't handle email notifications, focusing only on data validation."* |

## QUESTION 41

Answer – A), B), E)

Option A – Azure API Management is designed to manage APIs in a microservices architecture, providing monitoring, security, and scalability.
Option B – Role-Based Access Control (RBAC) is essential for securing access to various services and ensuring compliance with security standards.
Option C – While Azure SQL Database is a good data storage option, it does not directly address the need for microservices architecture or high availability.
Option D – Azure Functions can execute microservices, but for a full microservices architecture, a combination of services is needed.
Option E – Azure Traffic Manager helps distribute traffic across multiple regions, ensuring high availability and optimal performance.

| EXAM FOCUS | Use Azure API Management and RBAC to secure microservices architecture. |
|---|---|
| CAUTION ALERT | Azure SQL Database is good for data storage but doesn't address microservices architecture alone. |

## QUESTION 42

Answer – B), C), E)

Option A – Visualizing customer data without anonymization can lead to privacy breaches and is not a best practice for ensuring data privacy.
Option B – Dataverse supports GDPR compliance measures, helping to ensure that customer data privacy is maintained.
Option C – Azure Active Directory with SSO secures user access, ensuring that only authorized users can access sensitive information.
Option D – While Azure Data Lake provides centralized storage, it is more suitable for large-scale data analytics rather than secure storage of sensitive personal information.
Option E – Azure Policy enforces data handling standards and ensures compliance with ethical data practices.

| EXAM FOCUS | Implement GDPR compliance measures in Dataverse and use Azure AD for SSO. |
|---|---|
| CAUTION ALERT | Do not visualize customer data without anonymization; it risks privacy breaches. |

## QUESTION 43

Answer – A), C), D)

Option A – Power Automate can be used to trigger real-time data flows, ensuring timely processing.
Option B – Storing sensitive data in an unencrypted format is not secure and violates financial regulations.
Option C – Implementing data encryption at rest and in transit ensures data privacy and security, maintaining compliance.
Option D – Azure API Management provides the necessary tools to handle API integrations securely and efficiently.
Option E – While manual audits are useful, they do not ensure real-time data processing or continuous compliance monitoring.

| EXAM FOCUS | Implement Power Automate for real-time data flows and encrypt sensitive data. |
|---|---|
| CAUTION ALERT | Never store sensitive data unencrypted; it breaches regulations. |

## QUESTION 44

Answer – C)

Option A – Incorrect. Power BI is primarily for data visualization and analysis, not suited for real-time operational updates.
Option B – Incorrect. Canvas Apps are useful for creating custom applications but not specifically for managing real-time data flows or scalability.
Option C – Correct. Power Automate can be used to create automated flows that handle high transaction

Page | 77

volumes and ensure real-time data updates across platforms, ideal for inventory management.
Option D – Incorrect. While Common Data Service supports data management, it does not directly deal with real-time updates for high-volume transactions.
Option E – Incorrect. Power Virtual Agents are for creating intelligent chatbots and do not manage inventory or handle transaction volumes.

| EXAM FOCUS | "Please keep in mind, Power Automate ensures real-time updates and handles high transaction volumes for inventory management." |
| --- | --- |
| CAUTION ALERT | "Avoid using Power BI for real-time updates; it's designed for data analysis." |

## QUESTION 45

Answer – A), C), D)

Option A – Encrypting data during migration ensures the protection of sensitive financial information.
Option B – Power Automate is useful for automation but not ideal for large-scale data migration.
Option C – Implementing data quality rules in Dataverse helps maintain data integrity and consistency.
Option D – Conducting a pilot migration allows for process validation and troubleshooting.
Option E – Excel is not suitable for large-scale, secure data migration.

| EXAM FOCUS | Encrypt data during migration to protect sensitive financial information. |
| --- | --- |
| CAUTION ALERT | Power Automate is not ideal for large-scale data migration; use specialized tools. |

## QUESTION 46

Answer – A), B), C)

Option A – Using DLP policies helps protect sensitive data and prevent data leaks.
Option B – Implementing RBAC using Azure AD ensures effective management of user roles and access levels.
Option C – Regular security testing using Azure Security Center helps identify and mitigate security vulnerabilities.
Option D – Relying on default security settings is insufficient for ensuring robust security.
Option E – Conducting security validation once a year is not frequent enough to ensure continuous compliance and protection.

| EXAM FOCUS | "Implement DLP policies and RBAC with Azure AD for robust data privacy and protection." |
| --- | --- |
| CAUTION ALERT | "Relying on default security settings is insufficient for ensuring robust security." |

## QUESTION 47

Answer – A), B), D)

Option A – Azure DevOps provides tools for continuous integration and automated testing, ensuring ongoing quality assurance.
Option B – Conducting load testing using Azure Load Testing identifies how the system handles high usage, ensuring stability under load.

Option C – Implementing only manual security checks can miss automated attack scenarios; comprehensive security testing is required.
Option D – Using Microsoft Defender for Identity for security testing ensures the application is protected against identity-based attacks.
Option E – Skipping continuous quality monitoring would result in potential degradation of performance and security over time.

| EXAM FOCUS | *"Use Azure DevOps for continuous integration and automated testing to ensure ongoing quality assurance."* |
|---|---|
| CAUTION ALERT | *"Please keep in mind, skipping continuous quality monitoring can degrade performance and security over time."* |

## QUESTION 48

Answer – A), D)

Option A – Correct. Simplifying the user interface by reducing the number of controls and complexity can lead to faster load times and a smoother user experience.
Option B – Incorrect. Utilizing local collections can improve performance but only if data handling is also optimized to reduce overhead.
Option C – Incorrect. Control dependency structures can improve maintainability but not necessarily performance.
Option D – Correct. Enhancing formula efficiency by optimizing calculations and reducing reliance on complex multi-source formulas can significantly speed up app operations.
Option E – Incorrect. Adding non-delegable queries would degrade performance as they force the app to handle more data processing locally.

| EXAM FOCUS | *"Simplify user interface and enhance formula efficiency for a faster, more responsive Power Apps experience."* |
|---|---|
| CAUTION ALERT | *"Avoid adding non-delegable queries as they slow down app performance by processing data locally."* |

## QUESTION 49

Answer – A), B), D)

Option A – Correct. Regularly reviewing Microsoft's release notes helps identify deprecated features early, allowing for timely updates.
Option B – Correct. Azure DevOps is essential for version control and managing updates, ensuring that solutions remain sustainable.
Option C – Incorrect. Azure Service Health monitors service status but does not directly address deprecated features or version control.
Option D – Correct. The Power Platform Admin Center provides tools for managing and applying updates, ensuring that solutions remain current.
Option E – Incorrect. While code reviews are beneficial, they are not as directly related to managing deprecated features and updates as the other options.

| EXAM FOCUS | "Regularly review Microsoft's release notes to stay ahead of deprecated features and updates." |
| CAUTION ALERT | "Please keep in mind, failing to manage updates can lead to compatibility issues." |

## QUESTION 50

Answer – A), B), C)

Option A – Correct. Dynamics 365 Performance Insights provide valuable data on system performance.
Option B – Correct. Reviewing and optimizing custom plugins and workflows can help identify and resolve bottlenecks.
Option C – Correct. Azure Application Insights offers detailed monitoring capabilities, helping identify performance issues.
Option D – Incorrect. While useful for visualization, Power BI dashboards do not directly help in identifying or resolving performance issues.
Option E – Incorrect. Increasing infrastructure capacity may not address the root cause of performance issues.

| EXAM FOCUS | "Analyze system performance using Dynamics 365 Performance Insights to identify bottlenecks." |
| CAUTION ALERT | "Please keep in mind, increasing infrastructure capacity may not solve underlying performance issues." |

# PRACTICE TEST 3 - QUESTIONS ONLY

### QUESTION 1

A manufacturing company aims to enhance their inventory management system using Microsoft Power Platform. The business goals are to reduce inventory costs, minimize stockouts, and improve supply chain visibility. Specific challenges include:
- Lack of real-time inventory data.
- Inefficient restocking processes.
- Poor supply chain coordination.

How would you align the solution with the company's business goals and measure its impact? Select three correct answers.

A) Implement a Power BI dashboard for real-time inventory monitoring.
B) Use Power Automate to automate restocking workflows.
C) Develop a Dataverse-based app for inventory management.
D) Integrate IoT sensors with Azure for real-time data.
E) Use AI Builder to forecast inventory needs.

### QUESTION 2

A multinational corporation is facing challenges with the deployment of a Power Apps solution intended for global project management. The app performs well in headquarters but not in other regions. You are asked to identify factors that could be affecting performance.
- Analyze performance across different regions.
- Recommend solutions to improve global app performance.

What two aspects should be considered to enhance the app's usability across all regions?

A) Data localization strategies
B) Network latency
C) Custom API performance
D) User device capabilities
E) Network congestion

### QUESTION 3

A financial services firm is looking to enhance its loan approval process using Microsoft Power Platform. The project involves analyzing existing processes and identifying areas for automation. The specific challenges are:
- Manual data entry causing delays.
- Inconsistent approval criteria.
- Lack of real-time tracking of loan applications.

What solutions would you implement to address these challenges? Select three correct answers.

A) Use Power Automate to automate data entry from application forms.
B) Implement a Dataverse solution to standardize approval criteria.
C) Develop a Power BI dashboard for real-time loan application tracking.
D) Create a Canvas App for loan application submission.

E) Use AI Builder to validate application data.

## QUESTION 4

A logistics company is using Microsoft Dataverse to track shipments. The developer wrote JavaScript code that makes multiple RetrieveMultiple calls to check the status of each shipment, causing performance issues.
• The solution must reduce the number of RetrieveMultiple calls.
• It should enhance the performance of data retrieval.
What should you recommend the developer use to address this issue? Select two answers.

A) Alternate keys
B) OData $filter query
C) OData $select query
D) FetchXML query
E) Business rules

## QUESTION 5

A financial services firm wants to enhance its investment analysis system using Microsoft Power Platform. The project involves evaluating available technologies and conducting a cost-benefit analysis. The specific challenges are:
• Integrating with existing financial systems.
• Ensuring scalability to handle increasing data volumes.
• Conducting a cost-benefit analysis to justify technology choices.
What actions would you take to address these challenges? Select three correct answers.

A) Use Power BI to analyze investment data.
B) Implement Azure Data Factory for ETL processes.
C) Conduct a cost-benefit analysis to evaluate technology options.
D) Use Power Automate to integrate with financial systems.
E) Implement Dataverse to store and manage investment data.

## QUESTION 6

A manufacturing company is developing an IoT-based monitoring system using Microsoft Power Platform. The project involves identifying potential risks and contingency planning. The specific challenges are:
• Managing the risks associated with real-time data collection.
• Ensuring data integrity and accuracy.
• Preparing for potential data breaches.
What actions would you take to mitigate these risks? Select three correct answers.

A) Use Azure IoT Central for real-time data collection.
B) Implement DLP policies to protect data integrity.
C) Develop a data breach response plan.
D) Use Power Automate to validate data accuracy.
E) Conduct regular security audits using Azure Security Center.

## QUESTION 7

A manufacturing company is developing a new quality control system using Microsoft Power Platform. The project involves creating effective project plans and managing timelines. The specific challenges are:
• Developing a comprehensive project plan.
• Estimating realistic timelines for system implementation.
• Allocating resources for various project phases.
What actions would you take to address these challenges? Select three correct answers.

A) Use Azure DevOps to create a project plan.
B) Implement Dataverse for data management.
C) Use Power BI to estimate project timelines.
D) Allocate resources using Azure DevOps.
E) Conduct regular project status meetings.

## QUESTION 8

A retail company is planning to roll out a new customer engagement platform using Microsoft Power Platform. The project requires measuring and monitoring change impact. The specific challenges include:
• Defining key performance indicators (KPIs) to measure success.
• Setting up a monitoring system.
• Reporting the impact to stakeholders.
What actions would you take to address these challenges? Select three correct answers.

A) Use Power BI to create a dashboard for monitoring KPIs.
B) Define KPIs in collaboration with stakeholders.
C) Use Power Automate to automate data collection.
D) Implement a feedback loop using Microsoft Forms.
E) Develop custom reports using Dataverse.

## QUESTION 9

A healthcare provider is integrating their patient management system with Dynamics 365 using Microsoft Power Platform. The project involves load testing and capacity planning. The specific challenges are:
• Conducting load testing to simulate peak usage.
• Planning capacity to handle peak loads.
• Balancing cost with performance.
What actions would you take to address these challenges? Select three correct answers.

A) Use Azure Load Testing to simulate peak usage.
B) Implement capacity planning using Azure Monitor.
C) Use Power Virtual Agents for patient interactions.
D) Develop cost-performance models using Azure Cost Management.
E) Implement scaling strategies using Azure Logic Apps.

## QUESTION 10

A healthcare provider is implementing a new patient management system using Microsoft Power

Platform. The project requires regular status updates and reporting. The specific challenges are:
- Providing accurate and timely updates.
- Ensuring all stakeholders are informed.
- Maintaining transparency throughout the project.

What steps would you take to address these challenges? Select three correct answers.

A) Use Power BI for real-time status dashboards.
B) Schedule bi-weekly status meetings.
C) Implement Azure Logic Apps for data integration.
D) Use Power Automate for sending regular email updates.
E) Use Power Virtual Agents for automated reporting.

## QUESTION 11

A retail company is upgrading its inventory management system using Microsoft Power Platform and Azure services. The specific challenges are:
- Selecting vendors with robust IoT integration capabilities.
- Ensuring the solution can scale with business growth.
- Managing vendor relationships effectively.

What steps would you take to address these challenges? Select three correct answers.

A) Use a structured RFP process to gather detailed vendor information on IoT capabilities.
B) Implement Azure IoT Hub for initial integration testing.
C) Compare technology solutions using Power BI for scalability analysis.
D) Use Power Virtual Agents to handle vendor queries.
E) Schedule regular performance reviews with vendors.

## QUESTION 12

A manufacturing company wants to implement an IoT solution to monitor equipment health and predict maintenance needs. They plan to use Microsoft Power Platform for this project.
- The solution must support real-time data processing.
- It should integrate with Dynamics 365 Field Service to manage maintenance schedules.

What components should be included in your solution design?

A) Azure IoT Hub, Power BI, Dynamics 365 Field Service, Power Automate
B) Power Apps, Power BI, Dynamics 365 Field Service, Power Virtual Agents
C) Azure IoT Central, Power BI, Dynamics 365 Field Service, Power Automate
D) Azure Event Hub, Power BI, Dynamics 365 Field Service, Power Automate
E) Azure IoT Hub, Power BI, Dynamics 365 Field Service, Microsoft Dataverse

## QUESTION 13

A government agency wants to adopt emerging technologies to improve citizen services. The challenges include:
- Staying current with industry trends.
- Evaluating and adopting new technologies.
- Fostering an innovative mindset.

What technologies and strategies should you recommend to address these challenges? Select three correct answers.

A) Integrate Azure Cognitive Services for enhanced citizen interaction.
B) Use Dynamics 365 for case management.
C) Implement Power Virtual Agents for automated responses.
D) Use AI Builder for data insights.
E) Conduct regular training on emerging technologies.

## QUESTION 14

A healthcare provider is transitioning to a new patient management system using the Microsoft Power Platform. The challenges include:
- Handling deployment challenges.
- Managing user transition during deployment.
- Post-deployment monitoring and support.

What strategies should you implement to address these challenges? Select three correct answers.

A) Use Azure DevOps for tracking deployment progress and issues.
B) Conduct user training sessions prior to deployment.
C) Implement a phased deployment approach.
D) Develop a post-deployment support plan.
E) Utilize AI Builder for predictive analytics and performance monitoring.

## QUESTION 15

You are managing a team of developers working on a Dynamics 365 project. The challenges include:
- Building effective project teams.
- Using tools and techniques for team communication.
- Managing remote and distributed team members.

Which approaches should you take to ensure effective team management? Select three correct answers.

A) Implement Microsoft Teams for real-time communication.
B) Use Azure DevOps for project tracking and collaboration.
C) Develop a communication plan for the team.
D) Assign specific roles and responsibilities using Dataverse.
E) Utilize Power BI to create a team performance dashboard.

## QUESTION 16

A healthcare provider is building a patient management system using Microsoft Power Platform. The system needs to integrate with an existing electronic health record (EHR) system and ensure secure handling of patient data.
- The solution must comply with HIPAA regulations.
- It should provide real-time updates and analytics.

Which components should be included in the solution design?

A) Power Apps, Power Automate, Power BI, Azure API Management
B) Power Apps, Power Automate, Azure Synapse Analytics, Azure Logic Apps
C) Power Apps, Power Automate, Power BI, Azure Logic Apps

D) Power Apps, Power Automate, Power BI, Microsoft Dataverse
E) Power Apps, Power Automate, Power BI, Azure SQL Database

## QUESTION 17

An e-commerce company is implementing a new logistics management system using Microsoft Power Platform. The challenges include:
- Assessing environmental impact of solutions.
- Designing for sustainability.
- Long-term sustainability planning.

Which strategies should you implement to address these challenges? Select three correct answers.

A) Use Power BI to analyze current logistics processes and identify areas for environmental impact reduction.
B) Develop a detailed sustainability plan using Power Apps.
C) Implement user training sessions to ensure efficient use of the new system.
D) Customize Power Apps extensively to fit specific sustainability needs.
E) Use Azure Logic Apps to automate integration with environmental monitoring systems.

## QUESTION 18

A healthcare organization is deploying a patient management system using Microsoft Power Platform. The system must:
- Be adaptable to regulatory changes.
- Scale with the increasing number of patients.
- Ensure long-term sustainability and relevance.

You need to choose two strategies to adopt in the solution design. Which two strategies should you choose? (Select two)

A) Use Dataverse to manage patient data and ensure compliance.
B) Implement Power Automate for adaptable workflows.
C) Develop custom APIs for future regulatory changes.
D) Use model-driven apps for core functionalities.
E) Implement role-based security to manage user access.

## QUESTION 19

A healthcare provider is developing a new patient management system using Microsoft Power Platform. The solution must:
- Gather detailed patient insights.
- Develop user personas for different types of patients.
- Ensure the design is user-centric.

Which three actions should you prioritize to achieve these goals? (Select three)

A) Conduct focus groups with patients.
B) Use AI Builder to analyze patient data.
C) Create patient personas based on demographics.
D) Implement Power Automate for patient feedback collection.
E) Develop model-driven apps for patient interactions.

## QUESTION 20

A logistics company wants to create a data model in Microsoft Dataverse to track shipments and deliveries. They need to ensure that the data model can support complex relationships and hierarchies.
- The solution must handle one-to-many and many-to-many relationships.
- It should support hierarchical data structures.

Which components should be included in the data model design? Select two answers.

A) Lookups
B) Option sets
C) Polymorphic relationships
D) Hierarchical relationship settings
E) Business rules

## QUESTION 21

A healthcare organization is planning to implement a new solution using Power Platform. The solution must:
- Align with enterprise architecture.
- Balance innovation with existing systems.
- Follow architectural standards and best practices.

Which two measures should you implement? (Select two)

A) Use Dataverse for unified data storage.
B) Implement Azure Cognitive Services for advanced analytics.
C) Develop a governance framework for Power Platform.
D) Utilize Model-Driven Apps for complex business processes.
E) Conduct a pilot program to test the solution.

## QUESTION 22

A financial services firm is moving to a cloud-based Power Platform solution with Azure integration. The solution must:
- Comply with financial regulations.
- Ensure data privacy and protection.
- Optimize operational costs.

Which two actions should you take? (Select two)

A) Use Dataverse for secure data storage and management.
B) Implement Data Loss Prevention (DLP) policies using Microsoft 365.
C) Use Azure Key Vault for data encryption.
D) Enable Azure Cost Management and Billing.
E) Use Power Automate for workflow automation.

## QUESTION 23

A healthcare provider is deploying a Power Platform solution with a robust ALM strategy to comply with regulatory standards. The solution must:
- Implement CI/CD for rapid deployments.

- Ensure data protection and privacy.
- Manage version control of solutions.

Which two tools or practices should you recommend? (Select two)

A) Use Azure DevOps for CI/CD.
B) Implement Dataverse for secure data storage.
C) Use GitHub for version control.
D) Use Power BI for monitoring.
E) Implement DLP policies.

## QUESTION 24

A nonprofit organization is developing a donation management system using Microsoft Dataverse. They need to ensure that when a donor record is deleted, all related donation records are also deleted.
- The solution must automate the deletion of related records.
- It should maintain referential integrity.

Which type of relationship behavior should you configure? Select two answers.

A) Referential
B) Parental
C) Custom
D) Referential, Restrict Delete
E) Cascade Delete

## QUESTION 25

A retail chain wants to create a mobile solution with Power Apps to manage inventory. The app needs to:
- Work seamlessly across various devices.
- Provide offline capabilities for remote stores.
- Ensure secure data transmission.

Which two components should be prioritized in the solution? (Select two)

A) Canvas Apps for custom UI design.
B) Dataverse for secure data storage.
C) Power Automate for real-time data updates.
D) Azure Logic Apps for workflow automation.
E) Azure Cognitive Services for image recognition.

## QUESTION 26

A financial institution wants to implement Power Automate to streamline loan approval processes. The solution must:
- Validate loan applications using AI.
- Automate the approval workflow.
- Ensure compliance with regulatory requirements.

What three Power Automate features or components should be used? (Select three)

A) AI Builder for validating loan applications.
B) Power Automate Cloud Flow for automating the approval workflow.

C) Power Automate Desktop for local validations.
D) Data Loss Prevention (DLP) policies for ensuring compliance.
E) Azure DevOps for continuous integration.

## QUESTION 27

A healthcare provider wants to use Power Platform for patient management while ensuring HIPAA compliance. The solution must:
• Audit user activities.
• Ensure data encryption.
• Manage user access based on roles.
Which three components are critical for this solution? (Select three)

A) Azure Policy for compliance auditing.
B) Dataverse for secure data storage.
C) Power BI for data analysis.
D) Azure AD for RBAC.
E) Azure Key Vault for encryption.

## QUESTION 28

A nonprofit organization uses Power Apps to manage donor information and donations. They want to create a more interactive and user-friendly experience for their staff when entering donation details. What type of Power App should they use to achieve this?

A) Model-driven App
B) Portal App
C) Canvas App
D) Dynamics 365 Sales
E) Power Automate

## QUESTION 29

Your client is looking to optimize resource utilization for their Power Platform solution. They are particularly focused on minimizing costs while maintaining high performance and reliability.
 1. Assessing current resource usage and identifying inefficiencies.
 2. Implementing solutions that provide cost savings without compromising performance.
 3. Ensuring scalability for future growth.
What measures would you implement to achieve optimal resource utilization for the client? Select two answers.

A) Conduct a detailed analysis of resource usage using Power Platform analytics tools.
B) Optimize data storage by archiving old data and using Power BI dataflows.
C) Increase resource allocation to ensure peak performance at all times.
D) Use Azure Logic Apps for automating tasks that do not require high performance.
E) Implement premium features and services to guarantee reliability.

## QUESTION 30

Your client is planning to negotiate contracts with multiple vendors for a large-scale Power Platform deployment. They want to ensure they get the best value and maintain good vendor relationships.
1. Securing favorable terms and conditions in vendor contracts.
2. Ensuring vendors meet performance expectations.
3. Establishing a framework for ongoing vendor management.

What actions would you take to negotiate and manage vendor contracts effectively? Select two answers.

A) Focus on negotiating the lowest possible price.
B) Include performance-based incentives in vendor contracts.
C) Use Power Automate to streamline contract management processes.
D) Negotiate clear terms for dispute resolution and contract termination.
E) Select vendors who agree to provide free additional services.

## QUESTION 31

Your client is a logistics company looking to use IoT solutions to track their fleet in real-time. They need to process real-time data and ensure the system is scalable and performs well.
1. Integrating IoT devices for real-time fleet tracking.
2. Ensuring the scalability and performance of the IoT system.
3. Generating actionable insights to optimize logistics operations.

What measures would you implement to achieve these goals? Select two answers.

A) Use Power BI to integrate and visualize real-time tracking data.
B) Implement Azure IoT Central for device management and data processing.
C) Store tracking data in a local SQL database.
D) Use Azure Stream Analytics for real-time data processing.
E) Implement custom IoT solutions for each vehicle.

## QUESTION 32

A retail company uses Dynamics 365 Customer Service for handling customer inquiries and complaints. They want to enhance their customer service by integrating an AI chatbot that can provide instant responses to common queries. The chatbot must access data from Dynamics 365 in real-time and ensure high availability. Which solution should they implement to integrate the AI chatbot with Dynamics 365?

A) Use Power Virtual Agents
B) Use Azure Bot Service with Direct Line API
C) Use Power Automate
D) Use Dynamics 365 for Marketing
E) Use Microsoft Teams

## QUESTION 33

Your client is launching a new Power Platform solution and wants to ensure it promotes sustainability and reduces environmental impact. They also aim to comply with relevant green standards.
1. Ensuring sustainability in solution design.

2. Reducing environmental impact through efficient technology use.
3. Complying with green standards and regulations.
What strategies would you implement to achieve these objectives? Select two answers.

A) Use Azure Logic Apps to automate eco-friendly business processes.
B) Implement Azure Cognitive Services to optimize resource usage.
C) Conduct regular audits to ensure compliance with green standards.
D) Avoid sustainability measures to reduce costs.
E) Select renewable energy sources for data centers.

## QUESTION 34

During a legacy system integration project, you need to bridge the technology gap between an old on-premises database and a new cloud-based solution using Microsoft technologies. The project requires:
• Secure data transfer.
• Minimal changes to the existing system.
• Efficient data transformation and loading. What strategies should you use? (Select 3 answers)

A) Implement Azure Data Factory for ETL processes.
B) Use Azure Service Bus to handle messaging and data transfer.
C) Develop custom ETL scripts using Azure Functions.
D) Utilize Azure Logic Apps to automate workflows.
E) Apply Azure Cognitive Services for data transformation.

## QUESTION 35

During a large-scale Dynamics 365 implementation, you need to ensure that all stakeholders are informed and trained on the new system. The knowledge transfer process must:
• Provide comprehensive training materials.
• Ensure all users understand their roles and responsibilities.
• Enable continuous learning and support. What strategies should you adopt? (Select 3 answers)

A) Develop detailed user manuals and role-based guides.
B) Organize regular training sessions and webinars.
C) Create an online learning portal with training modules.
D) Use a ticketing system for ongoing support and issue resolution.
E) Provide one-time training sessions at the beginning of the project.

## QUESTION 36

A financial services firm uses Dynamics 365 Finance for managing their accounting operations. They want to automate the process of detecting and flagging fraudulent transactions in real-time using historical transaction data. What approach should they use to implement this solution?

A) Use Power Automate with Dataverse
B) Use Dynamics 365 Fraud Protection
C) Implement a Custom AI Model in Azure Machine Learning
D) Use AI Builder with Power Apps
E) Use Azure Logic Apps

## QUESTION 37

During a cross-functional Power Platform implementation, you need to ensure that data flows and processes are consistent and secure. The project requirements include:
- Consistent data flows across all functions.
- Secure access to data based on roles.
- Minimal disruption to ongoing operations. What strategies should be implemented? (Select 3 answers)

A) Use Dataverse with role-based access controls (RBAC).
B) Implement Power Automate for automated data flows.
C) Use shared Excel sheets for data management.
D) Utilize Azure Logic Apps for integration.
E) Schedule integration tasks during off-peak hours.

## QUESTION 38

Your team is tasked with fostering a culture of innovation within the organization using Power Platform. The initiative must:
- Encourage the use of cutting-edge technologies.
- Balance innovation with practical business needs.
- Ensure new solutions are scalable and maintainable. What actions should you take? (Select 3 answers)

A) Establish an innovation lab for experimenting with new technologies.
B) Implement ALM practices to manage new solutions.
C) Use a single instance for all experiments to minimize costs.
D) Encourage cross-functional teams to collaborate on innovative projects.
E) Regularly review and scale successful innovations to production environments.

## QUESTION 39

Your company is deploying a global Power Platform solution with strict data security requirements. The solution must:
- Secure data at rest and in transit.
- Implement advanced threat protection.
- Conduct regular security evaluations. What steps should you take? (Select 2 answers)

A) Use Azure Security Center for continuous security monitoring.
B) Encrypt data in Dataverse at rest and in transit.
C) Implement a single layer of security at the application level.
D) Use Azure Service Bus for secure communication between services.
E) Schedule regular penetration testing and vulnerability assessments.

## QUESTION 40

An insurance company uses Dynamics 365 Customer Service to handle claims processing. They want to implement an AI solution to automatically categorize incoming claims based on text analysis and route them to the appropriate department. The solution must integrate seamlessly with Dynamics 365. Which tool should they use?

A) Power Automate with AI Builder

B) Azure Cognitive Services
C) Dynamics 365 Marketing
D) Power Virtual Agents
E) Microsoft Power BI

## QUESTION 41

An e-commerce company wants to transition to a cloud-native architecture to improve scalability and performance. The solution must:
- Leverage containerization.
- Ensure automated scaling based on demand.
- Provide robust monitoring and logging. What steps should you take? (Select 3 answers)

A) Use Azure Kubernetes Service (AKS) for container orchestration.
B) Implement Azure Monitor for monitoring and logging.
C) Use Azure DevOps for CI/CD pipelines.
D) Utilize Azure Logic Apps for scaling applications.
E) Use Azure Functions with Event Grid for automated scaling.

## QUESTION 42

A financial institution is deploying a Power Platform solution to handle financial transactions and customer information. The solution must:
- Ensure privacy and security of financial data.
- Implement privacy by design principles.
- Manage and secure sensitive customer data. What measures should be taken? (Select 3 answers)

A) Use Azure Logic Apps for automating transaction processing without encryption.
B) Implement Dataverse with role-based access control (RBAC) and data encryption.
C) Use Azure Sentinel for real-time threat detection and response.
D) Store encryption keys in Azure Key Vault.
E) Use Power Automate to send transaction data via email without encryption.

## QUESTION 43

An e-commerce company needs to integrate a third-party payment gateway with their Power Platform solution. They must:
- Ensure secure transactions.
- Handle high transaction volumes efficiently.
- Maintain compliance with payment processing regulations. What approaches should they take? (Select 3 answers)

A) Use Azure Functions to handle transaction processing.
B) Implement PCI DSS compliance measures.
C) Store credit card information in plain text for easy access.
D) Use Power Automate to schedule batch processing of transactions.
E) Use Azure API Management to manage API calls to the payment gateway.

## QUESTION 44

A multinational corporation requires a Microsoft Power Platform solution that automates data processing across various global departments with strict compliance to data sovereignty laws. The solution must efficiently manage and segregate data based on regional regulations.
• Compliance with data sovereignty laws.
• Efficient management and segregation of data by region.
What architecture should you implement to meet these needs effectively?

A) Multi-tenant architecture
B) Single-tenant architecture
C) Hybrid cloud environment
D) Distributed services
E) Automated data flows

## QUESTION 45

A healthcare provider is migrating patient records to Dynamics 365. They need to:
• Ensure compliance with healthcare regulations.
• Maintain data integrity and quality.
• Efficiently handle large volumes of patient data. What methods should they use? (Select 3 answers)

A) Use Azure Data Factory for large-scale data migration.
B) Implement data encryption to ensure compliance with healthcare regulations.
C) Use manual data entry for accurate migration.
D) Apply data validation rules in Dataverse to ensure data quality.
E) Use Power BI to validate data accuracy post-migration.

## QUESTION 46

An educational institution is deploying a new Dynamics 365 solution. They must:
• Implement security protocols to protect student data.
• Ensure compliance with data privacy regulations.
• Validate security measures regularly. What actions should they take?

A) Use GDPR compliance tools in Dynamics 365.
B) Implement role-based access control with Azure AD.
C) Conduct regular security assessments using Power BI dashboards.
D) Use manual processes for compliance validation.
E) Ignore compliance checks.

## QUESTION 47

A healthcare organization is deploying a Power BI solution for analytics. They need to:
• Ensure data integrity and quality.
• Optimize performance for large datasets.
• Validate post-migration data. What are the best practices they should follow?
Select 2 answers.

A) Use Power Query for data transformation and cleansing.

B) Load entire datasets into memory without partitioning.
C) Implement incremental data refresh in Power BI.
D) Validate data using Power BI dataflows.
E) Skip data validation after migration.

## QUESTION 48

A manufacturing company complains about the slow performance of their Power Apps solution used for tracking production lines. The app integrates complex data from multiple sources and displays extensive analytics on multiple screens.
- Reduce app load times.
- Ensure data is processed efficiently.

What two solutions would best improve the app's performance?

A) Introduce data caching
B) Minimize control usage
C) Implement asynchronous data loading
D) Increase data polling intervals
E) Optimize data models

## QUESTION 49

An educational institution is using Power Apps and Dataverse for managing student records. To ensure long-term sustainability, the institution must handle routine maintenance, apply updates, and manage version control. The key requirements are:
- Ensuring regular maintenance and updates.
- Managing version control and rollback processes.
- Addressing potential data loss during updates.

What strategies should you employ? (Select 2 answers)

A) Implement automated backup procedures using Power Automate.
B) Use Azure DevOps for version control and managing updates.
C) Schedule regular maintenance windows for updates.
D) Utilize Dataverse's built-in data loss prevention (DLP) policies.
E) Conduct manual backups before applying any updates.

## QUESTION 50

Your organization relies on Power Virtual Agents for customer support. Recently, customers have reported that the chatbot is providing incorrect or incomplete answers. As a solution architect, you need to troubleshoot and resolve these issues. The key requirements are:
- Identifying the source of incorrect answers.
- Ensuring the chatbot provides accurate and complete information.
- Implementing changes without downtime.

What steps should you take? (Select 3 answers)

A) Review the Power Virtual Agents' topic configurations.
B) Use AI Builder to improve the natural language understanding (NLU) model.
C) Analyze customer conversations to identify patterns of incorrect answers.
D) Implement a fallback topic to handle unrecognized queries.
E) Use Dataverse to log and track customer feedback.

# PRACTICE TEST 3 - ANSWERS ONLY

## QUESTION 1

Answer – A), B), E)

Option A – Real-time monitoring helps visibility and addresses the lack of real-time inventory data.
Option B – Automating restocking helps efficiency, addressing inefficient restocking processes.
Option C – A Dataverse-based app centralizes data but does not ensure real-time updates or coordination.
Option D – IoT sensors provide real-time data but do not address restocking or forecasting.
Option E – AI Builder can forecast inventory needs, reducing costs and stockouts, aligning with business goals.

| | |
|---|---|
| **EXAM FOCUS** | *Use Power BI for real-time inventory monitoring, automate restocking with Power Automate, and forecast with AI Builder for optimal results.* |
| **CAUTION ALERT** | *Remember, centralizing data alone won't provide real-time updates or improve restocking efficiency.* |

## QUESTION 2

Answer – A), B)

Option A – Correct. Implementing data localization strategies by hosting data closer to where users are located can significantly reduce load times and improve performance.
Option B – Correct. Network latency is a crucial factor in app performance, particularly when accessing apps across great distances, and should be minimized to enhance usability.
Option C – Incorrect. While API performance is important, it does not address the regional disparities in app performance.
Option D – Incorrect. User device capabilities could impact performance but are not a primary concern when addressing regional performance issues.
Option E – Incorrect. Network congestion is a broader issue that might not specifically affect international app deployment unless it is region-specific.

| | |
|---|---|
| **EXAM FOCUS** | *"Use data localization strategies and minimize network latency to improve global app performance."* |
| **CAUTION ALERT** | *"API performance isn't the main issue for regional disparities."* |

## QUESTION 3

Answer – A), B), C)

Option A – Automating data entry with Power Automate reduces delays.
Option B – A Dataverse solution can standardize approval criteria, ensuring consistency.
Option C – A Power BI dashboard allows for real-time tracking of loan applications.
Option D – A Canvas App for submission is useful but does not address data entry or approval criteria.
Option E – AI Builder for data validation is useful but not as critical as the other options for this scenario.

**EXAM FOCUS** *Automate data entry with Power Automate, standardize approval criteria with Dataverse, and track*

| CAUTION ALERT | loans with Power BI.<br>*Remember, a Canvas App is useful for submission but won't solve data entry or approval consistency issues.* |
|---|---|

## QUESTION 4

Answer – B), D)

Option A – Alternate keys are useful for unique identifier-based retrieval but do not reduce the number of calls.
Option B – Correct choice as OData $filter query can retrieve specific records more efficiently.
Option C – OData $select query is used to select specific columns but does not reduce the number of calls.
Option D – Correct choice as FetchXML query can retrieve multiple records based on complex criteria efficiently.
Option E – Business rules enforce validation rules but do not optimize data retrieval.

| EXAM FOCUS | *"FetchXML query can efficiently retrieve multiple records based on complex criteria."* |
|---|---|
| CAUTION ALERT | *"You should stay cautious, multiple RetrieveMultiple calls can degrade performance significantly."* |

## QUESTION 5

Answer – B), C), D)

Option A – Power BI is useful for data analysis but does not address integration or ETL processes.
Option B – Azure Data Factory is ideal for ETL processes, ensuring scalability.
Option C – Conducting a cost-benefit analysis helps in evaluating and justifying technology choices.
Option D – Power Automate can integrate with existing financial systems, ensuring seamless operation.
Option E – Dataverse is useful for managing data but does not address ETL processes or integration directly.

| EXAM FOCUS | *Use Azure Data Factory for scalable ETL processes and Power Automate for seamless system integration.* |
|---|---|
| CAUTION ALERT | *Please keep in mind, Power BI is useful for analysis but doesn't handle ETL or integration directly.* |

## QUESTION 6

Answer – A), C), E)

Option A – Azure IoT Central handles real-time data collection, mitigating risks associated with it.
Option B – DLP policies ensure data protection but do not directly address real-time collection or data breaches.
Option C – Developing a data breach response plan prepares the company for potential breaches.
Option D – Power Automate is useful for data validation but does not address real-time collection or breach response.
Option E – Conducting regular security audits ensures ongoing assessment and mitigation of security risks.

| EXAM FOCUS | Use Azure IoT Central for real-time data, develop a breach response plan, and conduct regular security audits. |
|---|---|
| CAUTION ALERT | Please keep in mind, Power Automate won't address real-time data collection or breach response effectively. |

## QUESTION 7

Answer – A), C), D)

Option A – Azure DevOps can be used to create a comprehensive project plan.
Option B – Dataverse is useful for data management but does not address project planning or timeline estimation.
Option C – Power BI can be used to estimate realistic project timelines.
Option D – Allocating resources using Azure DevOps ensures efficient management.
Option E – Regular project status meetings are important but do not address initial planning and timeline estimation.

| EXAM FOCUS | Use Azure DevOps for comprehensive project planning and Power BI for realistic timeline estimation. |
|---|---|
| CAUTION ALERT | Stay cautious, Dataverse won't address project planning or timeline estimation effectively. |

## QUESTION 8

Answer – A), B), C)

Option A – Power BI can be used to create a dashboard for monitoring KPIs.
Option B – Defining KPIs in collaboration with stakeholders ensures they are aligned with business goals.
Option C – Using Power Automate to automate data collection ensures efficient monitoring.
Option D – Implementing a feedback loop using Microsoft Forms helps gather feedback but is not directly related to measuring KPIs.
Option E – Dataverse is useful for data management but not directly related to creating custom reports for monitoring change impact.

| EXAM FOCUS | Use Power BI for KPI monitoring, define KPIs with stakeholders, and automate data collection with Power Automate. |
|---|---|
| CAUTION ALERT | Stay cautious, feedback loops alone won't measure KPIs effectively. |

## QUESTION 9

Answer – A), B), D)

Option A – Azure Load Testing simulates peak usage effectively.
Option B – Implementing capacity planning using Azure Monitor helps in planning resources.
Option C – Power Virtual Agents is useful for interactions but not directly related to load testing.
Option D – Developing cost-performance models using Azure Cost Management helps balance cost with performance.

Option E – Azure Logic Apps are useful for workflows but not directly related to scaling strategies.

| EXAM FOCUS | Use Azure Load Testing and Azure Monitor for capacity planning and cost-performance modeling with Azure Cost Management. |
|---|---|
| CAUTION ALERT | Stay cautious, Power Virtual Agents are not used for load testing or capacity planning. |

## QUESTION 10

Answer – A), B), D)

Option A – Using Power BI ensures real-time status updates.
Option B – Scheduling bi-weekly status meetings ensures stakeholders are informed.
Option C – Azure Logic Apps is useful for data integration but not directly related to status updates and reporting.
Option D – Power Automate can automate the process of sending regular email updates.
Option E – Power Virtual Agents is useful for automated interactions but not directly related to regular status updates and reporting.

| EXAM FOCUS | Use Power BI for real-time status updates and Power Automate for regular email notifications. |
|---|---|
| CAUTION ALERT | Remember, Azure Logic Apps are useful for data integration but not for regular status updates. |

## QUESTION 11

Answer – A), C), E)

Option A – Using a structured RFP process ensures thorough vendor assessments.
Option B – Azure IoT Hub is useful for integration testing but not for vendor selection.
Option C – Using Power BI for scalability analysis ensures the solution can meet growth requirements.
Option D – Power Virtual Agents can be helpful for handling queries but not critical for assessment.
Option E – Regular performance reviews ensure ongoing effective vendor management.

| EXAM FOCUS | Use a structured RFP process and Power BI for scalability analysis to select the right vendor. |
|---|---|
| CAUTION ALERT | Stay cautious, Azure IoT Hub is useful for integration testing but not for vendor selection. |

## QUESTION 12

Answer – C)

Option A – Azure IoT Hub is good but IoT Central provides a more managed solution.
Option B – Lacks real-time data ingestion capabilities.
Option C – Correct choice as Azure IoT Central handles real-time data, and Power BI and Power Automate provide analytics and workflows.
Option D – Azure Event Hub can handle real-time data but is more complex than IoT Central for this use case.
Option E – Microsoft Dataverse is unnecessary for this scenario.

| EXAM FOCUS | "Azure IoT Central simplifies real-time data processing and integration with Dynamics 365." |
|---|---|

| CAUTION ALERT | *"Be cautious, solutions without real-time data ingestion won't meet requirements."* |

## QUESTION 13

Answer – A), C), D)

Option A – Azure Cognitive Services enhance citizen interaction with advanced technology.
Option B – Dynamics 365 is useful but more for case management than innovation.
Option C – Power Virtual Agents for automated responses foster an innovative mindset.
Option D – AI Builder provides data insights and helps in adopting new technologies.
Option E – Regular training on emerging technologies ensures the team stays current with trends.

| EXAM FOCUS | *Implement Azure Cognitive Services and AI Builder to stay current and innovative in government services.* |
|---|---|
| CAUTION ALERT | *Please keep in mind, focusing only on case management may hinder innovative solutions.* |

## QUESTION 14

Answer – A), B), D)

Option A – Azure DevOps is crucial for tracking deployment progress and issues.
Option B – User training sessions prior to deployment help manage user transition.
Option C – A phased deployment approach helps manage deployment challenges but is less critical than other options.
Option D – A post-deployment support plan is essential for continuous monitoring and support.
Option E – AI Builder is useful for analytics but not directly for handling deployment challenges.

| EXAM FOCUS | *Use Azure DevOps for tracking deployment progress and issues, and conduct user training sessions prior to deployment.* |
|---|---|
| CAUTION ALERT | *You should avoid neglecting post-deployment support, as it is crucial for continuous improvement.* |

## QUESTION 15

Answer – A), B), C)

Option A – Microsoft Teams is essential for real-time communication, enhancing team collaboration.
Option B – Azure DevOps provides project tracking and collaboration tools, crucial for managing remote and distributed teams.
Option C – Developing a communication plan ensures clear and effective communication within the team.
Option D – Dataverse is useful for assigning roles but less critical for team communication.
Option E – Power BI is useful for performance monitoring but less critical for enhancing team communication and management.

| EXAM FOCUS | *Please keep in mind, Azure DevOps is crucial for managing remote and distributed teams effectively.* |
|---|---|
| CAUTION ALERT | *Avoid relying solely on Dataverse for assigning roles without a clear communication plan.* |

## QUESTION 16

Answer – A)

Option A – Correct choice as it includes secure API management (Azure API Management), real-time updates (Power Automate), and analytics (Power BI).
Option B – Azure Synapse Analytics is overkill for this scenario.
Option C – Lacks the specific security component (Azure API Management) to ensure HIPAA compliance.
Option D – Microsoft Dataverse is useful but not necessary for this specific integration.
Option E – Azure SQL Database is not needed as the data is already managed within the EHR system.

| EXAM FOCUS | "Use Azure API Management for secure integrations and ensure compliance with HIPAA." |
|---|---|
| CAUTION ALERT | "Remember, Azure Synapse Analytics might be overkill for this scenario." |

## QUESTION 17

Answer – A), B), E)

Option A – Using Power BI to analyze current logistics processes helps identify areas for environmental impact reduction.
Option B – Developing a detailed sustainability plan using Power Apps aids in long-term sustainability planning.
Option C – Implementing user training sessions ensures users are prepared for the transition but does not directly address environmental impact and sustainability.
Option D – Customizing Power Apps extensively increases complexity and should be avoided unless necessary.
Option E – Using Azure Logic Apps for automation helps streamline processes and environmental monitoring.

| EXAM FOCUS | Use Power BI to identify environmental impact areas, create a sustainability plan, and automate with Azure Logic Apps. |
|---|---|
| CAUTION ALERT | Extensive customization of Power Apps increases complexity; avoid unless necessary. |

## QUESTION 18

Answer – A), B)

Option A – Using Dataverse ensures patient data management and compliance.
Option B – Implementing Power Automate allows adaptable workflows that can change with regulations.
Option C – Developing custom APIs adds complexity and may not be necessary for flexibility.
Option D – Using model-driven apps provides a robust and scalable solution for core functionalities but might be overkill depending on the specific needs.
Option E – Role-based security manages user access but does not directly address adaptability and scalability.

| EXAM FOCUS | Dataverse ensures compliance and scalability; Power Automate allows adaptable workflows for regulatory changes. |
|---|---|
| CAUTION ALERT | Custom APIs add complexity; use only if necessary. |

## QUESTION 19

Answer – A), C), D)

Option A – Conducting focus groups with patients gathers detailed patient insights.
Option B – Using AI Builder analyzes patient data but might not directly gather detailed insights or develop personas.
Option C – Creating patient personas based on demographics helps in developing user personas.
Option D – Implementing Power Automate for patient feedback collection ensures the design is user-centric.
Option E – Developing model-driven apps for patient interactions supports interactions but might not gather detailed insights or develop personas.

| | |
|---|---|
| EXAM FOCUS | *Conduct focus groups and create patient personas; use Power Automate for collecting patient feedback.* |
| CAUTION ALERT | *Avoid skipping direct patient interactions; they provide critical insights.* |

## QUESTION 20

Answer – A), D)

Option A – Correct choice as Lookups handle one-to-many and many-to-many relationships.
Option B – Option sets are used for picklist values, not relationships.
Option C – Polymorphic relationships are useful but not as common as Lookups.
Option D – Correct choice as Hierarchical relationship settings support hierarchical data structures.
Option E – Business rules enforce validation but don't define relationships.

| | |
|---|---|
| EXAM FOCUS | "Leverage Lookups and Hierarchical relationship settings for complex relationships and data hierarchies." |
| CAUTION ALERT | "Polymorphic relationships are less common; prioritize Lookups and Hierarchical settings for relationships." |

## QUESTION 21

Answer – A), C)

Option A – Dataverse provides unified data storage, aligning with enterprise architecture.
Option B – Azure Cognitive Services is innovative but does not directly align with enterprise architecture.
Option C – Developing a governance framework ensures adherence to architectural standards and best practices.
Option D – Model-Driven Apps are useful but do not directly address the requirements.
Option E – Pilot programs help in testing but are not directly related to alignment or best practices.

| | |
|---|---|
| EXAM FOCUS | *Use Dataverse for data storage and develop a governance framework.* |
| CAUTION ALERT | *Ensure architectural standards and best practices are followed to avoid future issues.* |

## QUESTION 22

Answer – A), C)

Option A – Dataverse ensures secure data storage and management, complying with financial regulations.
Option B – DLP policies are useful for data protection but do not directly address cost optimization.
Option C – Azure Key Vault ensures data encryption, ensuring data privacy and protection.
Option D – Azure Cost Management and Billing optimizes costs but does not directly address data privacy and protection.
Option E – Power Automate helps with workflow automation but does not directly address data privacy or cost optimization.

| | |
|---|---|
| EXAM FOCUS | *Please keep in mind, Dataverse and Azure Key Vault are essential for secure data management and encryption in financial services.* |
| CAUTION ALERT | *Don't confuse DLP policies or cost management tools with direct solutions for data privacy or cost optimization.* |

## QUESTION 23

Answer – A), C)

Option A – Azure DevOps provides robust CI/CD capabilities for rapid deployments.
Option B – Dataverse ensures secure data storage but does not directly contribute to CI/CD or version control.
Option C – GitHub offers version control and integrates well with CI/CD pipelines.
Option D – Power BI is useful for monitoring but not directly for CI/CD or version control.
Option E – DLP policies are essential for data protection but do not contribute to CI/CD or version control.

| | |
|---|---|
| EXAM FOCUS | *Implement Azure DevOps and GitHub for robust CI/CD and version control, ensuring compliance and rapid deployments.* |
| CAUTION ALERT | *Be cautious about relying solely on Dataverse or Power BI; they don't handle CI/CD or version control directly.* |

## QUESTION 24

Answer – B), E)

Option A – Referential relationships enforce referential integrity but do not automatically delete related records.
Option B – Correct choice as Parental relationships automatically delete related records.
Option C – Custom relationships can be configured for specific behaviors but are more complex.
Option D – Referential, Restrict Delete prevents deletion if there are related records, but does not automate deletion.
Option E – Correct choice as Cascade Delete will automatically delete related records.

| | |
|---|---|
| EXAM FOCUS | *"Leverage Parental and Cascade Delete to maintain referential integrity and automate deletion."* |
| CAUTION ALERT | *"Avoid using Custom or Referential relationships for automatic deletion."* |

## QUESTION 25

Answer – A), B)

Option A – Canvas Apps are crucial for creating a custom UI that works across various devices.
Option B – Dataverse ensures secure data storage and supports offline capabilities.
Option C – Power Automate is useful for real-time data updates but not necessarily for offline capabilities.
Option D – Azure Logic Apps are useful for workflow automation but not critical for this scenario.
Option E – Azure Cognitive Services are beneficial for image recognition but not directly related to the requirements of this solution.

| | |
|---|---|
| **EXAM FOCUS** | *Prioritize Canvas Apps and Dataverse for secure, seamless, cross-device functionality with offline capabilities.* |
| **CAUTION ALERT** | *Avoid depending solely on Power Automate for real-time updates; it does not address offline capabilities.* |

## QUESTION 26

Answer – A), B), D)

Option A – AI Builder can validate loan applications using AI capabilities.
Option B – Power Automate Cloud Flow can automate the loan approval workflow.
Option C – Power Automate Desktop is not necessary for this cloud-based workflow.
Option D – Data Loss Prevention (DLP) policies ensure compliance with regulatory requirements.
Option E – Azure DevOps is useful for continuous integration but not directly related to loan approval processes.

| | |
|---|---|
| **EXAM FOCUS** | *Remember to use AI Builder, Cloud Flow, and DLP policies for validating applications, automating workflows, and ensuring compliance.* |
| **CAUTION ALERT** | *Be cautious about using Power Automate Desktop; it's not necessary for cloud-based workflows.* |

## QUESTION 27

Answer – B), D), E)

Option A – Azure Policy is useful for compliance auditing but not specific to HIPAA directly.
Option B – Dataverse provides secure data storage.
Option C – Power BI is for analysis and does not directly manage compliance requirements.
Option D – Azure AD is critical for managing user access based on roles.
Option E – Azure Key Vault is essential for ensuring data encryption.

| | |
|---|---|
| **EXAM FOCUS** | *Ensure HIPAA compliance with Dataverse for storage, Azure AD for RBAC, and Azure Key Vault for encryption.* |
| **CAUTION ALERT** | *Don't rely on Power BI for HIPAA compliance; it focuses on data analysis, not security or access management.* |

## QUESTION 28

Answer – C)

Option A – Model-driven Apps are data-driven and less flexible for creating highly interactive user interfaces.
Option B – Portal Apps are used for external users, not internal staff.
Option C – Canvas Apps allow for a highly customizable and interactive user interface, making it ideal for entering donation details.
Option D – Dynamics 365 Sales is not specifically designed for managing donation entries.
Option E – Power Automate is used for automating workflows, not for building interactive user interfaces.

| EXAM FOCUS | *"Canvas Apps provide a highly customizable interface for entering donation details."* |
|---|---|
| CAUTION ALERT | *"Model-driven Apps are less flexible for creating interactive UIs."* |

## QUESTION 29

Answer – A), B)

Option A – Correct. Detailed analysis using analytics tools helps in identifying and eliminating inefficiencies.
Option B – Correct. Optimizing data storage reduces costs and improves efficiency.
Option C – Incorrect. Increasing resource allocation unnecessarily can lead to higher costs.
Option D – Incorrect. While Logic Apps can be useful, it may not be necessary for tasks that do not need automation.
Option E – Incorrect. Premium features are costly and should be used judiciously.

| EXAM FOCUS | *Conduct a detailed analysis of resource usage and optimize data storage to reduce costs.* |
|---|---|
| CAUTION ALERT | *Increasing resource allocation unnecessarily can lead to higher costs.* |

## QUESTION 30

Answer – B), D)

Option A – Incorrect. Focusing only on price may lead to compromises in quality.
Option B – Correct. Performance-based incentives ensure vendors meet expectations.
Option C – Incorrect. Power Automate can help but is not directly related to contract negotiation.
Option D – Correct. Clear terms for dispute resolution and termination are crucial.
Option E – Incorrect. Free services should not be a deciding factor.

| EXAM FOCUS | *Include performance-based incentives and clear dispute resolution terms in contracts.* |
|---|---|
| CAUTION ALERT | *Focusing only on price may compromise quality and long-term relationships.* |

## QUESTION 31

Answer – B), D)

Option A – Incorrect. Power BI is useful for visualization but not for real-time data processing.

Option B – Correct. Azure IoT Central provides integrated device management and data processing.
Option C – Incorrect. Storing data locally limits scalability and performance.
Option D – Correct. Azure Stream Analytics is ideal for real-time data processing.
Option E – Incorrect. Custom solutions increase complexity and are not necessary with Azure IoT services.

| EXAM FOCUS | Implement Azure IoT Central and Stream Analytics for integrated device management. |
|---|---|
| CAUTION ALERT | Storing data in a local database limits scalability and performance. |

## QUESTION 32

Answer – A)

Option A – Power Virtual Agents allows for easy creation and integration of AI chatbots with Dynamics 365, ensuring real-time data access and high availability.
Option B – Azure Bot Service with Direct Line API requires more complex setup and does not integrate as seamlessly with Dynamics 365.
Option C – Power Automate can be used for workflows but is not designed for creating AI chatbots.
Option D – Dynamics 365 for Marketing is focused on marketing automation, not customer service chatbots.
Option E – Microsoft Teams can facilitate communication but is not specifically designed for AI chatbots.

| EXAM FOCUS | "Power Virtual Agents provides seamless AI chatbot integration with Dynamics 365." |
|---|---|
| CAUTION ALERT | "Azure Bot Service requires more complex setup compared to Power Virtual Agents." |

## QUESTION 33

Answer – C), E)

Option A – Incorrect. Azure Logic Apps are useful for automation but not primarily for eco-friendly processes.
Option B – Incorrect. Azure Cognitive Services are useful but not the primary tool for resource optimization.
Option C – Correct. Regular audits ensure compliance with green standards.
Option D – Incorrect. Avoiding sustainability measures can lead to non-compliance and environmental impact.
Option E – Correct. Selecting renewable energy sources for data centers promotes sustainability.

| EXAM FOCUS | Regular audits and renewable energy sources ensure green compliance and sustainability. |
|---|---|
| CAUTION ALERT | Avoiding sustainability measures can lead to non-compliance and increased environmental impact. |

## QUESTION 34

Answer – A), B), D)

Option A – Azure Data Factory is ideal for ETL processes and efficient data transformation.
Option B – Azure Service Bus ensures secure and reliable data transfer.

Option C – Custom ETL scripts may require significant changes and maintenance.
Option D – Azure Logic Apps automate workflows and integrate different services efficiently.
Option E – Azure Cognitive Services are not typically used for data transformation in ETL processes.

| | |
|---|---|
| **EXAM FOCUS** | *You should utilize Azure Data Factory and Logic Apps for secure data transfer and efficient workflow automation.* |
| **CAUTION ALERT** | *Be cautious, custom ETL scripts can lead to significant maintenance and changes to the existing system.* |

## QUESTION 35

Answer – A), B), C)

Option A – Detailed user manuals and role-based guides are essential for comprehensive training.
Option B – Regular training sessions and webinars ensure continuous learning.
Option C – An online learning portal provides easy access to training materials and supports continuous learning.
Option D – A ticketing system is useful for support but does not replace training materials.
Option E – One-time training is insufficient for large-scale implementations.

| | |
|---|---|
| **EXAM FOCUS** | *Develop comprehensive training materials and use online learning portals to ensure continuous learning and support.* |
| **CAUTION ALERT** | *One-time training sessions are insufficient for large-scale implementations; ensure ongoing training and support.* |

## QUESTION 36

Answer – B)

Option A – Power Automate can automate workflows but is not specifically designed for fraud detection.
Option B – Dynamics 365 Fraud Protection provides real-time fraud detection capabilities tailored for financial services.
Option C – Custom AI Model in Azure Machine Learning is powerful but requires extensive AI expertise and setup.
Option D – AI Builder can help build AI models, but Dynamics 365 Fraud Protection is specifically optimized for fraud detection.
Option E – Azure Logic Apps are used for workflow automation, not specifically for fraud detection.

| | |
|---|---|
| **EXAM FOCUS** | *"Dynamics 365 Fraud Protection offers specialized real-time fraud detection for financial services."* |
| **CAUTION ALERT** | *"Power Automate is not specifically designed for fraud detection and may lack necessary features."* |

## QUESTION 37

Answer – A), B), E)

Option A – Dataverse with RBAC ensures secure and consistent data access.
Option B – Power Automate facilitates automated and consistent data flows.
Option C – Shared Excel sheets are not secure or reliable for data management.

Option D – Azure Logic Apps are useful but may require complex configurations.
Option E – Scheduling integration tasks during off-peak hours minimizes disruption to ongoing operations.

| EXAM FOCUS | *Implement Dataverse with role-based access and Power Automate for automated, consistent data flows.* |
|---|---|
| **CAUTION ALERT** | *Avoid using shared Excel sheets; they are not secure or reliable for data management.* |

## QUESTION 38

Answer – A), B), E)

Option A – An innovation lab allows for experimentation with new technologies.
Option B – ALM practices ensure new solutions are scalable and maintainable.
Option C – A single instance can limit scalability and experimentation.
Option D – Cross-functional collaboration fosters innovation but needs proper management.
Option E – Regularly reviewing and scaling successful innovations balances innovation with practical business needs.

| EXAM FOCUS | *Establish an innovation lab and implement ALM practices to manage scalable and maintainable solutions.* |
|---|---|
| **CAUTION ALERT** | *A single instance for experiments limits scalability and hinders proper evaluation.* |

## QUESTION 39

Answer – A), B)

Option A – Azure Security Center provides continuous security monitoring and threat protection.
Option B – Encrypting data in Dataverse ensures security at rest and in transit.
Option C – A single layer of security is not sufficient; multiple layers should be implemented.
Option D – Azure Service Bus can help secure communication but may not be enough alone.
Option E – Regular penetration testing and vulnerability assessments ensure ongoing security evaluations.

| EXAM FOCUS | *Use Azure Security Center for continuous monitoring and encrypt data in Dataverse at rest and in transit.* |
|---|---|
| **CAUTION ALERT** | *A single layer of security is not sufficient; implement multiple layers to enhance security.* |

## QUESTION 40

Answer – A)

Option A – Power Automate with AI Builder can automate the categorization of claims based on text analysis and integrate directly with Dynamics 365.
Option B – Azure Cognitive Services provides advanced AI capabilities but requires more complex integration.

Option C – Dynamics 365 Marketing is focused on marketing automation, not claims processing.
Option D – Power Virtual Agents are used for chatbots, not for categorizing and routing claims.
Option E – Power BI is for data visualization and analysis, not for automating claims categorization.

| EXAM FOCUS | "Leverage Power Automate with AI Builder for seamless AI integration and categorization." |
|---|---|
| CAUTION ALERT | "Azure Cognitive Services need more complex integration than AI Builder." |

## QUESTION 41

Answer – A), B), E)

Option A – Azure Kubernetes Service (AKS) is designed for container orchestration, making it suitable for managing containerized applications.
Option B – Azure Monitor provides comprehensive monitoring and logging capabilities, which are crucial for maintaining robust monitoring and logging.
Option C – Azure DevOps is useful for CI/CD pipelines but does not directly address containerization, automated scaling, or robust monitoring.
Option D – Azure Logic Apps is more suited for workflow automation rather than scaling applications.
Option E – Azure Functions with Event Grid can handle automated scaling based on events, ensuring scalability according to demand.

| EXAM FOCUS | Use AKS for container orchestration and Azure Monitor for comprehensive logging. |
|---|---|
| CAUTION ALERT | Avoid relying solely on Azure DevOps for containerization and automated scaling. |

## QUESTION 42

Answer – B), C), D)

Option A – Automating transaction processing without encryption compromises data privacy and security.
Option B – Dataverse with RBAC and data encryption ensures that financial data is securely managed and access is restricted to authorized personnel only.
Option C – Azure Sentinel provides real-time threat detection and response, enhancing the security of financial transactions and customer information.
Option D – Storing encryption keys in Azure Key Vault secures the encryption keys, ensuring that sensitive customer data is protected.
Option E – Sending transaction data via email without encryption poses a significant security risk and violates data privacy principles.

| EXAM FOCUS | Use Dataverse with RBAC, Azure Sentinel, and Azure Key Vault for security and compliance. |
|---|---|
| CAUTION ALERT | Never process or send financial data without encryption. |

## QUESTION 43

Answer – A), B), E)

Option A – Azure Functions can efficiently handle high transaction volumes with serverless architecture,

ensuring scalability.
Option B – Implementing PCI DSS compliance measures ensures that transactions are secure and meet regulatory requirements.
Option C – Storing credit card information in plain text is highly insecure and violates payment processing regulations.
Option D – While Power Automate can schedule batch processing, it is not ideal for handling real-time, high-volume transactions.
Option E – Azure API Management provides robust tools to manage and secure API calls, ensuring reliable and secure integration with the payment gateway.

| EXAM FOCUS | *Use Azure Functions for transactions and implement PCI DSS measures.* |
|---|---|
| CAUTION ALERT | *Do not store credit card information in plain text; it's insecure.* |

## QUESTION 44

Answer – B)

Option A – Incorrect. Multi-tenant architecture might not provide the necessary segregation for compliance with data sovereignty laws.
Option B – Correct. Single-tenant architecture ensures data is stored and processed within dedicated environments, which can be tailored to meet regional regulations and ensure compliance.
Option C – Incorrect. Hybrid cloud environments offer flexibility but can complicate compliance with data sovereignty without proper configuration.
Option D – Incorrect. Distributed services can help manage data across locations but do not inherently provide compliance to specific regional laws.
Option E – Incorrect. Automated data flows streamline processes but do not address the core need for data segregation and compliance with sovereignty laws.

| EXAM FOCUS | *"You should stay cautious, Single-tenant architecture helps meet regional compliance and data sovereignty laws effectively."* |
|---|---|
| CAUTION ALERT | *"Multi-tenant setups may complicate data sovereignty compliance; choose single-tenant for clear segregation."* |

## QUESTION 45

Answer – A), B), D)

Option A – Azure Data Factory is designed for large-scale data migration, ensuring efficiency.
Option B – Data encryption is crucial for compliance with healthcare regulations such as HIPAA.
Option C – Manual data entry is impractical for large volumes and prone to errors.
Option D – Data validation rules in Dataverse ensure data integrity and quality.
Option E – Power BI is primarily used for reporting and analysis, not data migration validation.

| EXAM FOCUS | *Implement data encryption to ensure compliance with healthcare regulations.* |
|---|---|
| CAUTION ALERT | *Manual data entry is impractical for large volumes and prone to errors.* |

## QUESTION 46

Answer – A), B), C)

Option A – Using GDPR compliance tools in Dynamics 365 helps ensure data privacy and protection for student data.
Option B – Implementing RBAC with Azure AD ensures secure access management.
Option C – Regular security assessments using Power BI dashboards help monitor and validate the effectiveness of security measures.
Option D – Manual processes for compliance validation are less efficient and reliable.
Option E – Ignoring compliance checks is not acceptable as it can lead to regulatory breaches and data protection issues.

| EXAM FOCUS | *"Use GDPR compliance tools and regular security assessments with Power BI dashboards."* |
|---|---|
| CAUTION ALERT | *"Manual compliance validation processes are less efficient and reliable."* |

## QUESTION 47

Answer – A), C)

Option A – Using Power Query for data transformation and cleansing ensures that data is accurate and clean before loading into Power BI.
Option B – Loading entire datasets without partitioning can lead to performance issues; partitioning is essential for handling large datasets efficiently.
Option C – Implementing incremental data refresh improves performance by only updating data that has changed, reducing load times.
Option D – Validating data using Power BI dataflows helps ensure data accuracy and integrity throughout the ETL process.
Option E – Skipping data validation after migration risks data inaccuracies and quality issues in the new environment.

| EXAM FOCUS | *"Remember, using Power Query for data transformation ensures data accuracy before loading into Power BI."* |
|---|---|
| CAUTION ALERT | *"You should stay cautious, loading entire datasets without partitioning can lead to performance issues."* |

## QUESTION 48

Answer – C), E)

Option A – Incorrect. Data caching can improve performance but might not be sufficient alone to handle complex multi-source integrations efficiently.
Option B – Incorrect. Minimizing control usage helps, but the scenario suggests the need for a more substantial approach to handling data efficiently.
Option C – Correct. Implementing asynchronous data loading allows the app to remain responsive while handling data requests in the background, improving user experience during complex operations.
Option D – Incorrect. Increasing data polling intervals might reduce load but could lead to less current data being available in a manufacturing context.
Option E – Correct. Optimizing data models to streamline how data is processed and integrated can significantly boost performance.

| EXAM FOCUS | *"Implement asynchronous data loading and optimize data models for efficient data processing and reduced load times."* |
|---|---|
| CAUTION ALERT | *"Don't rely solely on minimizing controls; focus on data handling efficiency for best results."* |

## QUESTION 49

Answer – B), C)

Option A – Incorrect. While automated backups are useful, Power Automate alone does not provide comprehensive version control or update management.
Option B – Correct. Azure DevOps is essential for version control and managing updates, ensuring rollback capabilities if issues arise.
Option C – Correct. Scheduling regular maintenance windows helps ensure that updates are applied systematically without disrupting operations.
Option D – Incorrect. DLP policies are important for data protection but do not address version control or update management.
Option E – Incorrect. Manual backups are less efficient and reliable compared to automated procedures combined with robust version control systems like Azure DevOps.

| EXAM FOCUS | *"Use Azure DevOps for managing updates and version control to ensure rollback capabilities."* |
|---|---|
| CAUTION ALERT | *"You should stay cautious, ignoring regular maintenance can disrupt business operations."* |

## QUESTION 50

Answer – A), B), C)

Option A – Correct. Reviewing topic configurations helps ensure that the chatbot is set up correctly.
Option B – Correct. Improving the NLU model with AI Builder can enhance the chatbot's understanding and accuracy.
Option C – Correct. Analyzing conversations helps identify patterns and sources of incorrect answers.
Option D – Incorrect. While useful for handling unrecognized queries, it does not directly address the issue of incorrect answers.
Option E – Incorrect. Logging feedback in Dataverse is helpful for tracking, but does not directly resolve the issue of incorrect answers.

| EXAM FOCUS | *"Review Power Virtual Agents' topic configurations to ensure accuracy."* |
|---|---|
| CAUTION ALERT | *"You should stay cautious, incorrect chatbot responses can frustrate customers and damage trust."* |

# PRACTICE TEST 4 - QUESTIONS ONLY

## QUESTION 1

A healthcare organization wants to improve patient care and operational efficiency using Microsoft Power Platform. Their business goals include enhancing patient engagement, reducing administrative overhead, and ensuring data privacy. Specific challenges are:
- Limited patient interaction channels.
- High administrative workload.
- Data privacy concerns.

Which solutions best align with their business goals while addressing these challenges? Select two correct answers.

A) Use Power Virtual Agents for patient interactions.
B) Implement Power Automate to reduce administrative tasks.
C) Develop a Power Apps portal for patient access to information.
D) Use Dataverse for secure data management.
E) Create Power BI reports for operational insights.

## QUESTION 2

During the rollout of a new Power Apps-based solution for a logistics company, users in different countries report varying performance levels, affecting operational efficiency. You are tasked with optimizing the app globally.
- Optimize app globally.
- Ensure consistent operational efficiency.

Which two factors would you prioritize to address these international performance disparities?

A) Implementing global accelerator technologies
B) Network latency
C) Enhancing data architecture
D) Application feature reduction
E) Increasing server capacity

## QUESTION 3

A manufacturing company wants to implement an IoT-based monitoring system using Microsoft Power Platform. They need to analyze existing processes and map out new workflows. The specific challenges are:
- Manual data collection from machines.
- Lack of integration with ERP systems.
- Difficulty in real-time monitoring and reporting.

Which solutions would best address these challenges? Select two correct answers.

A) Use Azure IoT Central to collect data from machines.
B) Implement Power Automate to integrate with ERP systems.
C) Develop a Power BI dashboard for real-time monitoring.
D) Create a Dataverse-based app for data management.

E) Use AI Builder for predictive maintenance.

## QUESTION 4

An educational institution is building a student management system using Microsoft Dataverse. The developer is using multiple RetrieveMultiple calls in JavaScript to get student records based on their IDs, which affects performance.
- The solution must optimize data retrieval.
- It should simplify the code.

What should you recommend the developer use to achieve this? Select two answers.

A) Alternate keys
B) OData $filter query
C) OData $expand query
D) FetchXML query
E) Calculated columns

## QUESTION 5

A manufacturing company wants to implement an IoT-based monitoring system using Microsoft Power Platform. The project involves evaluating available technologies and ensuring they match the solution requirements. The specific challenges are:
- Collecting real-time data from various IoT devices.
- Integrating with existing ERP systems.
- Future-proofing the technology decisions.

Which solutions would best address these challenges? Select two correct answers.

A) Use Azure IoT Central to collect real-time data from IoT devices.
B) Implement Azure Logic Apps for integration with ERP systems.
C) Conduct a technology evaluation to ensure future-proofing.
D) Develop a Power Apps solution for data visualization.
E) Use Dataverse to store IoT data.

## QUESTION 6

An educational institution is implementing a new student information system using Microsoft Power Platform. The project requires continuous risk monitoring and assessment. The specific challenges are:
- Identifying risks in data handling and storage.
- Ensuring the system can handle peak usage times.
- Regularly assessing system security.

Which solutions would best address these challenges? Select two correct answers.

A) Use Dataverse to store and manage student data securely.
B) Implement Power BI to monitor system usage.
C) Use Azure Monitor for continuous risk assessment.
D) Develop a contingency plan for peak usage times.
E) Implement RBAC to control access to student data.

## QUESTION 7

An educational institution is implementing a new student information system using Microsoft Power Platform. The project requires effective timeline estimation and scheduling. The specific challenges are:
- Estimating the time required for system development.
- Scheduling regular progress reviews.
- Ensuring the project stays on track.

Which solutions would best address these challenges? Select two correct answers.

A) Use Power BI to create a project timeline.
B) Implement Power Automate to schedule progress reviews.
C) Develop a Gantt chart to track project progress.
D) Use Dataverse to manage student data.
E) Conduct regular team meetings using Microsoft Teams.

## QUESTION 8

A government agency is implementing a new document management system using Microsoft Power Platform. The project involves stakeholder involvement in the change process. The specific challenges are:
- Identifying key stakeholders.
- Ensuring stakeholders are engaged throughout the process.
- Addressing stakeholder concerns.

Which solutions would best address these challenges? Select three correct answers.

A) Use Power Apps to develop a prototype for stakeholder review.
B) Conduct stakeholder analysis to identify key stakeholders.
C) Use Power Automate to streamline stakeholder communications.
D) Develop a stakeholder engagement plan.
E) Implement feedback sessions using Microsoft Teams.

## QUESTION 9

A logistics company is scaling its tracking system using Microsoft Power Platform. The project requires implementing scaling strategies for growth. The specific challenges are:
- Ensuring the system can scale efficiently.
- Implementing strategies for automatic scaling.
- Monitoring performance during scaling.

What actions would you take to address these challenges? Select three correct answers.

A) Use Azure Functions for serverless scaling.
B) Implement Azure Monitor for performance monitoring.
C) Use Power BI for tracking system usage.
D) Develop autoscaling policies using Azure Autoscale.
E) Implement Azure API Management for managing API traffic.

## QUESTION 10

A retail company is deploying a new e-commerce platform using Microsoft Power Platform. The project

requires building and maintaining stakeholder relationships. The specific challenges are:
• Engaging stakeholders throughout the project lifecycle.
• Building trust and rapport.
• Addressing stakeholder concerns and feedback.
What steps would you take to address these challenges? Select three correct answers.

A) Schedule regular one-on-one meetings with key stakeholders.
B) Use Dynamics 365 for tracking stakeholder interactions.
C) Implement Power Automate for workflow management.
D) Use Power BI for tracking project performance.
E) Conduct stakeholder surveys.

## QUESTION 11

A government agency is deploying a new citizen services portal using Dynamics 365 and Microsoft Power Platform. The specific challenges are:
• Ensuring vendors meet stringent security and compliance requirements.
• Assessing vendor solutions for scalability and performance.
• Negotiating favorable terms for long-term support and maintenance.
What steps would you take to address these challenges? Select three correct answers.

A) Conduct a detailed security and compliance assessment using Azure Security Center.
B) Use Power Automate to streamline the vendor selection process.
C) Compare scalability and performance metrics of different solutions using Power BI.
D) Use Power Apps to create a compliance checklist for vendors.
E) Engage legal experts to negotiate terms and long-term support.

## QUESTION 12

A multinational corporation is designing a Power Platform solution for their sales teams in Europe and North America. The solution needs to ensure optimal performance and data compliance across regions.
• The company has one development environment and two production environments: one in Europe and one in North America.
• They need to deploy from the development environment to the production environments without issues.
Which region should you host the development environment in?

A) Canada
B) Europe
C) Japan
D) North America
E) Australia

## QUESTION 13

A financial services company wants to ensure its IT team stays ahead of industry trends and can predict future changes. The challenges include:
• Staying current with industry trends.
• Balancing innovation with practicality.

- Predicting and preparing for future changes.

What best practices should you follow to address these challenges? Select two correct answers.

A) Subscribe to industry research reports and newsletters.
B) Use Azure DevOps to manage innovation projects.
C) Implement Power BI to monitor industry trends.
D) Develop a continuous learning program.
E) Schedule bi-annual innovation summits.

## QUESTION 14

A manufacturing company is implementing a new inventory management system using the Microsoft Power Platform. The challenges include:
- Planning deployment phases.
- Handling deployment challenges.
- Strategies for successful rollouts.

What practices and tools should you recommend to ensure a successful deployment? Select three correct answers.

A) Implement Azure DevOps for CI/CD and version control.
B) Conduct regular deployment status meetings.
C) Use Power BI for real-time deployment monitoring.
D) Develop a comprehensive deployment checklist.
E) Utilize Power Virtual Agents for deployment support.

## QUESTION 15

A healthcare provider is using Microsoft Power Platform to develop a new patient management system. The team faces challenges such as:
- Enhancing collaboration and teamwork.
- Resolving team conflicts and challenges.
- Using appropriate tools for team communication.

What steps should you take to address these challenges? Select three correct answers.

A) Use Microsoft Teams for team meetings and communication.
B) Implement Azure DevOps for project management.
C) Develop conflict resolution training for the team.
D) Utilize Power BI for tracking project progress.
E) Assign Data Steward roles in Dataverse.

## QUESTION 16

A logistics company is designing an ALM strategy for their Power Platform solution, which includes Power Apps, Power Automate, and Power BI. The solution needs to ensure smooth deployment across development, test, and production environments.
- The ALM process should support version control and continuous integration.
- It must allow rollback in case of deployment failures.

Which tools would you recommend for implementing this ALM strategy? Select all that apply.

A) Azure Pipelines in Azure DevOps
B) Microsoft Power Platform Pipelines
C) ALM Accelerator
D) Manual ALM
E) Power Automate Desktop

## QUESTION 17

A healthcare provider is planning to implement a new patient management system using Microsoft Power Platform. The team faces challenges such as:
- Assessing environmental impact of solutions.
- Compliance with environmental standards.
- Long-term sustainability planning.

What steps should you take to address these challenges? Select three correct answers.

A) Conduct an environmental readiness assessment using Power BI for data analysis.
B) Develop a comprehensive sustainability plan involving all stakeholders.
C) Implement a pilot program to test the new system and assess environmental implications.
D) Customize Power Apps to fit specific environmental needs.
E) Use Azure DevOps to manage project tasks and track environmental progress.

## QUESTION 18

A multinational corporation is deploying a new document management system using Microsoft Power Platform. The solution must:
- Be flexible enough to adapt to varying regional compliance requirements.
- Scale to accommodate the growing volume of documents.
- Remain stable while integrating with existing systems.

You need to select three design considerations to meet these requirements. Which three considerations should you include? (Select three)

A) Use Dataverse for centralized and scalable data storage.
B) Implement Power Automate to manage document workflows.
C) Develop custom connectors for integration with existing systems.
D) Use Power BI for compliance reporting.
E) Develop a single comprehensive model-driven app.

## QUESTION 19

A technology company is revamping its employee intranet using Microsoft Power Platform. The solution must:
- Gather employee feedback and insights.
- Develop personas for different user groups.
- Incorporate these insights into the design.

Which two approaches should you take to meet these requirements? (Select two)

A) Use Power Automate to distribute and collect surveys.
B) Implement Dataverse to analyze employee behavior.
C) Create Power BI dashboards to visualize feedback.

D) Conduct workshops to gather detailed feedback.
E) Develop canvas apps for specific user groups.

## QUESTION 20

A retail company is designing a solution using Microsoft Dataverse to manage inventory and sales data. They want to ensure that the data model can provide real-time insights and analytics.
• The solution must support real-time data updates and reporting.
• It should integrate with Power BI for advanced analytics.
Which components should you include in the solution? Select three answers.

A) Real-time workflows
B) Calculated columns
C) Rollup columns
D) Power BI dataflows
E) Scheduled cloud flows

## QUESTION 21

A multinational corporation wants to ensure their Power Platform solutions are integrated with their existing systems and adhere to best practices. The solution must:
• Integrate with existing IT infrastructure.
• Follow architectural standards and best practices.
• Balance innovation with existing systems.
Which two actions should you take? (Select two)

A) Implement Azure Logic Apps for workflow automation.
B) Use AI Builder for predictive analytics.
C) Adopt a microservices architecture using Power Apps.
D) Establish a Center of Excellence (CoE) for Power Platform.
E) Utilize Azure Functions for custom logic.

## QUESTION 22

A healthcare provider needs a hybrid Power Platform solution with Azure integration. The solution must:
• Ensure compliance with HIPAA regulations.
• Provide secure data access and storage.
• Enable seamless integration with on-premises systems.
Which two components should you use? (Select two)

A) Use Azure Logic Apps for hybrid integration.
B) Implement Azure AD Conditional Access for secure data access.
C) Use Azure Cognitive Services for data analysis.
D) Use Azure DevOps for continuous integration and deployment.
E) Implement Azure Key Vault for secure data storage.

## QUESTION 23

A retail company wants to establish an ALM strategy for their Power Platform applications. They need to

manage environments, automate deployments, and ensure best practices in version control. The solution must:
• Use CI/CD pipelines.
• Automate environment management.
• Ensure application quality.
Which two tools should you use? (Select two)

A) Use Azure DevOps for CI/CD pipelines.
B) Use Power Apps Test Studio for automated testing.
C) Implement Dataverse for data management.
D) Use Power Automate for deployment.
E) Use Power Platform Build Tools.

## QUESTION 24

A logistics company is using Microsoft Dataverse to track shipments and deliveries. They need to ensure that related shipment items are not deleted when the main shipment record is deleted to preserve historical data.
• The solution must prevent deletion of related records.
• It should maintain referential integrity.
Which type of relationship behavior should you configure? Select two answers.

A) Referential
B) Custom
C) Parental
D) Referential, Restrict Delete
E) Delete Cascade

## QUESTION 25

A financial services company needs a cross-platform mobile app to allow clients to access account information and perform transactions securely. The app must:
• Handle peak loads efficiently.
• Provide high security for financial transactions.
• Ensure seamless integration with existing systems.
What three components or strategies should be implemented? (Select three)

A) Use Azure API Management for API handling.
B) Implement horizontal scaling for Power Apps.
C) Use Azure Functions for backend processing.
D) Enable data encryption.
E) Conduct regular security audits.

## QUESTION 26

A retail business wants to enhance their inventory management using Power Automate. The solution must:
• Monitor stock levels in real-time.
• Automatically reorder items when stock is low.

• Integrate with their existing ERP system.
What three strategies should you prioritize? (Select three)

A) Power Automate Cloud Flow for monitoring stock levels.
B) Power Automate approvals for reordering items.
C) ERP Connector for integrating with the existing system.
D) Power BI for inventory reports.
E) Azure Logic Apps for complex integrations.

## QUESTION 27

A multinational corporation needs to implement a comprehensive IT governance strategy using Power Platform. The solution must:
• Enforce data governance policies.
• Monitor compliance across regions.
• Provide role-based access controls.
Which components should be included? (Select three)

A) Power Platform Admin Center for policy enforcement.
B) Azure Monitor for compliance monitoring.
C) Azure AD for managing roles and access.
D) Power Virtual Agents for user interaction.
E) AI Builder for data analysis.

## QUESTION 28

A technology company uses Power BI to create dashboards for their sales performance. They want to ensure that their Power BI data is always up-to-date with minimal latency. What data connectivity mode should they use?

A) Import Mode
B) DirectQuery Mode
C) Composite Mode
D) Live Connection
E) Dataflow

## QUESTION 29

A client needs assistance with financial planning for their Power Platform deployment. They are worried about the long-term financial sustainability of their solution and want to ensure they are making cost-effective decisions.
1. Estimating the Total Cost of Ownership (TCO) for their Power Platform solution.
2. Identifying areas where they can reduce costs without impacting functionality.
3. Ensuring their financial plan supports future growth and scalability.
How would you guide the client in their financial planning? Select two answers.

A) Use Power BI to create financial models that project future costs and savings.
B) Regularly audit the Power Platform environment to identify and eliminate unnecessary costs.
C) Encourage the client to invest in high-cost add-ons for future-proofing.

D) Implement Azure Cost Management to provide insights and control over spending.
E) Suggest the use of external consultants for continuous financial planning.

## QUESTION 30

A government client requires assistance in evaluating and selecting vendors for a critical Power Platform project. They need to ensure the vendors can meet strict regulatory and performance requirements.
1. Evaluating vendor compliance with government regulations.
2. Assessing vendor capabilities to meet performance SLAs.
3. Integrating vendor solutions with existing Power Platform infrastructure.
What steps would you recommend for evaluating and selecting vendors for this project? Select three answers.

A) Conduct a detailed compliance assessment of potential vendors.
B) Use Power BI to track vendor performance metrics.
C) Select vendors who can provide the lowest bid.
D) Evaluate vendor technical capabilities and past project performance.
E) Negotiate contracts that include detailed SLAs and performance metrics.

## QUESTION 31

A healthcare client wants to implement IoT solutions to monitor patient vitals in real-time. They need a solution that ensures data privacy and security, as well as scalability and performance.
1. Integrating IoT devices to monitor patient vitals in real-time.
2. Ensuring data privacy and security in compliance with healthcare regulations.
3. Ensuring the system is scalable and performs well.
What actions would you recommend to achieve these objectives? Select three answers.

A) Use Azure IoT Hub to manage and secure IoT devices.
B) Implement Azure Stream Analytics for real-time data processing.
C) Apply AI Builder to develop basic predictive models.
D) Use Azure Security Center to ensure compliance with healthcare regulations.
E) Store patient data in a single Excel file for simplicity.

## QUESTION 32

A tech startup uses Dynamics 365 Sales to manage their sales pipeline. They want to implement a solution that automatically updates sales opportunities based on interactions recorded in an external CRM system. The integration should ensure data consistency and minimize manual data entry. What is the best approach to achieve this integration?

A) Use Power Automate with Common Data Service (Dataverse) connector
B) Use Azure Data Factory
C) Implement Data Export Service
D) Use Dynamics 365 App for Outlook
E) Use LinkedIn Sales Navigator

## QUESTION 33

A government client is implementing a Power Platform solution to improve public services while ensuring the solution is sustainable and eco-friendly. They need to reduce the environmental impact and comply with green standards.
1. Designing sustainable solutions.
2. Reducing environmental impact of public services.
3. Ensuring compliance with green standards and regulations.
What measures would you take to achieve these goals? Select three answers.

A) Use Power BI to analyze and monitor the environmental impact of public services.
B) Implement Azure Functions to optimize resource usage.
C) Select cloud services with low carbon footprints and energy-efficient hardware.
D) Ignore green standards to focus on service efficiency.
E) Conduct training sessions on sustainable practices for employees.

## QUESTION 34

Your company is planning a phased approach to integrate its legacy financial system with Dynamics 365 Finance and Operations (F&O). The initial phase must:
• Ensure data consistency between systems.
• Allow parallel operations during transition.
• Facilitate user adoption of the new system. What are the best strategies to achieve these goals? (Select 2 answers)

A) Implement a dual-write feature to synchronize data between systems.
B) Use Azure DevOps for continuous integration and deployment.
C) Develop a comprehensive training program for end-users.
D) Conduct a full data migration before switching systems.
E) Utilize Power BI for reporting to compare data between systems.

## QUESTION 35

Your organization is implementing a new Power BI solution and needs to document the data sources, models, and reports. The documentation must be:
• Clear and understandable by non-technical users.
• Regularly updated with changes.
• Accessible for training and support purposes. What are the best practices to ensure this documentation meets the requirements? (Select 2 answers)

A) Use a standardized template for all documentation.
B) Maintain documentation in a cloud-based repository like OneDrive or SharePoint.
C) Include detailed technical jargon and code snippets.
D) Create visual aids like flowcharts and diagrams.
E) Restrict access to documentation to only technical team members.

## QUESTION 36

A retail chain uses Dynamics 365 for Retail to manage their inventory across multiple stores. They want to optimize stock levels by predicting future demand based on historical sales data. The solution must integrate seamlessly with Dynamics 365 and provide actionable insights. What tool should they use?

A) Power BI with R Scripts
B) Azure Machine Learning
C) AI Builder with Dynamics 365
D) Power Automate
E) Dynamics 365 Supply Chain Management

## QUESTION 37

Your team is tasked with integrating multiple departmental systems using Power Platform to create a unified solution. The integration must:
- Balance specialized needs of each department with the overall architecture.
- Ensure data integrity.
- Support future scalability. What are the best practices to achieve these goals? (Select 2 answers)

A) Implement Dataverse as the common data platform.
B) Use Power Apps to create department-specific applications.
C) Maintain separate databases for each department.
D) Implement Azure Data Factory for ETL processes.
E) Use manual processes for data integration.

## QUESTION 38

An organization wants to stay ahead by exploring the use of AI and machine learning within their Power Platform solutions. The initiative should:
- Evaluate the potential business impact of AI.
- Implement practical AI solutions.
- Foster a culture of continuous improvement. What strategies should you use? (Select 2 answers)

A) Use AI Builder to integrate machine learning models into Power Apps.
B) Develop a roadmap for AI adoption in business processes.
C) Implement AI solutions without a pilot phase.
D) Conduct regular training sessions on AI technologies for employees.
E) Focus on cutting-edge AI technologies regardless of current business needs.

## QUESTION 39

A manufacturing company is designing a Power Platform solution that involves secure data exchange between IoT devices and cloud services. The solution must:
- Ensure data integrity and confidentiality.
- Use secure communication protocols.
- Regularly update security measures. What strategies should you adopt? (Select 3 answers)

A) Use HTTPS for all data transmissions.
B) Implement Azure IoT Hub for secure device communication.
C) Use unencrypted MQTT for device communication.
D) Regularly update device firmware and security patches.

E) Implement rotating encryption keys for all communications.

## QUESTION 40

A manufacturing firm uses Dynamics 365 Supply Chain Management for inventory tracking. They need to integrate their system with a third-party warehouse management system (WMS) to synchronize inventory levels. The integration must ensure real-time updates and high availability. What approach should they use?

A) Use Azure Logic Apps for integration.
B) Implement Power Automate with HTTP connector.
C) Use Dual-write for real-time synchronization.
D) Develop a custom API to handle the integration.
E) Use Power Apps to manually update inventory levels.

## QUESTION 41

A healthcare provider is adopting cloud-native solutions to enhance their patient management system. The solution must:
- Use serverless architecture for specific functions.
- Ensure compliance with healthcare data regulations.
- Integrate with existing on-premises systems. What should you implement? (Select 2 answers)

A) Use Azure Functions for serverless operations.
B) Implement Azure Policy for compliance management.
C) Use Power Automate for on-premises integration.
D) Use Azure Service Bus for reliable messaging between cloud and on-premises systems.
E) Use Power Virtual Agents for patient interactions.

## QUESTION 42

A global enterprise is designing a Power Platform solution to manage employee data across multiple regions. The solution must:
- Comply with international data privacy standards.
- Secure sensitive employee information.
- Implement ethical data handling practices. What steps should be taken? (Select 3 answers)

A) Use Power BI to share detailed employee data across all regions without restriction.
B) Implement GDPR and CCPA compliance measures using Dataverse.
C) Use Azure AD Conditional Access to secure access based on user location.
D) Store all employee data in on-premises databases to avoid cloud storage.
E) Use Azure Information Protection to classify and protect sensitive data.

## QUESTION 43

A logistics company wants to integrate their Power Platform solution with a third-party GPS tracking service. They need to:
- Ensure real-time data updates.
- Secure data transmission.

• Maintain system performance. What steps should they take? (Select 3 answers)

A) Use Azure Logic Apps to automate data integration workflows.
B) Implement HTTPS for secure data transmission.
C) Store GPS data in an unencrypted format for faster access.
D) Use Azure API Management to manage and secure API interactions.
E) Rely on manual data entry for GPS coordinates.

## QUESTION 44

You need to design a Power Platform solution for a logistics company that aims to optimize its supply chain management. The solution must predict supply chain disruptions and provide actionable insights based on historical data analysis.
• Predictive analytics for supply chain disruptions.
• Actionable insights based on historical data.
Which Power Platform tool should you focus on to maximize the effectiveness of the solution?

A) AI Builder
B) Power BI
C) Power Apps
D) Power Automate
E) Common Data Service

## QUESTION 45

An e-commerce company is migrating sales data to Dynamics 365. They must:
• Ensure data consistency across multiple platforms.
• Handle large datasets without performance issues.
• Validate and troubleshoot data post-migration. What actions should they take? (Select 3 answers)

A) Use Azure Data Factory for efficient data migration.
B) Perform data validation using Dataverse rules.
C) Use manual checks to ensure data consistency.
D) Implement Azure Logic Apps for data transformation.
E) Conduct post-migration validation using Power BI.

## QUESTION 46

A healthcare provider is rolling out a new patient management system using Dynamics 365. Their requirements include:
• Protecting patient data with robust security measures.
• Implementing role-based access control.
• Ensuring compliance with healthcare regulations. How should they proceed?

A) Implement data encryption at rest and in transit.
B) Use RBAC to manage user permissions.
C) Conduct security compliance audits using Power BI.
D) Assign roles manually.
E) Validate compliance only during initial deployment.

## QUESTION 47

An educational institution is implementing Dynamics 365 for student management. To ensure security, they must:
- Implement role-based access controls (RBAC).
- Conduct security testing.
- Ensure compliance with data protection regulations. What measures should they take?

Select 2 answers.

A) Use Azure AD for role-based access control.
B) Skip security testing if using a trusted platform.
C) Implement data encryption at rest and in transit.
D) Use Dynamics 365 built-in security roles without customization.
E) Conduct regular security audits and assessments.

## QUESTION 48

An HR department uses a Power Apps canvas app for employee onboarding that has become progressively slower as more features were added. The app is crucial for day-to-day operations but suffers from long loading times and lag.
- Improve operational efficiency.
- Enhance the onboarding experience.

Which two actions should you take to optimize the app's performance?

A) Optimize screen navigation
B) Reduce external API calls
C) Compress images and media
D) Streamline data connections
E) Implement lazy loading

## QUESTION 49

A retail company uses a combination of Power Apps, Power Automate, and Dynamics 365 to manage inventory and sales. They need to ensure that their solutions remain sustainable and up to date. The key requirements are:
- Managing and applying updates.
- Handling deprecated features.
- Implementing rollback processes in case of update failures.

Which actions should you prioritize? (Select 3 answers)

A) Regularly monitor Microsoft's product lifecycle announcements.
B) Use Azure DevOps for CI/CD and version control.
C) Configure alerts for deprecated features in the Power Platform Admin Center.
D) Develop a rollback strategy using solution exports and backups.
E) Integrate Power BI to monitor system performance and update status.

## QUESTION 50

A retail company is using Power Apps for inventory management. Users report that the app crashes frequently during peak hours. As a solution architect, you need to identify and resolve the issue. The key requirements are:
- Identifying the root cause of the crashes.
- Implementing a fix to prevent future crashes.
- Ensuring minimal disruption to users.

What actions should you take? (Select 3 answers)

A) Use the Monitor tool in Power Apps to analyze app performance.
B) Review and optimize the app's formulas and data queries.
C) Increase the app's data capacity in Dataverse.
D) Implement error handling and logging within the app.
E) Use Azure DevOps to deploy updates during off-peak hours.

# PRACTICE TEST 4 - ANSWERS ONLY

## QUESTION 1

Answer – B), D)

Option A – Virtual Agents improve interactions but do not address administrative overhead or data privacy.
Option B – Automating tasks reduces workload, addressing high administrative workload.
Option C – A Power Apps portal enhances access but does not address administrative overhead or privacy.
Option D – Dataverse provides secure data management, ensuring privacy and operational efficiency.
Option E – Power BI reports offer insights but do not directly enhance patient engagement or reduce overhead.

| 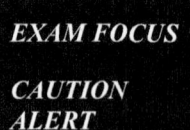 | |
|---|---|
| EXAM FOCUS | *Implement Power Automate to reduce administrative workload and use Dataverse for secure data management to improve patient care.* |
| CAUTION ALERT | *Stay cautious, relying on Virtual Agents and portals alone won't address data privacy or administrative overhead.* |

## QUESTION 2

Answer – A), B)

Option A – Correct. Global accelerator technologies like Azure Front Door or Azure Traffic Manager can optimize app traffic and improve performance by routing users to the nearest data center.
Option B – Correct. Minimizing network latency is fundamental to improving app performance, especially for users located far from the app's hosted server.
Option C – Incorrect. While enhancing data architecture can improve performance, it does not directly address the issue of international disparities.
Option D – Incorrect. Reducing application features may simplify the app but won't necessarily resolve issues related to geographical differences in app performance.
Option E – Incorrect. Increasing server capacity can handle more load but won't necessarily improve performance for distant users without addressing network latency or routing.

| 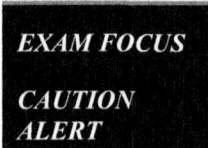 | |
|---|---|
| EXAM FOCUS | *"Implement global accelerator technologies and reduce network latency to optimize global performance."* |
| CAUTION ALERT | *"Increasing server capacity alone won't address geographical performance differences."* |

## QUESTION 3

Answer – A), B)

Option A – Azure IoT Central can automate data collection from machines.
Option B – Power Automate can integrate collected data with ERP systems.
Option C – A Power BI dashboard is useful for monitoring but does not address data collection or integration.

Option D – A Dataverse-based app is useful but not critical for initial data collection and integration.
Option E – AI Builder for predictive maintenance is advanced but might not be the first step.

| EXAM FOCUS | Implement Azure IoT Central for data collection and Power Automate for ERP integration to improve process efficiency. |
|---|---|
| CAUTION ALERT | Stay cautious, focusing on monitoring alone won't solve data collection and integration challenges. |

## QUESTION 4

Answer – A), B)

Option A – Correct choice as Alternate keys simplify data retrieval by providing a unique identifier other than the primary key.
Option B – Correct choice as OData $filter query can retrieve specific records more efficiently.
Option C – OData $expand query is used to retrieve related entity data, which is not required in this scenario.
Option D – FetchXML query can retrieve data but is more complex than using alternate keys and $filter.
Option E – Calculated columns perform calculations within Dataverse but do not simplify data retrieval in JavaScript.

| EXAM FOCUS | "Leveraging OData $filter query simplifies code and enhances performance." |
|---|---|
| CAUTION ALERT | "Remember, multiple RetrieveMultiple calls can lead to performance issues." |

## QUESTION 5

Answer – A), C)

Option A – Azure IoT Central can handle real-time data collection from various IoT devices.
Option B – Azure Logic Apps is useful for integration but may increase complexity and cost.
Option C – Conducting a technology evaluation helps ensure the selected technologies are future-proof.
Option D – A Power Apps solution is useful for data visualization but does not address real-time data collection or integration.
Option E – Dataverse is useful for storing data but does not address real-time data collection or integration directly.

| EXAM FOCUS | Azure IoT Central for real-time data collection and a technology evaluation for future-proofing are key. |
|---|---|
| CAUTION ALERT | Stay cautious, Azure Logic Apps might add complexity and cost without guaranteeing long-term benefits. |

## QUESTION 6

Answer – C), E)

Option A – Dataverse provides secure storage for student data but does not directly address risk monitoring.
Option B – Power BI is useful for monitoring system usage but does not ensure continuous risk

assessment.

Option C – Azure Monitor provides continuous risk assessment.

Option D – Developing a contingency plan is essential but does not address continuous risk monitoring.

Option E – RBAC controls access to student data, ensuring secure data handling.

| | |
|---|---|
| **EXAM FOCUS** | *Utilize Azure Monitor for continuous risk assessment and RBAC for secure data handling to manage risks.* |
| **CAUTION ALERT** | *Remember, Power BI is useful for monitoring but not for continuous risk assessment or secure data handling.* |

## QUESTION 7

Answer – A), C)

Option A – Power BI can be used to create a detailed project timeline.

Option B – Power Automate is useful for scheduling tasks but does not address timeline estimation directly.

Option C – Developing a Gantt chart to track project progress helps ensure the project stays on track.

Option D – Dataverse is useful for managing data but does not address timeline estimation or scheduling.

Option E – Regular team meetings are important but do not address initial timeline estimation.

| | |
|---|---|
| **EXAM FOCUS** | *Use Power BI for detailed project timelines and develop Gantt charts for tracking progress.* |
| **CAUTION ALERT** | *Remember, regular meetings are important but won't address initial timeline estimation effectively.* |

## QUESTION 8

Answer – B), D), E)

Option A – Power Apps can be used to develop a prototype but not directly related to stakeholder involvement.

Option B – Conducting stakeholder analysis helps identify key stakeholders.

Option C – Power Automate is useful for streamlining communications but not directly related to ensuring engagement.

Option D – Developing a stakeholder engagement plan ensures continuous engagement.

Option E – Implementing feedback sessions using Microsoft Teams addresses stakeholder concerns.

| | |
|---|---|
| **EXAM FOCUS** | *Conduct stakeholder analysis, develop an engagement plan, and use Teams for feedback sessions.* |
| **CAUTION ALERT** | *Remember, Power Apps prototypes are useful but won't ensure stakeholder engagement.* |

## QUESTION 9

Answer – A), B), D)

Option A – Azure Functions provide serverless scaling that can handle growth efficiently.

Option B – Implementing Azure Monitor helps in monitoring performance during scaling.

Option C – Power BI is useful for tracking system usage but not directly related to scaling strategies.

Option D – Developing autoscaling policies using Azure Autoscale ensures the system can scale automatically.

Option E – Azure API Management is useful for managing API traffic but not directly related to scaling strategies.

| EXAM FOCUS | *Implement serverless scaling with Azure Functions, monitor performance with Azure Monitor, and use Azure Autoscale policies.* |
|---|---|
| CAUTION ALERT | *Remember, Power BI is great for tracking usage but not for implementing scaling strategies.* |

## QUESTION 10

Answer – A), B), E)

Option A – Regular one-on-one meetings help in building trust and rapport.
Option B – Using Dynamics 365 helps in tracking stakeholder interactions effectively.
Option C – Power Automate is useful for workflow management but not directly related to building stakeholder relationships.
Option D – Power BI is useful for tracking performance but not directly related to building relationships.
Option E – Conducting stakeholder surveys helps in gathering feedback and addressing concerns.

| EXAM FOCUS | *Schedule one-on-one meetings, use Dynamics 365 for tracking, and conduct stakeholder surveys for effective engagement.* |
|---|---|
| CAUTION ALERT | *Stay cautious, Power Automate is for workflow management, not for building relationships.* |

## QUESTION 11

Answer – A), C), E)

Option A – Conducting a security and compliance assessment ensures vendors meet requirements.
Option B – Power Automate can streamline the process but is not essential for selection.
Option C – Comparing scalability and performance metrics using Power BI ensures the solution meets performance requirements.
Option D – Power Apps can create checklists but is not essential for assessment.
Option E – Engaging legal experts ensures favorable terms and long-term support.

| EXAM FOCUS | *Conduct detailed security assessments and use Power BI for performance metrics to ensure vendor reliability.* |
|---|---|
| CAUTION ALERT | *Remember, Power Automate is helpful but not essential for vendor selection processes.* |

## QUESTION 12

Answer – B)

Option A – Canada is not optimal as it is neither Europe nor North America.
Option B – Correct choice as it ensures compliance and performance for European users.
Option C – Japan is not relevant to the given regions.
Option D – While North America is a valid choice, Europe ensures better compliance and performance

for European operations.

Option E – Australia is not relevant to the given regions.

| EXAM FOCUS | "Host development in Europe to ensure compliance and optimal performance for European users." |
|---|---|
| CAUTION ALERT | "Remember, hosting outside the target regions can affect compliance and performance." |

## QUESTION 13

Answer – A), D)

Option A – Subscribing to industry research reports and newsletters helps in staying current with trends.
Option B – Azure DevOps is useful but more for managing projects than predicting trends.
Option C – Power BI can monitor trends but is more a tool than a strategy.
Option D – A continuous learning program ensures the team stays ahead of trends and prepares for future changes.
Option E – Innovation summits are useful but not as crucial as continuous learning and research.

| EXAM FOCUS | You should subscribe to industry research reports and develop a continuous learning program for the IT team. |
|---|---|
| CAUTION ALERT | Stay cautious, relying solely on tools like Azure DevOps for trend prediction can be limiting. |

## QUESTION 14

Answer – A), B), D)

Option A – Azure DevOps for CI/CD and version control is crucial for successful deployments.
Option B – Regular deployment status meetings help handle deployment challenges.
Option C – Power BI is useful for monitoring but not as critical as other options for deployment strategies.
Option D – A comprehensive deployment checklist ensures all aspects of deployment are covered.
Option E – Power Virtual Agents are useful for support but less critical than other options for deployment strategies.

| EXAM FOCUS | Implement Azure DevOps for CI/CD and version control, and conduct regular deployment status meetings. |
|---|---|
| CAUTION ALERT | Please keep in mind, relying solely on monitoring tools like Power BI without a comprehensive checklist can miss key steps. |

## QUESTION 15

Answer – A), B), C)

Option A – Microsoft Teams is essential for team meetings and communication, enhancing collaboration.
Option B – Azure DevOps is crucial for project management, helping in collaboration and teamwork.
Option C – Conflict resolution training helps in resolving team conflicts and challenges.
Option D – Power BI is useful for tracking progress but less critical for team communication.
Option E – Data Steward roles in Dataverse are relevant for data management but less critical for

enhancing collaboration and communication.

| EXAM FOCUS | *You should use Microsoft Teams for team meetings to enhance collaboration and communication.* |
| CAUTION ALERT | *Remember, Power BI is useful for tracking progress but less critical for resolving team conflicts.* |

## QUESTION 16

Answer – A), B), C)

Option A – Correct choice as Azure Pipelines in Azure DevOps supports CI/CD and version control.
Option B – Correct choice as Microsoft Power Platform Pipelines provide native support for deploying Power Platform components.
Option C – Correct choice as ALM Accelerator supports CI/CD and version control in Power Platform.
Option D – Manual ALM does not support the required automation and scalability.
Option E – Power Automate Desktop is not suitable for ALM strategy implementation.

| EXAM FOCUS | *"Combine Azure Pipelines, Power Platform Pipelines, and ALM Accelerator for a comprehensive ALM strategy."* |
| CAUTION ALERT | *"Manual ALM is insufficient for modern, automated deployment requirements."* |

## QUESTION 17

Answer – A), B), C)

Option A – Conducting an environmental readiness assessment using Power BI allows for data-driven analysis.
Option B – Developing a comprehensive sustainability plan ensures all stakeholders are involved and prepared.
Option C – Implementing a pilot program allows for testing and assessing environmental implications before full deployment.
Option D – Customizing Power Apps adds complexity and should be avoided unless necessary.
Option E – While Azure DevOps is useful for project management, it does not directly address environmental impact and sustainability planning.

| EXAM FOCUS | *Conduct an environmental readiness assessment with Power BI, develop a sustainability plan, and pilot the system.* |
| CAUTION ALERT | *Avoid unnecessary customizations in Power Apps; focus on core functionalities.* |

## QUESTION 18

Answer – A), B), C)

Option A – Using Dataverse ensures centralized and scalable data storage.
Option B – Implementing Power Automate manages document workflows and adapts to changing requirements.
Option C – Developing custom connectors ensures seamless integration with existing systems.

Option D – Power BI is useful for reporting but does not directly address flexibility and adaptability.
Option E – Developing a single comprehensive model-driven app can hinder flexibility and scalability.

| | |
|---|---|
| **EXAM FOCUS** | *Use Dataverse for centralized storage; Power Automate for workflows; custom connectors for integration.* |
| **CAUTION ALERT** | *Single comprehensive apps hinder flexibility and scalability.* |

## QUESTION 19

Answer – A), D)

Option A – Using Power Automate to distribute and collect surveys gathers employee feedback and insights.
Option B – Implementing Dataverse analyzes behavior but might not directly gather feedback or develop personas.
Option C – Creating Power BI dashboards visualizes feedback but might not gather detailed feedback or develop personas.
Option D – Conducting workshops gathers detailed feedback and helps in developing personas.
Option E – Developing canvas apps supports user groups but might not gather feedback or develop personas effectively.

| | |
|---|---|
| **EXAM FOCUS** | *Use Power Automate for surveys and conduct workshops to gather detailed employee feedback.* |
| **CAUTION ALERT** | *Relying solely on automated tools without direct engagement can miss nuanced feedback.* |

## QUESTION 20

Answer – A), B), D)

Option A – Correct choice as Real-time workflows support real-time data updates.
Option B – Correct choice as Calculated columns provide dynamic calculations.
Option C – Rollup columns aggregate data over time, not in real-time.
Option D – Correct choice as Power BI dataflows integrate Dataverse data with Power BI.
Option E – Scheduled cloud flows are for periodic updates, not real-time.

| | |
|---|---|
| **EXAM FOCUS** | *"Combine Real-time workflows, Calculated columns, and Power BI dataflows for real-time insights and analytics."* |
| **CAUTION ALERT** | *"Scheduled cloud flows only support periodic updates, not real-time data needs."* |

## QUESTION 21

Answer – A), D)

Option A – Azure Logic Apps facilitate workflow automation and integration with existing systems.
Option B – AI Builder is useful for predictive analytics but does not directly address integration or best practices.
Option C – Microservices architecture can be beneficial but is not the primary focus for integration and

best practices.

Option D – Establishing a Center of Excellence (CoE) ensures adherence to best practices and governance.

Option E – Azure Functions provide custom logic but do not directly address integration or best practices.

| | |
|---|---|
| **EXAM FOCUS** | *Azure Logic Apps for workflow automation and establish a Center of Excellence.* |
| **CAUTION ALERT** | *Neglecting best practices can lead to integration issues; ensure adherence.* |

## QUESTION 22

Answer – A), B)

Option A – Azure Logic Apps ensure seamless integration with on-premises systems.
Option B – Azure AD Conditional Access provides secure data access, complying with HIPAA regulations.
Option C – Azure Cognitive Services is useful for data analysis but not specifically for secure data access or integration.
Option D – Azure DevOps helps with continuous integration and deployment but does not address secure data access or storage.
Option E – Azure Key Vault ensures secure data storage but does not directly address hybrid integration.

| | |
|---|---|
| **EXAM FOCUS** | *For healthcare solutions, Azure Logic Apps and Azure AD Conditional Access ensure HIPAA compliance and secure integration.* |
| **CAUTION ALERT** | *Avoid choosing options like Azure Cognitive Services that don't directly address secure access or hybrid integration.* |

## QUESTION 23

Answer – A), E)

Option A – Azure DevOps is ideal for managing CI/CD pipelines and version control.
Option B – Power Apps Test Studio is useful for automated testing but not for CI/CD or environment management.
Option C – Dataverse is used for data management, not specifically for CI/CD or environment management.
Option D – Power Automate can be used for deployment automation but does not encompass full CI/CD pipeline capabilities.
Option E – Power Platform Build Tools help manage environments, automate deployments, and ensure application quality.

| | |
|---|---|
| **EXAM FOCUS** | *Please keep in mind, Azure DevOps and Power Platform Build Tools are crucial for managing CI/CD and ensuring application quality.* |
| **CAUTION ALERT** | *Do not use tools like Dataverse for CI/CD pipelines; they are meant for data management.* |

## QUESTION 24

Answer – A), D)

Option A – Correct choice as Referential relationships enforce referential integrity and do not automatically delete related records.
Option B – Custom relationships can be configured for specific behaviors but are more complex.
Option C – Parental relationships automatically delete related records.
Option D – Correct choice as Referential, Restrict Delete prevents deletion if there are related records, maintaining referential integrity.
Option E – Delete Cascade will automatically delete related records, which is not desired.

| | |
|---|---|
| **EXAM FOCUS** | *"Use Referential and Restrict Delete to prevent deletion of related records."* |
| **CAUTION ALERT** | *"Parental and Delete Cascade settings will delete related records, which is not desired."* |

## QUESTION 25

Answer – A), D), E)

Option A – Azure API Management is essential for handling APIs and ensuring integration with existing systems.
Option B – Horizontal scaling for Power Apps ensures the app can handle peak loads efficiently.
Option C – Azure Functions are useful for backend processing but not directly related to security for financial transactions.
Option D – Enabling data encryption ensures high security for financial transactions.
Option E – Conducting regular security audits ensures the app remains secure and compliant with financial regulations.

| | |
|---|---|
| **EXAM FOCUS** | *Use Azure API Management, data encryption, and regular security audits for efficient handling, security, and compliance.* |
| **CAUTION ALERT** | *Be cautious about using only Azure Functions; they help with backend processing but not directly with transaction security.* |

## QUESTION 26

Answer – A), C), E)

Option A – Power Automate Cloud Flow can monitor stock levels in real-time.
Option B – Power Automate approvals are useful but not necessary for automatic reordering.
Option C – ERP Connector facilitates integration with the existing ERP system.
Option D – Power BI is useful for generating reports but not directly related to real-time monitoring and reordering.
Option E – Azure Logic Apps can handle complex integrations between Power Automate and the ERP system.

| | |
|---|---|
| **EXAM FOCUS** | *Use Cloud Flow, ERP Connector, and Logic Apps for real-time monitoring, ERP integration, and complex workflows.* |
| **CAUTION ALERT** | *Don't rely on Power Automate approvals alone for reordering items; focus on automatic triggers.* |

## QUESTION 27

Answer – A), B), C)

Option A – Power Platform Admin Center is used for policy enforcement.
Option B – Azure Monitor helps in compliance monitoring.
Option C – Azure AD is crucial for managing roles and access.
Option D – Power Virtual Agents is for user interaction and not directly related to governance.
Option E – AI Builder is for data analysis and not directly related to governance and policy management.

| | |
|---|---|
| **EXAM FOCUS** | *Use Power Platform Admin Center, Azure Monitor, and Azure AD to enforce policies, monitor compliance, and manage roles.* |
| **CAUTION ALERT** | *Be cautious about using Power Virtual Agents for governance tasks; it's for user interaction.* |

## QUESTION 28

Answer – B)

Option A – Import Mode involves scheduled refreshes and may not provide the real-time data updates required.
Option B – DirectQuery Mode allows for real-time data queries, ensuring the data in Power BI is always up-to-date with minimal latency.
Option C – Composite Mode is a mix of Import and DirectQuery but may not be as efficient as DirectQuery for real-time updates.
Option D – Live Connection is typically used with SSAS and may not be applicable for all data sources.
Option E – Dataflow is used for data preparation and ETL processes, not specifically for real-time data connectivity.

| | |
|---|---|
| **EXAM FOCUS** | *"DirectQuery Mode ensures Power BI data is always up-to-date with minimal latency."* |
| **CAUTION ALERT** | *"Import Mode involves scheduled refreshes and may not provide real-time updates."* |

## QUESTION 29

Answer – A), D)

Option A – Correct. Financial models in Power BI can help project costs and identify savings.
Option B – Incorrect. Regular audits are helpful but may not be the most efficient first step.
Option C – Incorrect. High-cost add-ons may not be necessary and can increase costs.
Option D – Correct. Azure Cost Management provides tools for monitoring and controlling costs.
Option E – Incorrect. While external consultants can be helpful, it may not be cost-effective for all clients.

| | |
|---|---|
| **EXAM FOCUS** | *Use Power BI to create financial models and Azure Cost Management for cost control.* |
| **CAUTION ALERT** | *Avoid investing in high-cost add-ons without evaluating necessity.* |

## QUESTION 30

Answer – A), D), E)

Option A – Correct. Compliance assessments ensure vendors meet regulatory requirements.
Option B – Incorrect. Tracking performance is important but not the first step.
Option C – Incorrect. Cost should not be the sole criterion.
Option D – Correct. Evaluating technical capabilities ensures vendors can meet project needs.
Option E – Correct. Detailed SLAs and performance metrics ensure accountability.

| EXAM FOCUS | *Conduct detailed compliance assessments and evaluate technical capabilities.* |
|---|---|
| CAUTION ALERT | *Cost alone should not drive vendor selection; consider compliance and performance metrics.* |

## QUESTION 31

Answer – A), B), D)

Option A – Correct. Azure IoT Hub manages and secures IoT devices effectively.
Option B – Correct. Azure Stream Analytics processes real-time data efficiently.
Option C – Incorrect. AI Builder may not provide the necessary capabilities for this scenario.
Option D – Correct. Azure Security Center ensures compliance with healthcare data regulations.
Option E – Incorrect. Storing data in Excel is not secure or scalable enough for healthcare data.

| EXAM FOCUS | *Use Azure IoT Hub for device management and Azure Security Center for compliance.* |
|---|---|
| CAUTION ALERT | *Excel is not suitable for storing secure, scalable healthcare data.* |

## QUESTION 32

Answer – A)

Option A – Power Automate with Common Data Service (Dataverse) connector allows for real-time integration and automation, ensuring data consistency and reducing manual data entry.
Option B – Azure Data Factory is primarily used for data integration and ETL processes but may not provide real-time updates.
Option C – Data Export Service is used for exporting data to Azure SQL Database, not for real-time integration.
Option D – Dynamics 365 App for Outlook is useful for tracking emails and appointments but not for CRM integration.
Option E – LinkedIn Sales Navigator is a sales tool that provides insights but does not facilitate CRM integration.

| EXAM FOCUS | *"Use Power Automate with Dataverse connector for real-time CRM integration."* |
|---|---|
| CAUTION ALERT | *"Azure Data Factory may not provide real-time updates required for CRM integration."* |

## QUESTION 33

Answer – A), C), E)

Option A – Correct. Power BI can effectively analyze and monitor environmental impact.

Option B – Incorrect. Azure Functions are useful but not the primary tool for optimizing resource usage.
Option C – Correct. Selecting cloud services with low carbon footprints and energy-efficient hardware reduces environmental impact.
Option D – Incorrect. Ignoring green standards can lead to non-compliance and increased environmental impact.
Option E – Correct. Training sessions on sustainable practices promote eco-friendly solutions.

| | |
|---|---|
| **EXAM FOCUS** | *Use Power BI to monitor impact and train employees on sustainable practices.* |
| **CAUTION ALERT** | *Ignoring green standards can lead to non-compliance and increased environmental impact.* |

## QUESTION 34

Answer – A), C)

Option A – Dual-write ensures real-time data consistency between systems.
Option B – Azure DevOps is useful for CI/CD but not directly for phased integration.
Option C – Training programs facilitate user adoption during the transition.
Option D – Full migration before switching can cause disruptions.
Option E – Power BI reporting is helpful but not critical for achieving data consistency and user adoption.

| | |
|---|---|
| **EXAM FOCUS** | *Implement dual-write for real-time data consistency and develop comprehensive training programs to facilitate user adoption.* |
| **CAUTION ALERT** | *Avoid full data migration before switching; it can cause major disruptions and data inconsistencies.* |

## QUESTION 35

Answer – A), D)

Option A – Standardized templates ensure consistency and clarity.
Option B – Cloud-based repositories are useful but must be coupled with other practices.
Option C – Detailed technical jargon and code snippets may not be understandable by non-technical users.
Option D – Visual aids like flowcharts and diagrams help non-technical users understand the documentation.
Option E – Restricting access limits the documentation's usefulness for training.

| | |
|---|---|
| **EXAM FOCUS** | *Standardize documentation templates and use visual aids like flowcharts for clarity to non-technical users.* |
| **CAUTION ALERT** | *Avoid overloading documentation with technical jargon; it must be understandable by all users.* |

## QUESTION 36

Answer – C)

Option A – Power BI with R Scripts can provide insights but requires advanced statistical knowledge and

setup.
Option B – Azure Machine Learning is powerful but requires more expertise and integration effort.
Option C – AI Builder with Dynamics 365 provides an easy-to-use solution for predicting demand based on historical data and integrates seamlessly with Dynamics 365.
Option D – Power Automate is used for workflow automation, not for demand prediction.
Option E – Dynamics 365 Supply Chain Management helps manage supply chains but does not specifically provide demand prediction based on AI.

| EXAM FOCUS | "AI Builder with Dynamics 365 easily integrates for demand prediction and actionable insights." |
|---|---|
| CAUTION ALERT | "Power BI with R Scripts requires advanced statistical knowledge and may be complex to set up." |

## QUESTION 37

Answer – A), D)

Option A – Dataverse as the common data platform ensures data integrity and supports scalability.
Option B – Power Apps for department-specific applications is useful but must be integrated properly.
Option C – Separate databases can lead to data inconsistencies.
Option D – Azure Data Factory handles ETL processes efficiently, supporting data integration and scalability.
Option E – Manual processes are inefficient and error-prone.

| EXAM FOCUS | Use Dataverse as a common data platform and Azure Data Factory for efficient ETL processes. |
|---|---|
| CAUTION ALERT | Separate databases can lead to data inconsistencies and management difficulties. |

## QUESTION 38

Answer – A), B)

Option A – AI Builder integrates machine learning models into Power Apps, making AI practical.
Option B – A roadmap for AI adoption helps evaluate and plan the business impact.
Option C – Implementing AI solutions without a pilot phase can lead to unforeseen issues.
Option D – Regular training sessions foster continuous improvement but may need to be paired with practical implementations.
Option E – Focusing solely on cutting-edge AI technologies may neglect current business needs.

| EXAM FOCUS | Use AI Builder to integrate machine learning models and develop a roadmap for AI adoption. |
|---|---|
| CAUTION ALERT | Avoid implementing AI solutions without a pilot phase; it can lead to unforeseen issues. |

## QUESTION 39

Answer – A), B), D)

Option A – HTTPS ensures secure data transmission.
Option B – Azure IoT Hub provides secure communication between IoT devices and cloud services.
Option C – Unencrypted MQTT is not secure for device communication.
Option D – Regularly updating firmware and security patches helps maintain security.

Option E – Rotating encryption keys provide better security compared to static keys.

| EXAM FOCUS | *Use HTTPS for data transmissions and Azure IoT Hub for secure device communication.* |
| --- | --- |
| CAUTION ALERT | *Avoid using unencrypted MQTT for device communication; it is not secure.* |

## QUESTION 40

Answer – C)

Option A – Azure Logic Apps can handle integration but may not provide the real-time synchronization needed.
Option B – Power Automate with HTTP connector can work but might not be as robust for high availability and real-time updates.
Option C – Dual-write provides seamless, real-time synchronization between Dynamics 365 and third-party systems.
Option D – Developing a custom API requires significant development and maintenance effort.
Option E – Manually updating inventory levels is not feasible for real-time synchronization and high availability.

| EXAM FOCUS | *"Dual-write offers seamless, real-time synchronization with high availability."* |
| --- | --- |
| CAUTION ALERT | *"Manual updates are not feasible for ensuring real-time synchronization."* |

## QUESTION 41

Answer – A), D)

Option A – Azure Functions provides a serverless architecture that is ideal for scalable and efficient operations.
Option B – Azure Policy helps manage and ensure compliance, but it does not address serverless architecture or integration with on-premises systems.
Option C – Power Automate is useful for automation but is not the best choice for on-premises system integration.
Option D – Azure Service Bus facilitates reliable messaging and integration between cloud and on-premises systems, ensuring smooth data flow and operations.
Option E – Power Virtual Agents can enhance patient interactions but is not related to serverless architecture or integration requirements.

| EXAM FOCUS | *Use Azure Functions for serverless operations and Service Bus for cloud-on-prem integration.* |
| --- | --- |
| CAUTION ALERT | *Power Automate is not the best choice for on-premises integration.* |

## QUESTION 42

Answer – B), C), E)

Option A – Sharing detailed employee data without restriction violates data privacy standards and ethical considerations.
Option B – Dataverse supports compliance with GDPR and CCPA, ensuring that the solution adheres to

international data privacy standards.

Option C – Azure AD Conditional Access secures access to sensitive data based on user location, enhancing security and compliance.

Option D – Storing all data on-premises limits the scalability and flexibility of the solution, and it may not leverage the advanced security features of cloud storage.

Option E – Azure Information Protection helps classify and protect sensitive data, ensuring that employee information is handled ethically and securely.

| EXAM FOCUS | *Implement GDPR and CCPA measures in Dataverse, and use Azure Information Protection.* |
|---|---|
| CAUTION ALERT | *Sharing detailed employee data without restriction violates privacy standards.* |

## QUESTION 43

Answer – A), B), D)

Option A – Azure Logic Apps is effective for automating data integration workflows, ensuring real-time updates.

Option B – Implementing HTTPS ensures that data transmission is secure.

Option C – Storing GPS data in an unencrypted format is insecure and can lead to data breaches.

Option D – Azure API Management helps manage and secure API interactions, maintaining system performance.

Option E – Manual data entry is not feasible for real-time updates and can lead to errors.

| EXAM FOCUS | *Utilize Azure Logic Apps for real-time updates and HTTPS for security.* |
|---|---|
| CAUTION ALERT | *Manual data entry is error-prone; use automated systems instead.* |

## QUESTION 44

Answer – A)

Option A – Correct. AI Builder provides capabilities to build and train AI models that can predict supply chain disruptions using historical data, perfectly aligning with the need for predictive analytics and actionable insights.

Option B – Incorrect. Power BI is excellent for data visualization and analysis but lacks the machine learning capabilities needed for predictive analytics.

Option C – Incorrect. Power Apps allows for the creation of custom applications but does not specialize in data analysis or predictive modeling.

Option D – Incorrect. Power Automate automates workflows but is not suited for deep analytics or predictions.

Option E – Incorrect. Common Data Service manages data but does not provide predictive analytics or actionable insights on its own.

| EXAM FOCUS | *"Remember, AI Builder provides predictive analytics and actionable insights for supply chain management."* |
|---|---|
| CAUTION ALERT | *"Don't rely solely on Power BI for predictive analytics; use AI Builder for deeper insights."* |

## QUESTION 45

Answer – A), B), D)

Option A – Azure Data Factory provides a scalable and efficient solution for large dataset migration.
Option B – Dataverse rules can be used for automated data validation, ensuring consistency.
Option C – Manual checks are inefficient and prone to errors, especially with large datasets.
Option D – Azure Logic Apps are useful for transforming data during the migration process.
Option E – Power BI is better suited for reporting and analysis, not direct validation and troubleshooting of migrated data.

| | |
|---|---|
| EXAM FOCUS | Use Azure Data Factory for scalable data migration and Dataverse for validation. |
| CAUTION ALERT | Manual checks are inefficient and error-prone for large datasets. |

## QUESTION 46

Answer – A), B), C)

Option A – Implementing data encryption at rest and in transit protects patient data from unauthorized access and breaches.
Option B – Using RBAC to manage user permissions ensures secure and appropriate access to sensitive data.
Option C – Conducting security compliance audits using Power BI helps ensure the solution meets healthcare regulations.
Option D – Assigning roles manually can be error-prone and inefficient.
Option E – Validating compliance only during initial deployment is insufficient for ensuring continuous compliance and data protection.

| | |
|---|---|
| EXAM FOCUS | "Implement data encryption at rest and in transit, and conduct regular compliance audits." |
| CAUTION ALERT | "Assigning roles manually can be error-prone and inefficient." |

## QUESTION 47

Answer – A), E)

Option A – Using Azure AD for role-based access control provides a robust and scalable solution for managing user access.
Option B – Skipping security testing, even on a trusted platform, is not advisable as vulnerabilities can still exist.
Option C – Implementing data encryption at rest and in transit ensures data is protected both when stored and during transmission.
Option D – Using built-in security roles without customization may not meet all specific security requirements; custom roles should be considered.
Option E – Conducting regular security audits and assessments helps identify and address potential security weaknesses continuously.

| | |
|---|---|
| EXAM FOCUS | "Implement Azure AD for RBAC to ensure secure access management." |
| CAUTION ALERT | "Skipping security testing, even on a trusted platform, can still leave vulnerabilities." |

## QUESTION 48

Answer – D), E)

Option A – Incorrect. Optimizing screen navigation improves the user experience but doesn't address the root causes of performance issues.
Option B – Incorrect. Reducing external API calls can help, but it's not mentioned as a major factor in this scenario.
Option C – Incorrect. Compressing images and media can reduce load times but is not cited as a primary issue with this app.
Option D – Correct. Streamlining data connections by reducing the complexity and number of connections can directly improve loading times and overall app responsiveness.
Option E – Correct. Implementing lazy loading techniques ensures that only necessary data is loaded when required, significantly enhancing performance by not overwhelming the system at startup.

| | |
|---|---|
| **EXAM FOCUS** | *"Streamline data connections and implement lazy loading to enhance app performance and user experience."* |
| **CAUTION ALERT** | *"Reducing external API calls helps but focus more on data connection optimization and lazy loading."* |

## QUESTION 49

Answer – A), B), D)

Option A – Correct. Monitoring Microsoft's product lifecycle announcements helps keep track of deprecated features and necessary updates.
Option B – Correct. Azure DevOps provides CI/CD capabilities and version control, essential for managing updates and ensuring rollback processes.
Option C – Incorrect. While configuring alerts is useful, it does not directly address managing updates or rollback processes.
Option D – Correct. Developing a rollback strategy using solution exports and backups ensures that the company can revert to a stable version if updates fail.
Option E – Incorrect. Power BI is useful for monitoring performance but is less relevant for managing updates and handling deprecated features.

| | |
|---|---|
| **EXAM FOCUS** | *"Monitor Microsoft's product lifecycle announcements to keep track of deprecated features and updates."* |
| **CAUTION ALERT** | *"Remember, neglecting rollback strategies can result in prolonged downtime."* |

## QUESTION 50

Answer – A), B), D)

Option A – Correct. The Monitor tool in Power Apps helps analyze app performance and identify issues.
Option B – Correct. Reviewing and optimizing formulas and data queries can help prevent crashes.
Option C – Incorrect. Increasing data capacity may not address the root cause of crashes related to app performance.

Option D – Correct. Implementing error handling and logging helps identify and resolve issues proactively.

Option E – Incorrect. While useful for minimizing disruption, deploying updates during off-peak hours does not directly address the root cause of crashes.

| EXAM FOCUS | *"Use the Monitor tool in Power Apps to analyze app performance effectively."* |
|---|---|
| CAUTION ALERT | *"Remember, failing to optimize app formulas and data queries can lead to frequent crashes."* |

# PRACTICE TEST 5 - QUESTIONS ONLY

## QUESTION 1

An educational institution seeks to modernize its student management system using Microsoft Power Platform. Their business objectives are to improve student engagement, streamline administrative processes, and enhance data analytics. Specific challenges include:
- Disconnected student information systems.
- Manual administrative processes.
- Limited insights into student performance.

What solutions would best align with these goals and address the challenges? Select three correct answers.

A) Implement Power BI for student performance analytics.
B) Use Power Automate to automate administrative workflows.
C) Develop a unified student management app with Power Apps.
D) Integrate AI Builder for predictive analytics on student performance.
E) Use Dataverse to centralize student data.

## QUESTION 2

A healthcare organization is deploying Dynamics 365 to manage patient interactions across multiple clinics. The system must support real-time data updates and integrate with existing health record systems. Given these requirements, which Dynamics 365 products should you recommend? Select up to 2 answers.

A) Dynamics 365 Customer Service
B) Dynamics 365 Field Service
C) Dynamics 365 Customer Insights - Journeys
D) Dynamics 365 Sales

## QUESTION 3

An educational institution seeks to modernize its student management system using Microsoft Power Platform. The project requires analyzing current processes and integrating with existing workflows. The specific challenges include:
- Disconnected student information systems.
- Manual administrative processes.
- Limited insights into student performance.

What actions would you take to integrate and improve the student management system? Select three correct answers.

A) Implement Dataverse to centralize student information.
B) Use Power Automate to automate administrative workflows.
C) Develop a Power BI dashboard to analyze student performance.
D) Create a Canvas App for student information access.
E) Use AI Builder for predictive analytics on student performance.

## QUESTION 4

A healthcare provider is developing a patient management system using Microsoft Dataverse. The developer's JavaScript code makes several RetrieveMultiple calls to fetch patient data based on various attributes, leading to performance issues.
• The solution must improve data retrieval performance.
• It should leverage Dataverse capabilities to streamline the code.
What should you recommend the developer use to enhance performance? Select two answers.

A) FetchXML query
B) OData $filter query
C) Alternate keys
D) Business process flow
E) OData $expand query

## QUESTION 5

An educational institution is developing a new student information system using Microsoft Power Platform. The project requires selecting the right technologies to ensure scalability and cost-efficiency. The specific challenges include:
• Integrating with existing student management systems.
• Ensuring the system can scale to accommodate future growth.
• Conducting a cost-benefit analysis of different technology options.
What actions would you take to address these challenges? Select three correct answers.

A) Implement Dataverse to store and manage student data.
B) Use Power Automate to integrate with existing systems.
C) Conduct a cost-benefit analysis to evaluate different technologies.
D) Develop a Power BI dashboard for data analysis.
E) Use Azure Functions to handle complex processing tasks.

## QUESTION 6

A retail company is developing a new customer loyalty program using Microsoft Power Platform. The project involves identifying potential risks and developing strategies for risk mitigation. The specific challenges include:
• Protecting customer data privacy.
• Ensuring system reliability and availability.
• Preparing for potential system failures.
What actions would you take to mitigate these risks? Select three correct answers.

A) Implement Dataverse to securely store customer data.
B) Use Power Automate to automate backup processes.
C) Develop a system reliability plan.
D) Apply DLP policies to protect customer data privacy.
E) Conduct regular system performance audits using Azure Monitor.

## QUESTION 7

A retail company is implementing a new customer relationship management (CRM) system using Microsoft Power Platform. The project involves creating effective project plans and resource allocation. The specific challenges include:
- Allocating resources to high-priority tasks.
- Estimating the timeline for each project phase.
- Setting milestones to ensure timely completion.

What actions would you take to address these challenges? Select three correct answers.

A) Use Azure DevOps to manage resource allocation.
B) Use Power BI to estimate timelines for each project phase.
C) Develop a detailed project plan using Azure DevOps.
D) Implement Power Automate to automate milestone tracking.
E) Conduct regular project reviews.

## QUESTION 8

An educational institution is transitioning to a new learning management system using Microsoft Power Platform. The project requires communicating change effectively. The specific challenges are:
- Informing all stakeholders about the upcoming changes.
- Ensuring clear and consistent messaging.
- Addressing any questions or concerns.

What actions would you take to address these challenges? Select three correct answers.

A) Use Power BI to create informative dashboards.
B) Develop a detailed communication plan.
C) Conduct informational webinars using Microsoft Teams.
D) Use Power Automate to send regular updates.
E) Create a FAQ section using Power Virtual Agents.

## QUESTION 9

A manufacturing firm is upgrading its ERP system using Microsoft Power Platform. The project involves balancing performance with cost. The specific challenges are:
- Ensuring high performance under load.
- Minimizing costs while maintaining performance.
- Implementing cost-effective scaling strategies.

What actions would you take to address these challenges? Select three correct answers.

A) Use Azure Logic Apps for cost-effective integration.
B) Implement Azure Cost Management for cost tracking.
C) Use Azure DevOps for continuous performance testing.
D) Develop cost-performance models using Power BI.
E) Implement Azure Autoscale for dynamic scaling.

## QUESTION 10

A technology company is implementing a new enterprise resource planning (ERP) system using Microsoft Power Platform. The project requires conflict resolution and negotiation with stakeholders. The specific challenges are:
- Resolving conflicts between different stakeholder groups.
- Negotiating project scope and deliverables.
- Ensuring stakeholder buy-in and support.

What steps would you take to address these challenges? Select two correct answers.

A) Use Azure DevOps for tracking project tasks.
B) Implement a conflict resolution framework.
C) Conduct mediation sessions with conflicting parties.
D) Use Power BI for project transparency.
E) Use Power Virtual Agents for stakeholder engagement.

## QUESTION 11

An educational institution is deploying a new learning management system (LMS) using Microsoft Power Platform. The specific challenges are:
- Evaluating vendors based on their LMS integration capabilities with Azure AD.
- Ensuring compliance with FERPA regulations.
- Negotiating service-level agreements (SLAs) that include uptime and support guarantees.

What steps would you take to address these challenges? Select three correct answers.

A) Develop a vendor evaluation matrix focusing on LMS integration capabilities with Azure AD and compliance.
B) Use Power Automate to collect and manage vendor responses.
C) Implement Azure AD for initial integration testing.
D) Compare vendor SLAs focusing on uptime and support guarantees.
E) Use Power BI to visualize and compare vendor capabilities.

## QUESTION 12

A financial institution is developing a loan management system using Microsoft Power Platform. The system needs to integrate with their existing CRM and provide a seamless experience for users across different regions.
- The system must support high data volume and provide real-time processing.
- It should ensure data compliance with financial regulations.

What components would you recommend for this solution?

A) Power Apps, Power Automate, Power BI, Azure SQL Database
B) Power Apps, Power Automate, Power BI, Azure Data Lake
C) Power Apps, Power Automate, Power BI, Azure Service Bus
D) Power Apps, Power Automate, Power BI, Azure Functions
E) Power Apps, Power Automate, Power BI, Azure Logic Apps

## QUESTION 13

A manufacturing company aims to adopt emerging trends to stay competitive. The challenges include:
- Evaluating and adopting new technologies.
- Fostering an innovative mindset.
- Balancing innovation with practicality.

What steps should you take to address these challenges? Select three correct answers.

A) Implement Azure Machine Learning for predictive maintenance.
B) Use Power Automate to streamline operations.
C) Conduct regular innovation workshops.
D) Use Dataverse for centralized data management.
E) Develop a strategic innovation plan.

## QUESTION 14

A technology company is deploying a new enterprise resource planning (ERP) system using the Microsoft Power Platform. The challenges include:
- Handling deployment challenges.
- Post-deployment monitoring and support.
- Managing user transition during deployment.

What strategies should you implement to address these challenges? Select three correct answers.

A) Conduct a pilot deployment to identify potential issues.
B) Develop detailed user guides and training materials.
C) Use Azure Functions to automate deployment tasks.
D) Implement a feedback loop for continuous improvement.
E) Establish a dedicated post-deployment support team.

## QUESTION 15

An e-commerce company is using Microsoft Power Platform to enhance its inventory management system. The team faces challenges such as:
- Building effective project teams.
- Managing remote and distributed team members.
- Using tools and techniques for team communication.

What strategies should you implement to address these challenges? Select three correct answers.

A) Develop a remote work policy for the team.
B) Use Microsoft Teams for daily stand-up meetings.
C) Implement Power Automate for task notifications and updates.
D) Create a team performance dashboard in Power BI.
E) Assign project roles using Dynamics 365.

## QUESTION 16

A multinational corporation is setting up a new Dynamics 365 Customer Service environment. They need to design an environment strategy that ensures optimal performance and data compliance across regions.

- The solution must comply with data residency laws in each region.
- It should provide high availability and disaster recovery capabilities.

Which environment setup should you recommend?

A) Single global production environment with geo-redundant storage
B) Multiple production environments hosted in each region
C) One global production environment with regional data gateways
D) Multiple sandbox environments for each region
E) One production environment with daily backups and a cold standby in a different region

## QUESTION 17

A government agency is transitioning to a new document management system using Microsoft Power Platform. The challenges include:
- Assessing environmental impact of solutions.
- Implementing eco-friendly practices.
- Long-term sustainability planning.

What strategies should you adopt to address these challenges? Select three correct answers.

A) Conduct a comprehensive environmental impact assessment using Power BI.
B) Use Azure Cognitive Services to automate document classification and save resources.
C) Develop a communication plan to keep all stakeholders informed throughout the transition.
D) Implement training programs to ensure all users are comfortable with the new system.
E) Use custom workflows in Power Automate to handle document approvals and reduce manual workload.

## QUESTION 18

A retail company is implementing a new inventory management system using Microsoft Power Platform. The solution must:
- Be adaptable to future changes in inventory processes.
- Scale with the increasing number of products.
- Maintain stability and relevance over time.

You need to choose two actions to design a solution that meets these requirements. Which two actions should you take? (Select two)

A) Use Dataverse for inventory data storage to ensure scalability.
B) Implement Power Automate for adaptable inventory workflows.
C) Develop custom APIs for future process changes.
D) Use model-driven apps for core inventory functions.
E) Implement ALM practices using Azure DevOps.

## QUESTION 19

A nonprofit organization is designing a volunteer management system using Microsoft Power Platform. The solution must:
- Understand volunteer behavior and preferences.
- Incorporate user-centric design principles.
- Continuously improve based on feedback.

Which three steps should you take to ensure these objectives are met? (Select three)

A) Conduct volunteer interviews and focus groups.
B) Use Power BI to analyze volunteer activity data.
C) Implement AI Builder for predictive analytics.
D) Develop user personas for different volunteer roles.
E) Use Power Automate to gather continuous feedback.

## QUESTION 20

A nonprofit organization is using Microsoft Dataverse to manage donor information and track donations. They want to ensure that the data model is optimized for performance and scalability.
• The solution must handle large volumes of data efficiently.
• It should support complex queries and reporting.
Which components should be included in the data model design? Select two answers.

A) Indexed columns
B) Option sets
C) Lookup columns
D) Alternate keys
E) Business rules

## QUESTION 21

An IT company is planning to deploy Power Platform solutions to enhance their existing IT infrastructure. The solution must:
• Align with enterprise architecture.
• Ensure long-term architectural strategy.
• Integrate with existing systems.
Which two measures should you implement? (Select two)

A) Use Power Automate for process automation.
B) Implement a scalable data architecture with Dataverse.
C) Develop a roadmap for technology adoption.
D) Conduct training sessions for IT staff.
E) Utilize Azure API Management for API integration.

## QUESTION 22

A government agency requires a Power Platform solution with Azure integration. The solution must:
• Comply with strict data protection regulations.
• Ensure high system performance.
• Provide cost-effective operations.
Which two measures should you implement? (Select two)

A) Use Azure SQL Database with performance tiers.
B) Implement Azure Policy for regulatory compliance.
C) Use Azure DevOps for application lifecycle management.
D) Enable Dataverse for data management.

E) Implement Azure Key Vault for data encryption.

## QUESTION 23

An educational institution is planning to implement an ALM strategy for their Power Platform solutions to streamline development and deployment processes. The solution must:
- Implement version control.
- Automate deployment and testing.
- Ensure high application quality.

Which two tools or strategies should you implement? (Select two)

A) Use Azure DevOps for automated deployment.
B) Implement GitHub for version control.
C) Use Dataverse for storing test data.
D) Implement Power Apps Solution Checker.
E) Use Dynamics 365 for ALM.

## QUESTION 24

A financial services firm is implementing a client management system using Microsoft Dataverse. They need to ensure that when a client record is deleted, all associated financial transactions remain in the system for auditing purposes.
- The solution must maintain the financial transaction records.
- It should prevent deletion of related records.

Which type of relationship behavior should you configure? Select two answers.

A) Parental
B) Referential
C) Referential, Restrict Delete
D) Cascade Delete
E) Custom

## QUESTION 25

An educational institution is developing a mobile app using Power Apps to provide students with access to course materials and grades. The solution must:
- Be compatible with various mobile devices.
- Provide offline access to course materials.
- Synchronize data once connected to the internet.

Which three features should you prioritize in the app's design? (Select three)

A) Use responsive design for compatibility.
B) Implement local caching for offline access.
C) Use Azure API Management for secure API handling.
D) Use Dataverse for data storage and synchronization.
E) Implement Power Virtual Agents for customer support.

## QUESTION 26

An IT service company wants to use Power Automate to improve their incident management process. The solution must:
• Automatically categorize incidents based on severity.
• Trigger alerts for high-priority incidents.
• Generate detailed incident reports.
Which three components should you implement? (Select three)

A) Power Automate Cloud Flow for categorizing incidents.
B) AI Builder for categorizing incidents based on severity.
C) Power Automate approvals for triggering alerts.
D) Power BI for detailed incident reports.
E) Azure Functions for custom logic.

## QUESTION 27

A government agency needs to ensure its Power Platform solutions adhere to strict governance and compliance requirements. The solution must:
• Automate compliance reporting.
• Manage data access and security.
• Enforce data loss prevention policies.
What are the best components and practices to implement? (Select three)

A) Power Automate for compliance workflows.
B) Power BI for compliance dashboards.
C) Dataverse for secure data management.
D) Power Platform Admin Center for DLP policies.
E) Azure Policy for compliance automation.

## QUESTION 28

A large enterprise uses Dynamics 365 Finance and Operations for their accounting and finance operations. They need to implement a disaster recovery solution to ensure business continuity. Which Azure service should they use to set up a disaster recovery plan?

A) Azure Backup
B) Azure Site Recovery
C) Azure Blob Storage
D) Azure SQL Database
E) Azure DevOps

## QUESTION 29

During a project review, a client has expressed concerns about their budget allocation for their Power Platform solution. They want to ensure that their investment is providing the best value and want to explore ways to optimize their expenditures.
 1. Analyzing current expenditures to identify areas of high cost.
 2. Exploring alternative solutions that provide similar functionality at a lower cost.

3. Implementing cost-saving measures that do not compromise solution effectiveness.
What actions would you recommend? Select three answers.

A) Perform a cost-benefit analysis for all major expenditures.
B) Use Dataverse instead of high-cost third-party data storage solutions.
C) Implement governance policies to control and monitor resource usage.
D) Invest in extensive training for staff on all premium features.
E) Utilize Power Automate to streamline workflows and reduce manual effort.

## QUESTION 30

During a project review, a financial services client has expressed concerns about vendor performance and SLA management for their Power Platform solution. They want to ensure vendors are meeting their contractual obligations and maintaining high performance standards.
1. Monitoring vendor performance against agreed SLAs.
2. Conducting regular performance reviews and audits.
3. Ensuring vendors adhere to compliance and security standards.
What strategies would you recommend to address these concerns? Select two answers.

A) Use Power Automate to automate performance tracking and reporting.
B) Implement regular compliance and security audits.
C) Focus on renegotiating contracts to include higher penalties for non-compliance.
D) Use Dynamics 365 for vendor relationship and performance management.
E) Select vendors who offer the lowest cost solutions.

## QUESTION 31

A smart city project aims to implement IoT solutions to monitor and manage urban infrastructure in real-time. They need to ensure the system is scalable, performs well, and maintains data privacy and security.
1. Integrating IoT devices for real-time monitoring of urban infrastructure.
2. Ensuring scalability and performance of the IoT system.
3. Maintaining data privacy and security.
What measures would you take to achieve these goals? Select two answers.

A) Use Azure IoT Hub for device management and data security.
B) Implement Azure Data Factory for data integration from multiple sources.
C) Use Azure Stream Analytics for real-time data processing.
D) Store data in a shared network drive for easy access.
E) Develop custom applications for each aspect of urban management.

## QUESTION 32

A logistics company uses Dynamics 365 Field Service to manage their field operations. They want to integrate IoT data from their delivery vehicles to monitor vehicle health and optimize maintenance schedules. The solution must provide real-time data analysis and trigger automated workflows based on the data. What Microsoft technology should they use to achieve this integration?

A) Azure IoT Central
B) Power BI Dataflows

C) Power Apps
D) Azure SQL Database
E) Microsoft Power Virtual Agents

## QUESTION 33

During a project review, a healthcare client has expressed concerns about the sustainability of their new Power Platform solution. They want to ensure the solution is eco-friendly and complies with green standards.
1. Ensuring the solution is sustainable and reduces environmental impact.
2. Promoting eco-friendly practices in technology use.
3. Complying with relevant green standards and regulations.
What actions would you recommend to address these concerns? Select two answers.

A) Use Azure DevOps to manage and track sustainability initiatives.
B) Conduct regular sustainability audits and reviews.
C) Focus solely on functionality without considering environmental impact.
D) Implement Power Virtual Agents to promote eco-friendly practices.
E) Select energy-efficient hardware and cloud services.

## QUESTION 34

To minimize disruption during the integration of a legacy inventory management system with Dynamics 365, your project must:
- Ensure continuous system availability.
- Perform data migration without halting operations.
- Validate data accuracy during the migration process. What actions should you take? (Select 3 answers)

A) Schedule migration during non-business hours.
B) Use Azure Data Factory to automate and manage the migration process.
C) Perform real-time data validation using Power Automate.
D) Implement a rollback strategy in case of failures.
E) Use Azure DevOps for monitoring and reporting on migration progress.

## QUESTION 35

Your team has completed a Power Automate project and needs to ensure that the solution is well-documented and knowledge is transferred to the operations team. The documentation should:
- Describe the workflow configurations.
- Include troubleshooting guides.
- Be easy to update as changes occur. What actions should you take to achieve these objectives? (Select 2 answers)

A) Use a shared document repository with access controls.
B) Create a comprehensive FAQ section in the documentation.
C) Conduct one-time handover sessions with the operations team.
D) Implement a change management process to keep documentation current.
E) Use email to notify the operations team of changes.

## QUESTION 36

A transportation company uses Dynamics 365 for Customer Service to manage customer inquiries and complaints. They want to implement a solution that automatically categorizes and prioritizes incoming emails based on their content, ensuring urgent issues are addressed promptly. The solution must integrate with Dynamics 365 and provide real-time processing. What tool should they use?

A) Power Automate with AI Builder
B) Dynamics 365 Marketing
C) Azure Cognitive Services
D) Power BI
E) Azure Logic Apps

## QUESTION 37

A healthcare organization is using Power Platform to integrate various functions, including patient management, billing, and inventory. The solution must:
- Ensure compliance with data governance policies.
- Facilitate seamless data flows across functions.
- Maintain data accuracy and integrity. What steps should be taken to meet these requirements? (Select 3 answers)

A) Use Dataverse with data governance policies implemented.
B) Implement Power Automate for seamless data flows.
C) Use Azure DevOps for managing solution development and deployment.
D) Conduct regular data audits to ensure accuracy.
E) Use separate systems for each function to maintain data integrity.

## QUESTION 38

A financial services company wants to implement innovative solutions using Power Platform to enhance customer experience. The solutions must:
- Balance the use of new technologies with regulatory compliance.
- Ensure data security and privacy.
- Provide a seamless user experience. What steps should you take? (Select 3 answers)

A) Use Power Virtual Agents to provide automated customer support.
B) Integrate AI Builder for fraud detection and prevention.
C) Store customer data in a public cloud without encryption.
D) Ensure compliance with financial regulations through Dataverse security roles.
E) Develop a user-friendly interface using Power Apps.

## QUESTION 39

Your organization is implementing a Power Platform solution for a government agency. The solution must:
- Comply with stringent data security regulations.
- Implement secure communication and data transmission.
- Regularly assess and update security protocols. What actions should you take? (Select 3 answers)

A) Use Dataverse with government community cloud (GCC) compliance.
B) Encrypt data at rest and in transit using advanced encryption standards (AES).
C) Use public Wi-Fi for data transmission.
D) Conduct regular security training for all users.
E) Implement multi-factor authentication (MFA) for all users.

## QUESTION 40

A retail chain uses Power Apps to manage customer loyalty programs. They want to implement a process where customers can check their loyalty points and redeem rewards through a mobile app. The solution must be secure and provide real-time updates to the loyalty points. What should they use to develop this solution?

A) Create a canvas app with Dataverse.
B) Develop a model-driven app.
C) Use Power Automate to update loyalty points.
D) Integrate with Dynamics 365 Commerce.
E) Use Azure SQL Database to store loyalty points.

## QUESTION 41

A tech startup wants to build a cloud-native application to support its rapid growth. The solution must:
- Utilize microservices.
- Ensure high performance and low latency.
- Implement a continuous delivery pipeline. What components should you use? (Select 3 answers)

A) Deploy microservices using Azure Kubernetes Service (AKS).
B) Use Azure DevOps for continuous delivery.
C) Implement Azure Cosmos DB for low-latency data access.
D) Use Power BI for application performance monitoring.
E) Implement Azure Functions for critical compute tasks.

## QUESTION 42

A tech company is implementing a Power Platform solution to manage customer support data. They need to ensure:
- Privacy and security of support tickets.
- Ethical data handling practices.
- Compliance with data protection regulations. What strategies should be used? (Select 3 answers)

A) Use Power Apps to display sensitive support ticket details to all users.
B) Implement role-based access control (RBAC) in Dataverse to restrict access to sensitive data.
C) Use Azure Security Center for continuous compliance monitoring.
D) Store support ticket data in a publicly accessible SharePoint site.
E) Use Azure Data Factory to anonymize data before analysis.

## QUESTION 43

A telecommunications company is integrating their Power Platform solution with a third-party billing

system. They need to:
- Ensure seamless data exchange.
- Maintain compliance with industry standards.
- Securely handle billing information. What strategies should they use? (Select 3 answers)

A) Use Azure Data Factory for ETL processes.
B) Implement role-based access control (RBAC) for secure data handling.
C) Use plain text for storing billing information for easy access.
D) Use Azure API Management to manage API calls and ensure compliance.
E) Perform manual data transfers to the billing system.

## QUESTION 44

You are developing a Microsoft Power Platform solution for a healthcare provider that needs to ensure compliance with data privacy regulations while synchronizing patient data across systems. The synchronization has recently failed, causing discrepancies in patient records.
- Ensure compliance with data privacy regulations.
- Accurate data synchronization.

What should you use to diagnose the issue?

A) Dataverse auditing
B) Microsoft Power Apps activity logging
C) Trace logging
D) WorkflowLog
E) Power Automate analytics

## QUESTION 45

A manufacturing firm is migrating their operational data to Dynamics 365. They need to:
- Handle large volumes of data efficiently.
- Ensure data integrity during migration.
- Perform thorough post-migration validation. What strategies should they consider? (Select 3 answers)

A) Use Azure Data Factory to manage and transfer large datasets.
B) Implement data validation rules within Dataverse.
C) Use manual data entry to ensure accuracy.
D) Conduct a pilot migration to identify potential issues.
E) Skip post-migration validation to save time.

## QUESTION 46

A financial services company is deploying a new Dynamics 365 solution. They need to:
- Implement stringent security protocols.
- Protect sensitive financial data.
- Ensure ongoing compliance with financial regulations. What measures should they implement?

A) Use Data Loss Prevention (DLP) policies to protect sensitive data.
B) Implement RBAC with Azure AD.
C) Conduct regular security testing and audits.

D) Use default security settings.
E) Perform compliance checks only during the initial rollout.

## QUESTION 47

A logistics company is using Power Automate for process automation. To ensure optimal performance, they must:
• Identify performance bottlenecks.
• Monitor performance metrics.
• Continuously improve process performance. What actions should they take?
Select 3 answers.

A) Use Power Automate analytics for performance monitoring.
B) Implement logging and tracing for flow activities.
C) Ignore performance metrics and focus on functionality.
D) Optimize flows by reducing unnecessary actions.
E) Conduct regular performance reviews and optimizations.

## QUESTION 48

A healthcare organization requires integration of their Dynamics 365 system with external laboratory services using Microsoft Power Platform. The process involves configuring secure data exchange and automating patient data updates. You must recommend automation strategies to enhance the integration's reliability and efficiency.
• Secure data exchange required.
• Automate patient data updates.
Which two automation tasks would you prioritize to meet these requirements?

A) Connection management
B) Service endpoint configuration
C) Team records creation
D) Upsert of reference data
E) Webhook configuration

## QUESTION 49

Your organization relies heavily on Power Virtual Agents and AI Builder for customer support solutions. To ensure the long-term sustainability of these solutions, you need to focus on routine maintenance, managing updates, and addressing deprecated features. The key requirements are:
• Implementing automated maintenance procedures.
• Ensuring updates are applied without disrupting services.
• Monitoring for deprecated features and updates.
What measures should you implement? (Select 3 answers)

A) Use Azure DevOps for automated deployment and version control.
B) Implement a monitoring system using Azure Application Insights.
C) Schedule regular update windows to minimize disruption.
D) Use Power Platform's Solution Checker for regular maintenance.
E) Regularly review Microsoft's product release notes and update logs.

## QUESTION 50

Your organization has implemented a Power BI solution for executive reporting. Users report that some reports are taking too long to load. As a solution architect, you need to troubleshoot and optimize the performance of these reports. The key requirements are:
- Identifying performance bottlenecks.
- Optimizing report performance.
- Ensuring a smooth user experience.

What steps should you take? (Select 3 answers)

A) Use Power BI Performance Analyzer to identify bottlenecks.
B) Optimize DAX queries in the reports.
C) Increase the Power BI capacity in the Power BI admin portal.
D) Implement incremental data refresh for large datasets.
E) Use Azure Data Factory to preprocess data before loading into Power BI.

# PRACTICE TEST 5 - ANSWERS ONLY

## QUESTION 1

Answer – A), B), C)

Option A – Analytics improve insights, addressing limited insights into student performance.
Option B – Automating workflows reduces manual effort, addressing manual administrative processes.
Option C – A unified app with Power Apps centralizes information, addressing disconnected student information systems.
Option D – Predictive analytics enhance insights but do not address disconnected systems or manual processes.
Option E – Centralizing data helps unify systems but does not directly improve engagement or streamline processes.

| | |
|---|---|
| **EXAM FOCUS** | *Implement Power BI for performance analytics, automate workflows with Power Automate, and develop a unified app for better student engagement.* |
| **CAUTION ALERT** | *Please keep in mind that predictive analytics won't address disconnected systems or manual processes effectively.* |

## QUESTION 2

Answer – A), C)

Option A – Correct. Dynamics 365 Customer Service provides the capabilities necessary for managing patient interactions efficiently, ensuring that all queries and issues are tracked and resolved promptly.
Option B – Incorrect. Dynamics 365 Field Service is geared towards managing field operations and doesn't align closely with the requirements for managing patient interactions in a healthcare setting.
Option C – Correct. Dynamics 365 Customer Insights - Journeys can help the healthcare organization understand and optimize patient interactions based on data from integrated health record systems.
Option D – Incorrect. Dynamics 365 Sales focuses on streamlining sales processes and is not tailored to the specific needs of patient interaction management in a healthcare context.

| | |
|---|---|
| **EXAM FOCUS** | "Use Dynamics 365 Customer Service and Customer Insights - Journeys to manage patient interactions and optimize engagement." |
| **CAUTION ALERT** | "Field Service and Sales modules aren't designed for patient interaction management." |

## QUESTION 3

Answer – A), B), C)

Option A – Centralizing student information with Dataverse addresses disconnected systems.
Option B – Automating administrative workflows with Power Automate reduces manual processes.
Option C – A Power BI dashboard provides insights into student performance.
Option D – A Canvas App for access is useful but does not address integration or automation.
Option E – AI Builder for predictive analytics is advanced but might not be necessary initially.

| EXAM FOCUS | *Centralize student information with Dataverse, automate workflows with Power Automate, and use Power BI for insights.* |
| --- | --- |
| CAUTION ALERT | *Please keep in mind, creating a Canvas App for access is useful but won't solve integration or automation issues.* |

## QUESTION 4

Answer – A), B)

Option A – Correct choice as FetchXML query can efficiently retrieve multiple records based on complex criteria.
Option B – Correct choice as OData $filter query can retrieve specific records more efficiently.
Option C – Alternate keys are useful for unique identifier-based retrieval but may not address various attributes.
Option D – Business process flow guides users through processes but does not optimize data retrieval.
Option E – OData $expand query retrieves related data, which may not be necessary for improving performance in this scenario.

| EXAM FOCUS | *"Using FetchXML query can efficiently handle multiple record retrieval."* |
| --- | --- |
| CAUTION ALERT | *"You should stay cautious, improper data retrieval methods can cause performance bottlenecks."* |

## QUESTION 5

Answer – A), B), C)

Option A – Dataverse provides scalable storage and management of student data.
Option B – Power Automate can integrate with existing systems, ensuring seamless operation.
Option C – Conducting a cost-benefit analysis helps in evaluating and justifying technology choices.
Option D – A Power BI dashboard is useful for data analysis but does not address integration or scalability directly.
Option E – Azure Functions is useful for complex processing but may increase complexity and cost.

| EXAM FOCUS | *Use Dataverse for scalable data storage and Power Automate for integration with existing systems.* |
| --- | --- |
| CAUTION ALERT | *Remember, Power BI dashboards are great for analysis but won't ensure scalability or integration.* |

## QUESTION 6

Answer – A), D), E)

Option A – Dataverse provides secure storage for customer data, protecting privacy.
Option B – Power Automate is useful for backup processes but does not directly address system reliability or availability.
Option C – Developing a system reliability plan ensures the system remains reliable and available.
Option D – DLP policies protect customer data privacy.
Option E – Conducting regular system performance audits ensures ongoing assessment of system reliability and performance.

| EXAM FOCUS | Implement Dataverse for secure storage, DLP policies for privacy, and conduct regular audits with Azure Monitor. |
|---|---|
| CAUTION ALERT | Stay cautious, Power Automate alone won't ensure system reliability or availability effectively. |

## QUESTION 7

Answer – A), B), C)

Option A – Azure DevOps can be used to manage resource allocation effectively.
Option B – Power BI can be used to estimate realistic timelines for each project phase.
Option C – Developing a detailed project plan using Azure DevOps helps ensure comprehensive planning.
Option D – Power Automate is useful for automating tasks but does not address initial planning directly.
Option E – Regular project reviews are important but do not address initial resource allocation or timeline estimation.

| EXAM FOCUS | Manage resources and timelines with Azure DevOps and estimate project phases with Power BI for effective planning. |
|---|---|
| CAUTION ALERT | Please keep in mind, Power Automate alone won't address initial project planning or resource allocation. |

## QUESTION 8

Answer – B), C), D)

Option A – Power BI can be used for creating dashboards but not directly related to communicating change.
Option B – Developing a detailed communication plan ensures clear and consistent messaging.
Option C – Conducting informational webinars using Microsoft Teams helps inform stakeholders.
Option D – Using Power Automate to send regular updates ensures ongoing communication.
Option E – Creating a FAQ section using Power Virtual Agents is useful but not directly related to communicating change.

| EXAM FOCUS | Develop a communication plan, conduct webinars via Teams, and send regular updates using Power Automate. |
|---|---|
| CAUTION ALERT | Please keep in mind, Power BI dashboards won't address communication needs directly. |

## QUESTION 9

Answer – B), C), E)

Option A – Azure Logic Apps are useful for integration but not directly related to performance.
Option B – Implementing Azure Cost Management helps track and minimize costs.
Option C – Using Azure DevOps for continuous performance testing ensures high performance.
Option D – Power BI is useful for developing models but not directly related to balancing performance with cost.
Option E – Implementing Azure Autoscale for dynamic scaling ensures cost-effective scaling strategies.

| EXAM FOCUS | Track costs with Azure Cost Management, test performance continuously with Azure DevOps, and use Azure Autoscale for scaling. |
|---|---|
| CAUTION ALERT | Please keep in mind, Power BI alone won't balance performance with cost effectively. |

## QUESTION 10

Answer – B), C)

Option A – Azure DevOps is useful for tracking tasks but not directly related to conflict resolution and negotiation.
Option B – Implementing a conflict resolution framework provides a structured approach to resolving conflicts.
Option C – Conducting mediation sessions helps in negotiating and resolving conflicts.
Option D – Power BI is useful for project transparency but not directly related to conflict resolution.
Option E – Power Virtual Agents is useful for engagement but not directly related to conflict resolution and negotiation.

| EXAM FOCUS | Implement a conflict resolution framework and conduct mediation sessions to resolve stakeholder conflicts. |
|---|---|
| CAUTION ALERT | Remember, Azure DevOps tracks tasks but does not directly resolve conflicts. |

## QUESTION 11

Answer – A), D), E)

Option A – Developing a vendor evaluation matrix ensures all critical factors are considered.
Option B – Power Automate can manage responses but is not critical for initial evaluation.
Option C – Azure AD is useful for testing but not essential for assessment.
Option D – Comparing vendor SLAs ensures uptime and support guarantees.
Option E – Using Power BI to visualize and compare capabilities ensures comprehensive evaluation.

| EXAM FOCUS | Create an evaluation matrix and compare SLAs with Power BI to ensure compliance and performance. |
|---|---|
| CAUTION ALERT | Please keep in mind, Power Automate is useful for managing responses but not critical for initial evaluation. |

## QUESTION 12

Answer – B)

Option A – Azure SQL Database may not be the best for handling high volumes of data compared to Azure Data Lake.
Option B – Correct choice as Azure Data Lake handles high volumes of data, and Power BI and Power Automate provide dashboards and workflows.
Option C – Azure Service Bus is not necessary for this scenario.
Option D – Azure Functions is useful but not essential for this specific solution.

Option E – Azure Logic Apps is good but Azure Data Lake is more suited for high data volumes.

| EXAM FOCUS | "Azure Data Lake is ideal for handling high data volumes with real-time processing." |
|---|---|
| CAUTION ALERT | "Azure SQL Database might struggle with high volumes compared to Data Lake." |

## QUESTION 13

Answer – A), C), E)

Option A – Implementing Azure Machine Learning for predictive maintenance helps adopt new technologies.
Option B – Power Automate is useful but more for streamlining operations than innovation.
Option C – Regular innovation workshops foster an innovative mindset.
Option D – Dataverse is useful for data management but not directly related to innovation.
Option E – Developing a strategic innovation plan balances innovation with practicality.

| EXAM FOCUS | Conduct regular innovation workshops and implement Azure Machine Learning for predictive maintenance. |
|---|---|
| CAUTION ALERT | Remember, streamlining operations with Power Automate should not replace strategic innovation planning. |

## QUESTION 14

Answer – A), B), E)

Option A – A pilot deployment helps identify and handle potential deployment challenges early.
Option B – Detailed user guides and training materials help manage user transition.
Option C – Azure Functions can automate tasks but are less critical than other options for deployment challenges.
Option D – A feedback loop for continuous improvement is useful but less critical than other options for deployment challenges.
Option E – A dedicated post-deployment support team is crucial for continuous monitoring and support.

| EXAM FOCUS | Conduct a pilot deployment to identify potential issues and develop detailed user guides and training materials. |
|---|---|
| CAUTION ALERT | Remember, automating tasks with Azure Functions is helpful but secondary to user transition management. |

## QUESTION 15

Answer – A), B), C)

Option A – Developing a remote work policy helps in managing remote and distributed team members effectively.
Option B – Using Microsoft Teams for daily stand-up meetings enhances communication and collaboration.
Option C – Power Automate can automate task notifications and updates, ensuring efficient communication.

Option D – Power BI is useful for performance monitoring but less critical for communication and team management.

Option E – Dynamics 365 is useful for assigning roles but less critical for managing remote and distributed teams.

| EXAM FOCUS | *Implement a remote work policy and use Microsoft Teams for daily stand-ups to manage remote teams.* |
|---|---|
| CAUTION ALERT | *Please keep in mind, focusing solely on Power BI for performance monitoring can miss critical communication aspects.* |

## QUESTION 16

Answer – B)

Option A – A single global environment may not comply with regional data residency laws.

Option B – Correct choice as it ensures compliance with data residency laws and provides high availability by hosting environments in each region.

Option C – Regional data gateways may not fully address compliance and availability needs.

Option D – Sandbox environments are not suitable for production use.

Option E – Daily backups and a cold standby provide disaster recovery but not high availability or compliance with data residency laws.

| EXAM FOCUS | *"Multiple regional production environments ensure compliance and high availability."* |
|---|---|
| CAUTION ALERT | *"Single global environments may fail to comply with regional data residency laws."* |

## QUESTION 17

Answer – A), B), E)

Option A – Conducting a comprehensive environmental impact assessment using Power BI helps understand the environmental implications.

Option B – Using Azure Cognitive Services to automate document classification can save resources.

Option C – Developing a communication plan is useful but does not directly address environmental impact and sustainability.

Option D – Implementing training programs ensures all users are comfortable with the new system but does not directly address environmental impact and sustainability.

Option E – Using custom workflows in Power Automate helps reduce manual workload and save resources.

| EXAM FOCUS | *Conduct an environmental impact assessment with Power BI, automate with Azure Cognitive Services, and use Power Automate workflows.* |
|---|---|
| CAUTION ALERT | *Training programs are important but do not directly address environmental impact and sustainability.* |

## QUESTION 18

Answer – A), B)

Option A – Using Dataverse ensures scalable inventory data storage.

Option B – Implementing Power Automate allows adaptable workflows that can change with processes.
Option C – Developing custom APIs adds unnecessary complexity.
Option D – Using model-driven apps provides robust and scalable solutions for core inventory functions but might not always be necessary.
Option E – Implementing ALM practices ensures continuous improvement and relevance.

| | |
|---|---|
| EXAM FOCUS | *Dataverse ensures scalable storage; Power Automate for adaptable workflows.* |
| CAUTION ALERT | *Custom APIs increase complexity; avoid unless necessary.* |

## QUESTION 19

Answer – A), D), E)

Option A – Conducting volunteer interviews and focus groups gathers behavior and preferences.
Option B – Using Power BI analyzes activity data but might not directly gather behavior or preferences.
Option C – Implementing AI Builder provides predictive analytics but might not directly gather behavior or incorporate user-centric design principles.
Option D – Developing user personas for different volunteer roles helps in understanding behavior and incorporating user-centric design principles.
Option E – Using Power Automate gathers continuous feedback and ensures continuous improvement.

| | |
|---|---|
| EXAM FOCUS | *Conduct volunteer interviews and develop personas; use Power Automate for continuous feedback.* |
| CAUTION ALERT | *Ignoring direct volunteer interactions can lead to incomplete understanding of preferences.* |

## QUESTION 20

Answer – A), D)

Option A – Correct choice as Indexed columns improve query performance.
Option B – Option sets are used for picklists, not performance optimization.
Option C – Lookup columns define relationships but don't directly improve performance.
Option D – Correct choice as Alternate keys improve query efficiency and data integrity.
Option E – Business rules enforce validation but don't optimize performance.

| | |
|---|---|
| EXAM FOCUS | "Index columns and use Alternate keys to enhance performance and query efficiency in large datasets." |
| CAUTION ALERT | "Option sets and Business rules do not directly improve performance or scalability." |

## QUESTION 21

Answer – B), E)

Option A – Power Automate helps with process automation but does not directly address architectural alignment.
Option B – Dataverse provides a scalable data architecture, aligning with enterprise strategy.
Option C – Developing a roadmap is useful but not directly for architectural alignment.
Option D – Training sessions help but do not directly address integration or architectural strategy.

Option E – Azure API Management facilitates API integration, ensuring long-term strategy and alignment.

| EXAM FOCUS | *Implement Dataverse for scalable architecture and Azure API Management for integration.* |
|---|---|
| CAUTION ALERT | *Training alone is not enough; focus on aligning with architectural strategy.* |

## QUESTION 22

Answer – A), E)

Option A – Azure SQL Database with performance tiers ensures high system performance.
Option B – Azure Policy helps with regulatory compliance but does not directly ensure high system performance.
Option C – Azure DevOps helps with application lifecycle management but does not directly address system performance or data protection.
Option D – Dataverse is useful for data management but does not directly ensure high system performance.
Option E – Azure Key Vault ensures data encryption, complying with strict data protection regulations.

| EXAM FOCUS | *You should use Azure SQL Database with performance tiers and Azure Key Vault for compliance and high performance.* |
|---|---|
| CAUTION ALERT | *Remember, Azure Policy and Dataverse alone don't guarantee high system performance or data protection.* |

## QUESTION 23

Answer – A), B)

Option A – Azure DevOps supports automated deployment and testing, ensuring high application quality.
Option B – GitHub provides version control capabilities essential for ALM.
Option C – Dataverse can be used for storing test data but does not contribute to version control or deployment automation.
Option D – Power Apps Solution Checker ensures solution quality but does not handle version control or deployment.
Option E – Dynamics 365 is not specifically designed for ALM in the context of Power Platform solutions.

| EXAM FOCUS | *Remember, Azure DevOps and GitHub are essential for automated deployment and version control, ensuring high application quality.* |
|---|---|
| CAUTION ALERT | *Avoid using Dynamics 365 for ALM; it is not specifically designed for Power Platform solutions.* |

## QUESTION 24

Answer – B), C)

Option A – Parental relationships automatically delete related records, which is not desired.
Option B – Correct choice as Referential relationships enforce referential integrity but do not automatically delete related records.
Option C – Correct choice as Referential, Restrict Delete prevents deletion if there are related records.

Option D – Cascade Delete will automatically delete related records, which is not desired.
Option E – Custom relationships can be configured for specific behaviors but are more complex.

| EXAM FOCUS | *"Select Referential and Restrict Delete to ensure related records are preserved for auditing."* |
|---|---|
| CAUTION ALERT | *"Parental and Cascade Delete will remove related records, which is not suitable for auditing."* |

## QUESTION 25

Answer – A), B), D)

Option A – Using responsive design ensures the app is compatible with various mobile devices.
Option B – Implementing local caching allows offline access to course materials.
Option C – Azure API Management is useful for secure API handling but not directly related to offline access.
Option D – Using Dataverse for data storage and synchronization ensures that data is synchronized once connected to the internet.
Option E – Implementing Power Virtual Agents is beneficial for customer support but not critical for the app's primary requirements.

| EXAM FOCUS | *Use responsive design, local caching, and Dataverse for compatibility, offline access, and synchronization.* |
|---|---|
| CAUTION ALERT | *Avoid relying on Azure API Management for offline access; it focuses on secure API handling.* |

## QUESTION 26

Answer – A), B), C)

Option A – Power Automate Cloud Flow can categorize incidents.
Option B – AI Builder can be used to categorize incidents based on severity using AI.
Option C – Power Automate approvals can trigger alerts for high-priority incidents.
Option D – Power BI is useful for generating reports but not directly for categorizing or triggering alerts.
Option E – Azure Functions can be used for custom logic but may not be required if Power Automate and AI Builder are implemented effectively.

| EXAM FOCUS | *Utilize Cloud Flow, AI Builder, and approvals for categorizing incidents, using AI for severity, and triggering alerts.* |
|---|---|
| CAUTION ALERT | *Avoid assuming Power BI handles incident categorization or alerts; it's for reporting.* |

## QUESTION 27

Answer – C), D), E)

Option A – Power Automate can be used for workflows but not directly for governance and compliance.
Option B – Power BI is useful for creating dashboards but not directly for enforcing compliance.
Option C – Dataverse is critical for secure data management.
Option D – Power Platform Admin Center is necessary for enforcing DLP policies.

Option E – Azure Policy helps automate compliance reporting.

| EXAM FOCUS | *Implement Dataverse, Power Platform Admin Center, and Azure Policy for secure data management, DLP policies, and compliance automation.* |
|---|---|
| CAUTION ALERT | *Don't depend on Power BI for enforcing compliance; it's designed for dashboards and reports.* |

## QUESTION 28

Answer – B)

Option A – Azure Backup is used for backing up data but does not provide a full disaster recovery solution.
Option B – Azure Site Recovery offers comprehensive disaster recovery capabilities, including failover and failback, ensuring business continuity.
Option C – Azure Blob Storage is used for storing unstructured data and is not a disaster recovery solution.
Option D – Azure SQL Database provides high availability and disaster recovery for SQL databases but not for a full ERP system like Dynamics 365 Finance and Operations.
Option E – Azure DevOps is used for development and CI/CD processes, not for disaster recovery.

| EXAM FOCUS | "Azure Site Recovery offers comprehensive disaster recovery capabilities for business continuity." |
|---|---|
| CAUTION ALERT | "Azure Backup is not a full disaster recovery solution." |

## QUESTION 29

Answer – A), B), E)

Option A – Correct. Cost-benefit analysis helps in making informed financial decisions.
Option B – Correct. Dataverse provides a cost-effective and integrated data storage solution.
Option C – Incorrect. Governance policies are helpful but may not directly impact immediate costs.
Option D – Incorrect. Training on premium features is beneficial but could increase costs initially.
Option E – Correct. Power Automate can reduce manual effort and operational costs.

| EXAM FOCUS | *Perform cost-benefit analysis and use Dataverse for cost-effective data storage.* |
|---|---|
| CAUTION ALERT | *Governance policies help, but they may not directly impact immediate costs.* |

## QUESTION 30

Answer – B), D)

Option A – Incorrect. Power Automate can help with automation but is not a primary strategy.
Option B – Correct. Regular audits ensure compliance and security standards are met.
Option C – Incorrect. Renegotiating contracts can be useful but should not be the only focus.
Option D – Correct. Dynamics 365 is effective for managing vendor relationships and performance.
Option E – Incorrect. Cost should not be the sole criterion.

| EXAM FOCUS | Implement regular audits and use Dynamics 365 for managing vendor relationships. |
| CAUTION ALERT | Avoid focusing solely on renegotiating contracts; ensure ongoing performance management. |

## QUESTION 31

Answer – A), C)

Option A – Correct. Azure IoT Hub provides device management and ensures data security.
Option B – Incorrect. Azure Data Factory is useful for data integration but not primarily for real-time data processing.
Option C – Correct. Azure Stream Analytics is ideal for real-time data processing.
Option D – Incorrect. Storing data in a shared drive is not secure or scalable.
Option E – Incorrect. Custom applications can increase complexity and are not necessary with Azure IoT solutions.

| EXAM FOCUS | Use Azure IoT Hub for device security and Stream Analytics for real-time processing. |
| CAUTION ALERT | Shared network drives are not secure or scalable for data storage. |

## QUESTION 32

Answer – A)

Option A – Azure IoT Central is designed for integrating IoT data with real-time analysis and can trigger automated workflows in Dynamics 365 Field Service.
Option B – Power BI Dataflows are used for data preparation and ETL processes, not for real-time IoT data integration.
Option C – Power Apps is used for building custom applications but not for IoT data integration.
Option D – Azure SQL Database is used for storing structured data but does not provide real-time IoT integration capabilities.
Option E – Microsoft Power Virtual Agents is used for creating AI chatbots, not for IoT data integration.

| EXAM FOCUS | "Azure IoT Central offers ready-to-use IoT data integration and analysis." |
| CAUTION ALERT | "Power BI Dataflows are not designed for real-time IoT data integration." |

## QUESTION 33

Answer – B), E)

Option A – Incorrect. Azure DevOps is useful for project management but not primarily for sustainability initiatives.
Option B – Correct. Regular sustainability audits and reviews ensure compliance and promote eco-friendly practices.
Option C – Incorrect. Ignoring environmental impact can lead to unsustainable practices.
Option D – Incorrect. Power Virtual Agents are useful but not the primary tool for promoting eco-friendly practices.
Option E – Correct. Selecting energy-efficient hardware and cloud services reduces environmental impact.

| EXAM FOCUS | Conduct sustainability audits regularly and select energy-efficient hardware and cloud services. |
|---|---|
| CAUTION ALERT | Ignoring environmental impact can lead to unsustainable practices. |

## QUESTION 34

Answer – A), B), D)

Option A – Scheduling migration during non-business hours minimizes operational disruption.
Option B – Azure Data Factory efficiently manages and automates the migration process.
Option C – Real-time validation using Power Automate may be complex and less reliable.
Option D – A rollback strategy ensures recovery in case of failures.
Option E – Azure DevOps is useful for monitoring but not directly for minimizing disruption.

| EXAM FOCUS | Schedule migrations during non-business hours and use Azure Data Factory for automated processes to ensure continuous availability. |
|---|---|
| CAUTION ALERT | Implement a rollback strategy to recover in case of failures; this is crucial for minimizing risks. |

## QUESTION 35

Answer – A), D)

Option A – A shared document repository with access controls ensures secure and accessible documentation.
Option B – An FAQ section is helpful but should be part of comprehensive documentation.
Option C – One-time handover sessions are insufficient for ongoing knowledge transfer.
Option D – A change management process ensures documentation is kept current and relevant.
Option E – Email notifications alone are not sufficient to keep documentation updated.

| EXAM FOCUS | Use a shared document repository with access controls and implement change management for keeping documentation current. |
|---|---|
| CAUTION ALERT | One-time handover sessions are insufficient; ensure ongoing documentation updates. |

## QUESTION 36

Answer – A)

Option A – Power Automate with AI Builder allows for automatic categorization and prioritization of emails based on content and integrates seamlessly with Dynamics 365 for real-time processing.
Option B – Dynamics 365 Marketing is focused on marketing campaigns, not customer service email processing.
Option C – Azure Cognitive Services provides powerful AI capabilities but requires more complex integration and setup compared to AI Builder.
Option D – Power BI is used for data visualization and analysis, not for processing incoming emails.
Option E – Azure Logic Apps can automate workflows but do not offer built-in AI capabilities for categorizing and prioritizing emails.

| EXAM FOCUS | "Power Automate with AI Builder efficiently categorizes and prioritizes emails in real-time." |
|---|---|
| CAUTION ALERT | "Azure Cognitive Services requires more complex setup compared to AI Builder." |

## QUESTION 37

Answer – A), B), D)

Option A – Dataverse with data governance policies ensures compliance and data integrity.
Option B – Power Automate facilitates seamless data flows across functions.
Option C – Azure DevOps helps with development and deployment but not directly with data flows and governance.
Option D – Regular data audits ensure data accuracy.
Option E – Separate systems can hinder seamless data flows and lead to data inconsistencies.

| EXAM FOCUS | *Implement Dataverse with data governance policies and Power Automate for seamless data flows.* |
|---|---|
| CAUTION ALERT | *Separate systems can hinder seamless data flows and lead to data inconsistencies.* |

## QUESTION 38

Answer – A), B), D)

Option A – Power Virtual Agents enhance customer experience through automated support.
Option B – AI Builder aids in fraud detection and prevention.
Option C – Storing data without encryption violates security and privacy requirements.
Option D – Dataverse security roles ensure compliance with financial regulations.
Option E – A user-friendly interface using Power Apps is important but must be paired with data security and compliance.

| EXAM FOCUS | *Use Power Virtual Agents for automated support and Dataverse security roles for compliance.* |
|---|---|
| CAUTION ALERT | *Do not store customer data in a public cloud without encryption; it violates security standards.* |

## QUESTION 39

Answer – A), B), E)

Option A – Dataverse with GCC compliance ensures adherence to government data security regulations.
Option B – AES encryption secures data at rest and in transit.
Option C – Public Wi-Fi is not secure for data transmission.
Option D – Regular security training is beneficial but not directly related to implementing secure communication and data transmission.
Option E – Multi-factor authentication (MFA) adds an extra layer of security for all users.

| EXAM FOCUS | *Use Dataverse with GCC compliance and AES encryption to meet stringent security regulations.* |
|---|---|
| CAUTION ALERT | *Do not use public Wi-Fi for data transmission; it is insecure and can lead to data breaches.* |

## QUESTION 40

Page | 176

Answer – A)

Option A – A canvas app with Dataverse allows for a customizable, secure, and real-time solution for managing customer loyalty points.
Option B – Model-driven apps are less flexible for mobile-specific use cases.
Option C – Power Automate can update loyalty points but is not sufficient on its own for developing a mobile app.
Option D – Dynamics 365 Commerce can manage retail operations but might be overkill for a simple loyalty program.
Option E – Azure SQL Database can store data but does not provide the app development capabilities needed for this solution.

| EXAM FOCUS | *"Canvas apps with Dataverse provide a flexible, real-time solution for mobile loyalty programs."* |
|---|---|
| CAUTION ALERT | *"Model-driven apps are less flexible for mobile-specific use cases."* |

## QUESTION 41

Answer – A), B), C)

Option A – Azure Kubernetes Service (AKS) is perfect for deploying microservices, ensuring scalability and manageability.
Option B – Azure DevOps is essential for implementing a continuous delivery pipeline, enabling rapid deployment and iteration.
Option C – Azure Cosmos DB provides high performance and low latency data access, which is crucial for a responsive application.
Option D – Power BI is excellent for data visualization but not ideal for monitoring application performance in real-time.
Option E – Azure Functions can handle compute tasks but are not specifically designed for microservices architecture or continuous delivery pipelines.

| EXAM FOCUS | *Deploy microservices with AKS and use Azure DevOps for continuous delivery.* |
|---|---|
| CAUTION ALERT | *Power BI is for data visualization, not real-time performance monitoring.* |

## QUESTION 42

Answer – B), C), E)

Option A – Displaying sensitive support ticket details to all users violates privacy principles and ethical data handling practices.
Option B – Implementing RBAC in Dataverse restricts access to sensitive data, ensuring privacy and security of support tickets.
Option C – Azure Security Center provides continuous compliance monitoring, ensuring that the solution adheres to data protection regulations.
Option D – Storing sensitive data in a publicly accessible site poses significant privacy and security risks.
Option E – Azure Data Factory can anonymize data before analysis, balancing data utility with privacy concerns and ensuring ethical data handling practices.

| EXAM FOCUS | Implement RBAC in Dataverse, use Azure Security Center, and Azure Data Factory for anonymization. |
|---|---|
| CAUTION ALERT | Avoid displaying sensitive data to all users; it compromises privacy. |

## QUESTION 43

Answer – A), B), D)

Option A – Azure Data Factory is suitable for ETL processes, ensuring seamless data exchange.
Option B – Implementing RBAC ensures that only authorized personnel have access to sensitive billing information, enhancing security.
Option C – Storing billing information in plain text is insecure and violates industry standards.
Option D – Azure API Management helps manage API calls and ensures compliance with industry standards.
Option E – Manual data transfers are prone to errors and do not ensure seamless data exchange.

| EXAM FOCUS | Implement Azure Data Factory for ETL and RBAC for secure data handling. |
|---|---|
| CAUTION ALERT | Storing billing information in plain text is insecure and non-compliant. |

## QUESTION 44

Answer – C)

Option A – Incorrect. Dataverse auditing tracks data changes within Dataverse but is not specialized in diagnosing synchronization issues between systems.
Option B – Incorrect. Microsoft Power Apps activity logging provides insights into user interactions within apps, not data synchronization processes.
Option C – Correct. Trace logging allows developers to view detailed logs that can help identify and diagnose issues in custom plugins and data synchronization processes.
Option D – Incorrect. WorkflowLog tracks workflows within Power Automate, which does not apply to custom plugin functionality in model-driven apps.
Option E – Incorrect. Power Automate analytics offers insights into the performance of automated workflows but doesn't provide the granular logging required for debugging custom plugins.

| EXAM FOCUS | "Please keep in mind, trace logging is essential to diagnose and resolve data synchronization issues." |
|---|---|
| CAUTION ALERT | "Avoid relying on activity logging; it doesn't provide detailed synchronization diagnostics." |

## QUESTION 45

Answer – A), B), D)

Option A – Azure Data Factory is designed to handle large volumes of data efficiently.
Option B – Data validation rules within Dataverse ensure data integrity during migration.
Option C – Manual data entry is not practical for large-scale migrations and is prone to errors.
Option D – Conducting a pilot migration helps identify and mitigate potential issues before full-scale migration.

Option E – Skipping post-migration validation can result in unnoticed data integrity issues, affecting overall data quality and reliability.

| EXAM FOCUS | Conduct a pilot migration to identify potential issues and ensure data integrity. |
|---|---|
| CAUTION ALERT | Skipping post-migration validation can result in unnoticed data integrity issues. |

## QUESTION 46

Answer – A), B), C)

Option A – Using DLP policies helps protect sensitive financial data from unauthorized access and data leaks.
Option B – Implementing RBAC with Azure AD ensures effective and secure management of user roles and permissions.
Option C – Regular security testing and audits help identify and mitigate security vulnerabilities and ensure compliance.
Option D – Using default security settings is not sufficient for ensuring robust security measures.
Option E – Performing compliance checks only during the initial rollout is insufficient for ensuring ongoing compliance and protection of sensitive data.

| EXAM FOCUS | "Use DLP policies and RBAC with Azure AD, and conduct regular security audits." |
|---|---|
| CAUTION ALERT | "Using default security settings is not sufficient for ensuring robust security." |

## QUESTION 47

Answer – A), B), E)

Option A – Using Power Automate analytics helps in monitoring the performance of workflows and identifying issues.
Option B – Implementing logging and tracing for flow activities provides detailed insights into the execution of flows, aiding in troubleshooting and optimization.
Option C – Ignoring performance metrics can lead to inefficiencies and unaddressed performance issues.
Option D – Optimizing flows by reducing unnecessary actions ensures more efficient execution and better performance.
Option E – Conducting regular performance reviews and optimizations ensures that the processes remain efficient and effective over time.

| EXAM FOCUS | "You should use Power Automate analytics to monitor workflow performance effectively." |
|---|---|
| CAUTION ALERT | "Ignoring performance metrics can lead to inefficiencies and unresolved issues." |

## QUESTION 48

Answer – A), E)

Option A – Correct. Automating connection management ensures that the integration maintains consistent and secure connections without manual intervention, essential for healthcare data.
Option B – Incorrect. While service endpoint configuration is important, it's generally a one-time setup

and not a repetitive task that benefits significantly from automation.
Option C – Incorrect. Team records creation is less critical to the integration's performance and security.
Option D – Incorrect. Although upsert of reference data is crucial, it's not as impactful on security and automation of patient updates as other options.
Option E – Correct. Configuring webhooks to automate patient data updates enables real-time data synchronization, which is crucial for timely medical responses.

| EXAM FOCUS | "Automate connection management and configure webhooks for secure and reliable healthcare data exchange." |
|---|---|
| CAUTION ALERT | "Service endpoint configuration is essential but not as impactful for ongoing automation needs." |

## QUESTION 49

Answer – A), C), E)

Option A – Correct. Azure DevOps provides automated deployment and version control, essential for maintaining and updating solutions.
Option B – Incorrect. Azure Application Insights is useful for monitoring application performance but does not directly manage updates or deprecated features.
Option C – Correct. Scheduling regular update windows ensures updates are applied systematically and with minimal disruption.
Option D – Incorrect. The Solution Checker is useful for identifying issues but does not directly handle automated maintenance or updates.
Option E – Correct. Regularly reviewing Microsoft's product release notes and update logs helps keep track of deprecated features and necessary updates.

| EXAM FOCUS | "Use Azure DevOps for automated deployment and version control to maintain solution sustainability." |
|---|---|
| CAUTION ALERT | "Please keep in mind, failing to monitor updates can lead to feature deprecation." |

## QUESTION 50

Answer – A), B), D)

Option A – Correct. The Power BI Performance Analyzer helps identify performance bottlenecks in reports.
Option B – Correct. Optimizing DAX queries can significantly improve report performance.
Option C – Incorrect. Increasing capacity may not address the root cause of performance issues in the reports.
Option D – Correct. Implementing incremental data refresh helps manage large datasets more efficiently, improving performance.
Option E – Incorrect. While preprocessing data can help, it is not directly related to optimizing Power BI report performance.

| EXAM FOCUS | "Use Power BI Performance Analyzer to pinpoint report bottlenecks." |
|---|---|
| CAUTION ALERT | "Please keep in mind, simply increasing capacity might not resolve performance issues." |

# PRACTICE TEST 6 - QUESTIONS ONLY

## QUESTION 1

Your client, a global retail chain, wants to enhance their customer relationship management system using Microsoft Power Platform. The key business objectives are to improve customer engagement, increase sales, and streamline marketing efforts. You are tasked with aligning the solution with their business goals. The specific challenges are:
- Current CRM lacks integration with social media channels.
- Marketing campaigns are not personalized.
- Customer data is fragmented across systems.

What solutions would you implement to align the solution with business goals and measure its impact on business outcomes? Select two correct answers.

A) Use Power Automate to integrate CRM with social media APIs.
B) Implement AI Builder to personalize marketing campaigns.
C) Consolidate customer data in Dataverse.
D) Develop a Power BI dashboard to track customer engagement metrics.
E) Implement a custom model-driven app for marketing management.

## QUESTION 2

An international retail company wants to enhance its customer service experience by integrating their Dynamics 365 system with social media platforms for better engagement and service issue tracking. Which Dynamics 365 products should you recommend to meet these requirements? Select up to 2 answers.

A) Dynamics 365 Customer Service
B) Dynamics 365 Marketing
C) Dynamics 365 Customer Insights
D) Dynamics 365 Sales

## QUESTION 3

A global retail company is using Microsoft Power Platform to enhance its sales data analysis. The project involves understanding data requirements and ensuring data accuracy. The specific challenges are:
- Inconsistent data from multiple sources.
- Difficulty in generating real-time sales reports.
- Ensuring data accuracy and reliability.

What solutions would you recommend to address these challenges and ensure data accuracy? Select two correct answers.

A) Use Power BI dataflows to consolidate data from multiple sources.
B) Implement Dataverse to store and manage sales data.
C) Use AI Builder to predict sales trends.
D) Develop a Canvas App for real-time sales report generation.
E) Use Power Automate to validate data accuracy.

## QUESTION 4

For a financial institution aiming to automate loan approval processes while ensuring data security, which Microsoft technologies should be integrated? Select up to two answers.

A) Dynamics 365 Finance
B) Azure Security Center
C) Power Automate
D) Microsoft Teams
E) Power Virtual Agents

## QUESTION 5

A financial services company wants to implement a new customer data management system using Microsoft Power Platform. The project requires addressing regulatory and compliance considerations. The specific challenges are:
• Ensuring compliance with data privacy laws such as GDPR.
• Incorporating security measures to protect sensitive financial data.
• Conducting compliance verification and audits.
What actions would you take to address these challenges? Select two correct answers.

A) Use Dataverse to securely store customer data.
B) Implement DLP policies to prevent data breaches.
C) Use Azure API Management to manage data access.
D) Conduct regular compliance audits using Power BI.
E) Implement RBAC to control data access.

## QUESTION 6

A retail company is implementing a new inventory management system using Microsoft Power Platform. The project requires accurate cost estimation and budgeting for the project lifecycle. The specific challenges are:
• Estimating the initial setup costs.
• Budgeting for ongoing maintenance and support.
• Analyzing the return on investment (ROI) over five years.
What actions would you take to address these challenges? Select two correct answers.

A) Use Power BI to create a detailed cost estimation model.
B) Implement Dataverse to store and manage inventory data.
C) Use Power Automate to schedule maintenance tasks.
D) Conduct an ROI analysis using Power BI.
E) Develop a budget plan including contingency funds.

## QUESTION 7

A healthcare provider is developing a patient management system using Microsoft Power Platform. The project requires developing prototypes and proofs of concept. The specific challenges are:
• Creating a prototype for stakeholder validation.
• Gathering feedback from end users.

• Iterating on the design based on feedback.
What actions would you take to address these challenges? Select two correct answers.

A) Use Power Apps to create a model-driven app prototype.
B) Use Dataverse to store patient data.
C) Use Power BI to visualize patient data.
D) Conduct user workshops for feedback.
E) Implement Azure DevOps for project tracking.

## QUESTION 8

A healthcare organization is integrating their patient management system with Dynamics 365 using Microsoft Power Platform. The project requires planning for system and data integration. The specific challenges are:
• Ensuring seamless data flow between systems.
• Addressing security and compliance requirements.
• Handling data format differences.
What actions would you take to address these challenges? Select two correct answers.

A) Use Power Automate to create data integration flows.
B) Implement Dataverse as a central data repository.
C) Use Power BI to create compliance reports.
D) Develop custom connectors using Azure API Management.
E) Implement Azure Functions for data transformation.

## QUESTION 9

A multinational company is implementing a customer management system using Microsoft Power Platform. The project requires incorporating security and privacy by design. The specific challenges are:
• Ensuring data privacy for customer information.
• Implementing security measures at each development stage.
• Complying with global privacy laws.
What steps would you take to address these challenges? Select two correct answers.

A) Use Azure Security Center for security monitoring.
B) Implement RBAC for access control.
C) Use Power Automate for data processing.
D) Integrate Data Loss Prevention (DLP) policies.
E) Use Power Virtual Agents for customer support.

## QUESTION 10

A retail company is implementing a new inventory management system using Microsoft Power Platform. The project requires effective QA planning. The specific challenges are:
• Ensuring the solution meets quality standards.
• Implementing continuous quality improvement.
• Defining quality metrics and standards.
What steps would you take to address these challenges? Select three correct answers.

A) Develop a QA strategy aligned with project requirements.
B) Use Power Automate to automate testing processes.
C) Implement Power BI dashboards to monitor quality metrics.
D) Schedule regular QA reviews and feedback sessions.
E) Use Power Apps for real-time defect tracking.

**QUESTION 11**

A manufacturing company is implementing a new inventory management solution using Microsoft Power Platform. The specific challenges are:
• Managing multiple versions of the solution during development.
• Ensuring smooth release management.
• Planning for end-of-life migration of the legacy system.
What steps would you take to address these challenges? Select two correct answers.

A) Implement ALM using Azure DevOps for version control.
B) Use Power Automate for release notifications.
C) Develop a migration strategy for the legacy system using Dataverse.
D) Utilize Power BI to monitor solution performance.
E) Engage with stakeholders to ensure smooth transition.

**QUESTION 12**

A company is implementing Dynamics 365 Customer Service and needs to ensure seamless integration with their existing ERP system for customer data synchronization.
• The integration must be able to handle real-time data updates.
• The solution should ensure data security and compliance with industry standards.
As a solution architect, what components would you recommend for this integration?

A) Power Automate, Azure Logic Apps, Azure Key Vault
B) Data Export Service, Azure Service Bus, Power BI
C) Azure Data Factory, Power Automate, Azure AD
D) Power Automate, Azure API Management, Azure SQL Database
E) Azure Logic Apps, Azure API Management, Azure Key Vault

**QUESTION 13**

A software development company is adopting agile methodologies for its new project using the Microsoft Power Platform. As a solution architect, you need to address the following challenges:
• Implementing agile methodologies.
• Managing agile projects.
• Adapting to changes in agile environments.
Which tools and practices should you recommend to address these challenges? Select three correct answers.

A) Use Azure DevOps for sprint planning and tracking.
B) Implement Power Automate for automated workflows.
C) Use Dynamics 365 for project management.
D) Conduct daily stand-up meetings.

E) Utilize Dataverse for data storage and management.

## QUESTION 14

You are a solution architect tasked with implementing a data governance framework for a multinational corporation using Microsoft Power Platform. The challenges include:
- Establishing data governance frameworks.
- Defining roles and responsibilities in data stewardship.
- Ensuring compliance with data governance standards.

Which of the following steps should you prioritize? Select three correct answers.

A) Use Azure Policy to enforce data governance standards.
B) Assign Data Steward roles in Dataverse.
C) Implement Power BI for real-time data quality monitoring.
D) Develop a data governance policy document.
E) Utilize Azure Data Factory for ETL processes.

## QUESTION 15

You are leading a project to implement a custom CRM system using Microsoft Power Platform for a large retail company. The challenges include:
- Deciding between customization and configuration.
- Impact of customizations on maintenance.
- Balancing flexibility and standardization.

Which strategies should you adopt to address these challenges? Select three correct answers.

A) Use Power Apps model-driven apps for rapid application development with minimal customization.
B) Implement complex business logic using custom plugins.
C) Configure existing Dataverse entities instead of creating new ones.
D) Use Power Automate for workflow automation to minimize custom code.
E) Develop a custom API to integrate with external systems.

## QUESTION 16

A healthcare provider wants to streamline their patient intake process using Microsoft Power Platform. They need to validate patient information in real-time and send a confirmation email once the information is verified.
- The solution must integrate with their existing EHR system.
- It should automate the validation and email processes.

Which components should you use to implement this solution? Select two answers.

A) Power BI
B) Power Apps
C) Azure Logic Apps
D) Power Automate
E) Dynamics 365 Customer Service

## QUESTION 17

You are a solution architect tasked with implementing a new customer engagement solution using Microsoft Power Platform for a retail company. The project involves:
- Establishing governance structures for data management.
- Ensuring compliance with GDPR and other internal policies.
- Setting up auditing and reporting mechanisms.

Which approaches should you take to address these requirements? Select three correct answers.

A) Utilize Dataverse to centralize data management and ensure data integrity.
B) Implement DLP policies using Power Automate to prevent data loss.
C) Configure auditing in Power Apps to track data changes.
D) Use Azure Policy to enforce GDPR compliance.
E) Develop custom plugins to enhance data governance capabilities in Dynamics 365.

## QUESTION 18

A retail company is embarking on a digital transformation initiative using Microsoft Power Platform. The solution must:
- Support innovative approaches to solution design.
- Integrate disruptive technologies.
- Measure the success of the digital transformation.

You need to choose three actions to ensure the solution meets these requirements. Which three actions should you take? (Select three)

A) Utilize AI Builder to incorporate AI-driven insights.
B) Implement Azure IoT Hub for integrating IoT devices.
C) Use Power BI to create dashboards for measuring KPIs.
D) Develop custom APIs for integrating third-party systems.
E) Use Azure Functions to handle complex business logic.

## QUESTION 19

A healthcare organization is implementing a new patient data management system using Microsoft Power Platform. The solution must:
- Ensure data security.
- Comply with data protection laws.
- Prevent data breaches.

Which three actions should you take to meet these requirements? (Select three)

A) Implement Role-Based Access Control (RBAC) in Power Apps.
B) Use Power Automate to enforce data loss prevention (DLP) policies.
C) Encrypt data at rest using Dataverse.
D) Enable Multi-Factor Authentication (MFA) for all users.
E) Use AI Builder to analyze patient data.

## QUESTION 20

A retail company is developing a product catalog using Microsoft Dataverse. They need to ensure that

product information is categorized correctly and that products can be related to multiple categories.
• The solution must support many-to-many relationships.
• It should allow for easy updates to product categories.
Which components should you include in the data model design? Select two answers.

A) Lookups
B) Option sets
C) Many-to-many relationships
D) Rollup columns
E) Business rules

## QUESTION 21

You are designing a Power Platform solution for a multinational company that must comply with GDPR and ensure data security. The solution must:
• Implement data protection and privacy standards.
• Comply with GDPR regulations.
• Provide secure data access. Which three measures should you implement? (Select three)

A) Use Dataverse for secure data storage.
B) Implement role-based access control (RBAC) using Azure AD.
C) Enable Data Loss Prevention (DLP) policies.
D) Use Azure Cognitive Services for data processing.
E) Encrypt data at rest and in transit using Azure Key Vault.

## QUESTION 22

A global retail company is implementing a Power Platform solution integrated with Azure to handle large volumes of data generated from their stores worldwide. The solution must:
• Ensure data integrity and quality.
• Optimize data storage for performance.
• Implement advanced data modeling techniques.
Which two actions should you recommend? (Select two)

A) Use Dataverse for data storage and management.
B) Implement incremental data loads using Azure Data Factory.
C) Use Power BI for data visualization.
D) Apply Data Loss Prevention (DLP) policies.
E) Design data models using Power Query.

## QUESTION 23

You are designing a Power Platform solution for a global e-commerce company. They need to ensure that the user interface (UI) is intuitive and accessible to a diverse user base. The solution must:
• Adhere to principles of user-centered design.
• Be accessible and inclusive.
• Balance customization and standardization.
Which two approaches should you recommend? (Select two)

A) Conduct user persona workshops.
B) Use standard Power Platform templates without customization.
C) Implement WCAG (Web Content Accessibility Guidelines) standards.
D) Design interfaces with minimal user testing.
E) Use Power Virtual Agents for user feedback collection.

## QUESTION 24

A manufacturing company uses Dynamics 365 for managing its sales and customer service operations. They also have an existing on-premises ERP system. The company wants to integrate their ERP with Dynamics 365 to streamline their sales order processing. The integration needs to ensure data consistency and must be secure, scalable, and follow Microsoft's best practices. What integration approach should the company use to connect their on-premises ERP with Dynamics 365?

A) Use Data Export Service
B) Use Azure Service Bus
C) Use Power Automate with an on-premises data gateway
D) Use Direct SQL queries
E) Use Custom APIs

## QUESTION 25

A retail company wants to implement Power BI to analyze sales data and generate real-time business insights. The solution must:
• Provide interactive dashboards for different regions.
• Include AI-driven insights to forecast sales trends.
• Ensure data security and compliance.
What three strategies should you implement? (Select three)

A) Use Power BI Service for real-time dashboards.
B) Implement Azure Machine Learning for AI-driven insights.
C) Use Power Automate for data updates.
D) Enable Row-Level Security (RLS) in Power BI.
E) Utilize Data Loss Prevention (DLP) policies.

## QUESTION 26

A retail company wants to implement AI-driven product recommendations using Power Platform. The solution must:
• Analyze customer purchase history.
• Provide personalized recommendations.
• Integrate with the existing e-commerce platform.
Which components should you use? (Select three)

A) AI Builder for analyzing purchase history.
B) Power Automate for triggering recommendations.
C) Dataverse for storing customer data.
D) Azure Cognitive Services for recommendation algorithms.
E) Power BI for visualizing recommendations.

## QUESTION 27

A multinational corporation needs to implement a disaster recovery plan for its Power Platform solutions. The plan must:
• Ensure high availability of critical applications.
• Automate backup and recovery processes.
• Test and validate recovery procedures regularly.
Which components and practices should be included in the disaster recovery plan? (Select three)

A) Power Platform Admin Center for automated backups.
B) Azure Site Recovery for disaster recovery.
C) Power Automate for automated workflows.
D) Azure Backup for data protection.
E) Power BI for monitoring recovery procedures.

## QUESTION 28

A healthcare organization uses Dynamics 365 for managing patient records and appointments. They are implementing a new system to integrate with a third-party scheduling API. The integration must ensure real-time updates of patient appointments and follow strict data privacy regulations. You plan to use Power Automate to handle the integration. What trigger should you use to ensure that updates to patient appointments are processed in real-time?

A) Scheduled Flow
B) Manual Trigger
C) When a record is updated in Dataverse
D) Recurrence Trigger
E) When a new record is created in Dataverse

## QUESTION 29

You are a Microsoft Power Platform Solution Architect working on a project for a healthcare client. They need to navigate complex compliance and regulatory landscapes, particularly concerning data protection and privacy laws.
 1. Ensuring compliance with HIPAA regulations for patient data.
 2. Implementing tools for continuous compliance monitoring.
 3. Automating compliance reporting to reduce manual efforts.
 What measures should you implement to ensure the client meets these compliance requirements? Select two answers.

A) Use Dataverse to securely store patient data with role-based access controls.
B) Implement Power Automate flows for real-time compliance reporting.
C) Use third-party storage solutions to handle sensitive patient data.
D) Develop custom applications using Power Apps without integrating compliance checks.
E) Use Microsoft Compliance Manager to monitor and manage compliance.

## QUESTION 30

A client in the financial services sector wants to leverage advanced analytics to generate actionable

insights from their data. They need a solution that integrates external data sources and applies predictive analytics to improve decision-making.
1. Integrating multiple external data sources for comprehensive analysis.
2. Applying predictive analytics to forecast financial trends.
3. Ensuring the solution generates actionable insights for decision-making.
What solution would you recommend to achieve these objectives? Select two answers.

A) Use Power BI to create interactive dashboards integrating external data sources.
B) Implement AI Builder to develop predictive models for financial forecasting.
C) Store all data in a single Excel file for analysis.
D) Use Azure Data Factory to manage and integrate data from various sources.
E) Develop custom machine learning models outside the Power Platform.

## QUESTION 31

You are a Microsoft Power Platform Solution Architect working with a client who wants to implement a new solution using Power Platform. They are concerned about user adoption and potential resistance to change within their organization.
1. Facilitating organizational change to ensure smooth implementation.
2. Developing strategies to promote user adoption.
3. Managing resistance and promoting acceptance.
What steps would you recommend to address these concerns? Select two answers.

A) Conduct regular training sessions using Power Apps and Power Automate.
B) Implement change management strategies focusing on user engagement.
C) Ignore resistance and focus on technical implementation.
D) Use Power BI to measure user engagement and adoption rates.
E) Develop custom applications without involving end-users in the design process.

## QUESTION 32

A logistics company uses Dynamics 365 Field Service to manage its fleet and deliveries. They want to implement an IoT solution to monitor vehicle health in real-time and trigger maintenance workflows in Dynamics 365 based on specific thresholds. The solution must ensure seamless integration with Dynamics 365. Which service should they use to achieve this?

A) Azure IoT Central
B) Power Automate
C) Dynamics 365 Supply Chain Management
D) Power BI
E) Azure Synapse Analytics

## QUESTION 33

You are a Microsoft Power Platform Solution Architect working with a client who wants to implement advanced customization using Power Apps and Power Automate. They need a solution that includes custom connectors and API integrations while managing the complexity of the custom solutions.
1. Implementing advanced Power Apps and Power Automate customizations.
2. Integrating custom connectors and APIs.

3. Managing complexity in custom solutions.
What steps would you recommend to achieve these objectives? Select two answers.

A) Use Azure API Management to create and manage custom connectors.
B) Implement Dataverse for storing and managing data securely.
C) Ignore API integrations to reduce complexity.
D) Use Power BI to visualize and track custom solution performance.
E) Follow best practices for maintainable custom code including code reviews and documentation.

## QUESTION 34

Your company is integrating a legacy CRM system with Dynamics 365. You need to ensure that the data migration process minimizes disruption to ongoing operations. The project team must:
• Maintain data integrity and consistency.
• Ensure minimal downtime during migration.
• Address potential data quality issues pre-migration. What are the best approaches to achieve these objectives? (Select 2 answers)

A) Perform a big bang migration over a weekend.
B) Use an ETL tool to incrementally migrate data during off-peak hours.
C) Export data to CSV files and manually import them into Dynamics 365.
D) Develop custom scripts to migrate data in real-time.
E) Use Azure Data Factory for orchestrating and automating data migration.

## QUESTION 35

Your organization is implementing a Power Apps solution to manage customer interactions. The solution needs to scale to handle increased demand during peak times. The project requirements include:
• Efficiently scaling the solution without downtime.
• Ensuring optimal resource allocation.
• Planning for future growth. What strategies should you adopt? (Select 3 answers)

A) Implement auto-scaling using Azure App Services.
B) Use Power Automate to handle workflows dynamically.
C) Optimize database performance with Dataverse.
D) Utilize Azure Service Bus for message queuing.
E) Schedule regular manual scaling during peak times.

## QUESTION 36

A healthcare provider uses Dynamics 365 Customer Engagement to manage patient records. They want to integrate a third-party electronic health record (EHR) system to synchronize patient data. The integration must comply with health data privacy regulations and ensure real-time updates. Which categorizations should you consider for this integration?

A) Batch
B) Time-sensitive
C) Regulated
D) Volume

E) Licensed

## QUESTION 37

Your company is deploying a Power Platform solution globally. The deployment must:
- Ensure compliance with multi-region data residency laws.
- Optimize performance for users in different regions.
- Handle geo-redundancy for high availability. What strategies should you implement? (Select 3 answers)

A) Deploy separate instances of the solution in each region.
B) Use Dataverse with multi-geo capabilities.
C) Implement Azure Traffic Manager for load balancing.
D) Store all data in a central location.
E) Use Power BI with dataflows for regional data processing.

## QUESTION 38

Your organization is deploying a new Power Platform solution to enhance user experience in a customer service application. The solution must:
- Map and optimize the user journey.
- Personalize user interactions based on their profiles.
- Implement feedback loops for continuous improvement. What strategies should you adopt? (Select 3 answers)

A) Use Power Virtual Agents to automate and personalize customer interactions.
B) Implement AI Builder to analyze user feedback and identify improvement areas.
C) Use a static interface design for all users.
D) Create user journey maps to identify pain points and optimize processes.
E) Schedule periodic reviews and updates based on user feedback.

## QUESTION 39

You are designing a business continuity plan for a financial services company using the Power Platform. The solution must:
- Ensure critical business functions are maintained during a disruption.
- Identify potential business risks.
- Implement recovery strategies and plans. What steps should you take? (Select 3 answers)

A) Use Dataverse for secure and scalable data storage.
B) Implement Azure Site Recovery for disaster recovery.
C) Conduct a risk assessment to identify potential threats.
D) Use manual processes to manage business continuity.
E) Schedule regular drills to test the continuity plan.

## QUESTION 40

A global retail company uses Dynamics 365 Sales to manage their sales operations. They want to implement a solution where sales representatives can quickly generate quotes based on predefined templates and send them to customers for approval. The process must be automated and integrated with Dynamics 365. What should they use to achieve this?

A) Power Automate with Word Template action
B) Power Apps with manual email sending
C) Dynamics 365 Customer Insights
D) Azure Functions
E) Power BI with embedded reports

## QUESTION 41

A retail company is looking to scale their Power Platform solution to accommodate a growing user base and increasing data volume. The solution must:
• Utilize modular architecture for flexibility.
• Implement strategies for handling large data sets.
• Ensure performance tuning for scalability. What should you implement? (Select 3 answers)

A) Use Dataverse for scalable data storage.
B) Implement Azure Functions for processing large data sets.
C) Use Power BI Premium for enhanced data analytics.
D) Design modular components using Power Apps Component Framework (PCF).
E) Use Azure Monitor for performance tuning and monitoring.

## QUESTION 42

A manufacturing company has implemented a Power Platform solution to monitor equipment performance. To ensure long-term solution stability, they need to:
• Monitor solution health and performance continuously.
• Detect and resolve issues proactively.
• Perform regular maintenance and updates. What strategies should be implemented? (Select 3 answers)

A) Use Power BI to visualize performance data and set up alerts for anomalies.
B) Implement Dataverse with role-based access control (RBAC) for secure data management.
C) Use Azure Monitor to track solution health and performance metrics.
D) Rely on manual checks to identify and resolve issues.
E) Schedule regular updates and maintenance using Azure DevOps pipelines.

## QUESTION 43

A retail company wants to develop advanced reporting capabilities to analyze sales performance across multiple regions. They need to:
• Aggregate sales data from various sources.
• Provide real-time insights and intelligence.
• Create custom dashboards for different user roles. What tools and techniques should they use? (Select 3 answers)

A) Use Power BI to create interactive dashboards.
B) Implement Azure Data Factory for ETL processes.
C) Use Excel for manual data aggregation and analysis.

D) Utilize Power Automate to schedule data refreshes.
E) Store data in an unstructured format for easier access.

## QUESTION 44

A multinational corporation uses a custom-developed Power Platform solution to handle international transactions. Recently, discrepancies in transaction data have been reported post-synchronization between Power Platform and their ERP system.
• Handle international transactions.
• Ensure accurate data synchronization.
Which tool should you use to identify and resolve synchronization errors?

A) Power BI analytics
B) Microsoft Power Apps activity logging
C) Dataverse auditing
D) Entity store
E) Data integrator

## QUESTION 45

A company is implementing a new CRM system using Dynamics 365 and Power Platform. They need to ensure that users are properly trained to use the new system effectively. Their requirements include:
• Comprehensive training materials.
• Effective user support models.
• Feedback incorporation to improve training. How should they approach this task?

A) Develop interactive online training modules using Power Apps.
B) Use Power BI to create feedback surveys and analyze responses.
C) Provide a dedicated support team for ongoing user assistance.
D) Use a manual feedback collection process.
E) Implement one-time training sessions and no follow-up.

## QUESTION 46

You are tasked with optimizing the performance of a Power Platform solution that experiences significant delays during data processing. The key requirements are:
• Identify performance bottlenecks.
• Optimize resource usage.
• Monitor and improve performance metrics. What steps should you take to achieve these goals?

A) Use Power Platform's performance monitoring tools to identify bottlenecks.
B) Scale up the Azure SQL Database to handle increased load.
C) Implement caching mechanisms to reduce data retrieval times.
D) Avoid performance monitoring and focus on adding more resources.
E) Ignore the existing performance issues.

## QUESTION 47

A healthcare organization is implementing a Power BI solution to monitor patient data. To ensure

effective monitoring and analytics, they need to:
• Set up real-time monitoring and alerts.
• Analyze user behavior and feedback.
• Develop comprehensive reports and dashboards. What steps should they take?
Select 3 answers.

A) Use Power BI's real-time streaming capabilities.
B) Implement Azure Monitor for real-time alerts.
C) Ignore user feedback and focus only on data.
D) Create custom dashboards in Power BI.
E) Use Power BI's usage metrics to analyze user behavior.

## QUESTION 48

In a retail environment, a Power Platform solution is used to integrate point of sale (POS) systems across multiple stores with the central inventory management system. Frequent errors in data synchronization lead to inventory discrepancies. You need to streamline the synchronization process.
• Reduce data synchronization errors.
• Streamline inventory management.
What two automation activities would best achieve these improvements?

A) Webhook configuration
B) Service endpoint configuration
C) Connection management
D) Upsert of reference data
E) Automated testing of integrations

## QUESTION 49

Your organization is implementing a new Dynamics 365 Customer Engagement solution with customizations. As a solution architect, you need to manage these customizations efficiently. The key requirements are:
• Ensuring customizations do not disrupt future upgrades.
• Balancing custom and out-of-the-box features.
• Implementing lifecycle management of customizations.
What strategies should you implement? (Select 3 answers)

A) Use managed solutions for deploying customizations.
B) Regularly review and update customizations to align with new releases.
C) Implement Power Automate flows to handle lifecycle management.
D) Leverage out-of-the-box features before considering custom development.
E) Use Azure DevOps for version control and CI/CD.

## QUESTION 50

Your organization is implementing a new Power Platform solution with a focus on sustainability and eco-friendly practices. As a solution architect, you need to ensure the solution minimizes environmental impact and promotes eco-awareness. The key requirements are:
- Implementing sustainable technology practices.
- Reducing energy consumption.
- Promoting eco-awareness among users.

What strategies should you implement? (Select 3 answers)

A) Use Power BI to monitor and report on energy consumption metrics.
B) Implement serverless computing using Azure Functions to reduce energy use.
C) Develop an eco-awareness campaign using Power Virtual Agents.
D) Use Dataverse to track sustainability metrics.
E) Schedule regular downtime for maintenance to reduce energy usage.

# PRACTICE TEST 6 - ANSWERS ONLY

## QUESTION 1

Answer – B), C)

Option A – Integrating CRM with social media is useful but does not address personalized marketing or data consolidation.
Option B – AI Builder can analyze data and personalize marketing campaigns, aligning with business goals.
Option C – Consolidating customer data in Dataverse will improve data management, addressing one of the key challenges.
Option D – Power BI dashboards help measure impact but do not enhance engagement or sales directly.
Option E – A custom app for marketing management can streamline efforts but does not directly personalize campaigns.

| | |
|---|---|
| **EXAM FOCUS** | *You should integrate AI Builder to personalize marketing and consolidate data in Dataverse for enhanced CRM functionality.* |
| **CAUTION ALERT** | *Stay cautious, focusing on integration without addressing data fragmentation won't fully solve CRM challenges.* |

## QUESTION 2

Answer – A), B)

Option A – Correct. Dynamics 365 Customer Service offers tools and capabilities that allow seamless integration with social media platforms, enabling effective engagement and service issue resolution directly from social media inquiries.
Option B – Correct. Dynamics 365 Marketing includes features that enhance customer engagement through social media channels, complementing the customer service efforts by providing comprehensive tools for managing interactions and campaigns.
Option C – Incorrect. While Dynamics 365 Customer Insights provides valuable customer data and trend analysis, it does not directly facilitate social media integration for service management.
Option D – Incorrect. Dynamics 365 Sales is primarily focused on managing sales processes and does not directly support service issue tracking or social media integration.

| | |
|---|---|
| **EXAM FOCUS** | *"Dynamics 365 Customer Service and Marketing integrate well with social media for enhanced customer engagement."* |
| **CAUTION ALERT** | *"Customer Insights provides analysis but not direct social media integration."* |

## QUESTION 3

Answer – A), E)

Option A – Power BI dataflows can consolidate data from multiple sources, addressing inconsistency.
Option B – Dataverse helps manage data but does not address data consolidation directly.
Option C – AI Builder can predict trends but does not ensure data accuracy.

Page | 197

Option D – A Canvas App can generate reports but does not address data accuracy.
Option E – Power Automate can validate data accuracy, ensuring reliable data.

| EXAM FOCUS | *Consolidate sales data with Power BI dataflows and validate accuracy using Power Automate to ensure reliable data.* |
|---|---|
| CAUTION ALERT | *Remember, generating real-time reports alone won't address data consistency or accuracy challenges.* |

## QUESTION 4

Answer – A) & C)

Option A – Correct. Dynamics 365 Finance is ideal for handling financial operations and integrating with loan processing workflows.
Option B – Incorrect. Azure Security Center is crucial for security but does not directly integrate into workflow automation for loan processing.
Option C – Correct. Power Automate can be used to automate the loan approval processes efficiently.
Option D – Incorrect. Microsoft Teams is for collaboration, not specific to financial workflow automation.
Option E – Incorrect. Power Virtual Agents are for creating bots, not directly involved in the loan approval automation or integration.

| EXAM FOCUS | *"Dynamics 365 Finance integrates well with financial workflows, enhancing automation."* |
|---|---|
| CAUTION ALERT | *"Remember, Azure Security Center is crucial for security but not for loan processing workflows."* |

## QUESTION 5

Answer – A), E)

Option A – Dataverse provides secure storage for customer data, ensuring compliance with data privacy laws.
Option B – DLP policies prevent data breaches but do not address compliance verification.
Option C – Azure API Management is useful for managing data access but does not directly ensure compliance.
Option D – Power BI is useful for data analysis but not directly for conducting compliance audits.
Option E – RBAC controls data access, protecting sensitive financial data.

| EXAM FOCUS | *Use Dataverse for secure storage and RBAC for data access control to comply with privacy laws.* |
|---|---|
| CAUTION ALERT | *Please keep in mind, DLP policies are important but won't ensure compliance verification alone.* |

## QUESTION 6

Answer – A), E)

Option A – Power BI can be used to create a detailed cost estimation model.
Option B – Dataverse is useful for managing data but does not directly address cost estimation or budgeting.
Option C – Power Automate is useful for scheduling tasks but does not address cost estimation or

budgeting.
Option D – Power BI is useful for ROI analysis but not specifically for budgeting.
Option E – Developing a budget plan including contingency funds addresses ongoing maintenance and support costs.

| | |
|---|---|
| **EXAM FOCUS** | *Use Power BI for cost estimation and develop a budget plan with contingency funds to manage costs.* |
| **CAUTION ALERT** | *Please keep in mind, Dataverse won't directly address cost estimation or budgeting needs.* |

## QUESTION 7

Answer – A), D)

Option A – Power Apps can be used to create a model-driven app prototype for stakeholder validation.
Option B – Dataverse is useful for storing patient data but not directly related to prototyping.
Option C – Power BI is useful for data visualization but not directly for prototyping.
Option D – Conducting user workshops for feedback helps gather input from end users.
Option E – Azure DevOps is useful for project tracking but not directly related to prototyping.

| | |
|---|---|
| **EXAM FOCUS** | *Create prototypes with Power Apps and gather feedback through user workshops for effective iteration.* |
| **CAUTION ALERT** | *Remember, Dataverse is useful for data storage but not directly for prototyping or feedback gathering.* |

## QUESTION 8

Answer – A), B)

Option A – Power Automate can create data integration flows to ensure seamless data flow.
Option B – Implementing Dataverse as a central data repository helps address data format differences.
Option C – Power BI is useful for reporting but not directly related to planning for system and data integration.
Option D – Developing custom connectors using Azure API Management is useful but not a primary action for planning integration.
Option E – Azure Functions are useful for data transformation but not a primary action for planning integration.

| | |
|---|---|
| **EXAM FOCUS** | *Use Power Automate for integration flows and Dataverse as a central data repository for seamless integration.* |
| **CAUTION ALERT** | *Stay cautious, Power BI is for reporting, not planning integration.* |

## QUESTION 9

Answer – B), D)

Option A – Azure Security Center is useful for security monitoring but not directly related to incorporating security and privacy by design.
Option B – Implementing RBAC ensures access control, aligning with security measures.

Option C – Power Automate is useful for data processing but not directly related to security and privacy by design.
Option D – Integrating DLP policies helps in protecting sensitive data, aligning with privacy requirements.
Option E – Power Virtual Agents is useful for customer support but not directly related to security and privacy by design.

| EXAM FOCUS | Implement RBAC for access control and integrate DLP policies for data protection to comply with global privacy laws. |
|---|---|
| CAUTION ALERT | Stay cautious, Power Automate is useful for automation, not for ensuring security and privacy by design. |

## QUESTION 10

Answer – A), C), D)

Option A – Developing a QA strategy ensures alignment with project requirements.
Option B – Power Automate can automate processes, but not specifically testing.
Option C – Implementing Power BI dashboards helps monitor quality metrics in real-time.
Option D – Regular QA reviews ensure continuous quality improvement.
Option E – Power Apps can be used for defect tracking but does not directly address the main challenges.

| EXAM FOCUS | Develop a QA strategy, use Power BI for monitoring, and schedule regular QA reviews for continuous improvement. |
|---|---|
| CAUTION ALERT | Keep in mind, Power Automate can automate processes but not specifically testing. |

## QUESTION 11

Answer – A), C)

Option A – Implementing ALM using Azure DevOps ensures proper version control.
Option B – Power Automate can help with notifications but is not critical for release management.
Option C – Developing a migration strategy using Dataverse ensures smooth transition from legacy systems.
Option D – Power BI can monitor performance but is not directly related to lifecycle management.
Option E – Engaging with stakeholders is important but not specific to technical solution lifecycle management.

| EXAM FOCUS | Implement ALM with Azure DevOps and develop a migration strategy using Dataverse. |
|---|---|
| CAUTION ALERT | Stay cautious, Power Automate is useful for notifications but not critical for release management. |

## QUESTION 12

Answer – A)

Option A – Correct choice as Power Automate and Azure Logic Apps handle real-time updates and Azure Key Vault ensures data security.

Option B – Data Export Service and Azure Service Bus are not ideal for real-time updates.
Option C – Azure Data Factory is more suitable for batch processing.
Option D – Azure SQL Database may not be necessary if the data is already managed within the ERP and CRM systems.
Option E – While good for integration and security, Azure Logic Apps alone might not suffice for real-time synchronization without Power Automate.

| EXAM FOCUS | "Power Automate and Azure Logic Apps ensure real-time data synchronization securely." |
|---|---|
| CAUTION ALERT | "Avoid using solutions that can't handle real-time updates efficiently." |

## QUESTION 13

Answer – A), D), E)

Option A – Azure DevOps is essential for sprint planning and tracking.
Option B – Power Automate is useful but more for automated workflows than agile project management.
Option C – Dynamics 365 is useful but more for project management than agile methodologies.
Option D – Daily stand-up meetings are a core agile practice.
Option E – Dataverse is beneficial for data storage and management, aligning with agile environments.

| EXAM FOCUS | Use Azure DevOps for sprint planning and conduct daily stand-up meetings to manage agile projects effectively. |
|---|---|
| CAUTION ALERT | Please keep in mind, focusing only on automated workflows can overlook essential agile practices. |

## QUESTION 14

Answer – A), B), D)

Option A – Azure Policy helps enforce data governance standards across the organization.
Option B – Assigning Data Steward roles in Dataverse is crucial for defining responsibilities in data stewardship.
Option C – Power BI is useful for monitoring but not directly related to establishing a governance framework.
Option D – Developing a data governance policy document is essential for establishing a framework.
Option E – Azure Data Factory is useful for ETL processes but less critical for establishing data governance frameworks.

| EXAM FOCUS | Use Azure Policy to enforce standards, and assign Data Steward roles in Dataverse for effective data governance. |
|---|---|
| CAUTION ALERT | Stay cautious, focusing only on monitoring tools like Power BI can miss governance framework essentials. |

## QUESTION 15

Answer – A), C), D)

Option A – Power Apps model-driven apps allow rapid development with less customization, balancing flexibility and standardization.
Option B – Custom plugins increase maintenance complexity and should be avoided unless necessary.
Option C – Configuring existing Dataverse entities reduces customization, aiding in maintenance.
Option D – Power Automate provides workflow automation with less custom code, reducing maintenance burden.
Option E – Custom APIs increase complexity and maintenance efforts.

| EXAM FOCUS | Remember, Power Apps model-driven apps allow for rapid development with minimal customization. |
|---|---|
| CAUTION ALERT | Avoid unnecessary custom plugins as they increase maintenance complexity. |

## QUESTION 16

Answer – B), D)

Option A – Power BI is for analytics and reporting, not process automation.
Option B – Correct choice as Power Apps can be used to build the intake form.
Option C – Azure Logic Apps can be used for integration but requires more custom development.
Option D – Correct choice as Power Automate can handle real-time validation and sending confirmation emails.
Option E – Dynamics 365 Customer Service is more suited for customer support rather than process automation.

| EXAM FOCUS | "Power Apps and Power Automate effectively handle real-time validation and process automation." |
|---|---|
| CAUTION ALERT | "Don't overlook the need for automated processes; Power BI is not for process automation." |

## QUESTION 17

Answer – A), B), C)

Option A – Utilizing Dataverse helps centralize data management and maintain data integrity.
Option B – Implementing DLP policies using Power Automate prevents data loss and ensures compliance.
Option C – Configuring auditing in Power Apps allows for tracking data changes and maintaining compliance.
Option D – Azure Policy is useful but not directly integrated with Power Platform for GDPR compliance.
Option E – Developing custom plugins adds complexity and maintenance overhead.

| EXAM FOCUS | Use Dataverse for data management, implement DLP policies in Power Automate, and configure auditing in Power Apps. |
|---|---|
| CAUTION ALERT | Developing custom plugins increases complexity; avoid unless necessary for data governance. |

## QUESTION 18

Answer – A), B), C)

Option A – Utilizing AI Builder incorporates AI-driven insights, supporting innovation.
Option B – Implementing Azure IoT Hub integrates IoT devices, supporting disruptive technology

integration.
Option C – Using Power BI to create dashboards helps measure the success of the digital transformation.
Option D – Developing custom APIs can add complexity and may not be necessary for innovation.
Option E – Azure Functions handle complex business logic but do not directly support innovation and disruption in the solution.

| EXAM FOCUS | *AI Builder for AI insights; Azure IoT Hub for IoT integration; Power BI for KPI dashboards.* |
|---|---|
| CAUTION ALERT | *Custom APIs can add complexity; use built-in features when possible.* |

## QUESTION 19

Answer – A), B), D)

Option A – Implementing RBAC in Power Apps ensures data security.
Option B – Using Power Automate to enforce DLP policies helps in complying with data protection laws.
Option C – Encrypting data at rest is good but not essential for the primary requirements.
Option D – Enabling MFA for all users prevents data breaches.
Option E – Using AI Builder to analyze patient data does not directly address data security or compliance requirements.

| EXAM FOCUS | *Implement RBAC in Power Apps and use Power Automate for enforcing DLP policies.* |
|---|---|
| CAUTION ALERT | *Don't overlook the importance of enabling Multi-Factor Authentication (MFA).* |

## QUESTION 20

Answer – A), C)

Option A – Correct choice as Lookups can be used to define many-to-many relationships through intermediate tables.
Option B – Option sets are used for picklist values, not for defining relationships.
Option C – Correct choice as Many-to-many relationships directly support the requirement.
Option D – Rollup columns are for aggregating data, not for relationships.
Option E – Business rules enforce validation rules, not for defining relationships.

| EXAM FOCUS | *"Implement Lookups and Many-to-many relationships for flexible and dynamic data categorization."* |
|---|---|
| CAUTION ALERT | *"Option sets and Rollup columns are not designed for defining relationships between entities."* |

## QUESTION 21

Answer – A), B), E)

Option A – Dataverse ensures secure data storage, complying with GDPR.
Option B – RBAC using Azure AD provides secure data access.
Option C – DLP policies ensure data protection but are not sufficient alone for GDPR compliance.
Option D – Azure Cognitive Services is useful for data processing but not directly for GDPR compliance.
Option E – Encrypting data at rest and in transit using Azure Key Vault ensures data protection and privacy standards.

| EXAM FOCUS | Use Dataverse for secure data storage and Azure Key Vault for encryption. |
| --- | --- |
| CAUTION ALERT | Ensure compliance with GDPR by implementing robust data protection measures. |

## QUESTION 22

Answer – A), B)

Option A – Dataverse ensures data integrity and quality with managed data storage.
Option B – Incremental data loads using Azure Data Factory optimize data storage for performance.
Option C – Power BI is useful for data visualization but not directly for data integrity or storage optimization.
Option D – DLP policies are important for data protection but not directly for data integrity or advanced modeling.
Option E – Power Query helps with data transformation but not specifically with advanced data modeling techniques.

| EXAM FOCUS | Dataverse and Azure Data Factory are your go-to for maintaining data integrity and optimizing storage performance. |
| --- | --- |
| CAUTION ALERT | Don't be misled by options like DLP policies or Power BI that don't address core requirements like data integrity or advanced modeling. |

## QUESTION 23

Answer – A), C)

Option A – Conducting user persona workshops ensures that the design is user-centered and considers diverse needs.
Option B – Using standard templates without customization may not address specific user needs and may not be as intuitive.
Option C – Implementing WCAG standards ensures the interface is accessible and inclusive.
Option D – Designing interfaces with minimal user testing does not align with user-centered design principles.
Option E – Power Virtual Agents can be used for feedback but are not directly related to UI design.

| EXAM FOCUS | You should conduct user persona workshops and implement WCAG standards for intuitive and accessible UI design. |
| --- | --- |
| CAUTION ALERT | Stay cautious about using standard templates without customization; they might not meet specific user needs. |

## QUESTION 24

Answer – C)

Option A – Data Export Service is mainly used for exporting data to an Azure SQL database, not for real-time integration between systems.
Option B – Azure Service Bus is useful for messaging and decoupling applications but requires additional setup and isn't as straightforward as Power Automate for this scenario.
Option C – Power Automate with an on-premises data gateway allows for secure, scalable, and

Microsoft-recommended integration, ensuring data consistency between the on-premises ERP and Dynamics 365.

Option D – Direct SQL queries pose security risks and do not follow Microsoft's best practices for integration.

Option E – Custom APIs can be used but require extensive development and maintenance, making it less optimal compared to Power Automate.

| EXAM FOCUS | "Power Automate with an on-premises data gateway ensures secure and scalable integration." |
|---|---|
| CAUTION ALERT | "Avoid direct SQL queries due to security risks and lack of best practices." |

## QUESTION 25

Answer – A), B), D)

Option A – Power BI Service provides real-time dashboard capabilities.
Option B – Azure Machine Learning can be integrated for AI-driven insights and sales forecasting.
Option C – Power Automate is useful for data updates but not directly related to AI-driven insights or data security.
Option D – Enabling Row-Level Security (RLS) ensures data security and compliance by restricting data access based on user roles.
Option E – Data Loss Prevention (DLP) policies are essential for data security but not directly related to the key focus area of real-time analytics and AI-driven insights.

| EXAM FOCUS | Remember to use Power BI Service, Azure Machine Learning, and RLS for interactive, secure, and AI-driven insights. |
|---|---|
| CAUTION ALERT | Be cautious about overusing Power Automate; it's better suited for data updates, not AI-driven insights or security. |

## QUESTION 26

Answer – A), C), D)

Option A – AI Builder can analyze customer purchase history.
Option B – Power Automate can be used for triggering workflows but not specifically for recommendation algorithms.
Option C – Dataverse can store customer data.
Option D – Azure Cognitive Services provides advanced recommendation algorithms.
Option E – Power BI is useful for visualization but not for implementing recommendation logic.

| EXAM FOCUS | Employ AI Builder, Dataverse, and Cognitive Services for analyzing purchase history, storing customer data, and recommendations. |
|---|---|
| CAUTION ALERT | Be cautious about using Power Automate for recommendation algorithms; it's not designed for this purpose. |

## QUESTION 27

Answer – A), B), D)

Option A – Power Platform Admin Center allows configuration of automated backups.
Option B – Azure Site Recovery helps in implementing disaster recovery.
Option C – Power Automate is useful for workflows but not directly for disaster recovery.
Option D – Azure Backup is essential for data protection.
Option E – Power BI can be used for monitoring but not directly for implementing disaster recovery.

| EXAM FOCUS | *Use Power Platform Admin Center, Azure Site Recovery, and Azure Backup for automated backups, disaster recovery, and data protection.* |
|---|---|
| CAUTION ALERT | *Avoid relying on Power Automate for disaster recovery; it's better suited for workflow automation.* |

## QUESTION 28

Answer – C)

Option A – Scheduled Flow does not provide real-time updates as it runs at set intervals.
Option B – Manual Trigger requires user intervention and does not ensure real-time processing.
Option C – When a record is updated in Dataverse triggers the flow whenever an appointment record is updated, ensuring real-time integration.
Option D – Recurrence Trigger runs at set intervals and does not provide real-time updates.
Option E – When a new record is created in Dataverse triggers the flow only on record creation, not on updates.

| EXAM FOCUS | "Use the 'When a record is updated in Dataverse' trigger for real-time integration." |
|---|---|
| CAUTION ALERT | "Scheduled Flows and Recurrence Triggers do not ensure real-time updates." |

## QUESTION 29

Answer – A), E)

Option A – Correct. Dataverse provides secure storage with role-based access controls, crucial for HIPAA compliance.
Option B – Incorrect. While Power Automate is useful for automation, it is not primarily designed for compliance reporting.
Option C – Incorrect. Third-party storage solutions may not meet the same compliance standards.
Option D – Incorrect. Custom applications without compliance checks can lead to non-compliance.
Option E – Correct. Microsoft Compliance Manager is designed to monitor and manage compliance effectively.

| EXAM FOCUS | *Use Dataverse for secure storage and Microsoft Compliance Manager for monitoring compliance.* |
|---|---|
| CAUTION ALERT | *Custom applications without compliance checks can lead to non-compliance.* |

## QUESTION 30

Answer – A), D)

Option A – Correct. Power BI can integrate multiple data sources and create interactive dashboards.
Option B – Incorrect. AI Builder is useful but not the first choice for complex predictive analytics in this

scenario.

Option C – Incorrect. Storing data in Excel limits scalability and advanced analytics capabilities.

Option D – Correct. Azure Data Factory is designed for integrating and managing data from various sources.

Option E – Incorrect. Developing custom models outside the Power Platform may increase complexity and integration challenges.

| EXAM FOCUS | *Use Power BI for interactive dashboards and Azure Data Factory for data integration.* |
|---|---|
| CAUTION ALERT | *Storing data in Excel limits scalability and advanced analytics capabilities.* |

## QUESTION 31

Answer – A), B)

Option A – Correct. Regular training sessions help users understand and adopt new solutions.
Option B – Correct. Change management strategies focusing on user engagement are essential for promoting acceptance.
Option C – Incorrect. Ignoring resistance can lead to project failure.
Option D – Incorrect. Power BI can measure adoption but is not the primary solution.
Option E – Incorrect. Involving end-users in the design process is crucial for successful adoption.

| EXAM FOCUS | *Conduct regular training sessions and focus on user engagement strategies.* |
|---|---|
| CAUTION ALERT | *Ignoring resistance can lead to project failure.* |

## QUESTION 32

Answer – A)

Option A – Azure IoT Central provides a ready-to-use solution for integrating IoT data and triggering workflows in Dynamics 365.
Option B – Power Automate can automate workflows but is not designed for real-time IoT data integration.
Option C – Dynamics 365 Supply Chain Management is not specifically designed for IoT data integration.
Option D – Power BI is used for data visualization, not for triggering workflows based on IoT data.
Option E – Azure Synapse Analytics is used for data analytics, not for real-time IoT data integration and workflow automation.

| EXAM FOCUS | *"Azure IoT Central seamlessly integrates IoT data with Dynamics 365."* |
|---|---|
| CAUTION ALERT | *"Power Automate is not ideal for real-time IoT data integration."* |

## QUESTION 33

Answer – A), E)

Option A – Correct. Azure API Management helps create and manage custom connectors effectively.
Option B – Incorrect. While Dataverse is useful, it is not primarily for managing custom connectors and APIs.

Option C – Incorrect. Ignoring API integrations can limit functionality.

Option D – Incorrect. Power BI is useful for visualization but not for managing custom solution complexity.

Option E – Correct. Following best practices for maintainable custom code, including code reviews and documentation, helps manage complexity.

| | |
|---|---|
| EXAM FOCUS | Use Azure API Management for custom connectors and follow best coding practices for maintainability. |
| CAUTION ALERT | Ignoring API integrations can limit functionality and increase complexity. |

## QUESTION 34

Answer – B), E)

Option A – A big bang migration risks high downtime and data integrity issues.

Option B – Using an ETL tool for incremental migration minimizes downtime and maintains data integrity.

Option C – Manual CSV import is error-prone and inefficient for large datasets.

Option D – Custom scripts are complex and may not ensure data consistency.

Option E – Azure Data Factory is useful for orchestrating and automating the migration process.

| | |
|---|---|
| EXAM FOCUS | Use an ETL tool for incremental data migration during off-peak hours to ensure minimal disruption and data integrity. |
| CAUTION ALERT | Avoid manual CSV imports; they are error-prone and inefficient for large datasets. |

## QUESTION 35

Answer – A), C), D)

Option A – Auto-scaling with Azure App Services efficiently handles increased demand.

Option B – Power Automate handles workflows but not direct scaling.

Option C – Optimizing database performance with Dataverse ensures efficient data handling.

Option D – Azure Service Bus handles message queuing, aiding in load management.

Option E – Manual scaling is less efficient and prone to human error.

| | |
|---|---|
| EXAM FOCUS | Implement auto-scaling with Azure App Services and optimize database performance with Dataverse for efficient scaling. |
| CAUTION ALERT | Avoid manual scaling; it is prone to human error and inefficiency. |

## QUESTION 36

Answer – B), C), D)

Option A – Batch processing does not provide real-time updates and is not suitable for time-sensitive health data.

Option B – Time-sensitive integration is crucial for ensuring real-time updates of patient data.

Option C – Health data is regulated, requiring compliance with data privacy regulations.
Option D – The volume of patient data is significant and must be considered in the integration.
Option E – Licensing is important but not directly related to the technical requirements of real-time data synchronization.

| EXAM FOCUS | "Time-sensitive, regulated, and volume considerations are crucial for health data integrations." |
| --- | --- |
| CAUTION ALERT | "Batch processing is unsuitable for real-time health data updates." |

## QUESTION 37

Answer – A), B), C)

Option A – Separate instances in each region ensure compliance with data residency laws.
Option B – Dataverse with multi-geo capabilities supports data residency and performance optimization.
Option C – Azure Traffic Manager helps in balancing the load and optimizing performance.
Option D – Storing all data in a central location may violate data residency laws and affect performance.
Option E – Power BI with dataflows is useful for data processing but not for compliance and geo-redundancy.

| EXAM FOCUS | *Deploy separate instances in each region and use Azure Traffic Manager for load balancing.* |
| --- | --- |
| CAUTION ALERT | *Storing all data in a central location may violate data residency laws and affect performance.* |

## QUESTION 38

Answer – A), D), E)

Option A – Power Virtual Agents personalize and automate customer interactions.
Option B – AI Builder helps analyze feedback but may not directly implement improvements.
Option C – A static interface design does not cater to personalized interactions.
Option D – User journey maps help identify pain points and optimize processes.
Option E – Periodic reviews and updates ensure continuous improvement based on user feedback.

| EXAM FOCUS | Use Power Virtual Agents to automate interactions and create user journey maps to identify pain points. |
| --- | --- |
| CAUTION ALERT | Avoid using static interface designs; they do not cater to personalized interactions. |

## QUESTION 39

Answer – B), C), E)

Option A – Dataverse is important for secure and scalable data storage but does not directly address the broader aspects of business continuity, such as maintaining operations during a disruption or implementing recovery strategies.
Option B – Azure Site Recovery helps ensure that systems can be recovered quickly and effectively in the event of a disaster, which is critical for maintaining business functions.
Option C – Conducting a risk assessment is essential to identify and mitigate potential threats to business continuity. This helps in understanding what risks need to be addressed and how to prepare for

Page | 209

them.
Option D – Relying on manual processes for business continuity is not reliable as they can be slow, error-prone, and difficult to scale during large disruptions.
Option E – Regular drills are necessary to test the effectiveness of the continuity plan and to ensure that staff know what to do during an actual disruption. These drills help identify weaknesses in the plan and improve response times.

| EXAM FOCUS | *Implement Azure Site Recovery and conduct regular risk assessments to ensure business continuity during disruptions.* |
|---|---|
| CAUTION ALERT | *Manual processes for business continuity are unreliable; use automated solutions for better efficiency.* |

## QUESTION 40

Answer – A)

Option A – Power Automate with Word Template action allows sales representatives to generate quotes from predefined templates and automate the email sending process.
Option B – Power Apps can generate quotes but manual email sending is not automated.
Option C – Dynamics 365 Customer Insights is focused on customer data analysis, not quote generation.
Option D – Azure Functions require more development and are not necessary for this use case.
Option E – Power BI is for data visualization, not for generating and sending quotes.

| EXAM FOCUS | *"Power Automate with Word Template action automates quote generation and email sending."* |
|---|---|
| CAUTION ALERT | *"Manual email sending is not automated, missing the benefit of full automation."* |

## QUESTION 41

Answer – A), D), E)

Option A – Dataverse is designed for scalable and secure data storage, making it suitable for handling large data volumes.
Option B – While Azure Functions can process data, they are not specifically designed for handling large data sets in a scalable architecture.
Option C – Power BI Premium enhances data analytics but does not address modular architecture or performance tuning for scalability.
Option D – Power Apps Component Framework (PCF) allows for creating reusable and modular components, enhancing flexibility and scalability.
Option E – Azure Monitor provides comprehensive performance tuning and monitoring, essential for maintaining scalability as user base and data volumes grow.

| EXAM FOCUS | *Use Dataverse for scalable storage and PCF for modular architecture.* |
|---|---|
| CAUTION ALERT | *Azure Functions are not specifically designed for handling large data sets in a scalable way.* |

## QUESTION 42

Answer – A), C), E)

Option A – Power BI can visualize performance data and set up alerts for anomalies, aiding in proactive issue detection.
Option B – While RBAC is important for security, it does not directly address monitoring and maintenance.
Option C – Azure Monitor provides comprehensive tracking of solution health and performance metrics, enabling proactive maintenance.
Option D – Manual checks are not reliable for continuous monitoring and proactive issue detection.
Option E – Scheduling regular updates and maintenance using Azure DevOps pipelines ensures that the solution remains stable and up-to-date.

| | |
|---|---|
| **EXAM FOCUS** | *Use Power BI for visualization, Azure Monitor for health tracking, and Azure DevOps for updates.* |
| **CAUTION ALERT** | *Manual checks are unreliable; use continuous monitoring tools.* |

## QUESTION 43

Answer – A), B), D)

Option A – Power BI is ideal for creating interactive dashboards and providing real-time insights.
Option B – Azure Data Factory can handle ETL processes, aggregating data from various sources.
Option C – Using Excel for manual data aggregation is not scalable and does not provide real-time insights.
Option D – Power Automate can be used to schedule data refreshes, ensuring up-to-date information.
Option E – Storing data in an unstructured format can lead to inefficiencies and is not suitable for advanced reporting.

| | |
|---|---|
| **EXAM FOCUS** | *Use Power BI for dashboards and Azure Data Factory for ETL processes.* |
| **CAUTION ALERT** | *Manual data aggregation isn't scalable or real-time.* |

## QUESTION 44

Answer – C)

Option A – Incorrect. Power BI analytics is used for visualizing and analyzing data, not for troubleshooting synchronization issues.
Option B – Incorrect. Activity logging within Power Apps helps monitor user activities, not data flows between systems.
Option C – Correct. Dataverse auditing provides detailed data change history, helping identify and rectify issues in synchronization processes.
Option D – Incorrect. The entity store is used in Dynamics 365 for reporting purposes, not for diagnosing synchronization issues.
Option E – Incorrect. Data integrator facilitates data movement but does not provide tools to diagnose issues within the data synchronization process.

| | |
|---|---|
| **EXAM FOCUS** | "You should configure Dataverse auditing to identify and resolve synchronization errors between systems." |
| **CAUTION ALERT** | "Remember, Power BI analytics won't help diagnose synchronization issues." |

### QUESTION 45

Answer – A), B), C)

Option A – Interactive online training modules using Power Apps can effectively engage users and provide comprehensive training.
Option B – Power BI can be used to create and analyze feedback surveys, helping to improve training programs.
Option C – A dedicated support team ensures ongoing assistance and support for users.
Option D – Manual feedback collection is less efficient and may result in missed opportunities for improvement.
Option E – One-time training sessions without follow-up can lead to knowledge gaps and reduced user proficiency.

| EXAM FOCUS | *Develop interactive online training modules using Power Apps for effective engagement.* |
|---|---|
| CAUTION ALERT | *One-time training sessions without follow-up can lead to knowledge gaps.* |

### QUESTION 46

Answer – A), B), C)

Option A – Using Power Platform's performance monitoring tools helps identify where the delays and bottlenecks occur.
Option B – Scaling up the Azure SQL Database can provide more resources to handle increased data processing loads.
Option C – Implementing caching mechanisms can significantly reduce data retrieval times and improve overall performance.
Option D – Avoiding performance monitoring is not a viable solution as it prevents identifying and addressing the root causes of performance issues.
Option E – Ignoring performance issues will lead to continued or worsening delays and degrade the user experience.

| EXAM FOCUS | *"Use Power Platform performance monitoring tools and caching to improve performance."* |
|---|---|
| CAUTION ALERT | *"Avoid ignoring performance monitoring; it prevents addressing root causes."* |

### QUESTION 47

Answer – A), B), E)

Option A – Using Power BI's real-time streaming capabilities enables real-time data monitoring and alerts.
Option B – Implementing Azure Monitor for real-time alerts helps in promptly identifying and addressing issues.
Option C – Ignoring user feedback can lead to overlooking critical insights; user feedback is essential for continuous improvement.
Option D – Creating custom dashboards in Power BI provides tailored insights and reporting for specific needs.
Option E – Using Power BI's usage metrics to analyze user behavior helps in understanding how users

interact with the solution and identifying areas for improvement.

| EXAM FOCUS | *"Remember, using Power BI's real-time streaming capabilities enables timely data monitoring and alerts."* |
|---|---|
| CAUTION ALERT | *"Ignoring user feedback can lead to missed critical insights and improvement opportunities."* |

## QUESTION 48

Answer – C), D)

Option A – Incorrect. Webhook configuration is useful but doesn't directly address the core issue of inventory discrepancies.
Option B – Incorrect. Service endpoint configuration is typically a one-time setup and not the best area to focus on for ongoing synchronization issues.
Option C – Correct. Automating connection management ensures reliable data transmission between the POS systems and the central inventory, reducing errors.
Option D – Correct. Automating the upsert (update/insert) of reference data ensures that inventory records are consistently and correctly updated across all stores.
Option E – Incorrect. While automated testing is helpful, it does not directly resolve synchronization errors in a live environment.

| EXAM FOCUS | *"Automate connection management and upsert reference data to reduce synchronization errors in inventory management."* |
|---|---|
| CAUTION ALERT | *"Webhook configuration is useful but doesn't directly address synchronization issues."* |

## QUESTION 49

Answer – A), B), D)

Option A – Correct. Managed solutions ensure that customizations are packaged and can be easily updated or removed, reducing upgrade disruptions.
Option B – Correct. Regularly reviewing and updating customizations helps keep them compatible with new Dynamics 365 releases.
Option C – Incorrect. Power Automate flows are better suited for process automation rather than lifecycle management of customizations.
Option D – Correct. Leveraging out-of-the-box features reduces the need for custom development and minimizes the risk of future upgrade issues.
Option E – Incorrect. While Azure DevOps is excellent for version control and CI/CD, it is not specific to managing customizations in Dynamics 365.

| EXAM FOCUS | *"Use managed solutions for deploying customizations to ensure they do not disrupt future upgrades."* |
|---|---|
| CAUTION ALERT | *"You should stay cautious, relying heavily on customizations can complicate upgrades."* |

## QUESTION 50

Answer – A), B), C)

Option A – Correct. Power BI can effectively monitor and report on energy consumption metrics, helping track sustainability goals.

Option B – Correct. Serverless computing with Azure Functions can reduce energy consumption by scaling resources automatically based on demand.

Option C – Correct. Power Virtual Agents can be used to create an engaging eco-awareness campaign for users.

Option D – Incorrect. While useful for tracking data, Dataverse is not specifically geared towards tracking sustainability metrics.

Option E – Incorrect. Regular downtime might reduce energy usage but can disrupt operations and is not a sustainable practice in itself.

| | |
|---|---|
| **EXAM FOCUS** | *"Implement serverless computing using Azure Functions to reduce energy use."* |
| **CAUTION ALERT** | *"You should stay cautious, neglecting eco-friendly practices can increase your carbon footprint."* |

# PRACTICE TEST 7 - QUESTIONS ONLY

### QUESTION 1

A financial services company wants to optimize their loan approval process using Microsoft Power Platform. Their business goals include reducing processing time, ensuring regulatory compliance, and improving customer satisfaction. Specific challenges include:
- Manual data entry causing delays.
- Inconsistent compliance checks.
- Lack of real-time application status updates.

What solutions would best address these challenges while aligning with the company's business goals? Select two correct answers.

A) Use Power Automate to automate data entry from application forms.
B) Implement compliance workflows using Power Automate.
C) Develop a customer portal with Power Apps for real-time updates.
D) Create a Power BI report for regulatory compliance.
E) Integrate AI Builder for automatic data validation.

### QUESTION 2

A manufacturing company requires a solution to improve field service operations and equipment maintenance management. The solution must integrate with their existing inventory and ERP systems. Which Dynamics 365 products should you recommend to streamline their field service operations and maintenance management? Select up to 2 answers.

A) Dynamics 365 Field Service
B) Dynamics 365 Supply Chain Management
C) Dynamics 365 Customer Service
D) Dynamics 365 Finance

### QUESTION 3

A healthcare organization wants to improve its patient management system using Microsoft Power Platform. They need to collect and analyze patient data accurately. The specific challenges include:
- Disparate data sources for patient records.
- Ensuring compliance with data privacy regulations.
- Interpreting data for better patient care insights.

What actions would you take to collect and analyze patient data while ensuring compliance? Select three correct answers.

A) Implement Dataverse to centralize patient records.
B) Use Power Automate to ensure data compliance with privacy regulations.
C) Develop a Power BI dashboard for patient care insights.
D) Use AI Builder to analyze patient data.
E) Create a Power Apps solution for patient data entry.

## QUESTION 4

A healthcare provider wants to enhance patient engagement and streamline appointment scheduling across multiple platforms. Which Power Platform components should be utilized? Select up to two answers.

A) Power Apps
B) Power BI
C) Power Automate
D) Microsoft Dataverse
E) Dynamics 365 Health

## QUESTION 5

A healthcare organization is adopting a new patient management system using Microsoft Power Platform. The project requires incorporating compliance into the solution design. The specific challenges include:
• Ensuring compliance with HIPAA regulations.
• Protecting patient data from unauthorized access.
• Verifying compliance through regular audits.
What actions would you take to incorporate compliance into the solution design? Select three correct answers.

A) Implement Dataverse to store patient data securely.
B) Use Power Automate to enforce compliance workflows.
C) Apply DLP policies to ensure data privacy.
D) Conduct compliance audits using Power BI.
E) Implement RBAC to control access to patient data.

## QUESTION 6

A healthcare organization is planning to implement a new patient management system using Microsoft Power Platform. The project requires techniques for accurate cost estimation and handling potential cost overruns. The specific challenges include:
• Estimating costs for compliance with healthcare regulations.
• Budgeting for data storage and security.
• Preparing for potential cost overruns.
What actions would you take to address these challenges? Select three correct answers.

A) Implement Dataverse to store patient data securely.
B) Use Power BI to estimate compliance costs.
C) Apply DLP policies to ensure data security.
D) Develop a contingency budget for potential cost overruns.
E) Conduct a detailed cost analysis using Power BI.

## QUESTION 7

A financial institution is implementing a new loan approval system using Microsoft Power Platform. The project involves validating solution concepts with stakeholders. The specific challenges are:

- Demonstrating the solution concept to stakeholders.
- Gathering stakeholder feedback.
- Refining the solution based on feedback.

What actions would you take to address these challenges? Select two correct answers.

A) Use Power Automate to automate loan approval workflows.
B) Develop a canvas app prototype using Power Apps.
C) Use Power BI to create dashboards for stakeholder presentations.
D) Conduct stakeholder review meetings.
E) Implement Azure Logic Apps for integration.

## QUESTION 8

A retail company is implementing a new inventory management system using Microsoft Power Platform. The project requires designing the integration architecture. The specific challenges are:
- Defining the integration architecture.
- Ensuring data consistency.
- Handling real-time data updates.

What actions would you take to address these challenges? Select two correct answers.

A) Use Azure Logic Apps for integration orchestration.
B) Implement event-driven architecture using Azure Service Bus.
C) Use Power Virtual Agents to manage inventory queries.
D) Develop a unified data model using Dataverse.
E) Use Power BI for real-time reporting.

## QUESTION 9

A healthcare provider is upgrading its patient management system using Microsoft Power Platform. The project requires identifying security requirements. The specific challenges are:
- Defining security requirements for sensitive health data.
- Implementing security protocols for data access.
- Ensuring compliance with HIPAA regulations.

What steps would you take to address these challenges? Select three correct answers.

A) Use Azure Key Vault for managing encryption keys.
B) Implement Single Sign-On (SSO) for secure access.
C) Use Power BI for data visualization.
D) Implement Azure Active Directory (AAD) for identity management.
E) Use Azure DevOps for code deployment.

## QUESTION 10

A healthcare provider is deploying a new patient management system using Microsoft Power Platform. The project requires planning for quality control. The specific challenges are:
- Ensuring data integrity and accuracy.
- Defining quality metrics for patient data.
- Implementing continuous quality improvement.

What steps would you take to address these challenges? Select two correct answers.

A) Implement data validation rules in Power Apps.
B) Use Power Automate for automated data entry.
C) Create Power BI reports to monitor data quality.
D) Schedule regular training sessions for staff.
E) Use Azure DevOps for managing quality control processes.

## QUESTION 11

An e-commerce company needs to upgrade its CRM system using Dynamics 365 and Microsoft Power Platform. The specific challenges are:
- Handling version control and release management.
- Implementing continuous improvement processes.
- Managing legacy system end-of-life.

What steps would you take to address these challenges? Select three correct answers.

A) Use Azure DevOps for managing version control and release cycles.
B) Implement continuous integration and deployment (CI/CD) pipelines.
C) Create a detailed end-of-life plan for the legacy system.
D) Use Power Virtual Agents for customer support during migration.
E) Schedule regular review meetings to assess improvements.

## QUESTION 12

A retail company is using Microsoft Power Platform to build a solution for managing customer feedback. The solution needs to integrate with their Dynamics 365 Marketing application to automate email campaigns based on feedback received.
- The solution must support automatic triggers for email campaigns.
- It should provide analytics on campaign performance and customer feedback.

What components would you include in your solution design?

A) Power Automate, Power BI, Azure Synapse Analytics
B) Power Apps, Power Automate, Dynamics 365 Marketing
C) Power Automate, Power BI, Dynamics 365 Marketing
D) Power Virtual Agents, Power BI, Dynamics 365 Marketing
E) Power Apps, Power Automate, Power BI

## QUESTION 13

A financial services company is looking to implement iterative development for its new customer engagement platform using the Microsoft Power Platform. The challenges include:
- Benefits of iterative development.
- Continuous delivery and feedback loops.
- Adapting to changes in agile environments.

What strategies should you adopt to address these challenges? Select three correct answers.

A) Conduct regular user acceptance testing (UAT) sessions.
B) Implement Power BI for real-time analytics and feedback.
C) Use Azure Logic Apps for integrating continuous delivery.
D) Schedule sprint reviews and retrospectives.

E) Develop a continuous integration/continuous deployment (CI/CD) pipeline with Azure DevOps.

## QUESTION 14

A financial services firm needs to improve its data quality and consistency measures while ensuring compliance with data governance standards using the Microsoft Power Platform. The challenges include:
• Defining data quality and consistency measures.
• Ensuring compliance with data governance standards.
• Implementing effective data governance tools and technologies.
Which strategies should you adopt to address these challenges? Select three correct answers.

A) Use Power BI Dataflows for data transformation and quality checks.
B) Implement Azure Purview for data governance and cataloging.
C) Develop a data quality management plan.
D) Assign RBAC roles for data governance in Dynamics 365.
E) Utilize AI Builder for data quality predictions.

## QUESTION 15

A financial services firm is implementing a new solution using Microsoft Power Platform. The team faces challenges such as:
• Deciding between customization and configuration.
• Managing custom solutions.
• Best practices in system configuration.
Which approaches should you take to address these challenges? Select three correct answers.

A) Use out-of-the-box Power Apps functionalities wherever possible.
B) Develop custom connectors for every external system.
C) Configure security roles using Dataverse RBAC features.
D) Customize Dataverse entities for unique business needs.
E) Utilize Power BI for reporting instead of custom reporting tools.

## QUESTION 16

A manufacturing company is implementing a Dynamics 365 Finance and Operations solution. They need to ensure the data migration process from their legacy system is efficient and accurate.
• The migration tool must handle data transformations.
• It should support scheduled refreshes to ensure data consistency during the transition period.
Which tools should you use for the data migration process? Select two answers.

A) Data Import Wizard
B) Azure Data Factory
C) Dynamics 365 Data Export Service
D) Power Apps
E) Azure Synapse Analytics

## QUESTION 17

A financial services company is transitioning to a new ERP system using Microsoft Power Platform. The

implementation must:
• Establish governance structures.
• Comply with SOX and PCI-DSS requirements.
• Implement data governance and auditing.
What steps should you take to meet these requirements? Select three correct answers.

A) Implement RBAC in Dataverse to manage data access and permissions.
B) Use Power BI to create compliance reports and dashboards.
C) Configure Power Automate to enforce data governance policies.
D) Develop custom connectors to integrate with existing governance systems.
E) Utilize Azure Functions to automate compliance checks.

## QUESTION 18

A financial services firm is leading a digital transformation using Microsoft Power Platform. The solution must:
• Lead digital transformation initiatives.
• Drive innovation within the organization.
• Maintain compliance with financial regulations.
You need to select two strategies to achieve these goals. Which two strategies should you choose? (Select two)

A) Use Power Automate for automating regulatory compliance workflows.
B) Implement Azure Cognitive Services for advanced analytics.
C) Develop model-driven apps for core business processes.
D) Use Dataverse to manage customer data securely.
E) Incorporate Power Virtual Agents to enhance customer interactions.

## QUESTION 19

A financial services firm is deploying a new customer relationship management (CRM) system using Microsoft Power Platform. The solution must:
• Ensure ethical handling of sensitive data.
• Comply with internal and external data protection policies.
• Build trust with customers.
Which two measures should you implement? (Select two)

A) Conduct regular security audits using Power BI.
B) Implement Single Sign-On (SSO) with Azure AD.
C) Use Power Automate to automate compliance reporting.
D) Develop a user consent management process.
E) Implement data encryption in Dataverse.

## QUESTION 20

A financial services firm is implementing a compliance tracking solution using Microsoft Dataverse. They need to track and report on compliance activities across different departments.
• The solution must support complex queries and data aggregation.
• It should provide real-time compliance status updates.

Which components should you include in the data model design? Select three answers.

A) Calculated columns
B) Rollup columns
C) Real-time workflows
D) Virtual tables
E) Power BI dataflows

## QUESTION 21

A healthcare provider must ensure their Power Platform solution complies with HIPAA regulations. The solution must:
• Ensure data protection and privacy.
• Implement security policies.
• Comply with HIPAA regulations.
Which two actions should you take? (Select two)

A) Implement Multi-Factor Authentication (MFA) using Azure AD.
B) Use Power Automate to streamline data workflows.
C) Enable encryption of data at rest and in transit.
D) Use Canvas Apps for secure data entry.
E) Conduct regular security risk assessments using Azure Security Center.

## QUESTION 22

A financial institution needs to implement a Power Platform solution that complies with strict data governance policies and regulatory requirements. The solution must:
• Ensure data governance and lifecycle management.
• Implement role-based access control (RBAC).
• Provide advanced analytics capabilities.
Which two components should you use? (Select two)

A) Use Azure Policy for enforcing governance policies.
B) Implement Dataverse for data storage.
C) Use Azure Synapse Analytics for advanced analytics.
D) Apply RBAC using Azure AD.
E) Use Canvas Apps for user interfaces.

## QUESTION 23

A financial institution is developing a Power Platform solution to improve customer engagement. They want to ensure the interface is intuitive and accessible for all users, including those with disabilities. The solution must:
• Follow accessibility best practices.
• Provide a seamless user experience.
• Incorporate user feedback.
Which two strategies should you implement? (Select two)

A) Use Power Apps Component Framework (PCF) for custom controls.

B) Implement ARIA (Accessible Rich Internet Applications) landmarks.
C) Use AI Builder to analyze user behavior.
D) Conduct usability testing with diverse user groups.
E) Use Power Automate for process automation.

## QUESTION 24

A retail company uses Power BI to generate sales reports from multiple data sources. They want to enhance their data analytics capabilities by integrating AI-driven insights directly into their Power BI reports. Which tool should they use to achieve this integration?

A) Power Automate
B) Power Apps
C) AI Builder
D) Microsoft Dataverse
E) Azure Machine Learning

## QUESTION 25

An insurance firm wants to leverage Power BI to gain insights from customer data. The solution must:
- Generate comprehensive reports on customer claims.
- Provide real-time analytics on claim status.
- Integrate machine learning models for predictive analytics.

Which three Power BI features or components should you use? (Select three)

A) Power BI Dataflows for data preparation.
B) Power BI Embedded for custom analytics solutions.
C) Power BI AI Insights for integrating machine learning models.
D) Power BI Paginated Reports for detailed reporting.
E) Power BI Streaming Datasets for real-time analytics.

## QUESTION 26

A healthcare provider wants to use AI to improve patient diagnostics. The solution must:
- Analyze patient data using machine learning.
- Provide diagnostic suggestions to doctors.
- Ensure data privacy and compliance.

Which three components should be prioritized? (Select three)

A) AI Builder for machine learning models.
B) Power Virtual Agents for interactive diagnostics.
C) Azure Cognitive Services for advanced analytics.
D) Power Automate for workflow automation.
E) Azure Policy for data compliance.

## QUESTION 27

A financial institution must ensure business continuity for its Power Platform solutions in the event of a disaster. The solution must:

- Provide fault tolerance.
- Enable data synchronization across regions.
- Support role-based access control during recovery.

Which components should be configured to meet these requirements? (Select three)

A) Azure SQL Database for fault tolerance.
B) Azure Service Bus for data synchronization.
C) Azure AD for RBAC.
D) Dataverse for secure data storage.
E) Azure Functions for automated recovery processes.

## QUESTION 28

A financial services company is using Power Apps to build a custom application for loan processing. They need to ensure that the application validates all data inputs before any processing occurs to avoid data inconsistencies. Which Power Platform feature should be used to implement this validation?

A) Business Rules
B) Power Automate
C) Custom Connectors
D) Power BI Embedded
E) AI Builder

## QUESTION 29

A financial services client needs assistance in ensuring their Power Platform solution complies with industry-specific regulatory requirements. They are particularly concerned about data protection and privacy laws.
1. Implementing solutions that comply with GDPR regulations.
2. Automating compliance checks to ensure ongoing adherence.
3. Managing and protecting sensitive financial data.

What actions would you recommend to address these concerns? Select three answers.

A) Use Microsoft Purview for data governance and compliance.
B) Implement automated compliance checks using Power Automate.
C) Store sensitive data in Dataverse with encryption.
D) Use Azure Functions for handling data processes.
E) Implement role-based access control (RBAC) across all applications.

## QUESTION 30

A retail client wants to enhance their business intelligence capabilities by integrating external data sources and applying advanced data analysis techniques. They aim to generate insights that can drive sales and improve customer satisfaction.
1. Integrating customer data from various external sources.
2. Applying data modeling techniques to analyze sales patterns.
3. Generating actionable insights to enhance customer experience and drive sales.

What actions would you take to meet these objectives? Select three answers.

A) Use Power BI to create data models and visualize sales patterns.
B) Implement Azure Cognitive Services for advanced analytics.
C) Use Dataverse to store integrated customer data securely.
D) Apply AI Builder to develop models predicting customer behavior.
E) Use Azure DevOps to manage the analytics project.

## QUESTION 31

A client in the healthcare industry is implementing a new Power Platform solution. They need to develop a comprehensive communication and training plan to ensure successful user adoption.
1. Creating effective communication plans to inform users about the new solution.
2. Developing training programs to ensure users are proficient with the new tools.
3. Measuring the impact and success of the change initiative.
What actions would you recommend to achieve these objectives? Select three answers.

A) Use Power Automate to send regular updates and notifications to users.
B) Develop interactive training modules using Power Apps.
C) Implement Power BI dashboards to track training progress and user proficiency.
D) Focus solely on technical aspects and skip user training.
E) Conduct feedback sessions to gather user insights and improve training.

## QUESTION 32

A financial institution uses Dynamics 365 Finance to manage their financial operations. They need to integrate a third-party tax calculation service to automate tax computations during the invoice generation process. The integration must be seamless and adhere to security best practices. What approach should they use to implement this integration?

A) Use Power Automate with HTTP connector
B) Implement a Custom Connector
C) Use Azure Logic Apps
D) Use Dynamics 365 Business Central
E) Use Microsoft Graph API

## QUESTION 33

A client in the retail sector is adopting Microsoft Power Platform to enhance their operations. They want to ensure their solutions include advanced customization and are maintainable.
1. Implementing advanced customization in Power Apps and Power Automate.
2. Ensuring the solution is maintainable.
3. Managing the complexity of custom solutions.
What actions would you take to meet these objectives? Select three answers.

A) Use Power Automate to create complex workflows and automate business processes.
B) Implement custom connectors to integrate third-party APIs.
C) Follow coding best practices, including modular design and documentation.
D) Focus solely on adding features without considering maintainability.
E) Use Azure DevOps for version control and ALM.

## QUESTION 34

A manufacturing company is using an on-premises ERP system and wants to integrate it with Power Apps for improved workflow automation. The project requirements are:
• Securely connect to the ERP system from Power Apps.
• Ensure real-time data synchronization.
• Minimize custom development efforts. What are the best approaches to meet these requirements? (Select 2 answers)

A) Use Azure API Management to expose ERP data as APIs and connect them to Power Apps.
B) Develop custom connectors in Power Apps to integrate with the ERP system.
C) Use Power Automate to create workflows that synchronize data between ERP and Power Apps in real-time.
D) Implement Azure Logic Apps for integration and automation.
E) Export ERP data to Dataverse and access it through Power Apps.

## QUESTION 35

A retail company uses Dynamics 365 for their online store. They expect significant traffic spikes during sales events and need to ensure the system can handle the load. The project requirements include:
• Auto-scaling capabilities.
• Efficient load management.
• Continuous availability. What actions should you take to meet these requirements? (Select 2 answers)

A) Implement Azure Front Door to distribute traffic.
B) Use Azure Logic Apps to automate scaling.
C) Configure SQL Database elastic pools for resource optimization.
D) Use Azure DevOps for continuous integration and deployment.
E) Manually monitor and adjust resources during peak times.

## QUESTION 36

A retail company uses Dynamics 365 Commerce to manage online sales. They need to integrate their e-commerce platform with a third-party payment gateway to process transactions securely. The integration must handle high transaction volumes and comply with payment industry regulations. Which categorizations should you consider for this integration?

A) Volatility
B) Regulated
C) Licensed
D) Time-sensitive
E) Batch

## QUESTION 37

A multinational corporation is implementing a Dynamics 365 solution with Power Platform integration. The solution must:
• Provide a consistent user experience across regions.
• Comply with local data privacy regulations.

- Optimize performance globally. What actions should you take? (Select 2 answers)

A) Localize the user interface for each region.
B) Use Azure CDN to distribute static content globally.
C) Implement a single instance with centralized data storage.
D) Use Azure SQL Database with geo-replication.
E) Employ Azure Logic Apps for regional data processing.

## QUESTION 38

A retail company is implementing Power Apps to improve the user experience of their inventory management system. The solution must:
- Provide a seamless and intuitive UI.
- Enable personalization for different user roles.
- Measure and improve user satisfaction continuously. What steps should you take? (Select 3 answers)

A) Use Canvas Apps to design a user-friendly and intuitive UI.
B) Implement role-based access control (RBAC) in Dataverse.
C) Collect user feedback through in-app surveys.
D) Use a single interface for all users regardless of their role.
E) Schedule user training sessions to gather feedback and improve satisfaction.

## QUESTION 39

A manufacturing company is implementing a Power Platform solution that requires robust business continuity measures. The solution must:
- Mitigate potential risks.
- Ensure continuous operation during disruptions.
- Regularly update and test the continuity plan. What strategies should you implement? (Select 2 answers)

A) Use Azure Backup to protect critical data.
B) Conduct threat modeling to identify risks.
C) Use a single instance for all operations to simplify management.
D) Implement Power Automate to trigger alerts during disruptions.
E) Conduct regular continuity plan reviews and updates.

## QUESTION 40

A financial services company uses Dynamics 365 Finance to manage their accounting processes. They want to integrate with a third-party tax calculation service to automatically calculate taxes during invoice generation. The integration must comply with local tax regulations and be seamless. What approach should they use?

A) Use Power Automate with HTTP connector
B) Implement a Custom Connector
C) Use Dynamics 365 Fraud Protection
D) Use Azure Logic Apps
E) Integrate with Power BI for tax calculations

## QUESTION 41

A financial services firm needs to expand their Power Platform solution to new regions while ensuring high performance and low latency. The solution must:
- Utilize a modular architecture for easy expansion.
- Implement geo-redundancy.
- Optimize performance across regions. What components should you use? (Select 3 answers)

A) Deploy Azure Traffic Manager for load balancing.
B) Use Dataverse for multi-region data storage.
C) Implement Azure Front Door for global routing and acceleration.
D) Use Power Automate for integrating regional services.
E) Use Azure Service Bus for reliable messaging and geo-redundancy.

## QUESTION 42

A retail company is using a Power Platform solution to manage customer interactions and sales data. To ensure solution health and performance, they must:
- Monitor the solution continuously.
- Detect and resolve issues before they impact users.
- Perform regular updates and maintenance. What tools and techniques should be used? (Select 3 answers)

A) Use Power Automate to automate the resolution of detected issues.
B) Implement Application Insights to monitor solution performance and detect issues.
C) Use Azure Security Center for security monitoring and compliance checks.
D) Schedule regular solution updates and maintenance tasks using Azure DevOps.
E) Conduct manual performance reviews and updates quarterly.

## QUESTION 43

A financial institution needs to implement data analysis techniques to detect fraudulent transactions. They must:
- Analyze large volumes of transaction data.
- Provide actionable insights for fraud detection.
- Integrate with existing reporting tools. What approaches should they consider? (Select 3 answers)

A) Use AI Builder to create machine learning models for fraud detection.
B) Store transaction data in an unencrypted format for faster processing.
C) Implement Power BI for visualizing fraud patterns and trends.
D) Use Power Automate to trigger alerts for suspicious transactions.
E) Manually review all transaction data for potential fraud.

## QUESTION 44

You are tasked with resolving a data synchronization failure between Microsoft Power Platform and a third-party CRM system in a sales organization. The system needs to ensure real-time data accuracy.
- Real-time data accuracy.
- Diagnose synchronization failures.

What diagnostic approach should you employ to address the synchronization issues effectively?

A) Real-time dashboards
B) Custom logging via plugins
C) Microsoft Power Apps activity logging
D) Power Apps error notifications
E) Server-side synchronization

## QUESTION 45

An organization is rolling out a new Dynamics 365 application. They need to:
- Develop training materials that cater to different user roles.
- Establish an effective user support model.
- Continuously assess and improve training effectiveness. What strategies should they employ?

A) Create role-specific training materials using PowerPoint.
B) Use Power Virtual Agents for user support and FAQs.
C) Implement regular training effectiveness assessments using surveys in Power BI.
D) Collect feedback manually through email.
E) Conduct one-time training sessions for all users.

## QUESTION 46

A financial services firm is facing issues with slow report generation in Power BI. They need to:
- Optimize data models for better performance.
- Ensure efficient resource usage.
- Continuously monitor performance. How should they proceed?

A) Use query folding in Power Query to optimize data retrieval.
B) Simplify the data model by removing unnecessary columns and tables.
C) Enable Power BI Premium for better resource allocation.
D) Ignore performance metrics and focus on adding new features.
E) Avoid using performance optimization techniques.

## QUESTION 47

A retail company is using Power Apps for inventory management and needs to monitor solution performance and user feedback. They must:
- Set up solution monitoring systems.
- Analyze performance and usage insights.
- Collect and act on user feedback. What actions should they take?
Select 2 answers.

A) Integrate Power Apps with Azure Application Insights.
B) Use Power Automate to collect user feedback through forms.
C) Skip real-time monitoring and analyze data monthly.
D) Use Power BI to create performance and usage reports.
E) Focus solely on system logs for insights.

## QUESTION 48

You are leading a project to automate the onboarding process for new employees using Microsoft Power Platform. The process involves multiple departments with varying access needs to employee data. Simplifying and securing data flow between systems is a priority.
- Secure data handling.
- Simplify process automation.

Which two automation tasks should be implemented to efficiently manage and secure data flow in this scenario?

A) Connection management
B) Automated role-based access control setup
C) Service endpoint configuration
D) Team records creation
E) Upsert of reference data

## QUESTION 49

A financial services company is using Power Apps with significant customizations to manage client interactions. The company needs to ensure that these customizations are managed effectively and do not negatively impact system performance or upgrades. The key requirements are:
- Managing and applying updates.
- Handling deprecated features.
- Ensuring long-term sustainability.

Which measures should you implement? (Select 3 answers)

A) Use the Power Platform Admin Center to monitor system performance and apply updates.
B) Implement a strategy to regularly review and refactor customizations.
C) Utilize Dataverse for storing custom entities and managing relationships.
D) Develop custom connectors to replace deprecated features.
E) Use Solution Checker to identify potential issues in customizations.

## QUESTION 50

A manufacturing company is looking to implement a new Dynamics 365 solution with a focus on energy efficiency and sustainable resource utilization. As a solution architect, you need to ensure the solution supports these goals. The key requirements are:
- Utilizing energy-efficient cloud resources.
- Ensuring sustainable resource utilization.
- Integrating with existing sustainability tracking systems.

Which actions should you prioritize? (Select 3 answers)

A) Use Azure DevOps to automate deployment and ensure efficient use of resources.
B) Implement Power Automate to integrate with sustainability tracking systems.
C) Choose Azure regions with renewable energy sources for hosting.
D) Utilize Power BI to create dashboards for tracking resource utilization.
E) Develop custom connectors to link Dynamics 365 with existing sustainability systems.

# PRACTICE TEST 7 - ANSWERS ONLY

## QUESTION 1

Answer – A), E)

Option A – Automating data entry helps reduce delays, addressing one of the key challenges.
Option B – Compliance workflows ensure consistency but do not address data entry or real-time updates.
Option C – A customer portal improves satisfaction but does not address data entry or compliance.
Option D – Power BI reports help track compliance but do not optimize the process.
Option E – AI Builder can automate data validation, ensuring faster processing and compliance, aligning with business goals.

| | |
|---|---|
| **EXAM FOCUS** | *Use Power Automate to automate data entry and AI Builder for data validation to optimize loan approval processes.* |
| **CAUTION ALERT** | *Remember, customer portals alone won't address manual entry or compliance issues effectively.* |

## QUESTION 2

Answer – A), B)

Option A – Correct. Dynamics 365 Field Service is specifically designed to improve field service operations, offering capabilities for scheduling, dispatching, and ensuring that field agents have the necessary tools and information for equipment maintenance.
Option B – Correct. Dynamics 365 Supply Chain Management integrates well with ERP systems and can enhance inventory management, which is crucial for maintaining equipment and ensuring that parts are available for field service needs.
Option C – Incorrect. Dynamics 365 Customer Service focuses on customer interaction management and lacks the specific features required for field service operations and equipment maintenance.
Option D – Incorrect. Dynamics 365 Finance manages financial operations and does not offer specialized tools for field service management or equipment maintenance.

| | |
|---|---|
| **EXAM FOCUS** | *"Dynamics 365 Field Service and Supply Chain Management streamline field operations and integrate with inventory systems."* |
| **CAUTION ALERT** | *"Customer Service and Finance modules don't focus on field service or equipment maintenance."* |

## QUESTION 3

Answer – A), B), C)

Option A – Centralizing patient records in Dataverse addresses disparate data sources.
Option B – Power Automate ensures data compliance, addressing privacy concerns.
Option C – A Power BI dashboard helps interpret data for patient care insights.
Option D – AI Builder is useful for analysis but not critical for compliance.
Option E – A Power Apps solution is useful for data entry but does not address analysis or compliance

Page | 230

directly.

| EXAM FOCUS | Centralize patient records in Dataverse, ensure compliance with Power Automate, and use Power BI for care insights. |
|---|---|
| CAUTION ALERT | Stay cautious, relying on AI Builder alone for analysis won't address compliance or data centralization issues. |

## QUESTION 4

Answer – A) & C)

Option A – Correct. Power Apps can be used to develop versatile apps for scheduling and patient engagement.
Option B – Incorrect. Power BI is for analytics and does not contribute directly to appointment scheduling or patient engagement.
Option C – Correct. Power Automate to streamline processes and synchronize data across platforms.
Option D – Incorrect. Microsoft Dataverse stores data but doesn't address specific engagement or scheduling needs.
Option E – Incorrect. Dynamics 365 Health is specific to healthcare solutions but does not directly handle engagement or appointment scheduling.

| EXAM FOCUS | "Power Apps can develop versatile apps for scheduling and engagement." |
|---|---|
| CAUTION ALERT | "You should stay cautious, Power BI is for analytics, not for direct engagement or scheduling." |

## QUESTION 5

Answer – A), C), E)

Option A – Dataverse provides secure storage for patient data, ensuring compliance with HIPAA.
Option B – Power Automate is useful for workflows but does not directly ensure compliance.
Option C – DLP policies ensure data privacy and compliance.
Option D – Power BI is useful for data analysis but not directly for conducting compliance audits.
Option E – RBAC controls access to patient data, protecting it from unauthorized access.

| EXAM FOCUS | Implement Dataverse for secure patient data storage and DLP policies for data privacy compliance. |
|---|---|
| CAUTION ALERT | Stay cautious, relying solely on Power Automate won't fully address HIPAA compliance needs. |

## QUESTION 6

Answer – B), D), E)

Option A – Dataverse is useful for data storage but does not address cost estimation or budgeting.
Option B – Power BI can be used to estimate compliance costs.
Option C – DLP policies ensure data security but do not address cost estimation or budgeting.
Option D – Developing a contingency budget prepares for potential cost overruns.
Option E – Conducting a detailed cost analysis using Power BI helps in accurate cost estimation.

| EXAM FOCUS | Estimate compliance costs with Power BI and develop a contingency budget for potential overruns. |
|---|---|
| CAUTION ALERT | Remember, Dataverse is great for storage but won't address cost estimation or budget management. |

## QUESTION 7

Answer – B), D)

Option A – Power Automate is useful for automating workflows but not directly related to validating solution concepts.
Option B – Developing a canvas app prototype using Power Apps helps demonstrate the solution concept.
Option C – Power BI is useful for creating dashboards but not directly related to prototyping.
Option D – Conducting stakeholder review meetings helps gather feedback from stakeholders.
Option E – Azure Logic Apps is useful for integration but not directly related to validating solution concepts.

| EXAM FOCUS | Develop a canvas app prototype with Power Apps and conduct stakeholder review meetings for validation. |
|---|---|
| CAUTION ALERT | Stay cautious, Power Automate won't help with validating solution concepts directly. |

## QUESTION 8

Answer – A), B)

Option A – Azure Logic Apps can orchestrate integration workflows.
Option B – Implementing event-driven architecture using Azure Service Bus ensures real-time data updates.
Option C – Power Virtual Agents can manage queries but not directly related to integration architecture.
Option D – Developing a unified data model using Dataverse helps but is not a primary action for defining integration architecture.
Option E – Power BI is useful for reporting but not directly related to integration architecture.

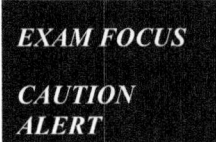

| EXAM FOCUS | Use Azure Logic Apps for integration and Service Bus for real-time updates to ensure data consistency. |
|---|---|
| CAUTION ALERT | Remember, Power Virtual Agents are for queries, not integration architecture. |

## QUESTION 9

Answer – A), B), D)

Option A – Using Azure Key Vault ensures encryption key management, aligning with security requirements.
Option B – Implementing SSO provides secure access to the system.
Option C – Power BI is useful for data visualization but not directly related to identifying security requirements.
Option D – Implementing AAD ensures proper identity management and secure access.

Page | 232

Option E – Azure DevOps is useful for code deployment but not directly related to identifying security requirements.

| EXAM FOCUS | Use Azure Key Vault for encryption keys, SSO for secure access, and AAD for identity management to meet security needs. |
|---|---|
| CAUTION ALERT | Remember, Power BI is for visualization, not for defining security requirements. |

## QUESTION 10

Answer – A), C)

Option A – Implementing data validation rules ensures data integrity and accuracy.
Option B – Power Automate is useful for automation but not directly related to quality control.
Option C – Creating Power BI reports helps in monitoring data quality.
Option D – Training sessions are useful but not directly related to the main challenges.
Option E – Azure DevOps is useful for managing processes but not specifically for quality control.

| EXAM FOCUS | Implement data validation rules in Power Apps and create Power BI reports to monitor data quality. |
|---|---|
| CAUTION ALERT | Remember, Power Automate is useful for automation but not directly for quality control. |

## QUESTION 11

Answer – A), B), C)

Option A – Using Azure DevOps for version control and release management ensures proper handling of versions.
Option B – Implementing CI/CD pipelines supports continuous improvement and efficient deployment.
Option C – Creating an end-of-life plan ensures a smooth transition from the legacy system.
Option D – Power Virtual Agents can assist with customer support but is not critical for handling lifecycle management.
Option E – Regular review meetings are beneficial but not specific to technical implementation.

| EXAM FOCUS | Use Azure DevOps for version control and CI/CD pipelines to handle continuous improvement and end-of-life planning. |
|---|---|
| CAUTION ALERT | Remember, Power Virtual Agents is useful for customer support but not critical for lifecycle management. |

## QUESTION 12

Answer – C)

Option A – Azure Synapse Analytics is not necessary for this solution.
Option B – Power Apps is not required for automating email campaigns.
Option C – Correct choice as Power Automate handles automation, Power BI provides analytics, and Dynamics 365 Marketing manages the email campaigns.
Option D – Power Virtual Agents is not needed for this scenario.
Option E – While Power Apps can be useful, it is not essential for this specific solution focused on

automation and analytics.

| EXAM FOCUS | *"Power Automate automates triggers, and Power BI provides analytics for Dynamics 365 Marketing."* |
|---|---|
| CAUTION ALERT | *"Don't overlook the need for automation in email campaigns."* |

## QUESTION 13

Answer – A), D), E)

Option A – Regular UAT sessions ensure continuous feedback and iterative development.
Option B – Power BI is useful for analytics but not directly for feedback loops.
Option C – Azure Logic Apps are more for integration than continuous delivery.
Option D – Sprint reviews and retrospectives are essential for adapting to changes in agile environments.
Option E – A CI/CD pipeline with Azure DevOps supports continuous delivery and iterative development.

| EXAM FOCUS | *Conduct regular UAT sessions and implement CI/CD pipelines with Azure DevOps for iterative development.* |
|---|---|
| CAUTION ALERT | *Stay cautious, integration tools like Azure Logic Apps are secondary to primary agile strategies.* |

## QUESTION 14

Answer – B), C), D)

Option A – Power BI Dataflows are useful but less critical than other options for data governance.
Option B – Azure Purview is essential for data governance and cataloging, ensuring compliance with standards.
Option C – Developing a data quality management plan is crucial for defining data quality measures.
Option D – Assigning RBAC roles in Dynamics 365 helps ensure compliance with data governance standards.
Option E – AI Builder can assist with predictions but is less critical for ensuring compliance and defining data quality measures.

| EXAM FOCUS | *Implement Azure Purview for data governance and develop a data quality management plan to ensure consistency.* |
|---|---|
| CAUTION ALERT | *You should avoid overlooking the importance of defining roles in data governance for compliance.* |

## QUESTION 15

Answer – A), C), E)

Option A – Using out-of-the-box functionalities minimizes customization and simplifies maintenance.
Option B – Developing custom connectors for every system increases complexity and should be avoided unless necessary.
Option C – Configuring security roles using Dataverse RBAC features follows best practices in system configuration.
Option D – Customizing entities should be limited to unique needs to avoid excessive customization.

Option E – Utilizing Power BI for reporting leverages existing tools and reduces the need for custom solutions.

| EXAM FOCUS | *You should use out-of-the-box Power Apps functionalities to minimize customization.* |
|---|---|
| CAUTION ALERT | *Stay cautious, developing custom connectors for every external system can increase complexity.* |

## QUESTION 16

Answer – B), E)

Option A – Data Import Wizard is not suitable for complex data transformations.
Option B – Correct choice as Azure Data Factory supports data transformations and scheduled refreshes.
Option C – Dynamics 365 Data Export Service is for exporting data, not importing.
Option D – Power Apps is for building applications, not for data migration.
Option E – Correct choice as Azure Synapse Analytics is powerful and supports complex data processing, though it adds complexity.

| EXAM FOCUS | *"Azure Data Factory supports complex transformations and scheduled refreshes for data migration."* |
|---|---|
| CAUTION ALERT | *"Data Import Wizard is too basic for handling complex data transformations and refreshes."* |

## QUESTION 17

Answer – A), B), C)

Option A – Implementing RBAC in Dataverse ensures proper data access and permissions management.
Option B – Using Power BI for compliance reports and dashboards helps in monitoring compliance.
Option C – Configuring Power Automate to enforce data governance policies ensures ongoing compliance.
Option D – Developing custom connectors adds unnecessary complexity.
Option E – Azure Functions are useful but may not directly integrate with Power Platform governance.

| EXAM FOCUS | *Implement RBAC in Dataverse, use Power BI for compliance reports, and enforce policies with Power Automate.* |
|---|---|
| CAUTION ALERT | *Custom connectors add unnecessary complexity; focus on integrated solutions.* |

## QUESTION 18

Answer – A), E)

Option A – Using Power Automate automates regulatory compliance workflows, ensuring compliance.
Option B – Implementing Azure Cognitive Services supports advanced analytics but might not directly drive innovation.
Option C – Developing model-driven apps supports core business processes but might not directly drive innovation.
Option D – Using Dataverse manages customer data securely but does not directly lead digital transformation initiatives.
Option E – Incorporating Power Virtual Agents enhances customer interactions and drives innovation

within the organization.

| EXAM FOCUS | Power Automate for regulatory compliance; Power Virtual Agents for enhanced interactions. |
| --- | --- |
| CAUTION ALERT | Custom connectors add complexity; focus on integrated solutions. |

## QUESTION 19

Answer – B), D)

Option A – Conducting regular security audits is good but not essential for the primary requirements.
Option B – Implementing SSO with Azure AD ensures secure access and builds trust.
Option C – Using Power Automate to automate compliance reporting supports compliance but does not directly ensure ethical handling.
Option D – Developing a user consent management process ensures ethical handling and builds trust.
Option E – Implementing data encryption in Dataverse is good but not essential for the primary requirements.

| EXAM FOCUS | Implement SSO with Azure AD for secure access and develop a user consent management process. |
| --- | --- |
| CAUTION ALERT | Avoid relying solely on automated compliance reporting for ethical data handling. |

## QUESTION 20

Answer – A), B), C)

Option A – Correct choice as Calculated columns provide dynamic calculations.
Option B – Correct choice as Rollup columns aggregate data.
Option C – Correct choice as Real-time workflows support real-time updates.
Option D – Virtual tables are used for integrating external data, not for complex queries and aggregation.
Option E – Power BI dataflows integrate Dataverse data with Power BI but are more relevant for analytics rather than compliance tracking.

| EXAM FOCUS | "Use Calculated columns, Rollup columns, and Real-time workflows for dynamic data aggregation and real-time updates." |
| --- | --- |
| CAUTION ALERT | "Virtual tables integrate external data but aren't ideal for complex queries and aggregation within Dataverse." |

## QUESTION 21

Answer – A), C)

Option A – MFA using Azure AD enhances security policies, ensuring compliance with HIPAA.
Option B – Power Automate helps streamline workflows but does not directly address HIPAA compliance.
Option C – Encryption of data at rest and in transit ensures data protection and privacy standards.
Option D – Canvas Apps are useful for data entry but do not directly address security policies.
Option E – Regular security risk assessments are important but not specific technical measures for HIPAA compliance.

| EXAM FOCUS | Implement MFA with Azure AD and ensure data encryption. |
| CAUTION ALERT | Regular security assessments are critical to maintaining HIPAA compliance. |

## QUESTION 22

Answer – B), D)

Option A – Azure Policy is useful for enforcing governance but not directly for data storage or RBAC.
Option B – Dataverse ensures data governance and lifecycle management.
Option C – Azure Synapse Analytics provides advanced analytics but does not directly address data governance or RBAC.
Option D – Applying RBAC using Azure AD ensures secure access control.
Option E – Canvas Apps are useful for user interfaces but do not address data governance or RBAC.

| EXAM FOCUS | Implement Dataverse for data governance and Azure AD RBAC for secure access control in financial institutions. |
| CAUTION ALERT | Be cautious about options like Azure Policy that don't directly manage data storage or access control. |

## QUESTION 23

Answer – B), D)

Option A – PCF is useful for custom controls but does not directly ensure accessibility.
Option B – Implementing ARIA landmarks helps make web applications accessible to people with disabilities.
Option C – AI Builder is useful for analyzing data but not directly related to accessibility.
Option D – Conducting usability testing with diverse user groups ensures the interface meets the needs of all users.
Option E – Power Automate is useful for process automation but not directly related to user experience design.

| EXAM FOCUS | Implement ARIA landmarks and conduct usability testing with diverse user groups for an accessible and user-friendly interface. |
| CAUTION ALERT | Don't rely on AI Builder for accessibility; it doesn't directly address user experience design principles. |

## QUESTION 24

Answer – C)

Option A – Power Automate is used for automating workflows, not for integrating AI insights directly into Power BI.
Option B – Power Apps is used for building custom apps and does not directly integrate AI insights into Power BI reports.
Option C – AI Builder allows users to integrate AI models directly into Power BI, enhancing data analytics with AI-driven insights.
Option D – Microsoft Dataverse is used for data storage and management, not for embedding AI insights

into Power BI reports.
Option E – Azure Machine Learning is powerful but requires more advanced setup and does not integrate as seamlessly with Power BI as AI Builder.

| EXAM FOCUS | "Use AI Builder to integrate AI insights directly into Power BI reports." |
|---|---|
| CAUTION ALERT | "Power Automate and Power Apps do not integrate AI insights into Power BI." |

## QUESTION 25

Answer – A), C), E)

Option A – Power BI Dataflows help in data preparation and transformation.
Option B – Power BI Embedded is useful for custom analytics solutions but not necessarily required for the given scenario.
Option C – Power BI AI Insights enables integration of machine learning models for predictive analytics.
Option D – Power BI Paginated Reports are ideal for detailed reporting but not specifically for real-time analytics or machine learning integration.
Option E – Power BI Streaming Datasets are essential for real-time analytics.

| EXAM FOCUS | Utilize Power BI Dataflows, AI Insights, and Streaming Datasets for comprehensive reporting, predictive analytics, and real-time insights. |
|---|---|
| CAUTION ALERT | Don't mistake Paginated Reports for real-time analytics; they are ideal for detailed reporting. |

## QUESTION 26

Answer – A), C), E)

Option A – AI Builder can be used to create machine learning models.
Option B – Power Virtual Agents is useful for interactive sessions but not directly for analytics.
Option C – Azure Cognitive Services provides advanced analytics capabilities.
Option D – Power Automate helps in workflow automation but not specifically for analytics.
Option E – Azure Policy ensures data compliance and privacy.

| EXAM FOCUS | Implement AI Builder, Cognitive Services, and Azure Policy for machine learning, advanced analytics, and data compliance. |
|---|---|
| CAUTION ALERT | Avoid using Power Virtual Agents solely for diagnostics; focus on AI analytics and compliance. |

## QUESTION 27

Answer – A), C), D)

Option A – Azure SQL Database provides fault tolerance.
Option B – Azure Service Bus is useful for messaging but not directly for data synchronization across regions.
Option C – Azure AD is crucial for managing RBAC.
Option D – Dataverse provides secure data storage.

Option E – Azure Functions can automate processes but are not directly related to the core requirements mentioned.

| EXAM FOCUS | Ensure business continuity with Azure SQL Database, Azure AD, and Dataverse for fault tolerance, RBAC, and secure storage. |
|---|---|
| CAUTION ALERT | Be cautious about using Azure Service Bus for synchronization; it's primarily for messaging. |

## QUESTION 28

Answer – A)

Option A – Business Rules allow for setting up data validation rules directly within the Power App, ensuring data consistency before processing.
Option B – Power Automate is used for automating workflows but is not primarily for data validation within Power Apps.
Option C – Custom Connectors are used for connecting to external data sources but do not provide data validation capabilities.
Option D – Power BI Embedded is used for embedding analytics, not for data validation.
Option E – AI Builder is used for adding AI capabilities to apps, not for data validation.

| EXAM FOCUS | "Implement Business Rules to enforce data validation within Power Apps." |
|---|---|
| CAUTION ALERT | "Power Automate is for workflows, not for direct data validation in apps." |

## QUESTION 29

Answer – A), C), E)

Option A – Correct. Microsoft Purview is a comprehensive solution for data governance and compliance.
Option B – Incorrect. Power Automate is useful but not primarily for automated compliance checks.
Option C – Correct. Dataverse provides secure, encrypted storage for sensitive data.
Option D – Incorrect. Azure Functions are useful for data processing but do not directly address compliance.
Option E – Correct. RBAC is crucial for managing access to sensitive data and ensuring compliance.

| EXAM FOCUS | Implement Microsoft Purview for data governance and Dataverse for secure storage. |
|---|---|
| CAUTION ALERT | Power Automate is useful but not primarily for automated compliance checks. |

## QUESTION 30

Answer – A), C), D)

Option A – Correct. Power BI can create data models and visualize sales patterns effectively.
Option B – Incorrect. While useful, Azure Cognitive Services might not be the first choice for this specific requirement.
Option C – Correct. Dataverse securely stores integrated customer data.
Option D – Correct. AI Builder can develop models to predict customer behavior and enhance insights.
Option E – Incorrect. Azure DevOps is useful for project management but not directly for analytics.

| EXAM FOCUS | Utilize Power BI for data modeling and AI Builder for predictive models. |
| CAUTION ALERT | Azure Cognitive Services is useful but might not be the first choice for this scenario. |

## QUESTION 31

Answer – B), C), E)

Option A – Incorrect. While useful, Power Automate is not the primary tool for communication and training.
Option B – Correct. Interactive training modules in Power Apps can engage users effectively.
Option C – Correct. Power BI dashboards help track progress and proficiency.
Option D – Incorrect. Skipping user training can lead to poor adoption.
Option E – Correct. Feedback sessions provide valuable insights to improve training and ensure successful adoption.

| EXAM FOCUS | Develop interactive training modules and use Power BI to track training progress. |
| CAUTION ALERT | Skipping user training can lead to poor adoption. |

## QUESTION 32

Answer – B)

Option A – Power Automate with HTTP connector can work but may not provide the seamless integration and security best practices required.
Option B – A Custom Connector allows for secure, seamless integration tailored to the specific third-party service.
Option C – Azure Logic Apps can also integrate services but may be more complex to set up compared to Custom Connectors.
Option D – Dynamics 365 Business Central is a different ERP system and not used for integrations in this context.
Option E – Microsoft Graph API is not designed for integrating third-party tax calculation services.

| EXAM FOCUS | "Custom Connectors provide secure, seamless integration with third-party services." |
| CAUTION ALERT | "Power Automate HTTP connector may not ensure the required security standards." |

## QUESTION 33

Answer – B), C), E)

Option A – Incorrect. Power Automate is useful for workflows but does not address all advanced customization needs.
Option B – Correct. Implementing custom connectors to integrate third-party APIs allows advanced customization.
Option C – Correct. Following coding best practices, including modular design and documentation, ensures maintainability.
Option D – Incorrect. Focusing solely on adding features can lead to unmanageable solutions.
Option E – Correct. Using Azure DevOps for version control and ALM helps manage complexity and

maintainability.

| EXAM FOCUS | Implement custom connectors and follow best practices for maintainable custom code using Azure DevOps. |
|---|---|
| CAUTION ALERT | Focusing solely on adding features can lead to unmanageable solutions. |

## QUESTION 34

Answer – A), C)

Option A – Using Azure API Management allows secure API exposure and easy integration.
Option B – Custom connectors require more development effort.
Option C – Power Automate can synchronize data in real-time with minimal custom development.
Option D – Azure Logic Apps are useful but may require more configuration.
Option E – Exporting data to Dataverse may not ensure real-time synchronization.

| EXAM FOCUS | Use Azure API Management for secure ERP data exposure and Power Automate for real-time data synchronization. |
|---|---|
| CAUTION ALERT | Custom connectors can require significant development effort; use standard solutions when possible. |

## QUESTION 35

Answer – A), C)

Option A – Azure Front Door efficiently distributes traffic and enhances load management.
Option B – Azure Logic Apps are useful but not primarily for auto-scaling.
Option C – SQL Database elastic pools optimize resources and handle load efficiently.
Option D – Azure DevOps is beneficial for CI/CD but not directly for auto-scaling.
Option E – Manual monitoring is less efficient and prone to delays.

| EXAM FOCUS | Use Azure Front Door to distribute traffic and SQL Database elastic pools for resource optimization during peak times. |
|---|---|
| CAUTION ALERT | Avoid manual monitoring and adjusting resources; automated solutions are more efficient. |

## QUESTION 36

Answer – B), C), D)

Option A – Volatility is less relevant compared to other considerations like compliance and transaction handling.
Option B – Payment transactions are regulated and must comply with industry standards.
Option C – Licensing for the payment gateway and e-commerce platform is essential.
Option D – Transactions must be processed in real-time, making the integration time-sensitive.
Option E – Batch processing is not suitable for real-time payment transactions.

| EXAM FOCUS | "Focus on regulated, licensed, and time-sensitive aspects for payment gateway integration." |
|---|---|
| CAUTION ALERT | "Batch processing cannot handle real-time payment transactions effectively." |

## QUESTION 37

Answer – A), D)

Option A – Localizing the user interface ensures a consistent user experience across regions.
Option B – Azure CDN is useful for distributing static content but does not handle data privacy regulations.
Option C – A single instance with centralized data storage may not comply with local data privacy regulations.
Option D – Azure SQL Database with geo-replication optimizes performance and ensures compliance.
Option E – Azure Logic Apps are useful for data processing but not for global optimization.

| EXAM FOCUS | Localize the user interface for each region and use Azure SQL Database with geo-replication. |
|---|---|
| CAUTION ALERT | A single instance with centralized data storage may not comply with local data privacy regulations. |

## QUESTION 38

Answer – A), B), C)

Option A – Canvas Apps allow for a customizable and user-friendly interface.
Option B – RBAC in Dataverse enables personalization based on user roles.
Option C – In-app surveys provide direct user feedback for continuous improvement.
Option D – A single interface for all users does not cater to personalized needs.
Option E – User training sessions help gather feedback but may not be as continuous or comprehensive as in-app surveys.

| EXAM FOCUS | Use Canvas Apps for intuitive UI and RBAC in Dataverse for personalization. |
|---|---|
| CAUTION ALERT | A single interface for all users does not address the needs of different roles. |

## QUESTION 39

Answer – A), E)

Option A – Azure Backup protects critical data, ensuring it can be restored in case of a disruption, which is fundamental for maintaining operations during unforeseen events.
Option B – Threat modeling helps identify risks but does not directly ensure continuous operation during disruptions. It is more of a preparatory measure than an operational one.
Option C – Using a single instance for all operations can create a single point of failure, making it a risky strategy for business continuity.
Option D – Power Automate can trigger alerts during disruptions, which is useful but does not encompass a full business continuity strategy. It does not ensure the continuation of operations, only alerts that there are issues.
Option E – Regular reviews and updates of the continuity plan ensure that it remains relevant and effective as the business and its environment evolve. This helps in mitigating potential risks and

preparing for future disruptions.

| EXAM FOCUS | *Use Azure Backup for data protection and conduct regular reviews of the continuity plan.* |
|---|---|
| CAUTION ALERT | *Avoid using a single instance for all operations; it creates a single point of failure.* |

## QUESTION 40

Answer – B)

Option A – Power Automate with HTTP connector can work but might not handle complex tax regulations effectively.
Option B – Implementing a Custom Connector allows for seamless and compliant integration with the third-party tax calculation service.
Option C – Dynamics 365 Fraud Protection is for fraud detection, not tax calculations.
Option D – Azure Logic Apps can integrate services but might be more complex than needed.
Option E – Power BI is for data visualization, not for real-time tax calculations.

| EXAM FOCUS | *"Custom Connector ensures compliant and seamless third-party tax service integration."* |
|---|---|
| CAUTION ALERT | *"Power Automate HTTP connector might struggle with complex tax regulations."* |

## QUESTION 41

Answer – A), C), E)

Option A – Azure Traffic Manager helps with load balancing and optimizing performance across different regions.
Option B – Dataverse is suitable for data storage but does not inherently provide multi-region support.
Option C – Azure Front Door provides global routing, ensuring low latency and high performance across regions.
Option D – Power Automate is more suited for workflow automation rather than managing regional service integration.
Option E – Azure Service Bus ensures reliable messaging and supports geo-redundancy, crucial for maintaining data integrity and availability across regions.

| EXAM FOCUS | *Use Azure Traffic Manager and Front Door for global optimization and geo-redundancy.* |
|---|---|
| CAUTION ALERT | *Power Automate is more suited for workflow automation, not regional service integration.* |

## QUESTION 42

Answer – B), C), D)

Option A – While Power Automate can help in automating processes, it is not specifically designed for monitoring and resolving issues.
Option B – Application Insights is a powerful tool for monitoring solution performance and detecting issues, making it essential for ensuring solution health.
Option C – Azure Security Center provides security monitoring and compliance checks, which are crucial for maintaining the overall health and performance of the solution.

Option D – Using Azure DevOps to schedule regular updates and maintenance tasks ensures that the solution is kept up-to-date and stable.
Option E – Manual performance reviews are not as effective as continuous monitoring tools like Application Insights.

| EXAM FOCUS CAUTION ALERT | *Implement Application Insights, Azure Security Center, and Azure DevOps for updates. Manual performance reviews are less effective than continuous monitoring.* |
|---|---|

## QUESTION 43

Answer – A), C), D)

Option A – AI Builder can create machine learning models to detect fraudulent transactions.
Option B – Storing data in an unencrypted format compromises security and is not advisable.
Option C – Power BI can visualize patterns and trends, providing insights into fraudulent activities.
Option D – Power Automate can trigger alerts for suspicious transactions, enabling timely action.
Option E – Manual review of all transactions is impractical and not scalable for large volumes of data.

| EXAM FOCUS CAUTION ALERT | *Use AI Builder for fraud detection and Power BI for visualization. Manual review of transactions isn't scalable for large volumes.* |
|---|---|

## QUESTION 44

Answer – B)

Option A – Incorrect. Real-time dashboards are useful for monitoring data but not for diagnosing synchronization issues.
Option B – Correct. Custom logging via plugins can provide targeted insights into the specific areas of failure within the synchronization process, making it highly effective for troubleshooting.
Option C – Incorrect. Power Apps activity logging monitors user interactions within apps and does not specifically address data integration issues.
Option D – Incorrect. Power Apps error notifications alert users to app-specific issues, not backend synchronization problems.
Option E – Incorrect. Server-side synchronization handles data transfer between Dynamics 365 and email servers, unrelated to diagnosing third-party CRM synchronization issues.

| EXAM FOCUS | "Custom logging via plugins gives detailed insights into synchronization issues, aiding in real-time data accuracy." |
|---|---|
| CAUTION ALERT | "Power Apps activity logging doesn't address backend synchronization issues." |

## QUESTION 45

Answer – A), B), C)

Option A – Creating role-specific training materials ensures that training is relevant and tailored to the needs of different user roles.
Option B – Power Virtual Agents can provide automated user support and answer frequently asked

questions, reducing the load on human support teams.
Option C – Regular training effectiveness assessments using Power BI surveys can help identify areas for improvement and ensure continuous learning.
Option D – Manual feedback collection through email is less efficient and harder to analyze.
Option E – One-time training sessions may not be sufficient to ensure long-term user proficiency.

| EXAM FOCUS | *Use Power Virtual Agents for automated user support and FAQs.* |
|---|---|
| CAUTION ALERT | *Manual feedback collection through email is less efficient.* |

## QUESTION 46

Answer – A), B), C)

Option A – Query folding optimizes data retrieval by pushing query logic to the data source, reducing the amount of data transferred.
Option B – Simplifying the data model by removing unnecessary columns and tables can improve performance by reducing the complexity and size of the model.
Option C – Enabling Power BI Premium provides dedicated resources and better performance for larger datasets and complex calculations.
Option D – Ignoring performance metrics is not advisable as it will lead to unresolved performance issues.
Option E – Avoiding performance optimization techniques will result in continued slow report generation and user dissatisfaction.

| EXAM FOCUS | *"Optimize data models and enable Power BI Premium for better performance and resource allocation."* |
|---|---|
| CAUTION ALERT | *"Ignoring performance metrics will lead to unresolved issues."* |

## QUESTION 47

Answer – A), D)

Option A – Integrating Power Apps with Azure Application Insights provides detailed performance monitoring and diagnostics.
Option B – Using Power Automate to collect user feedback through forms enables automated and systematic feedback collection.
Option C – Skipping real-time monitoring can result in delayed issue detection and resolution; real-time monitoring is crucial.
Option D – Using Power BI to create performance and usage reports provides comprehensive insights into system performance and user interactions.
Option E – Focusing solely on system logs may miss critical user feedback and performance insights; a combination of logs and user feedback is necessary.

| EXAM FOCUS | *"Integrate Power Apps with Azure Application Insights for detailed performance monitoring."* |
|---|---|
| CAUTION ALERT | *"Skipping real-time monitoring can delay issue detection and resolution."* |

## QUESTION 48

Answer – A), B)

Option A – Correct. Automating connection management helps secure and manage data flows across different departmental systems, ensuring that data handling is consistent and secure.
Option B – Correct. Setting up role-based access control automatically for new employees as part of the onboarding process ensures that employees receive appropriate access to systems, enhancing security and compliance.
Option C – Incorrect. While important, service endpoint configuration does not directly simplify the onboarding process.
Option D – Incorrect. Team records creation is less about security and more about organizational structure management.
Option E – Incorrect. Upsert of reference data is crucial for data integrity but less relevant to the specific needs of securing and simplifying the onboarding process.

| EXAM FOCUS | "Automate connection management and role-based access control for secure and simplified employee onboarding." |
|---|---|
| CAUTION ALERT | "Service endpoint configuration alone won't simplify the onboarding process." |

## QUESTION 49

Answer – A), B), E)

Option A – Correct. The Power Platform Admin Center provides tools to monitor performance and manage updates, ensuring the system remains healthy.
Option B – Correct. Regularly reviewing and refactoring customizations helps maintain performance and compatibility with new features.
Option C – Incorrect. While Dataverse is essential for managing data, it does not directly address customization management.
Option D – Incorrect. Developing custom connectors can be complex and should be considered only if there are no other alternatives.
Option E – Correct. Solution Checker helps identify issues in customizations, ensuring they do not negatively impact performance or upgrades.

| EXAM FOCUS | "Use the Power Platform Admin Center to monitor performance and apply updates efficiently." |
|---|---|
| CAUTION ALERT | "Remember, neglecting customization reviews can degrade system performance." |

## QUESTION 50

Answer – B), C), D)

Option A – Incorrect. While Azure DevOps can automate deployments, it does not directly contribute to energy efficiency or sustainability tracking.

Option B – Correct. Power Automate can integrate Dynamics 365 with existing sustainability tracking systems, ensuring seamless data flow.

Option C – Correct. Choosing Azure regions powered by renewable energy supports energy efficiency goals.

Option D – Correct. Power BI dashboards can track and visualize resource utilization, aiding in sustainable decision-making.

Option E – Incorrect. Developing custom connectors is beneficial but not as impactful as using built-in integrations and choosing energy-efficient hosting options.

| | |
|---|---|
| **EXAM FOCUS** | *"Choose Azure regions with renewable energy sources for hosting to support energy efficiency."* |
| **CAUTION ALERT** | *"Remember, overlooking integration with sustainability tracking systems can hinder your goals."* |

# PRACTICE TEST 8 - QUESTIONS ONLY

## QUESTION 1

A manufacturing company aims to enhance their inventory management system using Microsoft Power Platform. The business goals are to reduce inventory costs, minimize stockouts, and improve supply chain visibility. Specific challenges include:
- Lack of real-time inventory data.
- Inefficient restocking processes.
- Poor supply chain coordination.

How would you align the solution with the company's business goals and measure its impact? Select three correct answers.

A) Implement a Power BI dashboard for real-time inventory monitoring.
B) Use Power Automate to automate restocking workflows.
C) Develop a Dataverse-based app for inventory management.
D) Integrate IoT sensors with Azure for real-time data.
E) Use AI Builder to forecast inventory needs.

## QUESTION 2

A financial services firm is looking to enhance client engagement and manage client portfolios more effectively. They require a solution that provides detailed client insights and supports compliance with financial regulations. Which Dynamics 365 products should you recommend? Select up to 2 answers.

A) Dynamics 365 Customer Insights
B) Dynamics 365 Customer Service
C) Dynamics 365 Finance
D) Dynamics 365 Sales

## QUESTION 3

A financial services firm is looking to enhance its investment analysis process using Microsoft Power Platform. The project involves understanding data requirements and ensuring data-driven decision making. The specific challenges are:
- Lack of standardized data formats.
- Difficulty in interpreting complex investment data.
- Ensuring data reliability for decision making.

What solutions would you implement to address these challenges? Select three correct answers.

A) Use Power BI to create standardized data formats.
B) Implement Dataverse to store and manage investment data.
C) Develop a Power BI dashboard to interpret investment data.
D) Use Power Automate to automate data validation processes.
E) Utilize AI Builder to predict investment trends.

## QUESTION 4

To support a retail chain's demand forecasting and inventory management, which tools within the Microsoft ecosystem should be leveraged? Select up to three answers.

A) Dynamics 365 Commerce
B) Power BI
C) Azure Machine Learning
D) Power Apps
E) Microsoft Teams

## QUESTION 5

A manufacturing company wants to implement a new inventory tracking system using Microsoft Power Platform. The project involves understanding relevant legal and compliance issues. The specific challenges are:
- Complying with industry-specific regulatory requirements.
- Ensuring data privacy and security.
- Incorporating compliance verification into the solution.

What actions would you take to address these challenges? Select three correct answers.

A) Use Dataverse to securely store inventory data.
B) Implement DLP policies to ensure data security.
C) Use Azure API Management to manage data access.
D) Apply ALM practices to incorporate compliance.
E) Conduct compliance verification using Power BI.

## QUESTION 6

A manufacturing company is developing a new supply chain management system using Microsoft Power Platform. The project involves cost control strategies and ROI analysis. The specific challenges are:
- Controlling costs throughout the project lifecycle.
- Ensuring the system is scalable to meet future needs.
- Analyzing the ROI for different implementation options.

What actions would you take to address these challenges? Select three correct answers.

A) Use Azure DevOps to manage project costs.
B) Implement Dataverse for scalable data management.
C) Use Power BI to analyze ROI for different options.
D) Develop a cost control strategy using Power Automate.
E) Conduct scalability assessments using Power BI.

## QUESTION 7

A retail company is planning to implement a new inventory management system using Microsoft Power Platform. The project requires rapid prototyping techniques. The specific challenges include:
- Developing a prototype quickly.
- Validating the prototype with key stakeholders.
- Iterating based on stakeholder feedback.

What actions would you take to address these challenges? Select three correct answers.

A) Use Power Apps to create a quick prototype.
B) Use Dataverse to manage inventory data.
C) Conduct rapid prototyping sessions with stakeholders.
D) Use Power BI to visualize inventory levels.
E) Implement feedback loops for iteration.

## QUESTION 8

A financial institution is integrating their customer management system with a third-party service using Microsoft Power Platform. The project involves handling integration challenges. The specific challenges are:
- Ensuring secure data exchange.
- Handling API rate limits.
- Managing data transformation.

What actions would you take to address these challenges? Select three correct answers.

A) Use Azure API Management to handle API rate limits.
B) Implement data encryption using Azure Cognitive Services.
C) Use Power Automate for data transformation workflows.
D) Develop custom APIs for secure data exchange.
E) Implement retry logic using Azure Functions.

## QUESTION 9

A financial services company is integrating its transaction system with Dynamics 365 using Microsoft Power Platform. The project involves data privacy and protection strategies. The specific challenges are:
- Ensuring data encryption during transmission.
- Implementing data masking techniques.
- Complying with GDPR requirements.

What steps would you take to address these challenges? Select two correct answers.

A) Use Azure Information Protection for data classification.
B) Implement data masking using Azure SQL Database.
C) Use Power Automate for workflow automation.
D) Implement TLS/SSL for data encryption.
E) Use Power Virtual Agents for customer interactions.

## QUESTION 10

A financial institution is upgrading its CRM system using Dynamics 365 and Microsoft Power Platform. The project requires defining quality metrics and standards. The specific challenges are:
- Establishing clear quality benchmarks.
- Monitoring compliance with quality standards.
- Ensuring continuous quality improvement.

What steps would you take to address these challenges? Select three correct answers.

A) Use Power BI to create compliance dashboards.

B) Implement Power Automate for real-time alerts.
C) Define quality benchmarks in the project documentation.
D) Conduct regular QA audits.
E) Use Power Apps to collect feedback from users.

## QUESTION 11

A financial institution is deploying a new risk management system using Microsoft Power Platform. The specific challenges are:
- Ensuring robust version control during development.
- Planning for continuous updates and improvements.
- Managing the transition from a legacy system to the new solution.

What steps would you take to address these challenges? Select three correct answers.

A) Implement ALM practices using Azure DevOps.
B) Use Power Automate to schedule regular updates.
C) Develop a comprehensive migration strategy using Azure Data Factory.
D) Utilize Dataverse for data integration and management.
E) Engage with stakeholders to gather feedback and improve the solution.

## QUESTION 12

A multinational corporation is implementing a Dynamics 365 Finance and Operations solution. They need to ensure data residency compliance in multiple regions and optimize performance.
- The solution must comply with local data residency laws.
- It should ensure optimal performance for users in different regions.

Which strategy should you implement for the environment setup?

A) One global production environment hosted in North America
B) Multiple production environments hosted in each region
C) A single production environment with regional data gateways
D) Multiple sandbox environments for each region
E) One production environment with a centralized data management policy

## QUESTION 13

A healthcare provider is transitioning to agile methodologies for its patient management system development using the Microsoft Power Platform. The challenges include:
- Implementing agile methodologies.
- Continuous delivery and feedback loops.
- Managing agile projects.

What tools and methodologies should you recommend to address these challenges? Select three correct answers.

A) Use Azure DevOps for backlog management and sprint planning.
B) Implement Power Virtual Agents for patient interactions.
C) Conduct bi-weekly sprint reviews.
D) Utilize Dataverse for secure data storage.
E) Implement AI Builder for predictive analytics.

## QUESTION 14

You are responsible for managing data governance for a healthcare provider using Microsoft Power Platform. The challenges include:
- Establishing data governance frameworks.
- Ensuring data quality and consistency.
- Compliance with healthcare data regulations.

Which approaches should you take to ensure effective data governance? Select three correct answers.

A) Implement Dataverse for secure data storage and management.
B) Use Azure Data Factory for data integration and transformation.
C) Develop a comprehensive data governance policy.
D) Assign Data Steward roles for maintaining data quality.
E) Use Power Virtual Agents for data governance training.

## QUESTION 15

You are managing a Dynamics 365 project for a manufacturing company. The challenges include:
- Deciding between customization and configuration.
- Impact of customizations on maintenance.
- Balancing flexibility and standardization.

Which strategies should you implement to address these challenges? Select three correct answers.

A) Use Power Automate for process automation instead of custom plugins.
B) Customize Dynamics 365 forms to meet specific UI requirements.
C) Implement ALM practices to manage customizations.
D) Configure standard Dataverse tables for data storage.
E) Develop custom workflows using Azure Logic Apps.

## QUESTION 16

A retail company wants to implement a customer loyalty program using Microsoft Power Platform. The solution needs to track customer purchases and reward points, and send personalized offers based on purchase history.
- The solution must integrate with their existing POS system.
- It should automate the calculation of reward points and sending offers.

Which components should be included in your solution design? Select three answers.

A) Power BI, Dynamics 365 Marketing, Azure Logic Apps
B) Power Apps, Azure Functions, Dynamics 365 Customer Insights
C) Power Apps, Power Automate, Dynamics 365 Customer Insights
D) Power Automate, Dynamics 365 Sales, Power Virtual Agents
E) Power Apps, Power Automate, Power BI

## QUESTION 17

An e-commerce company is deploying a new CRM system using Microsoft Power Platform. The project must:
- Establish governance structures.

- Ensure compliance with CCPA and internal security policies.
- Implement auditing and reporting mechanisms.

Which strategies should you use to address these requirements? Select three correct answers.

A) Utilize Dataverse to manage and secure customer data.
B) Configure DLP policies in Power Automate to prevent unauthorized data access.
C) Use Power BI for detailed auditing and compliance reporting.
D) Develop custom APIs to integrate with third-party compliance tools.
E) Implement role-based security in Dynamics 365 to manage user access.

## QUESTION 18

A healthcare organization is transforming its patient management system using Microsoft Power Platform. The solution must:
- Integrate innovative technologies.
- Disrupt traditional processes for better efficiency.
- Measure the impact of the transformation on patient care.

You need to choose two actions to ensure the solution meets these requirements. Which two actions should you take? (Select two)

A) Use Power Automate to streamline patient workflows.
B) Implement Azure Cognitive Services for predictive analytics.
C) Develop custom connectors for legacy system integration.
D) Use Power BI to create patient care impact reports.
E) Utilize Power Apps component framework (PCF) for building reusable components.

## QUESTION 19

An educational institution is building a student information system using Microsoft Power Platform. The solution must:
- Prevent data breaches.
- Ensure compliance with data protection laws.
- Maintain data security during data transfers.

Which two strategies should you employ? (Select two)

A) Use Azure Logic Apps to automate data transfers.
B) Implement data encryption during data transfer using Dataverse.
C) Use Power Automate to monitor data access logs.
D) Enable data loss prevention (DLP) policies.
E) Use AI Builder to detect anomalies in data access.

## QUESTION 20

A manufacturing company wants to use Microsoft Dataverse to manage its supply chain operations. They need to model complex relationships between suppliers, products, and orders.
- The solution must support one-to-many and many-to-many relationships.
- It should enable tracking of product inventory levels in real-time.

Which components should be included in the data model design? Select three answers.

A) Lookups
B) Option sets
C) Many-to-many relationships
D) Hierarchical relationship settings
E) Real-time workflows

## QUESTION 21

An IT company needs to ensure their Power Platform solution is secure and complies with regulatory standards such as GDPR. The solution must:
- Implement role-based access control (RBAC).
- Ensure data encryption.
- Conduct security audits.

Which two actions should you take? (Select two)

A) Use Azure AD Conditional Access for RBAC.
B) Implement Data Loss Prevention (DLP) policies.
C) Enable Azure Security Center for threat detection.
D) Encrypt data using Azure Key Vault.
E) Use Dynamics 365 for customer relationship management.

## QUESTION 22

A healthcare provider needs a solution for managing large datasets from multiple sources while ensuring data integrity and compliance with healthcare regulations. The solution must:
- Integrate with existing on-premises systems.
- Ensure data quality and integrity.
- Provide big data analytics capabilities.

Which two measures should you implement? (Select two)

A) Use Azure Logic Apps for integration.
B) Implement Azure Data Factory for ETL processes.
C) Use Power Virtual Agents for patient interaction.
D) Implement Data Loss Prevention (DLP) policies.
E) Use Dataverse for data storage and quality management.

## QUESTION 23

A retail company is developing a Power Platform solution to enhance their customer service operations. They want to ensure the user experience (UX) is optimized for both their employees and customers. The solution must:
- Follow user-centered design principles.
- Provide customization options for different user roles.
- Incorporate iterative design based on feedback.

Which two practices should you follow? (Select two)

A) Implement Power Apps model-driven apps.
B) Use Dynamics 365 for user role management.
C) Conduct regular user feedback sessions.

D) Use pre-built Power BI dashboards without customization.
E) Implement Power Virtual Agents to gather real-time feedback.

## QUESTION 24

A financial services firm uses Dynamics 365 Customer Service for managing client interactions. They need to implement a new security model to ensure that only certain users have access to sensitive client data based on their role within the organization. What approach should they use to configure this security model in Dynamics 365?

A) Field-level security
B) Business units
C) Role-based security
D) Team-based security
E) Record ownership security

## QUESTION 25

A healthcare organization wants to use Power BI to monitor patient data. The solution must:
- Provide real-time updates on patient status.
- Use machine learning to predict patient readmissions.
- Ensure compliance with HIPAA regulations.

Which three components or strategies should you implement? (Select three)

A) Power BI Service for dashboard delivery.
B) Azure Cognitive Services for machine learning.
C) Power BI Row-Level Security (RLS) for compliance.
D) Power BI Premium for enhanced performance.
E) Azure Data Lake for data storage.

## QUESTION 26

A financial institution aims to integrate AI for fraud detection. The solution must:
- Monitor transactions in real-time.
- Identify suspicious activities using AI.
- Alert security teams immediately.

Which three components are essential? (Select three)

A) Azure Cognitive Services for fraud detection.
B) AI Builder for transaction analysis.
C) Power Automate for real-time alerts.
D) Dataverse for storing transaction data.
E) Power BI for fraud pattern visualization.

## QUESTION 27

A healthcare provider needs to implement a comprehensive disaster recovery plan for its patient management system built on Power Platform. The solution must:
- Ensure data integrity during disasters.

- Enable rapid recovery of services.
- Maintain compliance with HIPAA regulations.

Which three components are critical for this solution? (Select three)

A) Azure Policy for compliance auditing.
B) Dataverse for secure data storage.
C) Azure Site Recovery for rapid recovery.
D) Power BI for data analysis.
E) Azure Key Vault for encryption.

## QUESTION 28

A retail company uses Dynamics 365 Customer Engagement for managing their sales and customer interactions. They want to automate the process of sending follow-up emails to customers after a sales meeting is logged in the system. The emails should be personalized based on the customer's interaction history. Which tool should they use to implement this automation?

A) Power BI
B) Power Automate
C) Power Apps
D) Dynamics 365 Marketing
E) Azure Functions

## QUESTION 29

Your client is in the retail industry and needs to ensure their Power Platform solution complies with various data protection regulations. They want to automate their compliance processes to minimize manual intervention.
1. Ensuring compliance with CCPA regulations for customer data.
2. Automating data protection measures.
3. Continuously monitoring compliance status.

What measures would you implement to achieve these objectives? Select two answers.

A) Use Power Automate to create workflows for data protection compliance.
B) Implement Azure Policy to enforce compliance policies.
C) Store customer data in Dataverse with DLP policies.
D) Develop custom compliance monitoring tools.
E) Use Azure Monitor for continuous compliance monitoring.

## QUESTION 30

Your client is a manufacturing company looking to use predictive analytics and machine learning to optimize their supply chain operations. They need to integrate external data sources and generate actionable insights to improve efficiency.
1. Integrating supplier and logistics data from various external sources.
2. Applying machine learning models to predict supply chain disruptions.
3. Generating insights to optimize inventory levels and reduce costs.

What measures would you implement to achieve these goals? Select two answers.

A) Use Power BI to integrate and visualize supplier and logistics data.
B) Implement Azure Machine Learning for developing predictive models.
C) Store data in a local database for analysis.
D) Use AI Builder for basic predictive analytics.
E) Implement Azure Service Bus for real-time data integration.

## QUESTION 31

Your client is facing resistance from employees regarding the adoption of a new Dynamics 365 solution. They need strategies to manage this resistance and promote acceptance among users.
1. Addressing user concerns and managing resistance.
2. Promoting acceptance and ensuring a smooth transition.
3. Implementing measures to facilitate change and user adoption.
What strategies would you implement to manage resistance and promote acceptance? Select two answers.

A) Involve key stakeholders in the decision-making process.
B) Implement Power Virtual Agents to provide instant support and guidance.
C) Ignore user feedback and proceed with the implementation.
D) Develop a detailed change management plan focusing on user engagement.
E) Use AI Builder to predict potential resistance points.

## QUESTION 32

A healthcare provider uses Dynamics 365 Customer Service for managing patient inquiries. They need to integrate an AI-driven chatbot that can assist patients with common questions and schedule appointments based on availability in Dynamics 365. The chatbot must have real-time access to Dynamics 365 data. What solution should they implement?

A) Power Virtual Agents
B) Azure Bot Service
C) Power Automate
D) Dynamics 365 Marketing
E) Microsoft Teams

## QUESTION 33

Your client is launching a new Power Platform solution and wants to ensure it includes deep customization and scripting while managing complexity. They also aim to integrate various APIs.
1. Ensuring deep customization and scripting in Power Apps and Power Automate.
2. Integrating various APIs through custom connectors.
3. Managing the complexity of the custom solutions.
What strategies would you implement to achieve these objectives? Select two answers.

A) Use Azure Functions for complex server-side logic.
B) Implement Power Virtual Agents to automate customer interactions.
C) Create custom connectors to integrate external APIs.
D) Avoid deep customization to reduce complexity.
E) Follow best practices for scripting, including code reviews and continuous integration.

## QUESTION 34

During a legacy system integration project, you need to bridge the technology gap between an old on-premises database and a new cloud-based solution using Microsoft technologies. The project requires:
- Secure data transfer.
- Minimal changes to the existing system.
- Efficient data transformation and loading. What strategies should you use? (Select 3 answers)

A) Implement Azure Data Factory for ETL processes.
B) Use Azure Service Bus to handle messaging and data transfer.
C) Develop custom ETL scripts using Azure Functions.
D) Utilize Azure Logic Apps to automate workflows.
E) Apply Azure Cognitive Services for data transformation.

## QUESTION 35

During the implementation of a new Dynamics 365 solution, you need to ensure it scales efficiently with future growth. The solution should:
- Automatically adjust resources based on demand.
- Minimize costs while maximizing performance.
- Be resilient to traffic spikes. What are the best practices to achieve these goals? (Select 3 answers)

A) Use Azure Functions to handle background processes.
B) Implement auto-scaling rules in Azure App Services.
C) Optimize Dataverse performance settings.
D) Utilize Azure Traffic Manager to distribute traffic.
E) Conduct regular performance tuning and load testing.

## QUESTION 36

A financial institution uses Dynamics 365 Finance to manage accounting operations. They need to integrate a fraud detection service to monitor transactions in real-time. The integration must ensure compliance with financial regulations and handle large volumes of transaction data. Which categorizations should you consider for this integration?

A) Batch
B) Regulated
C) Time-sensitive
D) Volatility
E) Volume

## QUESTION 37

Your organization needs to deploy a Power Apps solution across multiple regions. The deployment must:
- Ensure data residency compliance.
- Provide high availability and disaster recovery.
- Optimize user experience and performance. What strategies should you adopt? (Select 2 answers)

A) Use Dataverse with multi-geo capabilities for data storage.
B) Deploy the solution in a single central region.

C) Implement Azure Site Recovery for disaster recovery.
D) Use Azure Front Door for global load balancing.
E) Enable manual failover processes for disaster recovery.

## QUESTION 38

A financial services company needs to enhance the customer experience in their mobile banking app using Power Platform. The solution must:
- Personalize user experience based on their transaction history.
- Continuously gather and analyze user feedback.
- Track KPIs for user engagement and satisfaction. What strategies should you implement? (Select 2 answers)

A) Use AI Builder to analyze transaction data and provide personalized insights.
B) Implement Power BI dashboards to track KPIs for user engagement.
C) Use a standard interface for all users.
D) Deploy Power Automate to send periodic surveys and gather feedback.
E) Collect feedback only during the initial phase of the app deployment.

## QUESTION 39

Your company is deploying a Power Platform solution globally and needs to plan for business continuity. The solution must:
- Secure data at rest and in transit.
- Implement recovery strategies.
- Regularly evaluate and update the continuity plan. What steps should you take? (Select 2 answers)

A) Use Azure Security Center for continuous security monitoring.
B) Encrypt data in Dataverse at rest and in transit.
C) Implement a single layer of security at the application level.
D) Use Azure Site Recovery to automate failover processes.
E) Schedule regular penetration testing and vulnerability assessments.

## QUESTION 40

A global non-profit organization uses Dynamics 365 Customer Service to manage donor interactions. They need to integrate a third-party email marketing platform to automatically add new donors to an email campaign when they donate. The integration must ensure compliance with data privacy regulations and provide real-time updates. What should they use to achieve this?

A) Power Automate with email marketing connector
B) Azure Logic Apps
C) Custom API integration
D) Data Export Service
E) Dynamics 365 Marketing

## QUESTION 41

An e-commerce company is preparing for a significant increase in traffic during a major sale event. The

solution must:
- Scale dynamically to handle traffic spikes.
- Ensure zero downtime during scaling.
- Monitor performance in real-time. What steps should you take? (Select 3 answers)

A) Use Azure Autoscale for automatic scaling of resources.
B) Implement Azure Load Balancer for distributing traffic.
C) Use Azure Monitor for real-time performance monitoring.
D) Deploy Azure API Management for handling API requests.
E) Use Power BI for real-time traffic analysis.

## QUESTION 42

An educational institution has deployed a Power Platform solution to manage student data and administrative processes. They need to:
- Ensure the solution remains stable over time.
- Perform proactive issue detection and resolution.
- Monitor and update the solution regularly. What steps should they take? (Select 3 answers)

A) Use Azure Logic Apps to automate maintenance tasks.
B) Implement Dataverse with data encryption for secure data storage.
C) Use Azure Monitor for real-time solution health tracking and alerts.
D) Schedule regular maintenance and updates using Azure DevOps.
E) Perform quarterly manual reviews to check for issues.

## QUESTION 43

A healthcare provider wants to integrate custom reports into their decision-making processes. They need to:
- Ensure compliance with healthcare regulations.
- Provide tailored reports for different departments.
- Maintain data security and privacy. What strategies should they implement? (Select 3 answers)

A) Use Power BI to create custom reports for each department.
B) Implement role-based access control (RBAC) to secure reports.
C) Store patient data in plain text for easier access.
D) Use Power Automate to automate report distribution.
E) Conduct manual audits to ensure data compliance.

## QUESTION 44

In a logistics company, a solution architect designs a Power Platform integration that pulls shipping data from multiple sources into a central system. After deployment, discrepancies in shipment records have been observed. The architect needs to identify the fault in data handling.
- Accurate data handling.
- Identify faults in integration.

What tool should you utilize to troubleshoot the issue?

A) Power BI audit logs

B) Trace logging
C) Microsoft Power Apps activity logging
D) Dataflow diagnostics
E) Common Data Service audit

## QUESTION 45

A financial institution is deploying a new system with Power Platform. They must:
• Ensure ongoing user training and support.
• Collect and incorporate user feedback effectively.
• Assess training program effectiveness regularly. What should they do?

A) Develop an interactive learning portal using Power Apps.
B) Use Microsoft Forms integrated with Power Automate to collect feedback.
C) Conduct quarterly training effectiveness reviews using Power BI.
D) Provide a support hotline for immediate assistance.
E) Rely on initial training sessions without follow-up.

## QUESTION 46

An e-commerce company is experiencing slow response times with their Power Apps application. Their requirements include:
• Identifying and addressing performance bottlenecks.
• Ensuring efficient resource management.
• Implementing continuous performance monitoring. What actions should they take?

A) Use the Power Apps Monitor tool to analyze app performance.
B) Optimize data source queries to reduce load times.
C) Implement Azure Application Insights for continuous monitoring.
D) Add more features without addressing performance issues.
E) Ignore performance issues and focus on functionality.

## QUESTION 47

An educational institution is deploying Dynamics 365 for student management. To effectively monitor and analyze the system, they must:
• Implement real-time monitoring and alerts.
• Use analytics for performance insights.
• Report on user behavior and feedback. What tools should they utilize?
Select 2 answers.

A) Use Dynamics 365 Customer Insights for analytics.
B) Implement Azure Monitor for real-time alerts.
C) Rely only on manual data collection for feedback.
D) Utilize Power BI for performance reporting.
E) Ignore user behavior analytics.

## QUESTION 48

A multinational corporation is deploying a new CRM system integrated with Microsoft Power Platform. The integration involves complex workflows and data from various global divisions. Automating certain aspects of the deployment could save time and reduce errors. You need to identify which integration-related tasks to automate.
• Reduce deployment errors.
• Save time on integration processes.
What two tasks would you automate to ensure a smooth deployment?

A) Connection management
B) Webhook configuration
C) Data validation checks
D) Service endpoint configuration
E) Team records creation

## QUESTION 49

An educational institution is using a combination of Power Apps and Dynamics 365 to manage student and faculty data. The institution needs to manage customizations effectively to ensure smooth upgrades and minimal disruptions. The key requirements are:
• Implementing version control for customizations.
• Balancing custom and out-of-the-box features.
• Addressing deprecated features.
What strategies should you employ? (Select 2 answers)

A) Use Azure DevOps for version control and managing customizations.
B) Implement managed solutions to package and deploy customizations.
C) Regularly review Microsoft's release notes to identify deprecated features.
D) Use Canvas Apps for custom features instead of Model-Driven Apps.
E) Implement automated testing for customizations using the Power Automate Test Framework.

## QUESTION 50

An educational institution is deploying a new Power Platform solution aimed at promoting eco-friendly practices and reducing its carbon footprint. The key requirements are:
• Implementing energy-efficient deployment strategies.
• Promoting sustainability among students and staff.
• Monitoring and reducing the carbon footprint of IT infrastructure.
What strategies should you employ? (Select 3 answers)

A) Use Azure Logic Apps to automate eco-friendly reminders and tips.
B) Implement AI Builder to analyze and optimize energy usage patterns.
C) Create a Power Apps portal to share sustainability initiatives and progress.
D) Use Azure Monitor to track the carbon footprint of IT resources.
E) Schedule cloud resource usage during off-peak hours to reduce energy consumption.

# PRACTICE TEST 8 - ANSWERS ONLY

## QUESTION 1

Answer – A), B), E)

Option A – Real-time monitoring helps visibility and addresses the lack of real-time inventory data.
Option B – Automating restocking helps efficiency, addressing inefficient restocking processes.
Option C – A Dataverse-based app centralizes data but does not ensure real-time updates or coordination.
Option D – IoT sensors provide real-time data but do not address restocking or forecasting.
Option E – AI Builder can forecast inventory needs, reducing costs and stockouts, aligning with business goals.

| | |
|---|---|
| **EXAM FOCUS** | *Implement Power BI for inventory monitoring, automate restocking with Power Automate, and forecast needs with AI Builder to reduce costs.* |
| **CAUTION ALERT** | *Please keep in mind, IoT sensors alone won't address restocking inefficiencies or inventory forecasting.* |

## QUESTION 2

Answer – A), D)

Option A – Correct. Dynamics 365 Customer Insights offers deep analytical capabilities that can help the firm understand client behaviors and preferences, enhancing client engagement through personalized experiences.
Option B – Incorrect. Dynamics 365 Customer Service is ideal for managing customer interactions but does not specifically cater to financial portfolio management or regulatory compliance.
Option C – Incorrect. Dynamics 365 Finance manages financial operations but does not provide client engagement features.
Option D – Correct. Dynamics 365 Sales enables effective management of client portfolios and interactions, ensuring that client relationships are managed efficiently and in compliance with financial regulations.

| | |
|---|---|
| **EXAM FOCUS** | *"Dynamics 365 Customer Insights and Sales provide client insights and portfolio management while ensuring regulatory compliance."* |
| **CAUTION ALERT** | *"Customer Service and Finance modules aren't tailored for client engagement or portfolio management."* |

## QUESTION 3

Answer – B), C), D)

Option A – Power BI can create visualizations but not standardized data formats.
Option B – Dataverse helps store and manage investment data, ensuring reliability.
Option C – A Power BI dashboard allows for interpreting complex investment data.
Option D – Power Automate can automate data validation, ensuring data reliability.
Option E – AI Builder for trend prediction is useful but not critical for data standardization or reliability.

| EXAM FOCUS | *Use Dataverse for data management, Power BI for interpreting data, and Power Automate for data validation.* |
|---|---|
| CAUTION ALERT | *Please keep in mind, creating standardized data formats in Power BI alone won't solve data reliability issues.* |

## QUESTION 4

Answer – A), B) & C)

Option A – Correct. Dynamics 365 Commerce integrates advanced retail solutions including inventory management.
Option B – Correct. Power BI for analyzing sales data and forecasting demand.
Option C – Correct. Azure Machine Learning can be used to enhance forecasting accuracy with advanced analytics.
Option D – Incorrect. Power Apps develops applications but is less involved in complex data analytics or forecasting.
Option E – Incorrect. Microsoft Teams is primarily for communication and does not directly contribute to inventory management or forecasting.

| EXAM FOCUS | *"Dynamics 365 Commerce integrates advanced retail solutions, including inventory management."* |
|---|---|
| CAUTION ALERT | *"Please keep in mind, Power Apps develops applications but is less involved in complex analytics."* |

## QUESTION 5

Answer – A), B), E)

Option A – Dataverse provides secure storage for inventory data, ensuring compliance with regulatory requirements.
Option B – DLP policies ensure data security and compliance.
Option C – Azure API Management is useful for managing data access but does not directly ensure compliance.
Option D – ALM practices are essential but do not directly address compliance verification.
Option E – Power BI is useful for conducting compliance verification.

| EXAM FOCUS | *Use Dataverse for secure data storage and DLP policies for data security compliance.* |
|---|---|
| CAUTION ALERT | *Remember, Azure API Management is useful but won't directly address compliance verification.* |

## QUESTION 6

Answer – A), C), D)

Option A – Azure DevOps can be used to manage project costs.
Option B – Dataverse is useful for scalable data management but does not directly address cost control or ROI analysis.
Option C – Power BI can be used to analyze ROI for different implementation options.
Option D – Developing a cost control strategy using Power Automate helps in managing costs throughout the project lifecycle.

Option E – Scalability assessments are useful but do not directly address cost control or ROI analysis.

| EXAM FOCUS | Manage project costs with Azure DevOps and analyze ROI using Power BI for effective cost control. |
|---|---|
| CAUTION ALERT | Stay cautious, focusing on data management alone won't control costs or analyze ROI comprehensively. |

## QUESTION 7

Answer – A), C), E)

Option A – Power Apps can be used to create a quick prototype for the inventory management system.
Option B – Dataverse is useful for managing inventory data but not directly related to rapid prototyping.
Option C – Conducting rapid prototyping sessions with stakeholders helps validate the prototype.
Option D – Power BI is useful for visualizing data but not directly related to rapid prototyping.
Option E – Implementing feedback loops for iteration ensures continuous improvement based on stakeholder feedback.

| EXAM FOCUS | Create quick prototypes with Power Apps and implement feedback loops for continuous improvement. |
|---|---|
| CAUTION ALERT | Please keep in mind, Dataverse is useful for data management but not for rapid prototyping. |

## QUESTION 8

Answer – A), C), E)

Option A – Azure API Management can handle API rate limits.
Option B – Data encryption is important but Azure Cognitive Services is not typically used for this purpose.
Option C – Power Automate can manage data transformation workflows.
Option D – Developing custom APIs can ensure secure data exchange but is not a primary action for handling integration challenges.
Option E – Implementing retry logic using Azure Functions helps manage API rate limits and data exchange.

| EXAM FOCUS | Use Azure API Management for rate limits, Power Automate for data transformation, and retry logic with Azure Functions. |
|---|---|
| CAUTION ALERT | Please keep in mind, Azure Cognitive Services is not typically used for encryption. |

## QUESTION 9

Answer – B), D)

Option A – Azure Information Protection is useful for data classification but not directly related to data privacy and protection strategies.
Option B – Implementing data masking using Azure SQL Database ensures data protection.
Option C – Power Automate is useful for workflow automation but not directly related to data privacy and protection.
Option D – Implementing TLS/SSL ensures data encryption during transmission.

Option E – Power Virtual Agents is useful for customer interactions but not directly related to data privacy and protection strategies.

| EXAM FOCUS | Use Azure SQL Database for data masking and TLS/SSL for data encryption to ensure data privacy and protection. |
|---|---|
| CAUTION ALERT | Please keep in mind, Power Automate does not address data privacy and protection directly. |

## QUESTION 10

Answer – A), C), D)

Option A – Using Power BI for compliance dashboards ensures clear monitoring.
Option B – Power Automate for alerts is useful but not specifically for monitoring compliance.
Option C – Defining quality benchmarks in documentation ensures clear standards.
Option D – Regular QA audits help in maintaining and improving quality.
Option E – Collecting feedback is useful but does not directly address the main challenges.

| EXAM FOCUS | Use Power BI for compliance dashboards, define benchmarks, and conduct regular QA audits. |
|---|---|
| CAUTION ALERT | Please keep in mind, Power Automate for alerts is useful but not for compliance monitoring. |

## QUESTION 11

Answer – A), C), E)

Option A – Implementing ALM practices using Azure DevOps ensures proper version control.
Option B – Power Automate can help schedule updates but is not directly related to managing continuous improvements.
Option C – Developing a migration strategy using Azure Data Factory ensures smooth data transition.
Option D – Utilizing Dataverse is important for data management but not specific to version control or migration strategy.
Option E – Engaging with stakeholders ensures continuous improvement through feedback.

| EXAM FOCUS | Implement ALM with Azure DevOps and develop a migration strategy using Azure Data Factory. |
|---|---|
| CAUTION ALERT | Keep in mind, Power Automate is useful for scheduling updates but not for managing continuous improvements. |

## QUESTION 12

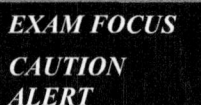

Answer – B)

Option A – A single global environment may not comply with local data residency laws.
Option B – Correct choice as it ensures compliance and performance by having environments in each region.
Option C – Regional data gateways can help but may not fully address compliance issues.
Option D – Sandbox environments are not suitable for production use.
Option E – Centralized data management policy alone may not ensure compliance and performance across regions.

| EXAM FOCUS | "Multiple regional production environments ensure compliance and performance." |
|---|---|
| CAUTION ALERT | "A single global environment might fail to meet local data residency laws." |

## QUESTION 13

Answer – A), C), D)

Option A – Azure DevOps is critical for backlog management and sprint planning in agile methodologies.
Option B – Power Virtual Agents are useful but not directly related to managing agile projects.
Option C – Bi-weekly sprint reviews ensure continuous delivery and feedback loops.
Option D – Dataverse provides secure data storage, aligning with agile projects.
Option E – AI Builder is beneficial for analytics but not directly for agile methodologies.

| EXAM FOCUS | Use Azure DevOps for sprint planning and conduct bi-weekly sprint reviews for continuous feedback. |
|---|---|
| CAUTION ALERT | Remember, Power Virtual Agents are useful but not core to managing agile methodologies. |

## QUESTION 14

Answer – A), C), D)

Option A – Dataverse is essential for secure data storage and management, ensuring data quality and consistency.
Option B – Azure Data Factory is useful for data integration but less critical for establishing a governance framework.
Option C – Developing a comprehensive data governance policy is crucial for effective data governance.
Option D – Assigning Data Steward roles is essential for maintaining data quality.
Option E – Power Virtual Agents are useful for training but less critical for effective data governance.

| EXAM FOCUS | Utilize Dataverse for secure data storage and develop a comprehensive data governance policy for effective governance. |
|---|---|
| CAUTION ALERT | Please keep in mind, relying solely on training tools like Power Virtual Agents may not ensure effective data stewardship. |

## QUESTION 15

Answer – A), C), D)

Option A – Using Power Automate for process automation reduces the need for custom plugins, simplifying maintenance.
Option B – Customizing forms increases maintenance efforts and should be minimized.
Option C – Implementing ALM practices helps manage and track customizations effectively.
Option D – Configuring standard Dataverse tables for data storage follows best practices and balances flexibility with standardization.
Option E – Custom workflows using Azure Logic Apps add complexity and should be avoided unless necessary.

| EXAM FOCUS | Remember, using Power Automate for process automation reduces the need for custom plugins. |
|---|---|
| CAUTION ALERT | Avoid customizing forms excessively as it increases maintenance efforts. |

## QUESTION 16

Answer – B), C), E)

Option A – While these tools are powerful, they do not directly address the need for automating rewards and offers.
Option B – Correct choice as Azure Functions can handle complex integrations, and Dynamics 365 Customer Insights for analyzing purchase history.
Option C – Correct choice as it includes Power Apps for data entry, Power Automate for automation, and Dynamics 365 Customer Insights for analyzing purchase history.
Option D – Dynamics 365 Sales is more suited for managing sales processes.
Option E – Correct choice as Power BI is for analytics, Power Automate for automation, and Power Apps for data entry.

| EXAM FOCUS | "Use Dynamics 365 Customer Insights to analyze purchase history and personalize offers." |
| --- | --- |
| CAUTION ALERT | "Azure Logic Apps alone may not suffice for comprehensive loyalty program automation." |

## QUESTION 17

Answer – A), B), C)

Option A – Utilizing Dataverse helps manage and secure customer data.
Option B – Configuring DLP policies in Power Automate prevents unauthorized data access and ensures compliance.
Option C – Using Power BI for auditing and compliance reporting provides insights into data usage and compliance.
Option D – Developing custom APIs increases complexity and maintenance overhead.
Option E – Implementing role-based security in Dynamics 365 is useful but not a primary strategy for governance.

| EXAM FOCUS | Use Dataverse for customer data, configure DLP policies in Power Automate, and use Power BI for compliance reporting. |
| --- | --- |
| CAUTION ALERT | Custom APIs increase complexity; use built-in capabilities whenever possible. |

## QUESTION 18

Answer – B), D)

Option A – Using Power Automate streamlines workflows but might not fully integrate innovative technologies.
Option B – Implementing Azure Cognitive Services provides predictive analytics, integrating innovative technologies.
Option C – Developing custom connectors integrates legacy systems but does not directly disrupt traditional processes.
Option D – Using Power BI to create reports measures the impact of the transformation on patient care.
Option E – Utilizing Power Apps component framework (PCF) builds reusable components but might not fully address the innovative and disruptive technology integration.

| EXAM FOCUS | Azure Cognitive Services for predictive analytics; Power BI for impact reports. |
| CAUTION ALERT | Custom connectors integrate legacy systems but don't disrupt processes. |

## QUESTION 19

Answer – B), D)

Option A – Using Azure Logic Apps to automate data transfers is good but not essential for preventing data breaches.
Option B – Implementing data encryption during data transfer using Dataverse ensures data security during transfers.
Option C – Using Power Automate to monitor data access logs supports security but is not essential for the primary requirements.
Option D – Enabling DLP policies ensures compliance with data protection laws.
Option E – Using AI Builder to detect anomalies supports security but is not essential for preventing data breaches.

| EXAM FOCUS | Use Dataverse for encryption and enable DLP policies to prevent data breaches and ensure compliance. |
| CAUTION ALERT | Avoid neglecting data transfer security measures like encryption during data transfer. |

## QUESTION 20

Answer – A), C), E)

Option A – Correct choice as Lookups handle one-to-many and many-to-many relationships.
Option B – Option sets are for picklists, not for defining relationships.
Option C – Correct choice as Many-to-many relationships are necessary for the model.
Option D – Hierarchical relationship settings are useful but less critical than real-time workflows.
Option E – Correct choice as Real-time workflows support real-time tracking of inventory levels.

| EXAM FOCUS | "Combine Lookups, Many-to-many relationships, and Real-time workflows for managing complex supply chain operations." |
| CAUTION ALERT | "Option sets are for picklists and not suitable for modeling relationships." |

## QUESTION 21

Answer – A), D)

Option A – Azure AD Conditional Access for RBAC ensures secure access control.
Option B – DLP policies are useful for data protection but not specific for role-based access control.
Option C – Azure Security Center helps with threat detection but does not directly address RBAC or encryption.
Option D – Encrypting data using Azure Key Vault ensures data protection.
Option E – Dynamics 365 is useful for customer relationship management but does not address security and compliance.

| EXAM FOCUS | Use Azure AD Conditional Access for RBAC and Azure Key Vault for encryption. |
|---|---|
| CAUTION ALERT | DLP policies alone are not sufficient; focus on comprehensive security measures. |

## QUESTION 22

Answer – B), E)

Option A – Azure Logic Apps are useful for integration but do not directly ensure data quality or provide big data analytics.
Option B – Azure Data Factory handles ETL processes, ensuring data quality and integrity.
Option C – Power Virtual Agents are useful for interaction but do not handle data quality or big data analytics.
Option D – DLP policies are important for data protection but do not directly ensure data quality or provide analytics.
Option E – Dataverse ensures data storage and quality management, supporting big data analytics.

| EXAM FOCUS | Utilize Azure Data Factory for ETL processes and Dataverse for quality data management in healthcare solutions. |
|---|---|
| CAUTION ALERT | Don't mistake Power Virtual Agents for tools that ensure data quality or provide big data analytics. |

## QUESTION 23

Answer – C), E)

Option A – Model-driven apps can be customized but do not directly address iterative design or feedback incorporation.
Option B – Dynamics 365 is useful for role management but does not directly address user-centered design principles.
Option C – Conducting regular user feedback sessions ensures the design remains user-centered and iterative.
Option D – Using pre-built dashboards without customization may not meet specific user needs.
Option E – Implementing Power Virtual Agents to gather real-time feedback supports iterative design.

| EXAM FOCUS | Remember to conduct regular user feedback sessions and use Power Virtual Agents for iterative design improvements. |
|---|---|
| CAUTION ALERT | Be cautious about using pre-built dashboards without customization; they might not suit all user roles. |

## QUESTION 24

Answer – C)

Option A – Field-level security is used to restrict access to specific fields within a record, not entire records based on roles.
Option B – Business units help organize users into manageable units but do not provide the granularity needed for role-based access control.
Option C – Role-based security allows for the creation of security roles that can be assigned to users to

control their access to sensitive data based on their roles.
Option D – Team-based security can complement role-based security but is not sufficient on its own for defining access based on roles.
Option E – Record ownership security manages access based on who owns the record, which is less flexible than role-based security for this scenario.

| EXAM FOCUS | "Configure Role-based security to control access to sensitive data based on user roles." |
| --- | --- |
| CAUTION ALERT | "Field-level and record ownership security lack the necessary granularity for role-based access." |

## QUESTION 25

Answer – A), B), C)

Option A – Power BI Service is crucial for delivering dashboards with real-time updates.
Option B – Azure Cognitive Services can be used for machine learning to predict patient readmissions.
Option C – Power BI Row-Level Security (RLS) ensures compliance with HIPAA by restricting data access.
Option D – Power BI Premium enhances performance but is not directly related to real-time updates or machine learning.
Option E – Azure Data Lake is useful for data storage but not directly related to real-time updates or compliance.

| EXAM FOCUS | Use Power BI Service, Azure Cognitive Services, and RLS to deliver real-time updates, predictive analytics, and ensure HIPAA compliance. |
| --- | --- |
| CAUTION ALERT | Avoid relying on Power BI Premium alone for performance; it doesn't address real-time updates or compliance directly. |

## QUESTION 26

Answer – A), B), C)

Option A – Azure Cognitive Services can be used for fraud detection algorithms.
Option B – AI Builder can analyze transactions for suspicious activities.
Option C – Power Automate can trigger real-time alerts.
Option D – Dataverse is useful for data storage but not specifically for real-time monitoring.
Option E – Power BI is useful for visualization but not for real-time detection and alerts.

| EXAM FOCUS | Use Cognitive Services, AI Builder, and Power Automate for fraud detection, transaction analysis, and real-time alerts. |
| --- | --- |
| CAUTION ALERT | Don't rely on Dataverse for real-time monitoring; it's for data storage. |

## QUESTION 27

Answer – B), C), E)

Option A – Azure Policy is useful for compliance auditing but not specific to disaster recovery.
Option B – Dataverse provides secure data storage.
Option C – Azure Site Recovery is critical for rapid recovery.

Option D – Power BI is for analysis and does not directly manage compliance requirements.
Option E – Azure Key Vault is essential for ensuring data encryption and maintaining compliance.

| | |
|---|---|
| EXAM FOCUS | *Implement Dataverse, Azure Site Recovery, and Azure Key Vault for secure storage, rapid recovery, and data encryption.* |
| CAUTION ALERT | *Don't use Power BI for disaster recovery planning; it's for data analysis.* |

## QUESTION 28

Answer – B)

Option A – Power BI is used for data visualization and analytics, not for email automation.
Option B – Power Automate can automate the sending of personalized follow-up emails based on triggers and conditions in Dynamics 365.
Option C – Power Apps is used for building custom applications, not for automating emails.
Option D – Dynamics 365 Marketing could be used for email campaigns but is more complex for simple follow-up email automation.
Option E – Azure Functions can be used for automation but requires coding and is more complex compared to Power Automate.

| | |
|---|---|
| EXAM FOCUS | *"Power Automate can automate personalized follow-up emails based on Dynamics 365 triggers."* |
| CAUTION ALERT | *"Power BI and Power Apps are not designed for email automation."* |

## QUESTION 29

Answer – C), E)

Option A – Incorrect. Power Automate is useful but not primarily designed for data protection compliance.
Option B – Incorrect. Azure Policy enforces policies but may not cover all compliance needs.
Option C – Correct. Dataverse with DLP policies ensures secure storage and compliance.
Option D – Incorrect. Custom tools can be costly and complex to maintain.
Option E – Correct. Azure Monitor provides continuous monitoring for compliance.

| | |
|---|---|
| EXAM FOCUS | *Store customer data in Dataverse with DLP policies and use Azure Monitor for continuous monitoring.* |
| CAUTION ALERT | *Custom tools can be costly and complex to maintain.* |

## QUESTION 30

Answer – A), B)

Option A – Correct. Power BI can integrate and visualize data effectively.
Option B – Correct. Azure Machine Learning is suitable for developing advanced predictive models.
Option C – Incorrect. Storing data locally limits the scope and scalability of analysis.
Option D – Incorrect. AI Builder may not provide the advanced analytics required for this scenario.

Option E – Incorrect. Azure Service Bus is useful for real-time integration but not primarily for predictive analytics.

| EXAM FOCUS | Integrate data using Power BI and develop predictive models with Azure Machine Learning. |
|---|---|
| CAUTION ALERT | Storing data locally limits scalability and advanced analytics. |

## QUESTION 31

Answer – A), D)

Option A – Correct. Involving key stakeholders helps address concerns and promote acceptance.
Option B – Incorrect. While useful, Power Virtual Agents alone cannot manage resistance.
Option C – Incorrect. Ignoring user feedback can lead to increased resistance.
Option D – Correct. A detailed change management plan focusing on user engagement is essential for managing resistance.
Option E – Incorrect. AI Builder is not designed for predicting resistance points.

| EXAM FOCUS | Involve key stakeholders and develop a detailed change management plan. |
|---|---|
| CAUTION ALERT | Ignoring user feedback can increase resistance. |

## QUESTION 32

Answer – A)

Option A – Power Virtual Agents allows for the easy creation of AI-driven chatbots with real-time access to Dynamics 365 data.
Option B – Azure Bot Service can also be used but requires more complex setup compared to Power Virtual Agents.
Option C – Power Automate is used for workflow automation, not for creating AI-driven chatbots.
Option D – Dynamics 365 Marketing is focused on marketing automation, not patient assistance chatbots.
Option E – Microsoft Teams is used for collaboration, not for creating AI-driven chatbots.

| EXAM FOCUS | "Power Virtual Agents ensures easy creation of AI-driven chatbots with Dynamics 365." |
|---|---|
| CAUTION ALERT | "Azure Bot Service setup is more complex than Power Virtual Agents." |

## QUESTION 33

Answer – A), E)

Option A – Correct. Azure Functions support complex server-side logic, enhancing customization.
Option B – Incorrect. Power Virtual Agents are useful but not primarily for deep customization and scripting.
Option C – Incorrect. While creating custom connectors is important, it is not sufficient alone.
Option D – Incorrect. Avoiding deep customization can limit solution capabilities.
Option E – Correct. Following best practices for scripting, including code reviews and continuous integration, helps manage complexity.

| EXAM FOCUS | Use Azure Functions for complex logic and follow best scripting practices, including code reviews. |
|---|---|
| CAUTION ALERT | Avoiding deep customization can limit solution capabilities and lead to incomplete implementations. |

## QUESTION 34

Answer – A), B), D)

Option A – Azure Data Factory is ideal for ETL processes and efficient data transformation.
Option B – Azure Service Bus ensures secure and reliable data transfer.
Option C – Custom ETL scripts may require significant changes and maintenance.
Option D – Azure Logic Apps automate workflows and integrate different services efficiently.
Option E – Azure Cognitive Services are not typically used for data transformation in ETL processes.

| EXAM FOCUS | Utilize Azure Data Factory for ETL processes and Azure Service Bus for secure data transfer with minimal system changes. |
|---|---|
| CAUTION ALERT | Custom ETL scripts can lead to high maintenance; prefer automated solutions like Azure Logic Apps. |

## QUESTION 35

Answer – B), C), E)

Option A – Azure Functions are useful for background processes but not directly for scaling.
Option B – Auto-scaling rules in Azure App Services ensure automatic resource adjustment.
Option C – Optimizing Dataverse performance settings maximizes efficiency.
Option D – Azure Traffic Manager helps with traffic distribution but not directly with auto-scaling.
Option E – Regular performance tuning and load testing ensure ongoing optimal performance.

| EXAM FOCUS | Implement auto-scaling in Azure App Services and optimize Dataverse settings for cost-effective, resilient scaling. |
|---|---|
| CAUTION ALERT | Avoid relying solely on manual performance tuning; implement automated solutions for scalability. |

## QUESTION 36

Answer – B), C), E)

Option A – Batch processing is not suitable for real-time fraud detection.
Option B – Financial data is regulated, requiring compliance with regulations.
Option C – Fraud detection must be performed in real-time, making it time-sensitive.
Option D – Volatility is less relevant compared to other factors.
Option E – The volume of transaction data is significant and must be managed effectively.

| EXAM FOCUS | "Real-time fraud detection integration must be regulated, time-sensitive, and handle large volumes." |
|---|---|
| CAUTION ALERT | "Batch processing is inadequate for real-time fraud detection needs." |

## QUESTION 37

Answer – A), D)

Option A – Dataverse with multi-geo capabilities ensures data residency compliance.
Option B – A single central region may not comply with data residency requirements and can affect performance.
Option C – Azure Site Recovery is useful for disaster recovery but not directly for data residency compliance.
Option D – Azure Front Door optimizes user experience and performance through global load balancing.
Option E – Manual failover processes are less efficient and reliable compared to automated solutions.

| EXAM FOCUS | *Use Dataverse with multi-geo capabilities and Azure Front Door for global load balancing.* |
|---|---|
| CAUTION ALERT | *A single central region deployment can affect performance and data residency compliance.* |

## QUESTION 38

Answer – A), D)

Option A – AI Builder helps personalize user experience based on transaction data.
Option B – Power BI dashboards track KPIs for user engagement and satisfaction.
Option C – A standard interface does not provide personalized user experience.
Option D – Power Automate can automate feedback collection through periodic surveys.
Option E – Collecting feedback only during the initial phase limits continuous improvement opportunities.

| EXAM FOCUS | *Use AI Builder for personalized insights and Power Automate for periodic feedback collection.* |
|---|---|
| CAUTION ALERT | *Collecting feedback only during the initial phase limits opportunities for continuous improvement.* |

## QUESTION 39

Answer – B), D)

Option A – Azure Security Center helps with continuous security monitoring but does not directly address data encryption or recovery strategies, which are essential for business continuity.
Option B – Encrypting data at rest and in transit using Dataverse ensures that data remains secure, reducing the risk of data breaches during disruptions. This is critical for maintaining trust and compliance.
Option C – Implementing a single layer of security is insufficient because it does not provide defense in depth. Multiple layers of security are necessary to protect against different types of threats.
Option D – Azure Site Recovery automates the failover process, ensuring that services can continue running with minimal downtime during disruptions, which is a key aspect of business continuity.
Option E – Regular penetration testing and vulnerability assessments are important for security but do not directly address the need for continuous operation and recovery strategies.

| EXAM FOCUS | *Encrypt data in Dataverse and use Azure Site Recovery for automated failover processes.* |
|---|---|
| CAUTION ALERT | *Do not rely solely on a single layer of security; use multiple layers for comprehensive protection.* |

## QUESTION 40

Answer – A)

Option A – Power Automate with an email marketing connector allows for easy, real-time integration and ensures compliance with data privacy regulations.
Option B – Azure Logic Apps can also handle integration but is more complex to set up.
Option C – Custom API integration requires significant development effort and maintenance.
Option D – Data Export Service is used for exporting data to an Azure SQL Database, not for real-time integration.
Option E – Dynamics 365 Marketing is more suited for managing campaigns directly within Dynamics 365, not integrating with third-party platforms.

| EXAM FOCUS | *"Power Automate with email marketing connector integrates easily and complies with privacy regulations."* |
|---|---|
| CAUTION ALERT | *"Custom API integration requires more effort and maintenance."* |

## QUESTION 41

Answer – A), B), C)

Option A – Azure Autoscale dynamically adjusts resources based on traffic, ensuring that the system can handle spikes effectively.
Option B – Azure Load Balancer distributes incoming traffic evenly across multiple servers, ensuring zero downtime and balanced loads.
Option C – Azure Monitor provides real-time insights into performance, enabling prompt response to issues.
Option D – Azure API Management is useful for managing APIs but does not directly address dynamic scaling or real-time performance monitoring.
Option E – Power BI is great for data analysis but not suited for real-time monitoring of traffic spikes and performance.

| EXAM FOCUS | *Use Azure Autoscale and Load Balancer for dynamic scaling and zero downtime.* |
|---|---|
| CAUTION ALERT | *Power BI is not suited for real-time performance monitoring.* |

## QUESTION 42

Answer – C), D), E)

Option A – Azure Logic Apps is more suited for integrating workflows and automating tasks rather than specifically for monitoring and maintenance.
Option B – While data encryption is crucial for security, it does not directly address solution health monitoring and maintenance.
Option C – Azure Monitor provides real-time tracking of solution health and performance, allowing for proactive issue detection and resolution.
Option D – Scheduling regular maintenance and updates using Azure DevOps ensures that the solution remains up-to-date and stable.
Option E – While not as effective as continuous monitoring, manual reviews can still be useful for

additional checks and ensuring solution stability.

| EXAM FOCUS | Use Azure Monitor for health tracking and Azure DevOps for regular updates. |
| CAUTION ALERT | Avoid relying solely on manual reviews; they are not as effective. |

## QUESTION 43

Answer – A), B), D)

Option A – Power BI can create custom reports tailored to different departments' needs.
Option B – Implementing RBAC ensures that only authorized personnel can access sensitive reports, maintaining data security.
Option C – Storing patient data in plain text is insecure and violates healthcare regulations.
Option D – Power Automate can automate the distribution of reports, ensuring timely delivery to relevant stakeholders.
Option E – While manual audits are useful, they do not ensure real-time compliance monitoring or the efficient distribution of reports.

| EXAM FOCUS | Create custom reports with Power BI and secure them with RBAC. |
| CAUTION ALERT | Storing patient data in plain text violates healthcare regulations. |

## QUESTION 44

Answer – B)

Option A – Incorrect. Power BI audit logs track user activities and data access within Power BI, not integration faults.
Option B – Correct. Trace logging provides detailed logging that can help pinpoint issues in data integration processes, especially when pulling data from multiple sources.
Option C – Incorrect. Power Apps activity logging monitors user interactions within apps and does not specifically address data integration issues.
Option D – Incorrect. Dataflow diagnostics help optimize data movement in Power BI dataflows, not Power Platform integrations.
Option E – Incorrect. Common Data Service auditing tracks data changes within the service but does not provide the detailed debugging capabilities needed for complex integrations.

| EXAM FOCUS | "Use trace logging to troubleshoot and identify faults in data integration processes." |
| CAUTION ALERT | "Avoid using Power BI audit logs for integration troubleshooting; they track user activities." |

## QUESTION 45

Answer – A), B), C)

Option A – An interactive learning portal using Power Apps can provide a centralized, engaging platform for ongoing training.
Option B – Microsoft Forms integrated with Power Automate can streamline feedback collection and ensure timely incorporation of user suggestions.

Option C – Quarterly training effectiveness reviews using Power BI can provide insights into the success of the training program and highlight areas for improvement.
Option D – A support hotline is useful but does not address the need for structured, ongoing training and feedback incorporation.
Option E – Relying solely on initial training sessions can lead to gaps in knowledge and reduced system adoption.

| EXAM FOCUS | *Create an interactive learning portal using Power Apps for ongoing training.* |
|---|---|
| CAUTION ALERT | *Relying solely on initial training sessions can lead to knowledge gaps.* |

## QUESTION 46

Answer – A), B), C)

Option A – Using the Power Apps Monitor tool helps identify and analyze performance bottlenecks within the application.
Option B – Optimizing data source queries can reduce load times and improve overall app responsiveness.
Option C – Implementing Azure Application Insights allows for continuous performance monitoring and proactive issue detection.
Option D – Adding more features without addressing performance issues will exacerbate the problem and degrade user experience.
Option E – Ignoring performance issues is not advisable as it will lead to a poor user experience and potential application failures.

| EXAM FOCUS | "Use Power Apps Monitor and Azure Application Insights for continuous performance monitoring." |
|---|---|
| CAUTION ALERT | "Ignoring performance issues will lead to a poor user experience." |

## QUESTION 47

Answer – B), D)

Option A – Dynamics 365 Customer Insights can provide analytics, but it is more suited for customer data rather than system performance.
Option B – Implementing Azure Monitor for real-time alerts ensures prompt detection of issues.
Option C – Relying only on manual data collection for feedback is inefficient and can miss critical insights.
Option D – Utilizing Power BI for performance reporting provides a comprehensive view of system performance and user interactions.
Option E – Ignoring user behavior analytics can lead to missed opportunities for improvement and better user experience.

| EXAM FOCUS | "Implement Azure Monitor for real-time alerts to ensure prompt issue detection." |
|---|---|
| CAUTION ALERT | "Ignoring user behavior analytics can miss opportunities for user experience improvement." |

## QUESTION 48

Answer – A), D)

Option A – Correct. Automating connection management ensures that all components of the new CRM system communicate effectively without manual setup errors, which is crucial for a multinational corporation.
Option B – Incorrect. Webhook configuration is essential but not as critical as ensuring fundamental communication pathways are error-free.
Option C – Incorrect. Data validation checks are important, but they do not contribute as directly to integration setup as connection management and endpoint configuration.
Option D – Correct. Automating service endpoint configuration ensures that data flows correctly between different systems and regions without manual configuration errors, essential for global operations.
Option E – Incorrect. Team records creation is important for internal management but less so for the technical deployment of a CRM system.

| | |
|---|---|
| **EXAM FOCUS** | *"Automate connection management and service endpoint configuration to ensure a smooth CRM deployment."* |
| **CAUTION ALERT** | *"Data validation checks are important but less impactful during initial setup compared to connection management."* |

## QUESTION 49

Answer – A), B)

Option A – Correct. Azure DevOps provides robust version control, essential for managing customizations and ensuring smooth upgrades.
Option B – Correct. Managed solutions help package customizations in a way that makes them easier to manage and upgrade.
Option C – Incorrect. While useful, reviewing release notes alone is not sufficient for managing customizations.
Option D – Incorrect. The choice between Canvas Apps and Model-Driven Apps depends on the use case and does not directly address customization management.
Option E – Incorrect. While automated testing is beneficial, it does not directly manage version control or address deprecated features.

| | |
|---|---|
| **EXAM FOCUS** | *"Use Azure DevOps for version control to manage customizations and ensure smooth upgrades."* |
| **CAUTION ALERT** | *"Please keep in mind, ignoring regular updates can lead to compatibility issues."* |

## QUESTION 50

Answer – B), C), D)

Option A – Incorrect. While useful for automation, Azure Logic Apps is not specifically aimed at promoting sustainability directly.

Option B – Correct. AI Builder can analyze and optimize energy usage patterns, contributing to energy efficiency.

Option C – Correct. A Power Apps portal can be used to share and promote sustainability initiatives among students and staff.

Option D – Correct. Azure Monitor can track the carbon footprint of IT resources, providing valuable insights for reduction efforts.

Option E – Incorrect. Scheduling resource usage during off-peak hours can help but is not a comprehensive energy-efficient deployment strategy.

| | |
|---|---|
| **EXAM FOCUS** | *"Develop an eco-awareness campaign using Power Virtual Agents to engage users."* |
| **CAUTION ALERT** | *"Please keep in mind, scheduling resource usage during off-peak hours is not a comprehensive strategy."* |

# PRACTICE TEST 9 - QUESTIONS ONLY

## QUESTION 1

A healthcare organization wants to improve patient care and operational efficiency using Microsoft Power Platform. Their business goals include enhancing patient engagement, reducing administrative overhead, and ensuring data privacy. Specific challenges are:
- Limited patient interaction channels.
- High administrative workload.
- Data privacy concerns.

Which solutions best align with their business goals while addressing these challenges? Select two correct answers.

A) Use Power Virtual Agents for patient interactions.
B) Implement Power Automate to reduce administrative tasks.
C) Develop a Power Apps portal for patient access to information.
D) Use Dataverse for secure data management.
E) Create Power BI reports for operational insights.

## QUESTION 2

You are leading the design of a customer service application using Microsoft Power Platform for a multinational corporation. The application must support multilingual user interfaces and real-time customer data synchronization across various regions. Select the appropriate services to achieve these requirements. Select up to two answers.

A) Power Apps portals
B) Power Automate
C) Azure AI Builder
D) Power BI
E) Dynamics 365 Customer Service

## QUESTION 3

A manufacturing company wants to use Microsoft Power Platform to enhance its production data analysis. They need to ensure data accuracy and reliability. The specific challenges are:
- Inconsistent production data from different sources.
- Difficulty in real-time monitoring of production metrics.
- Ensuring data accuracy for operational decisions.

Which solutions would best address these challenges? Select two correct answers.

A) Implement Power BI dataflows to consolidate production data.
B) Use Power Automate to automate data validation.
C) Develop a Power BI dashboard for real-time monitoring.
D) Create a Dataverse-based app for production data entry.
E) Use AI Builder to analyze production trends.

## QUESTION 4

As a solution architect, you need to design a system for a healthcare provider that ensures patient data confidentiality while allowing seamless data flow between departments. Which two technologies should you integrate to achieve this? Select up to two answers.

A) Microsoft Teams
B) Azure Active Directory
C) Power Automate
D) Microsoft Dataverse
E) Azure Security Center

## QUESTION 5

An educational institution wants to implement a new student information system using Microsoft Power Platform. The project requires ensuring compliance with educational data regulations. The specific challenges are:
- Ensuring compliance with FERPA regulations.
- Protecting student data from unauthorized access.
- Conducting regular compliance audits.

Which solutions would best address these challenges? Select two correct answers.

A) Use Dataverse to store and manage student data securely.
B) Implement DLP policies to protect data.
C) Use Power Automate to automate compliance workflows.
D) Conduct compliance audits using Power BI.
E) Implement RBAC to control access to student data.

## QUESTION 6

An educational institution is implementing a new learning management system using Microsoft Power Platform. The project requires budgeting for the project lifecycle and handling potential cost overruns. The specific challenges are:
- Estimating the costs for initial setup and training.
- Budgeting for ongoing system maintenance.
- Preparing for unexpected cost increases.

Which solutions would best address these challenges? Select two correct answers.

A) Use Power BI to create a detailed budget plan.
B) Implement Power Automate to schedule regular system maintenance.
C) Develop a contingency budget for unexpected cost increases.
D) Use Dataverse to manage training data.
E) Conduct regular budget reviews using Power BI.

## QUESTION 7

A government agency is implementing a citizen service portal using Microsoft Power Platform. The project involves transitioning from prototype to development. The specific challenges are:
- Ensuring the prototype meets user requirements.

- Gathering feedback from pilot users.
- Planning the transition to full-scale development.

Which solutions would best address these challenges? Select three correct answers.

A) Use Power Apps to develop the prototype.
B) Conduct a pilot test with a selected group of users.
C) Use Power BI to monitor prototype performance.
D) Plan the development phases using Azure DevOps.
E) Use AI Builder for predictive analysis.

## QUESTION 8

A manufacturing firm is integrating their ERP system with Dynamics 365 using Microsoft Power Platform. The project requires testing and validating integrations. The specific challenges are:
- Ensuring data accuracy.
- Validating integration workflows.
- Handling error scenarios.

What actions would you take to address these challenges? Select three correct answers.

A) Use Power Automate to test integration workflows.
B) Implement validation rules in Dataverse.
C) Use Power BI for data accuracy reports.
D) Develop automated test scripts using Azure DevOps.
E) Implement error handling using Azure Logic Apps.

## QUESTION 9

A logistics company is enhancing its tracking system using Microsoft Power Platform. The project requires security testing and validation. The specific challenges are:
- Conducting thorough security testing.
- Validating the security measures implemented.
- Ensuring no security gaps remain.

What actions would you take to address these challenges? Select three correct answers.

A) Use Azure Security Center for security assessments.
B) Implement Azure DevOps for continuous integration and delivery.
C) Conduct penetration testing using Azure Security Center.
D) Use Power BI for security monitoring dashboards.
E) Conduct vulnerability assessments.

## QUESTION 10

A technology company is implementing a new ERP system using Microsoft Power Platform. The project requires implementing continuous quality improvement. The specific challenges are:
- Establishing a continuous feedback loop.
- Integrating QA processes throughout the project lifecycle.
- Measuring improvement over time.

What steps would you take to address these challenges? Select three correct answers.

A) Schedule regular sprint reviews and retrospectives.
B) Use Power Automate for continuous feedback collection.
C) Implement Power BI for tracking improvement metrics.
D) Use Azure DevOps for managing QA processes.
E) Conduct user training and workshops.

## QUESTION 11

A healthcare provider is transitioning to a new patient management system using Dynamics 365 and Microsoft Power Platform. The specific challenges are:
- Managing solution versions and releases.
- Planning for continuous quality improvement.
- Migrating from the legacy system while ensuring compliance with healthcare regulations.

What steps would you take to address these challenges? Select three correct answers.

A) Use Azure DevOps for version control and release management.
B) Implement a continuous improvement process using Power Automate.
C) Develop a migration strategy using Azure Data Factory to ensure compliance.
D) Utilize Power BI for monitoring system performance.
E) Engage legal experts to ensure regulatory compliance.

## QUESTION 12

A financial services company wants to deploy a new Dynamics 365 Sales solution. They need to ensure the solution is highly available and meets disaster recovery requirements.
- The solution must provide continuous availability.
- It should have a robust disaster recovery plan to minimize downtime.

Which deployment strategy would you recommend?

A) Single production environment with daily backups
B) Production environment with a warm standby in a different region
C) Multiple production environments with active-active configuration
D) Production environment with a cold standby in a different region
E) Single production environment with geo-redundant storage

## QUESTION 13

A retail company wants to adopt agile methodologies for its e-commerce platform development using the Microsoft Power Platform. The challenges include:
- Implementing agile methodologies.
- Benefits of iterative development.
- Continuous delivery and feedback loops.

What practices and tools should you recommend to address these challenges? Select two correct answers.

A) Schedule regular sprint retrospectives.
B) Use Power Automate to automate testing.
C) Implement Azure DevOps for version control and CI/CD.
D) Conduct monthly project status meetings.

E) Utilize Power BI for project tracking.

**QUESTION 14**

A technology company is implementing a data governance framework using Microsoft Power Platform to comply with global data protection regulations. The challenges include:
• Establishing data governance frameworks.
• Ensuring compliance with data governance standards.
• Using appropriate data governance tools and technologies.
What steps should you take to address these challenges? Select three correct answers.

A) Use Power Automate to automate data governance processes.
B) Implement Azure Purview for data governance and cataloging.
C) Develop data stewardship guidelines and responsibilities.
D) Utilize Azure Policy for enforcing data governance standards.
E) Create a data quality dashboard in Power BI.

**QUESTION 15**

A healthcare provider is using Microsoft Power Platform to develop a new patient management system. The team faces challenges such as:
• Deciding between customization and configuration.
• Best practices in system configuration.
• Managing custom solutions.
What steps should you take to address these challenges? Select three correct answers.

A) Configure standard entities in Dataverse for patient data.
B) Use custom code for all business logic.
C) Utilize Power Virtual Agents for patient interactions.
D) Develop custom model-driven apps for unique business processes.
E) Implement Power BI for data analysis and reporting.

**QUESTION 16**

A financial services firm is developing a model-driven app to manage client portfolios using Microsoft Dataverse. They want to automate the process of validating client information and sending notifications to portfolio managers.
• The solution must ensure data accuracy and compliance with industry regulations.
• It should automate notifications based on validation results.
What components should be used to implement this workflow? Select two answers.

A) Business rule
B) Business process flow
C) Scheduled cloud flow
D) Power BI Dataflow
E) Virtual table

## QUESTION 17

A healthcare organization is implementing a patient management system using Microsoft Power Platform. The project must:
- Establish governance structures.
- Ensure compliance with HIPAA.
- Set up data auditing and reporting mechanisms.

What actions should you take to address these requirements? Select three correct answers.

A) Use Dataverse to centralize patient data and ensure data integrity.
B) Implement DLP policies using Power Automate to enforce data handling rules.
C) Configure auditing in Power Apps to monitor data changes.
D) Develop custom workflows to automate HIPAA compliance checks.
E) Use Azure Policy to enforce compliance across all data resources.

## QUESTION 18

A multinational corporation is deploying a new CRM system using Microsoft Power Platform. The solution must:
- Drive innovation within the organization.
- Measure success through key performance indicators (KPIs).
- Be adaptable to future technological advancements.

You need to select three actions to achieve these objectives. Which three actions should you take? (Select three)

A) Use Power BI to create KPI dashboards.
B) Implement AI Builder for AI-driven customer insights.
C) Develop model-driven apps for managing customer interactions.
D) Utilize Azure Logic Apps for seamless integration with other systems.
E) Implement ALM practices using Azure DevOps.

## QUESTION 19

A government agency is implementing a citizen services platform using Microsoft Power Platform. The solution must:
- Ensure data security.
- Handle sensitive data ethically.
- Build trust through transparent practices.

Which three practices should you implement? (Select three)

A) Implement Role-Based Access Control (RBAC) in Power Apps.
B) Use Power BI for transparent reporting.
C) Enable Multi-Factor Authentication (MFA) for all users.
D) Conduct regular data security training for employees.
E) Use Power Automate to enforce data retention policies.

## QUESTION 20

An educational institution wants to use Microsoft Dataverse to manage student information and course

enrollments. They need to ensure that the data model can support dynamic reporting and analysis of student performance.
• The solution must allow for real-time data updates.
• It should integrate with Power BI for advanced reporting.
Which components should you include in the solution design? Select three answers.

A) Real-time workflows
B) Calculated columns
C) Rollup columns
D) Power BI dataflows
E) Scheduled cloud flows

## QUESTION 21

A financial services firm needs to ensure their Power Platform solution complies with financial regulations and secures sensitive data. The solution must:
• Ensure data privacy.
• Implement security policies.
• Conduct regular audits.
Which two actions should you take? (Select two)

A) Use Dataverse for secure data management.
B) Implement RBAC using Azure AD.
C) Use Power BI for financial reporting.
D) Conduct regular security audits using Azure Security Center.
E) Implement Multi-Factor Authentication (MFA).

## QUESTION 22

A government agency is transitioning to a cloud-based Power Platform solution with Azure integration. The solution must:
• Ensure data integrity and compliance with government regulations.
• Optimize data storage for cost and performance.
• Implement advanced data modeling techniques.
Which two components should you use? (Select two)

A) Use Azure SQL Database with performance tiers.
B) Implement Dataverse for secure data storage.
C) Use Azure Cognitive Services for data analysis.
D) Apply Azure Policy for regulatory compliance.
E) Design data models using Power Query.

## QUESTION 23

An educational institution is using Power Platform to develop an application for student and faculty interaction. They need to ensure the application is user-friendly and accessible. The solution must:
• Follow accessibility standards.
• Be easy to navigate for all users.
• Incorporate feedback from both students and faculty.

Which two steps should you take? (Select two)

A) Use Canvas Apps for a flexible UI design.
B) Implement accessibility features such as high-contrast mode.
C) Use Dataverse for secure data storage.
D) Conduct user experience (UX) surveys regularly.
E) Use Azure Cognitive Services for sentiment analysis.

## QUESTION 24

A healthcare provider uses Dynamics 365 for patient management and wants to ensure high availability of their system to minimize downtime. What approach should they take to achieve this high availability?

A) Use a single data center with backup
B) Implement Geo-redundancy
C) Schedule regular maintenance windows
D) Use on-premises servers
E) Use only cloud-based solutions

## QUESTION 25

A financial services company wants to deploy Power BI for financial reporting. The solution must:
- Provide detailed financial reports.
- Enable real-time tracking of financial metrics.
- Integrate AI for anomaly detection in transactions.

What three Power BI features should be utilized? (Select three)

A) Power BI Paginated Reports for detailed reporting.
B) Power BI AI Insights for anomaly detection.
C) Power BI Streaming Datasets for real-time tracking.
D) Power BI Dataflows for data preparation.
E) Power BI Desktop for report creation.

## QUESTION 26

A manufacturing company wants to enhance its predictive maintenance system using AI. The solution must:
- Predict equipment failures before they occur.
- Integrate with the existing IoT platform.
- Optimize maintenance schedules.

What three strategies should be implemented? (Select three)

A) AI Builder for predictive models.
B) Power Automate for scheduling maintenance.
C) Azure IoT Central for device data integration.
D) Dataverse for maintenance data.
E) Azure Functions for custom logic.

## QUESTION 27

A government agency must create a business continuity strategy for its Power Platform solutions. The strategy must:
• Automate recovery workflows.
• Monitor system performance during recovery.
• Ensure high availability of critical services.
Which components should be included? (Select three)

A) Power Automate for automated recovery workflows.
B) Azure Monitor for performance monitoring.
C) Azure AD for managing user access.
D) Power Virtual Agents for user interaction.
E) Azure Site Recovery for high availability.

## QUESTION 28

A logistics company uses Power BI to track delivery performance metrics. They need to ensure that sensitive delivery data is accessible only to authorized personnel. What security feature in Power BI should they use to achieve this?

A) Power BI Embedded
B) Row-Level Security
C) Dataflows
D) Gateways
E) Power Query

## QUESTION 29

A client in the pharmaceutical industry is concerned about compliance with industry-specific regulations and data protection laws. They need a solution to ensure ongoing compliance and data security.
1. Navigating complex regulatory landscapes.
2. Ensuring data protection and privacy for sensitive data.
3. Implementing continuous compliance monitoring.
How would you assist the client in achieving compliance and data security? Select three answers.

A) Use Power BI for compliance reporting and monitoring.
B) Implement Microsoft Information Protection for data security.
C) Use Dataverse to store sensitive data with role-based access controls.
D) Develop custom compliance solutions.
E) Use Azure Sentinel for security monitoring and compliance.

## QUESTION 30

A client in the healthcare industry wants to implement a solution using advanced data analysis techniques to improve patient outcomes. They aim to integrate external health data sources and apply predictive analytics to identify at-risk patients.
1. Integrating patient data from various external health databases.
2. Applying predictive models to identify patients at risk of certain conditions.

3. Generating actionable insights for proactive healthcare management.
What actions would you recommend to achieve these objectives? Select three answers.

A) Use Power BI to visualize patient data and health trends.
B) Implement Azure Data Factory to integrate health data from multiple sources.
C) Apply AI Builder to develop basic predictive models.
D) Use Azure Cognitive Services for advanced analytics and insights.
E) Store patient data in a single Excel file for simplicity.

## QUESTION 31

A government client wants to implement a Power Platform solution to streamline their operations. They need to ensure that users adopt the new solution and that the impact of the change is measured effectively.
1. Developing strategies to promote user adoption.
2. Creating a communication and training plan.
3. Measuring the impact and success of the change initiative.
What measures would you take to achieve these goals? Select three answers.

A) Conduct training sessions using Power Apps to demonstrate the new solution.
B) Use Power BI to create dashboards tracking adoption rates and user feedback.
C) Implement a communication plan to keep users informed about the benefits and progress of the new solution.
D) Ignore user feedback and focus on technical implementation.
E) Develop a resistance management plan to address user concerns.

## QUESTION 32

A retail company uses Power Apps to manage their inventory and sales operations. They want to integrate their Power App with a legacy ERP system that does not have an API. The integration must automatically update inventory levels in the ERP system based on sales data entered in Power Apps. What solution should they use for this integration?

A) Attended Desktop Flow
B) Unattended Desktop Flow
C) Azure Functions
D) Power Automate with HTTP connector
E) Dynamics 365 Supply Chain Management

## QUESTION 33

A government client is implementing a Power Platform solution to improve public services and wants to ensure advanced customization and maintainability. They need to manage the complexity of custom solutions effectively.
1. Implementing advanced customization in Power Apps and Power Automate.
2. Ensuring maintainability of the solution.
3. Managing complexity in custom solutions.
What measures would you take to achieve these goals? Select three answers.

A) Use Azure API Management for custom connectors and API integrations.
B) Implement Power BI to track and monitor solution performance.
C) Follow best practices for coding and documentation.
D) Focus solely on functionality without considering maintainability.
E) Use Azure DevOps for continuous integration and version control.

## QUESTION 34

Your company is planning a phased approach to integrate its legacy financial system with Dynamics 365 Finance and Operations (F&O). The initial phase must:
• Ensure data consistency between systems.
• Allow parallel operations during transition.
• Facilitate user adoption of the new system. What are the best strategies to achieve these goals? (Select 2 answers)

A) Implement a dual-write feature to synchronize data between systems.
B) Use Azure DevOps for continuous integration and deployment.
C) Develop a comprehensive training program for end-users.
D) Conduct a full data migration before switching systems.
E) Utilize Power BI for reporting to compare data between systems.

## QUESTION 35

Your team is responsible for a Power BI implementation that needs to handle large datasets and multiple concurrent users. The solution must:
• Scale efficiently with increasing data volume.
• Provide high performance for users.
• Optimize resource usage. What strategies should you employ? (Select 2 answers)

A) Implement Power BI Premium for dedicated resources.
B) Use Power BI dataflows for ETL processes.
C) Schedule data refreshes during non-peak hours.
D) Enable query caching and aggregations.
E) Manually allocate additional resources during peak times.

## QUESTION 36

A logistics company uses Dynamics 365 Field Service to manage deliveries and fleet operations. They want to integrate an IoT solution to monitor vehicle conditions in real-time and trigger maintenance alerts. The integration must handle continuous data streams and ensure timely maintenance actions. Which categorizations should you consider for this integration?

A) Batch
B) Time-sensitive
C) Volume
D) Licensed
E) Volatility

## QUESTION 37

A global enterprise is using Power Platform to integrate various regional systems. The integration must:
• Handle data residency requirements.
• Ensure consistent performance across regions.
• Support regional customizations. What steps should you take? (Select 3 answers)

A) Use regional Dataverse instances with appropriate data governance policies.
B) Implement a global instance with regional data partitions.
C) Employ Azure API Management for secure regional API access.
D) Use Power Automate to manage cross-region data flows.
E) Configure Azure Traffic Manager for performance optimization.

## QUESTION 38

Your organization is designing a customer portal using Power Apps. The portal must:
• Provide a tailored experience for different customer segments.
• Include mechanisms for continuous feedback.
• Use metrics to measure the effectiveness of the user experience. What approaches should you consider? (Select 3 answers)

A) Use Power Virtual Agents to offer personalized support.
B) Implement Power BI to analyze user interaction metrics.
C) Develop static pages with identical content for all users.
D) Create dynamic content based on user profiles in Dataverse.
E) Use Azure Logic Apps to automate feedback collection processes.

## QUESTION 39

An e-commerce company is designing a Power Platform solution that involves secure data exchange and business continuity. The solution must:
• Ensure data integrity and confidentiality.
• Use secure communication protocols.
• Regularly update continuity measures. What strategies should you adopt? (Select 3 answers)

A) Use HTTPS for all data transmissions.
B) Implement Azure IoT Hub for secure device communication.
C) Conduct regular risk assessments.
D) Regularly update device firmware and security patches.
E) Use Azure DevOps to manage and automate continuity plan updates.

## QUESTION 40

A financial services company uses Dynamics 365 Finance to manage their accounting operations. They need to integrate their system with a third-party tax calculation service to automate tax computations during the invoice generation process. The integration must be seamless and adhere to security best practices. What approach should they use to implement this integration?

A) Use Power Automate with HTTP connector
B) Implement a Custom Connector

C) Use Azure Logic Apps
D) Use Dynamics 365 Business Central
E) Use Microsoft Graph API

## QUESTION 41

A healthcare provider wants to expand their patient management system using Power Platform. The solution must:
- Be scalable to handle an increasing number of patients.
- Ensure data security and compliance.
- Allow for easy integration of new features. What should you implement? (Select 3 answers)

A) Use Dataverse for secure and scalable data storage.
B) Implement Role-Based Access Control (RBAC) for security.
C) Use Power Apps Component Framework (PCF) for modular feature development.
D) Utilize Azure Logic Apps for workflow automation.
E) Use Azure DevOps for continuous integration and deployment.

## QUESTION 42

A financial services company is using a Power Platform solution to handle customer transactions. To maintain long-term stability and performance, they need to:
- Monitor solution health.
- Detect and address issues proactively.
- Perform regular updates and maintenance. What should be implemented? (Select 3 answers)

A) Use Azure Logic Apps to automate transaction processing.
B) Implement Dataverse with RBAC for secure data access.
C) Use Azure Monitor to continuously track solution health and set up alerts.
D) Schedule regular updates and maintenance using Azure DevOps pipelines.
E) Conduct manual quarterly performance reviews and updates.

## QUESTION 43

A manufacturing company wants to leverage data insights to optimize their supply chain operations. They need to:
- Analyze supply chain data from multiple sources.
- Develop dashboards to monitor key performance indicators (KPIs).
- Integrate these insights into their operational processes. What solutions should they use? (Select 3 answers)

A) Use Power BI to develop dashboards for monitoring KPIs.
B) Implement Azure Data Factory to aggregate supply chain data.
C) Store supply chain data in an unstructured format for flexibility.
D) Use Power Automate to integrate data insights into operational workflows.
E) Manually collect and analyze supply chain data.

## QUESTION 44

During a routine check, a solution architect discovers that a scheduled data import into Microsoft Dataverse from an external accounting system is not updating records as expected in a non-profit organization.
- Ensure data integrity.
- Diagnose data import issues.

What tool should be used to investigate the data discrepancies and ensure data integrity?

A) Dataverse auditing
B) Dataflow diagnostics
C) Trace logging
D) Power BI data integrity checks
E) Plugin trace logs

## QUESTION 45

A healthcare provider is implementing a new patient management system with Dynamics 365. They need to:
- Develop comprehensive training materials.
- Ensure effective user support.
- Continuously improve training based on feedback. What methods should they use?

A) Create detailed user manuals and video tutorials.
B) Use Power Virtual Agents for 24/7 support.
C) Implement a feedback loop using Power BI dashboards.
D) Collect feedback through periodic meetings only.
E) Conduct a single training session without follow-up.

## QUESTION 46

A healthcare provider's Dynamics 365 system is facing slow performance during peak hours. They need to:
- Identify performance bottlenecks.
- Implement resource scaling strategies.
- Continuously monitor performance metrics. What measures should they implement?

A) Use Dynamics 365 Performance Insights to identify bottlenecks.
B) Scale out resources by adding more instances.
C) Implement Azure Monitor for continuous performance tracking.
D) Focus only on functionality enhancements.
E) Avoid addressing performance issues during peak hours.

## QUESTION 47

A logistics company is implementing a new Power Automate workflow for order processing. To ensure optimal performance and user satisfaction, they must:
- Monitor workflow performance metrics.
- Set up real-time alerts for failures.

• Analyze user behavior and feedback. What measures should they take?
Select 3 answers.

A) Use Power Automate analytics to monitor workflow performance.
B) Set up alerts in Azure Monitor for workflow failures.
C) Ignore user feedback and focus only on system performance.
D) Collect user feedback through Power Apps forms.
E) Use Power BI to analyze performance metrics.

## QUESTION 48

As part of an initiative to improve data security and efficiency in a government agency, you are tasked with automating parts of a Power Platform implementation that involves sensitive data handling. The goal is to minimize human error and enhance security protocols.
• Enhance data security.
• Minimize human error.
Which two automation tasks would you prioritize to meet these objectives?

A) Connection management
B) Data encryption protocols
C) Webhook configuration
D) Service endpoint configuration
E) Automated compliance audits

## QUESTION 49

A healthcare organization is using Power Platform solutions with extensive customizations to manage patient data and workflows. To ensure long-term sustainability and compliance, the organization must manage these customizations carefully. The key requirements are:
• Ensuring customizations are compliant with healthcare regulations.
• Managing lifecycle and updates of customizations.
• Balancing the use of custom and out-of-the-box features.
Which actions should you prioritize? (Select 3 answers)

A) Use managed solutions to deploy and update customizations.
B) Implement compliance checks using Power Automate.
C) Leverage out-of-the-box features for workflows and processes.
D) Regularly audit customizations for compliance.
E) Use Azure Service Health to monitor the status of Power Platform services.

## QUESTION 50

A healthcare organization is looking to implement Power Platform solutions with a focus on sustainable technology practices. The key requirements are:
- Ensuring energy efficiency in solution deployment.
- Promoting eco-awareness among healthcare staff.
- Reducing the environmental impact of IT infrastructure.

Which measures should you implement? (Select 3 answers)

A) Use Power BI to create reports on the environmental impact of IT infrastructure.
B) Implement Azure Cognitive Services to optimize resource usage.
C) Develop training modules using Power Virtual Agents to promote eco-awareness.
D) Choose Azure services with a lower carbon footprint.
E) Use Power Automate to schedule and automate energy-saving tasks.

# PRACTICE TEST 9 - ANSWERS ONLY

## QUESTION 1

Answer – B), D)

Option A – Virtual Agents improve interactions but do not address administrative overhead or data privacy.
Option B – Automating tasks reduces workload, addressing high administrative workload.
Option C – A Power Apps portal enhances access but does not address administrative overhead or privacy.
Option D – Dataverse provides secure data management, ensuring privacy and operational efficiency.
Option E – Power BI reports offer insights but do not directly enhance patient engagement or reduce overhead.

| EXAM FOCUS | *Automate tasks with Power Automate and ensure secure data management with Dataverse to enhance patient care and efficiency.* |
|---|---|
| CAUTION ALERT | *Stay cautious, focusing on interaction channels alone won't address administrative overhead or data privacy.* |

## QUESTION 2

Answer – A) & E)

Option A – Correct. Power Apps portals support multilingual interfaces and can serve multiple regions effectively.
Option B – Incorrect. Power Automate is for automation and does not directly support UI requirements.
Option C – Incorrect. Azure AI Builder is for adding AI capabilities, not for UI or data synchronization.
Option D – Incorrect. Power BI is primarily an analytics tool, not suited for real-time data synchronization or UI management.
Option E – Correct. Dynamics 365 Customer Service provides real-time data synchronization and can be configured for multilingual support.

| EXAM FOCUS | *"Power Apps portals and Dynamics 365 Customer Service support multilingual interfaces and real-time data synchronization."* |
|---|---|
| CAUTION ALERT | *"Power Automate and Azure AI Builder do not directly address UI or real-time synchronization needs."* |

## QUESTION 3

Answer – A), B)

Option A – Power BI dataflows can consolidate data from different sources, addressing inconsistency.
Option B – Power Automate can automate data validation, ensuring data accuracy.
Option C – A Power BI dashboard is useful for monitoring but does not ensure data accuracy.
Option D – A Dataverse-based app is useful for data entry but does not address data consolidation or validation.
Option E – AI Builder for trend analysis is useful but not critical for data accuracy.

Page | 297

| EXAM FOCUS | *Consolidate production data with Power BI dataflows and automate validation with Power Automate to ensure accuracy.* |
|---|---|
| CAUTION ALERT | *Remember, real-time monitoring with Power BI alone won't address data consistency and validation.* |

## QUESTION 4

Answer – B) & E)

Option A – Incorrect. Microsoft Teams is primarily for communication and does not ensure data security.
Option B – Correct. Azure Active Directory can manage access and ensure that only authorized personnel can access sensitive data.
Option C – Incorrect. Power Automate automates workflows but is not focused on data security.
Option D – Incorrect. Microsoft Dataverse is useful for data storage but does not focus on inter-departmental data security.
Option E – Correct. Azure Security Center provides advanced security management and threat protection.

| EXAM FOCUS | *"Azure Active Directory manages access, ensuring authorized personnel can access sensitive data."* |
|---|---|
| CAUTION ALERT | *"You should stay cautious, Power Automate focuses on workflows, not on data security."* |

## QUESTION 5

Answer – A), E)

Option A – Dataverse provides secure storage and management of student data, ensuring compliance with FERPA.
Option B – DLP policies protect data but do not address regular compliance audits.
Option C – Power Automate is useful for automating workflows but does not directly ensure compliance.
Option D – Power BI is useful for conducting audits but is not a complete solution.
Option E – RBAC controls access to student data, protecting it from unauthorized access.

| EXAM FOCUS | *Implement Dataverse for secure storage and RBAC for access control to meet FERPA requirements.* |
|---|---|
| CAUTION ALERT | *Please keep in mind, DLP policies protect data but won't address compliance audits directly.* |

## QUESTION 6

Answer – A), C)

Option A – Power BI can be used to create a detailed budget plan for initial setup and training.
Option B – Power Automate is useful for scheduling maintenance but does not address cost estimation or budgeting.
Option C – Developing a contingency budget prepares for unexpected cost increases.
Option D – Dataverse is useful for managing data but does not address budgeting.
Option E – Regular budget reviews are useful but do not directly address initial setup or contingency planning.

| EXAM FOCUS | *Create a detailed budget with Power BI and develop a contingency plan for unexpected costs.* |
|---|---|

| CAUTION ALERT | Please keep in mind, Power Automate for scheduling won't address budgeting or unexpected cost planning. |

## QUESTION 7

Answer – A), B), D)

Option A – Power Apps can be used to develop the prototype for the citizen service portal.
Option B – Conducting a pilot test with a selected group of users helps gather feedback.
Option C – Power BI is useful for monitoring performance but not directly related to transitioning from prototype to development.
Option D – Planning the development phases using Azure DevOps ensures a smooth transition to full-scale development.
Option E – AI Builder is useful for predictive analysis but not directly related to transitioning from prototype to development.

| EXAM FOCUS | Use Power Apps for prototype development and conduct pilot tests to gather feedback for transition planning. |
| CAUTION ALERT | Remember, Power BI is useful for monitoring but not for transitioning from prototype to development. |

## QUESTION 8

Answer – A), B), D)

Option A – Power Automate can be used to test integration workflows.
Option B – Implementing validation rules in Dataverse ensures data accuracy.
Option C – Power BI is useful for reporting but not directly related to testing and validating integrations.
Option D – Developing automated test scripts using Azure DevOps helps ensure workflows are validated.
Option E – Implementing error handling using Azure Logic Apps is useful but not a primary action for testing and validating integrations.

| EXAM FOCUS | Test workflows with Power Automate, validate data in Dataverse, and develop test scripts with Azure DevOps. |
| CAUTION ALERT | Stay cautious, Power BI is for reporting, not direct integration testing. |

## QUESTION 9

Answer – A), C), E)

Option A – Using Azure Security Center ensures comprehensive security assessments.
Option B – Azure DevOps is useful for continuous integration and delivery but not directly related to security testing and validation.
Option C – Conducting penetration testing using Azure Security Center ensures thorough testing.
Option D – Power BI is useful for monitoring but not directly related to security testing.
Option E – Conducting vulnerability assessments ensures all security gaps are identified.

| EXAM FOCUS | Conduct security assessments and penetration testing with Azure Security Center, and perform regular vulnerability assessments. |
|---|---|
| CAUTION ALERT | Stay cautious, Power BI is for monitoring, not for conducting security testing. |

## QUESTION 10

Answer – A), C), D)

Option A – Regular sprint reviews and retrospectives establish a continuous feedback loop.
Option B – Power Automate is useful for feedback collection but not specifically for continuous quality improvement.
Option C – Implementing Power BI helps track improvement metrics over time.
Option D – Azure DevOps helps manage QA processes throughout the project lifecycle.
Option E – User training is useful but does not directly address the main challenges.

| EXAM FOCUS | Schedule regular sprint reviews, use Power BI for tracking, and Azure DevOps for managing QA processes. |
|---|---|
| CAUTION ALERT | Remember, Power Automate is useful for feedback collection but not for continuous quality improvement. |

## QUESTION 11

Answer – A), C), E)

Option A – Using Azure DevOps ensures proper version control and release management.
Option B – Power Automate can support continuous improvement but is not the primary tool for this purpose.
Option C – Developing a migration strategy using Azure Data Factory ensures compliance and smooth transition.
Option D – Power BI is useful for monitoring performance but not directly related to lifecycle management.
Option E – Engaging legal experts ensures compliance with healthcare regulations during migration.

| EXAM FOCUS | Use Azure DevOps for version control and engage legal experts to ensure regulatory compliance. |
|---|---|
| CAUTION ALERT | Remember, Power BI is useful for monitoring performance but not directly for lifecycle management. |

## QUESTION 12

Answer – C)

Option A – Daily backups do not ensure continuous availability.
Option B – Warm standby is good but does not provide active-active availability.
Option C – Correct choice as active-active configuration ensures high availability and robust disaster recovery.
Option D – Cold standby has longer recovery times.
Option E – Geo-redundant storage helps with data resilience but does not ensure application availability.

| EXAM FOCUS | "Active-active configuration ensures continuous availability and robust disaster recovery." |
|---|---|
| CAUTION ALERT | "Avoid single environments with only backups; they don't guarantee continuous availability." |

## QUESTION 13

Answer – A), C)

Option A – Regular sprint retrospectives are essential for iterative development and continuous feedback.
Option B – Power Automate is useful but more for automation than testing in agile methodologies.
Option C – Azure DevOps for version control and CI/CD supports agile methodologies and iterative development.
Option D – Monthly project status meetings are less frequent than needed for agile methodologies.
Option E – Power BI is useful for tracking but not directly related to agile methodologies.

| EXAM FOCUS | Schedule regular sprint retrospectives and use Azure DevOps for version control and CI/CD. |
|---|---|
| CAUTION ALERT | You should avoid infrequent meetings like monthly status updates for effective agile management. |

## QUESTION 14

Answer – B), C), D)

Option A – Power Automate is useful for automating processes but less critical than other options for data governance.
Option B – Azure Purview is essential for data governance and cataloging, ensuring compliance with standards.
Option C – Developing data stewardship guidelines is crucial for defining roles and responsibilities.
Option D – Azure Policy helps enforce data governance standards across the organization.
Option E – A data quality dashboard in Power BI is useful for monitoring but less critical for establishing a governance framework.

| EXAM FOCUS | Use Azure Purview for governance and develop data stewardship guidelines to comply with global data regulations. |
|---|---|
| CAUTION ALERT | Remember, automating processes with Power Automate is helpful but secondary to setting clear governance standards. |

## QUESTION 15

Answer – A), C), E)

Option A – Configuring standard entities in Dataverse reduces the need for customization, following best practices.
Option B – Using custom code for all business logic increases maintenance complexity and should be minimized.
Option C – Power Virtual Agents can handle patient interactions effectively with minimal customization.
Option D – Custom model-driven apps should be developed only when necessary to avoid excessive customization.

Option E – Implementing Power BI for data analysis and reporting leverages existing tools and reduces the need for custom solutions.

| EXAM FOCUS | *You should configure standard entities in Dataverse to reduce the need for customization.* |
|---|---|
| CAUTION ALERT | *Avoid relying heavily on custom code for business logic as it complicates maintenance.* |

## QUESTION 16

Answer – B), C)

Option A – Business rule is used for enforcing data validation rules within a single entity, not automation.
Option B – Correct choice as a business process flow can guide users through validation steps.
Option C – Correct choice as a scheduled cloud flow in Power Automate can handle validation and sending notifications.
Option D – Power BI Dataflow is for data aggregation, not process automation.
Option E – Virtual table is used for integrating data from external sources, not automation.

| EXAM FOCUS | *"Business process flow and scheduled cloud flow in Power Automate ensure compliance and automation."* |
|---|---|
| CAUTION ALERT | *"Business rules alone do not handle automation; focus on comprehensive workflows."* |

## QUESTION 17

Answer – A), B), C)

Option A – Using Dataverse centralizes patient data and ensures data integrity.
Option B – Implementing DLP policies using Power Automate enforces data handling rules and ensures compliance.
Option C – Configuring auditing in Power Apps allows monitoring of data changes and compliance.
Option D – Developing custom workflows adds unnecessary complexity.
Option E – Azure Policy is useful but may not directly integrate with Power Platform for HIPAA compliance.

| EXAM FOCUS | *Use Dataverse for patient data, implement DLP policies in Power Automate, and configure auditing in Power Apps.* |
|---|---|
| CAUTION ALERT | *Custom workflows add complexity; focus on built-in compliance features.* |

## QUESTION 18

Answer – A), B), D)

Option A – Using Power BI to create KPI dashboards measures success through key performance indicators.
Option B – Implementing AI Builder provides AI-driven customer insights, driving innovation.
Option C – Developing model-driven apps supports managing customer interactions but might not directly drive innovation.

Page | 302

Option D – Utilizing Azure Logic Apps ensures seamless integration with other systems and adaptability to future advancements.
Option E – Implementing ALM practices ensures continuous improvement but might not directly drive innovation within the organization.

| EXAM FOCUS | *Power BI for KPI dashboards; AI Builder for insights; Azure Logic Apps for integration.* |
|---|---|
| CAUTION ALERT | *Model-driven apps support interactions but don't drive innovation.* |

## QUESTION 19

Answer – A), C), D)

Option A – Implementing RBAC in Power Apps ensures data security.
Option B – Using Power BI for transparent reporting builds trust but is not essential for data security.
Option C – Enabling MFA for all users enhances data security.
Option D – Conducting regular data security training for employees ensures ethical handling of sensitive data.
Option E – Using Power Automate to enforce data retention policies supports data management but is not essential for the primary requirements.

| EXAM FOCUS | *Implement RBAC in Power Apps and enable MFA; conduct regular security training.* |
|---|---|
| CAUTION ALERT | *Transparent reporting is important but secondary to robust security measures.* |

## QUESTION 20

Answer – A), B), D)

Option A – Correct choice as Real-time workflows support real-time data updates.
Option B – Correct choice as Calculated columns provide dynamic calculations.
Option C – Rollup columns aggregate data over time but are not real-time.
Option D – Correct choice as Power BI dataflows integrate Dataverse data with Power BI.
Option E – Scheduled cloud flows are for periodic updates, not real-time.

| EXAM FOCUS | "Utilize Real-time workflows, Calculated columns, and Power BI dataflows for dynamic reporting and analysis." |
|---|---|
| CAUTION ALERT | "Scheduled cloud flows support periodic updates but not real-time data needs." |

## QUESTION 21

Answer – A), B)

Option A – Dataverse ensures secure data management, aligning with financial regulations.
Option B – RBAC using Azure AD provides secure access control.
Option C – Power BI helps with financial reporting but does not directly address data privacy or security policies.
Option D – Regular security audits using Azure Security Center are important but not specific technical measures for data privacy.

Option E – MFA enhances security but is not specifically required for financial regulations.

| EXAM FOCUS | Use Dataverse for secure data management and RBAC with Azure AD. |
|---|---|
| CAUTION ALERT | Regular security audits are essential but not the only measure for compliance. |

## QUESTION 22

Answer – B), D)

Option A – Azure SQL Database is useful for performance but does not directly address data integrity or compliance.
Option B – Dataverse ensures secure data storage and compliance with regulations.
Option C – Azure Cognitive Services provides data analysis but not specifically for data integrity or compliance.
Option D – Applying Azure Policy ensures regulatory compliance.
Option E – Power Query helps with data transformation but not specifically for advanced data modeling techniques.

| EXAM FOCUS | Use Dataverse and Azure Policy to ensure data integrity, compliance, and optimized data storage in government solutions. |
|---|---|
| CAUTION ALERT | Avoid options like Azure SQL Database that focus more on performance than data compliance. |

## QUESTION 23

Answer – B), D)

Option A – Canvas Apps offer flexibility but do not inherently address accessibility.
Option B – Implementing accessibility features like high-contrast mode ensures the application is accessible to users with visual impairments.
Option C – Dataverse is useful for data storage but does not directly address UX design.
Option D – Conducting UX surveys regularly helps gather feedback and improve the design iteratively.
Option E – Azure Cognitive Services for sentiment analysis is useful but not directly related to accessibility or navigation.

| EXAM FOCUS | Please keep in mind, implementing accessibility features and conducting UX surveys regularly ensures a user-friendly application. |
|---|---|
| CAUTION ALERT | Avoid using Dataverse solely for UX improvements; it's primarily for data storage. |

## QUESTION 24

Answer – B)

Option A – Using a single data center with backup does not ensure high availability as it does not protect against regional outages.
Option B – Implementing Geo-redundancy ensures that the system is replicated across multiple geographic locations, minimizing the risk of downtime.

Option C – Regular maintenance windows are necessary but do not contribute directly to high availability.
Option D – On-premises servers can offer high availability but require significant investment and management.
Option E – Using only cloud-based solutions is beneficial but does not guarantee high availability unless geo-redundancy is implemented.

| EXAM FOCUS | "Implement Geo-redundancy for high availability and minimal downtime." |
| --- | --- |
| CAUTION ALERT | "Single data center solutions do not ensure high availability in case of regional outages." |

## QUESTION 25

Answer – A), B), C)

Option A – Power BI Paginated Reports are ideal for detailed financial reporting.
Option B – Power BI AI Insights can be used for integrating AI models to detect anomalies in transactions.
Option C – Power BI Streaming Datasets enable real-time tracking of financial metrics.
Option D – Power BI Dataflows are useful for data preparation but not directly for anomaly detection or real-time tracking.
Option E – Power BI Desktop is essential for report creation but not specifically for anomaly detection or real-time tracking.

| EXAM FOCUS | Employ Paginated Reports, AI Insights, and Streaming Datasets in Power BI for detailed, real-time, and AI-integrated financial reporting. |
| --- | --- |
| CAUTION ALERT | Remember, Dataflows aid in preparation but are not directly for anomaly detection or real-time tracking. |

## QUESTION 26

Answer – A), C), E)

Option A – AI Builder can create predictive models for equipment failure.
Option B – Power Automate helps in scheduling but is not directly involved in predictive modeling.
Option C – Azure IoT Central can integrate device data for analysis.
Option D – Dataverse is useful for storing data but not directly for integration with IoT.
Option E – Azure Functions can implement custom logic for advanced scenarios.

| EXAM FOCUS | Utilize AI Builder, IoT Central, and Azure Functions for predictive maintenance, device data integration, and custom logic. |
| --- | --- |
| CAUTION ALERT | Avoid depending on Power Automate for predictive modeling; it's better suited for workflow automation. |

## QUESTION 27

Answer – A), B), E)

Option A – Power Automate can be used for automating recovery workflows.
Option B – Azure Monitor helps in monitoring system performance.

Option C – Azure AD is useful for managing user access but not directly related to monitoring and recovery.
Option D – Power Virtual Agents is for user interaction and not directly related to business continuity.
Option E – Azure Site Recovery is crucial for ensuring high availability.

| EXAM FOCUS | *Use Power Automate, Azure Monitor, and Azure Site Recovery for recovery workflows, performance monitoring, and high availability.* |
|---|---|
| CAUTION ALERT | *Avoid using Power Virtual Agents for business continuity; it's for user interaction.* |

## QUESTION 28

Answer – B)

Option A – Power BI Embedded is used to embed Power BI reports in applications, not for data security.
Option B – Row-Level Security allows defining security roles that control access to data at the row level, ensuring sensitive data is protected.
Option C – Dataflows are used for ETL processes, not for data security.
Option D – Gateways are used to connect on-premises data sources to Power BI but do not provide data security.
Option E – Power Query is used for data transformation, not for data security.

| EXAM FOCUS | *"Row-Level Security in Power BI controls data access at the row level."* |
|---|---|
| CAUTION ALERT | *"Power BI Embedded and Dataflows do not provide data security features."* |

## QUESTION 29

Answer – B), C), E)

Option A – Incorrect. Power BI is useful for reporting but not primarily for compliance monitoring.
Option B – Correct. Microsoft Information Protection provides robust data security measures.
Option C – Correct. Dataverse ensures secure storage with role-based access controls.
Option D – Incorrect. Custom solutions can be costly and complex to maintain.
Option E – Correct. Azure Sentinel provides comprehensive security monitoring and compliance.

| EXAM FOCUS | *Use Microsoft Information Protection and Azure Sentinel for robust data security and compliance monitoring.* |
|---|---|
| CAUTION ALERT | *Custom solutions can be costly and complex to maintain.* |

## QUESTION 30

Answer – A), B), D)

Option A – Correct. Power BI can visualize patient data and health trends effectively.
Option B – Correct. Azure Data Factory is ideal for integrating health data from multiple sources.
Option C – Incorrect. AI Builder may not provide the advanced predictive capabilities required.
Option D – Correct. Azure Cognitive Services can deliver advanced analytics and insights.

Option E – Incorrect. Storing data in Excel is not scalable or secure enough for healthcare data.

| EXAM FOCUS | *Use Power BI for visualization and Azure Data Factory for data integration.* |
|---|---|
| CAUTION ALERT | *Storing patient data in Excel is not scalable or secure for healthcare needs.* |

## QUESTION 31

Answer – A), B), C)

Option A – Correct. Training sessions using Power Apps help demonstrate the new solution to users.
Option B – Correct. Power BI dashboards can track adoption rates and user feedback effectively.
Option C – Correct. A communication plan keeps users informed and engaged.
Option D – Incorrect. Ignoring user feedback can lead to poor adoption.
Option E – Incorrect. While useful, a resistance management plan alone is not sufficient.

| EXAM FOCUS | *Conduct training sessions using Power Apps and implement a comprehensive communication plan.* |
|---|---|
| CAUTION ALERT | *Ignoring user feedback can lead to poor adoption.* |

## QUESTION 32

Answer – B)

Option A – Attended Desktop Flow requires user interaction, which does not meet the requirement for automatic updates.
Option B – Unattended Desktop Flow allows for automatic updates without user interaction, making it suitable for integrating with a legacy system without an API.
Option C – Azure Functions require coding and do not directly interact with desktop applications.
Option D – Power Automate with HTTP connector is not applicable as the legacy ERP system does not have an API.
Option E – Dynamics 365 Supply Chain Management is an ERP system and not a solution for integrating with another ERP.

| EXAM FOCUS | *"Use Unattended Desktop Flow for automatic updates without user interaction."* |
|---|---|
| CAUTION ALERT | *"Attended Desktop Flow requires user interaction, not suitable for automatic updates."* |

## QUESTION 33

Answer – A), C), E)

Option A – Correct. Azure API Management facilitates custom connectors and API integrations.
Option B – Incorrect. Power BI is useful for monitoring but not primarily for managing customization.
Option C – Correct. Following best practices for coding and documentation ensures maintainability.
Option D – Incorrect. Ignoring maintainability can lead to unmanageable solutions.
Option E – Correct. Using Azure DevOps for continuous integration and version control helps manage complexity.

| EXAM FOCUS | *Use Azure API Management for custom connectors and Azure DevOps for continuous integration.* |
|---|---|
| CAUTION ALERT | *Ignoring maintainability can lead to unmanageable solutions.* |

## QUESTION 34

Answer – A), C)

Option A – Dual-write ensures real-time data consistency between systems.
Option B – Azure DevOps is useful for CI/CD but not directly for phased integration.
Option C – Training programs facilitate user adoption during the transition.
Option D – Full migration before switching can cause disruptions.
Option E – Power BI reporting is helpful but not critical for achieving data consistency and user adoption.

| | |
|---|---|
| **EXAM FOCUS** | *Implement dual-write for real-time data consistency and provide extensive training for user adoption.* |
| **CAUTION ALERT** | *Conducting full migration before switching systems can cause disruptions; avoid this approach.* |

## QUESTION 35

Answer – A), D)

Option A – Power BI Premium provides dedicated resources for better performance and scalability.
Option B – Power BI dataflows assist with ETL but not directly with scaling.
Option C – Scheduling data refreshes helps but is not a primary scaling strategy.
Option D – Enabling query caching and aggregations improves performance and optimizes resource usage.
Option E – Manual allocation is less efficient and prone to delays.

| | |
|---|---|
| **EXAM FOCUS** | *Use Power BI Premium for dedicated resources and enable query caching to handle large datasets efficiently.* |
| **CAUTION ALERT** | *Avoid manual resource allocation; it is inefficient and can delay performance.* |

## QUESTION 36

Answer – B), C), E)

Option A – Batch processing is not suitable for real-time IoT data streams.
Option B – Timely maintenance actions require real-time data processing, making it time-sensitive.
Option C – The volume of data from IoT devices is significant and must be managed effectively.
Option D – Licensing is important but not directly related to the technical requirements of IoT data streams.
Option E – IoT data can be volatile and must be handled appropriately.

| | |
|---|---|
| **EXAM FOCUS** | *"IoT integration requires managing time-sensitive, high-volume, and volatile data streams."* |
| **CAUTION ALERT** | *"Batch processing is not suitable for real-time IoT data streams."* |

## QUESTION 37

Answer – A), C), E)

Option A – Regional Dataverse instances with data governance policies ensure compliance with data

residency requirements.
Option B – A global instance with regional data partitions may not fully address data residency and performance requirements.
Option C – Azure API Management ensures secure and efficient regional API access.
Option D – Power Automate is useful for managing data flows but not for performance optimization.
Option E – Azure Traffic Manager helps in optimizing performance across regions.

| EXAM FOCUS | *Use regional Dataverse instances and Azure API Management for secure API access.* |
|---|---|
| CAUTION ALERT | *A global instance with regional partitions may not fully address data residency and performance needs.* |

## QUESTION 38

Answer – A), B), D)

Option A – Power Virtual Agents provide personalized support for different customer segments.
Option B – Power BI helps analyze user interaction metrics for effectiveness.
Option C – Static pages with identical content do not cater to different customer segments.
Option D – Dynamic content based on user profiles ensures a tailored experience.
Option E – Azure Logic Apps can automate feedback collection but may not be as integrated as using Power Platform tools.

| EXAM FOCUS | *Use Power Virtual Agents for personalized support and Power BI for analyzing user metrics.* |
|---|---|
| CAUTION ALERT | *Static pages with identical content do not provide a tailored user experience.* |

## QUESTION 39

Answer – A), C), D)

Option A – HTTPS ensures that data transmissions are encrypted, maintaining data integrity and confidentiality during exchanges, which is crucial for secure communication.
Option B – Azure IoT Hub is useful for securing device communication but may not directly relate to the broader context of general data exchange and business continuity.
Option C – Regular risk assessments help identify potential threats and vulnerabilities, allowing the organization to proactively mitigate risks before they impact business continuity.
Option D – Regularly updating firmware and applying security patches ensures that all systems remain secure and are protected against known vulnerabilities, which supports continuous operation.
Option E – Azure DevOps can help manage updates to continuity plans, but it does not directly address ensuring data integrity and confidentiality or regular updates to continuity measures themselves.

| EXAM FOCUS | *Use HTTPS for data transmissions and conduct regular risk assessments to maintain data integrity.* |
|---|---|
| CAUTION ALERT | *Avoid using outdated firmware; regularly update device firmware to ensure security.* |

## QUESTION 40

Answer – B)

Option A – Power Automate with HTTP connector can work but may not provide the seamless integration and security best practices required.

Option B – A Custom Connector allows for secure, seamless integration tailored to the specific third-party service.

Option C – Azure Logic Apps can also integrate services but may be more complex to set up compared to Custom Connectors.

Option D – Dynamics 365 Business Central is a different ERP system and not used for integrations in this context.

Option E – Microsoft Graph API is not designed for integrating third-party tax calculation services.

| EXAM FOCUS | "Use a Custom Connector for secure, seamless integration with third-party tax services." |
| --- | --- |
| CAUTION ALERT | "Power Automate HTTP connector might not ensure the required level of security." |

## QUESTION 41

Answer – A), B), C)

Option A – Dataverse provides a secure and scalable data storage solution, suitable for managing patient data.

Option B – Role-Based Access Control (RBAC) ensures that only authorized personnel can access sensitive data, maintaining security and compliance.

Option C – Power Apps Component Framework (PCF) allows for the development of modular features, facilitating easy integration and expansion.

Option D – Azure Logic Apps is useful for workflow automation but does not directly address the need for scalable data storage or modular feature development.

Option E – Azure DevOps is great for CI/CD but is not specific to scalability or modular feature integration in the context of Power Platform.

| EXAM FOCUS | Use Dataverse for secure data storage and PCF for modular features. |
| --- | --- |
| CAUTION ALERT | Azure Logic Apps is for workflow automation, not directly for scalable storage or modular development. |

## QUESTION 42

Answer – C), D), E)

Option A – Azure Logic Apps is useful for automating workflows but not for monitoring solution health and performance.

Option B – RBAC in Dataverse is essential for secure data access but does not directly contribute to monitoring solution health and maintenance.

Option C – Azure Monitor is an effective tool for continuous tracking of solution health and setting up alerts for proactive issue detection.

Option D – Scheduling regular updates and maintenance using Azure DevOps pipelines ensures that the solution remains up-to-date and stable.

Option E – Conducting manual performance reviews can complement automated monitoring tools, ensuring comprehensive checks.

| EXAM FOCUS | Use Azure Monitor and DevOps for updates, and complement with manual reviews. |
| CAUTION ALERT | RBAC alone does not ensure overall solution health; use monitoring tools. |

## QUESTION 43

Answer – A), B), D)

Option A – Power BI is suitable for developing dashboards to monitor KPIs, providing visual insights.
Option B – Azure Data Factory can aggregate data from multiple sources, ensuring comprehensive analysis.
Option C – Storing data in an unstructured format is inefficient and not suitable for detailed analysis.
Option D – Power Automate can integrate data insights into workflows, streamlining operations.
Option E – Manual data collection and analysis are time-consuming and prone to errors, making them unsuitable for large-scale supply chain optimization.

| EXAM FOCUS | Develop dashboards with Power BI and use Azure Data Factory for data aggregation. |
| CAUTION ALERT | Unstructured data storage leads to inefficiencies and isn't suitable. |

## QUESTION 44

Answer – A)

Option A – Correct. Dataverse auditing provides a comprehensive log of all changes made within Dataverse, allowing for detailed examination of the data import process and identification of discrepancies.
Option B – Incorrect. Dataflow diagnostics are specific to Power BI and are used for optimizing data movement, not troubleshooting Dataverse imports.
Option C – Incorrect. Trace logging is useful for debugging but may not provide the specific data change history needed to diagnose import issues.
Option D – Incorrect. Power BI data integrity checks are used to ensure data quality within Power BI reports, not Dataverse imports.
Option E – Incorrect. Plugin trace logs provide detailed logs for custom plugin operations but are not directly used for auditing data imports.

| EXAM FOCUS | "Dataverse auditing ensures data integrity by providing comprehensive logs of all changes." |
| CAUTION ALERT | "Don't rely solely on trace logging; it might miss specific data change histories." |

## QUESTION 45

Answer – A), B), C)

Option A – Detailed user manuals and video tutorials provide comprehensive training resources that can be referenced as needed.
Option B – Power Virtual Agents can offer round-the-clock support, addressing user queries promptly.
Option C – A feedback loop using Power BI dashboards allows for continuous monitoring and improvement of the training program.
Option D – Collecting feedback through periodic meetings alone may miss real-time issues and

suggestions.
Option E – Conducting a single training session without follow-up is insufficient for ensuring long-term user competence and system adoption.

| EXAM FOCUS | *Detailed user manuals and video tutorials provide comprehensive training resources.* |
|---|---|
| CAUTION ALERT | *Conducting a single training session without follow-up is insufficient.* |

## QUESTION 46

Answer – A), B), C)

Option A – Using Dynamics 365 Performance Insights helps identify specific performance bottlenecks within the system.
Option B – Scaling out resources by adding more instances can help manage increased load during peak hours and improve performance.
Option C – Implementing Azure Monitor allows for continuous tracking of performance metrics and proactive issue resolution.
Option D – Focusing only on functionality enhancements without addressing performance issues will lead to continued slow performance during peak hours.
Option E – Avoiding addressing performance issues during peak hours will result in a poor user experience and potential system failures during critical times.

| EXAM FOCUS | *"Use Dynamics 365 Performance Insights and Azure Monitor for continuous tracking."* |
|---|---|
| CAUTION ALERT | *"Avoid addressing performance issues only during peak hours."* |

## QUESTION 47

Answer – A), B), E)

Option A – Using Power Automate analytics helps monitor the performance of workflows and identify issues.
Option B – Setting up alerts in Azure Monitor for workflow failures ensures prompt detection and resolution of issues.
Option C – Ignoring user feedback can lead to missed opportunities for improving the workflow and user satisfaction.
Option D – Collecting user feedback through Power Apps forms enables systematic feedback collection, contributing to continuous improvement.
Option E – Using Power BI to analyze performance metrics provides comprehensive insights into workflow performance and efficiency.

| EXAM FOCUS | *"Use Power Automate analytics to monitor and improve workflow performance continuously."* |
|---|---|
| CAUTION ALERT | *"Ignoring user feedback can result in missed improvement opportunities."* |

## QUESTION 48

Answer – A), E)

Option A – Correct. Automating connection management in a scenario involving sensitive data ensures that connections are consistently secure and properly managed, reducing the risk of human error.

Option B – Incorrect. While data encryption is critical for security, it is not specifically an "automation" task within Power Platform implementations.

Option C – Incorrect. Webhook configuration is more about functionality than security and error minimization.

Option D – Incorrect. Service endpoint configuration is vital but does not address the broader goal of minimizing human error across the system.

Option E – Correct. Automating compliance audits ensures ongoing adherence to security protocols without manual oversight, crucial for maintaining high security standards in government data handling.

| | |
|---|---|
| **EXAM FOCUS** | *"Automate connection management and compliance audits to enhance security and reduce human error in sensitive data handling."* |
| **CAUTION ALERT** | *"Service endpoint configuration is vital but doesn't minimize human error across the system."* |

## QUESTION 49

Answer – A), C), D)

Option A – Correct. Managed solutions help package customizations, making it easier to deploy and update them while ensuring compliance.

Option B – Incorrect. While Power Automate can automate processes, compliance checks need more rigorous methods.

Option C – Correct. Leveraging out-of-the-box features ensures that workflows and processes are built on stable, supported features, reducing the need for customizations.

Option D – Correct. Regular audits of customizations help ensure ongoing compliance with healthcare regulations.

Option E – Incorrect. Azure Service Health is useful for monitoring service status but does not directly address customization management or compliance.

| | |
|---|---|
| **EXAM FOCUS** | *"Use managed solutions to deploy customizations and ensure compliance with healthcare regulations."* |
| **CAUTION ALERT** | *"You should stay cautious, not auditing customizations can lead to compliance violations."* |

## QUESTION 50

Answer – A), C), D)

Option A – Correct. Power BI can create insightful reports on the environmental impact of IT infrastructure, helping track and manage sustainability efforts.

Option B – Incorrect. While Azure Cognitive Services can optimize resources, it is more suited for AI and analytics rather than direct resource optimization.

Option C – Correct. Power Virtual Agents can be used to develop engaging training modules to promote eco-awareness among healthcare staff.

Option D – Correct. Choosing Azure services with a lower carbon footprint supports energy efficiency and sustainability goals.

Option E – Incorrect. While useful, Power Automate is better suited for process automation rather than scheduling energy-saving tasks directly.

| | |
|---|---|
| **EXAM FOCUS** | *"Create training modules using Power Virtual Agents to promote eco-awareness."* |
| **CAUTION ALERT** | *"You should stay cautious, ignoring the carbon footprint of IT infrastructure can undermine sustainability efforts."* |

# PRACTICE TEST 10 - QUESTIONS ONLY

### QUESTION 1

An educational institution seeks to modernize its student management system using Microsoft Power Platform. Their business objectives are to improve student engagement, streamline administrative processes, and enhance data analytics. Specific challenges include:
- Disconnected student information systems.
- Manual administrative processes.
- Limited insights into student performance.

What solutions would best align with these goals and address the challenges? Select three correct answers.

A) Implement Power BI for student performance analytics.
B) Use Power Automate to automate administrative workflows.
C) Develop a unified student management app with Power Apps.
D) Integrate AI Builder for predictive analytics on student performance.
E) Use Dataverse to centralize student data.

### QUESTION 2

As a solution architect, you need to ensure a construction company's project management app integrates with external systems for real-time updates and adheres to strict data compliance standards. Which components should you incorporate into the Power Platform solution? Select up to three answers.

A) Power Apps
B) Power BI
C) Power Automate
D) Azure Logic Apps
E) Microsoft Dataverse

### QUESTION 3

An educational institution wants to improve its student performance analysis using Microsoft Power Platform. The project requires collecting and interpreting student data accurately. The specific challenges include:
- Disconnected data sources for student information.
- Ensuring data accuracy and reliability.
- Generating insights for data-driven decision making.

What actions would you take to integrate and analyze student data effectively? Select three correct answers.

A) Implement Dataverse to centralize student information.
B) Use Power Automate to ensure data accuracy.
C) Develop a Power BI dashboard to generate insights.
D) Create a Canvas App for student data entry.
E) Use AI Builder for predictive analysis of student performance.

## QUESTION 4

A financial institution wants to implement a solution to detect and respond to fraudulent transaction activities in real-time. Which Power Platform components should be used to develop this solution? Select up to three answers.

A) Power BI
B) Power Apps
C) Power Automate
D) Dynamics 365 Fraud Protection
E) Microsoft Dataverse

## QUESTION 5

A retail company is implementing a new customer feedback system using Microsoft Power Platform. The project requires understanding relevant legal and compliance issues. The specific challenges include:
• Ensuring compliance with GDPR regulations.
• Protecting customer data privacy.
• Incorporating compliance verification into the solution.
What actions would you take to ensure compliance with these requirements? Select three correct answers.

A) Implement Dataverse to securely store customer feedback data.
B) Use Power Automate to automate compliance workflows.
C) Apply DLP policies to protect data privacy.
D) Conduct regular compliance audits using Power BI.
E) Implement RBAC to control access to customer data.

## QUESTION 6

A retail company is implementing a new customer relationship management (CRM) system using Microsoft Power Platform. The project involves cost estimation and ROI analysis. The specific challenges include:
• Accurately estimating the costs for system implementation.
• Budgeting for future upgrades and enhancements.
• Analyzing the ROI over a five-year period.
What actions would you take to address these challenges? Select three correct answers.

A) Implement Dataverse to store and manage customer data.
B) Use Power BI to estimate implementation costs.
C) Develop a budget plan for future upgrades.
D) Conduct an ROI analysis using Power BI.
E) Use Power Automate to automate budgeting tasks.

## QUESTION 7

An educational institution is developing a student information system using Microsoft Power Platform. The project requires feedback gathering and iteration. The specific challenges are:
• Collecting feedback from end users.

- Incorporating feedback into the prototype.
- Iterating on the design for continuous improvement.

What actions would you take to address these challenges? Select three correct answers.

A) Use Power Apps to create an initial prototype.
B) Use Dataverse to store student data.
C) Conduct user feedback sessions.
D) Use Power Automate to streamline feedback collection.
E) Iterate on the design using user feedback.

## QUESTION 8

A logistics company is planning the integration of their tracking system with Dynamics 365 using Microsoft Power Platform. The project involves using tools and technologies for integration. The specific challenges are:
- Selecting appropriate integration tools.
- Ensuring scalability.
- Managing integration dependencies.

What actions would you take to address these challenges? Select three correct answers.

A) Use Azure Logic Apps for scalable integration workflows.
B) Implement Azure Functions for serverless integration.
C) Use Dataverse to manage integration dependencies.
D) Develop a microservices architecture using Azure Kubernetes Service.
E) Use Power Virtual Agents for tracking queries.

## QUESTION 9

A retail organization is expanding its e-commerce platform using Microsoft Power Platform. The project requires compliance with global privacy laws. The specific challenges are:
- Ensuring compliance with GDPR.
- Implementing data protection measures.
- Maintaining customer data privacy.

What actions would you take to address these challenges? Select three correct answers.

A) Use Azure Policy for compliance management.
B) Implement GDPR compliance using Azure Information Protection.
C) Use Power Automate for data processing.
D) Conduct regular audits for compliance validation.
E) Implement RBAC for access control.

## QUESTION 10

A manufacturing company is deploying a new supply chain management system using Microsoft Power Platform. The project requires planning for quality assurance. The specific challenges are:
- Implementing effective QA methodologies.
- Defining quality metrics.
- Ensuring quality control throughout the project lifecycle.

What steps would you take to address these challenges? Select two correct answers.

A) Develop a comprehensive QA plan.
B) Use Power Apps for defect tracking.
C) Implement automated testing with Power Automate.
D) Use Power BI for real-time quality monitoring.
E) Conduct regular stakeholder meetings.

## QUESTION 11

A government agency is implementing a new citizen services portal using Dynamics 365 and Microsoft Power Platform. The specific challenges are:
- Managing the solution lifecycle from development to deployment.
- Ensuring continuous updates and improvements.
- Planning for the end-of-life of the current system.

What steps would you take to address these challenges? Select three correct answers.

A) Implement ALM practices using Azure DevOps.
B) Use Power Automate to automate the release management process.
C) Develop a detailed migration and end-of-life plan for the current system.
D) Utilize Azure Functions to handle specific integration tasks.
E) Schedule regular stakeholder reviews to gather feedback.

## QUESTION 12

A technology company is developing a project management solution using Microsoft Power Platform. The solution needs to integrate with their existing SharePoint Online and Teams environments to enhance collaboration.
- The solution must allow project managers to automate task assignments and notifications.
- It should provide dashboards and reports for project tracking and performance analysis.

Which components would you use to build this solution?

A) Power Apps, Power Automate, Power BI, SharePoint Online, Teams
B) Power Apps, Power Automate, Azure Synapse Analytics, Teams
C) Power Automate, Power BI, Dynamics 365 Project Service Automation, Teams
D) Power Apps, Power Automate, Power BI, Dynamics 365 Project Service Automation
E) Power Automate, Power BI, SharePoint Online, Teams

## QUESTION 13

A manufacturing company is implementing agile methodologies for its inventory management system using the Microsoft Power Platform. The challenges include:
- Managing agile projects.
- Adapting to changes in agile environments.
- Continuous delivery and feedback loops.

What strategies and tools should you use to address these challenges? Select three correct answers.

A) Implement Azure DevOps for project tracking and CI/CD.
B) Conduct daily stand-up meetings.
C) Use Dynamics 365 for customer relationship management.
D) Schedule sprint planning and review meetings.

E) Utilize AI Builder for real-time analytics.

## QUESTION 14

An e-commerce company is deploying a data governance framework using Microsoft Power Platform to enhance data quality and compliance. The challenges include:
• Defining roles and responsibilities in data stewardship.
• Implementing data quality and consistency measures.
• Ensuring compliance with data governance standards.
What strategies should you implement to address these challenges? Select three correct answers.

A) Develop a data governance charter.
B) Assign Data Steward roles and responsibilities in Dataverse.
C) Use Power BI for data quality monitoring and reporting.
D) Implement Azure Policy to enforce data governance standards.
E) Utilize Azure Data Factory for data transformation and quality checks.

## QUESTION 15

An e-commerce company is using Microsoft Power Platform to enhance its inventory management system. The team faces challenges such as:
• Deciding between customization and configuration.
• Balancing flexibility and standardization.
• Impact of customizations on maintenance.
What strategies should you implement to address these challenges? Select three correct answers.

A) Use Power Automate for inventory updates and notifications.
B) Customize Dataverse schema extensively.
C) Leverage Power BI for inventory reporting.
D) Configure existing Dataverse entities to fit business needs.
E) Implement custom APIs for inventory management.

## QUESTION 16

A logistics company needs to improve its shipment tracking system by integrating real-time data from GPS devices into their Power Platform solution. They also want to send alerts to customers when their shipments are close to delivery.
• The solution must handle real-time data ingestion.
• It should automate the sending of alerts based on shipment status.
Which components should be included in your solution design? Select three answers.

A) Power Apps, Power Automate, Power BI, Azure IoT Hub
B) Power Automate, Azure Event Hub, Power BI
C) Power Apps, Power Automate, Power Virtual Agents
D) Power Automate, Azure Logic Apps, Power BI
E) Power Apps, Power Automate, Power BI, Azure Synapse Analytics

## QUESTION 17

A multinational corporation is implementing a new document management system using Microsoft Power Platform. The project involves:
- Establishing governance structures.
- Ensuring compliance with international data protection laws.
- Implementing auditing and reporting mechanisms.

What strategies should you adopt to address these requirements? Select three correct answers.

A) Utilize Dataverse for centralized data management and compliance tracking.
B) Implement Power Automate to enforce data governance policies.
C) Use Power BI for compliance reporting and auditing.
D) Develop custom connectors to integrate with existing compliance systems.
E) Configure role-based security in Power Apps to manage user access.

## QUESTION 18

A manufacturing company is leading a digital transformation initiative using Microsoft Power Platform. The solution must:
- Support innovative approaches to solution design.
- Integrate disruptive technologies.
- Drive continuous improvement in manufacturing processes.

You need to choose three strategies to ensure the solution meets these requirements. Which three strategies should you choose? (Select three)

A) Implement Azure IoT Hub for real-time equipment monitoring.
B) Use Power BI for real-time process analytics.
C) Develop custom APIs for integrating third-party manufacturing systems.
D) Use Power Virtual Agents to support employee training and development.
E) Implement Power Automate to streamline manufacturing workflows.

## QUESTION 19

A retail company is using Microsoft Power Platform to develop a customer loyalty program. The solution must:
- Comply with data protection laws.
- Prevent unauthorized data access.
- Ensure ethical handling of customer data.

Which three actions should you take? (Select three)

A) Implement data encryption at rest using Dataverse.
B) Use Power Automate to track data access and modifications.
C) Enable Role-Based Access Control (RBAC) in Power Apps.
D) Develop a clear data privacy policy and share it with customers.
E) Use Azure AD for secure user authentication.

## QUESTION 20

A government agency is using Microsoft Dataverse to track citizen service requests and responses. They

need to ensure the data model supports high performance and scalability for large volumes of data.
• The solution must handle complex queries efficiently.
• It should ensure data integrity and support data archival processes.
Which components should be included in the data model design? Select two answers.

A) Indexed columns
B) Option sets
C) Alternate keys
D) Hierarchical relationship settings
E) Business rules

## QUESTION 21

A government agency must comply with strict security protocols for their Power Platform solution. The solution must:
• Implement data protection standards.
• Ensure regulatory compliance (e.g., GDPR, HIPAA).
• Conduct security audits.
Which two measures should you implement? (Select two)

A) Use Dataverse for secure data management.
B) Implement Data Loss Prevention (DLP) policies.
C) Use Azure Functions for custom data processing.
D) Conduct regular security audits using Azure Security Center.
E) Implement role-based access control (RBAC) using Azure AD.

## QUESTION 22

A multinational corporation is deploying a Power Platform solution to manage and analyze data from various sources across its global branches. The solution must:
• Ensure data integrity and quality.
• Enable big data analytics.
• Support data governance and lifecycle management.
Which two actions should you recommend? (Select two)

A) Use Dataverse for data storage and quality management.
B) Implement Azure Data Factory for ETL processes.
C) Use Power BI for data visualization.
D) Apply Data Loss Prevention (DLP) policies.
E) Use Azure Synapse Analytics for big data analytics.

## QUESTION 23

A healthcare provider is designing a patient portal using Power Platform. They want to ensure the portal is user-friendly and accessible to patients of all ages and abilities. The solution must:
• Follow user-centered design principles.
• Be customizable for different patient needs.
• Include feedback mechanisms for continuous improvement.
Which two features should you implement? (Select two)

A) Use Power BI to create user-friendly dashboards.
B) Implement screen reader compatibility.
C) Use Power Apps for customizable patient forms.
D) Conduct accessibility testing with patients.
E) Use Power Automate to streamline backend processes.

## QUESTION 24

A logistics company uses Power Apps to manage their fleet operations. They need to integrate real-time GPS data from their vehicles into Power Apps to improve tracking and efficiency. What is the best approach to integrate this data?

A) Use a manual data entry system
B) Develop a custom connector for GPS data
C) Use Power BI for data visualization
D) Implement an Azure IoT Hub
E) Use Dynamics 365 Field Service

## QUESTION 25

A manufacturing company wants to use Power BI to improve its production efficiency. The solution must:
- Provide real-time analytics on production metrics.
- Utilize AI to predict equipment failures.
- Ensure secure access to data.

Which three components or strategies should you prioritize? (Select three)

A) Power BI Streaming Datasets for real-time analytics.
B) Azure Machine Learning for AI predictions.
C) Power BI Row-Level Security (RLS) for data security.
D) Power BI Embedded for custom solutions.
E) Azure API Management for API handling.

## QUESTION 26

A customer service organization wants to leverage AI to improve response times. The solution must:
- Automatically classify customer inquiries.
- Suggest responses to agents.
- Ensure ethical AI practices.

Which three components should be utilized? (Select three)

A) AI Builder for classifying inquiries.
B) Power Virtual Agents for suggesting responses.
C) Azure Cognitive Services for language understanding.
D) Dataverse for inquiry data.
E) Azure Policy for ethical AI guidelines.

## QUESTION 27

A retail company needs to ensure its Power Platform solutions have a robust disaster recovery plan. The plan must:
- Test and validate recovery procedures regularly.
- Back up critical data.
- Provide high availability for customer-facing applications.

What are the best components and practices to implement? (Select three)

A) Power Platform Admin Center for policy enforcement.
B) Azure Backup for data protection.
C) Power BI for compliance dashboards.
D) Azure Site Recovery for high availability.
E) Azure DevOps for testing and validating recovery plans.

## QUESTION 28

A manufacturing firm uses Dynamics 365 Supply Chain Management and wants to implement an IoT solution to monitor equipment health in real-time. They need to integrate this IoT data into Dynamics 365 to trigger maintenance workflows automatically. What Azure service should they use for this integration?

A) Azure Logic Apps
B) Azure IoT Hub
C) Azure Data Lake
D) Azure Machine Learning
E) Azure Cognitive Services

## QUESTION 29

A government client needs to ensure their Power Platform solution adheres to stringent compliance and regulatory requirements. They want to implement tools to automate and monitor compliance continuously.
1. Ensuring compliance with government regulations.
2. Automating compliance processes to reduce manual efforts.
3. Continuously monitoring compliance status.

What tools and strategies would you recommend to meet these needs? Select two answers.

A) Use Microsoft Compliance Manager to automate compliance tasks.
B) Store all data in third-party cloud solutions.
C) Implement Azure Policy to enforce compliance rules.
D) Use Power Automate for compliance process automation.
E) Use Dataverse for secure data storage and compliance.

## QUESTION 30

A government client wants to leverage data science and machine learning to enhance their public services. They aim to integrate various external data sources and apply predictive analytics to optimize resource allocation and improve service delivery.

1. Integrating data from multiple government agencies and external sources.
2. Applying machine learning models to predict service demand.
3. Generating actionable insights to optimize resource allocation.

What measures would you take to achieve these goals? Select two answers.

A) Use Power BI for data integration and visualization.
B) Implement Azure Data Factory for managing data from multiple sources.
C) Use Azure Machine Learning for developing predictive models.
D) Store data in a shared network drive for easy access.
E) Develop custom applications for data analysis and insights.

## QUESTION 31

During a project review, a financial services client has expressed concerns about the adoption of a new Power Platform solution. They want to ensure that the solution is well-received by users and that its impact is measured accurately.

1. Promoting user adoption and managing resistance.
2. Developing effective communication and training plans.
3. Measuring the impact and success of the new solution.

What actions would you recommend to address these concerns? Select two answers.

A) Use Power Automate to automate training notifications and reminders.
B) Conduct regular training sessions and provide ongoing support.
C) Develop a communication plan that includes success stories and benefits of the new solution.
D) Focus solely on technical deployment without considering user adoption.
E) Measure success through user surveys and adoption metrics tracked in Power BI.

## QUESTION 32

A government agency uses Dynamics 365 for managing citizen services. They want to integrate a third-party identity verification system to validate citizen identities during service requests. The integration must comply with government security standards and provide real-time validation results. What approach should they use?

A) Use Azure API Management
B) Implement a Custom Connector
C) Use Power Automate with HTTP connector
D) Use Azure Logic Apps
E) Use Microsoft Graph API

## QUESTION 33

During a project review, a financial services client has expressed concerns about the complexity and maintainability of their new Power Platform solution. They want to ensure the solution includes advanced customization and is maintainable.

1. Implementing advanced customization in Power Apps and Power Automate.
2. Ensuring maintainability of the solution.
3. Managing complexity in custom solutions.

What actions would you recommend to address these concerns? Select two answers.

A) Use Azure DevOps to manage version control and continuous integration.
B) Conduct regular code reviews and follow best practices for maintainable custom code.
C) Focus solely on adding new features to meet business needs.
D) Implement Power Virtual Agents to automate interactions.
E) Avoid using custom connectors to reduce complexity.

## QUESTION 34

To minimize disruption during the integration of a legacy inventory management system with Dynamics 365, your project must:
- Ensure continuous system availability.
- Perform data migration without halting operations.
- Validate data accuracy during the migration process. What actions should you take? (Select 3 answers)

A) Schedule migration during non-business hours.
B) Use Azure Data Factory to automate and manage the migration process.
C) Perform real-time data validation using Power Automate.
D) Implement a rollback strategy in case of failures.
E) Use Azure DevOps for monitoring and reporting on migration progress.

## QUESTION 35

An organization is using Power Automate to manage workflows for various business processes. They need to ensure the workflows can handle increased loads and remain responsive. The requirements are:
- Efficiently manage high-volume transactions.
- Optimize performance and resource allocation.
- Plan for future growth. What actions should you take? (Select 3 answers)

A) Use parallel branches in Power Automate to handle concurrent processes.
B) Implement Azure Logic Apps for complex workflows.
C) Optimize flow design to reduce execution time.
D) Utilize Azure Monitor to track performance metrics.
E) Schedule workflows during off-peak hours to balance the load.

## QUESTION 36

An educational institution uses Dynamics 365 to manage student records and academic activities. They want to integrate a learning management system (LMS) to synchronize course data and student grades. The integration must handle high volumes of data and ensure accuracy and compliance with educational standards. Which categorizations should you consider for this integration?

A) Batch
B) Licensed
C) Regulated
D) Volume
E) Time-sensitive

## QUESTION 37

Your company is deploying a Power BI solution to be used by employees across different regions. The solution must:
- Ensure data compliance and residency.
- Provide optimal performance for all users.
- Handle regional data processing efficiently. What strategies should you implement? (Select 3 answers)

A) Use Power BI Premium capacity for dedicated resources.
B) Implement regional Power BI dataflows.
C) Store all data in a single central database.
D) Use Azure Data Factory for ETL processes.
E) Deploy regional Power BI workspaces.

## QUESTION 38

An e-commerce company wants to enhance the user experience of their Power Apps-based order management system. The system must:
- Personalize the interface based on user roles.
- Continuously improve based on user feedback.
- Track key performance indicators (KPIs) for user experience. What strategies should be adopted? (Select 2 answers)

A) Use role-based views in Model-Driven Apps.
B) Implement Power BI to monitor KPIs related to user experience.
C) Collect feedback manually via emails.
D) Use static views for all user roles.
E) Implement AI Builder to predict and recommend improvements based on feedback data.

## QUESTION 39

Your organization is implementing a Power Platform solution for a healthcare agency. The solution must:
- Comply with stringent data security regulations.
- Ensure business continuity.
- Regularly assess and update security and continuity protocols. What actions should you take? (Select 3 answers)

A) Use Dataverse with government community cloud (GCC) compliance.
B) Encrypt data at rest and in transit using advanced encryption standards (AES).
C) Use public Wi-Fi for data transmission.
D) Conduct regular security and continuity training for all users.
E) Implement Azure Backup and Site Recovery for data protection and failover.

## QUESTION 40

A healthcare provider uses Dynamics 365 Customer Engagement to manage patient records. They want to integrate with an external patient portal to ensure that patient data is synchronized in real-time. The integration must avoid data duplication and keep all records current. Which data operation should you use in Power Automate to achieve this?

A) Create
B) Update
C) Upsert
D) Merge
E) Aggregate

## QUESTION 41

A tech startup is designing a Power Platform solution that must:
• Scale efficiently with user growth.
• Use modular architecture for rapid feature deployment.
• Ensure high performance and availability. What components should you use? (Select 3 answers)

A) Use Azure Kubernetes Service (AKS) for container orchestration.
B) Implement Azure DevOps for CI/CD pipelines.
C) Utilize Power Automate for workflow management.
D) Use Azure Functions for serverless compute tasks.
E) Use Dataverse for centralized data storage.

## QUESTION 42

A logistics company is managing its operations using a Power Platform solution. To ensure the solution's long-term stability and performance, they must:
• Continuously monitor solution health.
• Perform proactive issue detection and resolution.
• Regularly update and maintain the solution. What strategies should they use? (Select 3 answers)

A) Use Power BI to create dashboards for visualizing operational data.
B) Implement Azure Monitor to track solution health and performance metrics.
C) Use Azure Security Center for continuous security monitoring.
D) Schedule regular maintenance and updates through Azure DevOps pipelines.
E) Rely solely on annual manual reviews for performance checks.

## QUESTION 43

An educational institution aims to improve student performance analysis through advanced reporting. They need to:
• Collect and analyze student performance data.
• Create custom dashboards for teachers and administrators.
• Ensure data privacy and security. What steps should they take? (Select 3 answers)

A) Use Power BI to create dashboards for teachers and administrators.
B) Implement data encryption to protect student information.
C) Store performance data in an unencrypted format for easy access.
D) Use Power Automate to schedule regular data updates.
E) Conduct manual reviews of student performance data.

## QUESTION 44

A retail company uses Power Apps to manage inventory across multiple locations. The app has slowed significantly as new features were added. You need to optimize the app's performance to ensure quick and efficient inventory updates.
- Improve app performance.
- Efficient inventory management.

Which two actions should you take to enhance the app's responsiveness and user adoption?

A) Use the Concurrent function
B) Add non-delegable functions
C) Reduce the number of controls
D) Apply a control dependency
E) Increase data row limits

## QUESTION 45

A manufacturing company is deploying a new ERP system using Power Platform. They need to:
- Provide ongoing training to users.
- Establish an effective support strategy.
- Regularly assess the training program's effectiveness. What should they consider?

A) Develop a comprehensive e-learning platform using Power Apps.
B) Utilize Power BI to analyze training effectiveness and user feedback.
C) Implement a support ticketing system integrated with Dynamics 365.
D) Use email surveys for feedback collection.
E) Conduct a one-time training workshop for all users.

## QUESTION 46

A manufacturing company is implementing a new Power Automate solution to streamline operations. They must:
- Optimize the flow for performance.
- Manage resources effectively.
- Monitor and continuously improve performance. What steps should they take?

A) Use parallel branches in Power Automate to optimize flow performance.
B) Implement Azure Logic Apps for complex workflows.
C) Monitor flow performance using Power Platform Admin Center.
D) Add more steps to the flow without optimization.
E) Ignore resource management and focus on automation.

## QUESTION 47

A financial services firm is deploying a Power BI solution for financial analytics. To ensure robust monitoring and analytics, they must:
- Set up real-time monitoring systems.
- Analyze usage and performance insights.
- Develop comprehensive reports and dashboards. What steps should they take?

Select 2 answers.

A) Implement Power BI's real-time data streaming capabilities.
B) Use Azure Log Analytics for detailed monitoring.
C) Skip usage analysis and focus solely on performance.
D) Create detailed dashboards in Power BI.
E) Ignore user feedback and behavior analytics.

## QUESTION 48

A global retail company uses Power Apps to manage international sales data. A recent update to the app introduced performance issues, particularly noticeable at overseas locations. You need to analyze and recommend solutions to enhance performance and ensure uniform user experience.
• Enhance app performance internationally.
• Ensure uniform user experience across locations.
Which two factors should be evaluated to address the performance issues effectively?

A) Network latency
B) Microsoft Dataverse log capacity
C) Local data storage options
D) Service-level agreement (SLA)
E) Network bandwidth

## QUESTION 49

A retail company is implementing a new Power Platform solution to manage inventory and sales data. They need to ensure that their customizations are managed efficiently and do not hinder future upgrades. The key requirements are:
• Managing customizations lifecycle.
• Ensuring smooth upgrades.
• Balancing custom and out-of-the-box features.
What strategies should you implement? (Select 3 answers)

A) Use Azure DevOps for CI/CD and version control.
B) Implement managed solutions for customizations.
C) Develop a strategy to regularly review and update customizations.
D) Use Dataverse's built-in features for data management.
E) Implement automated testing for customizations using the Power Automate Test Framework.

## QUESTION 50

Your organization is adopting a new Power BI solution to monitor and promote sustainability initiatives. The key requirements are:
- Tracking sustainability metrics in real-time.
- Reducing energy consumption of data processing activities.
- Promoting sustainability practices among employees.

What steps should you take to meet these requirements? (Select 3 answers)

A) Use Power BI dataflows to preprocess data efficiently.
B) Implement incremental data refresh in Power BI to reduce processing loads.
C) Use Azure Functions to handle data processing tasks.
D) Create a Power BI dashboard to display real-time sustainability metrics.
E) Develop a Power Virtual Agents bot to educate employees on sustainability practices.

# PRACTICE TEST 10 - ANSWERS ONLY

## QUESTION 1

Answer – A), B), C)

Option A – Analytics improve insights, addressing limited insights into student performance.
Option B – Automating workflows reduces manual effort, addressing manual administrative processes.
Option C – A unified app with Power Apps centralizes information, addressing disconnected student information systems.
Option D – Predictive analytics enhance insights but do not address disconnected systems or manual processes.
Option E – Centralizing data helps unify systems but does not directly improve engagement or streamline processes.

| | |
|---|---|
| **EXAM FOCUS** | *Implement Power BI for analytics, automate workflows with Power Automate, and develop a unified app for improved student management.* |
| **CAUTION ALERT** | *Remember, centralizing data alone won't improve engagement or streamline administrative processes effectively.* |

## QUESTION 2

Answer – A), C) & E)

Option A – Correct. Power Apps for creating the app with necessary compliance features.
Option B – Incorrect. Power BI is mainly for data visualization, not integration or compliance.
Option C – Correct. Power Automate for automating data flows and ensuring real-time updates.
Option D – Incorrect. While Azure Logic Apps could help with integration, it's not a core component of the Power Platform.
Option E – Correct. Microsoft Dataverse to securely store and manage data according to compliance standards.

| | |
|---|---|
| **EXAM FOCUS** | *"Incorporate Power Apps, Power Automate, and Dataverse for integration, real-time updates, and compliance in project management."* |
| **CAUTION ALERT** | *"Power BI and Azure Logic Apps are not core components for integration or compliance in Power Platform."* |

## QUESTION 3

Answer – A), B), C)

Option A – Centralizing student information in Dataverse addresses disconnected data sources.
Option B – Power Automate can ensure data accuracy and reliability.
Option C – A Power BI dashboard helps generate insights for decision making.
Option D – A Canvas App is useful for data entry but does not address accuracy or analysis.
Option E – AI Builder for predictive analysis is useful but not critical for initial data collection and accuracy.

| EXAM FOCUS | Centralize student data with Dataverse, ensure accuracy with Power Automate, and use Power BI for insights. |
| --- | --- |
| CAUTION ALERT | Stay cautious, using a Canvas App for data entry alone won't address accuracy or disconnected data sources. |

## QUESTION 4

Answer – A), C) & D)

Option A – Correct. Power BI can be used to visualize transaction activities and detect anomalies.
Option B – Incorrect. Power Apps develops applications but is not specifically designed for fraud detection.
Option C – Correct. Power Automate can trigger responses and alerts based on detected anomalies.
Option D – Correct. Dynamics 365 Fraud Protection is specifically designed to help protect against fraud.
Option E – Incorrect. Microsoft Dataverse is a data platform, useful for data management but not specific to fraud detection.

| EXAM FOCUS | "Dynamics 365 Fraud Protection is designed to help protect against fraud." |
| --- | --- |
| CAUTION ALERT | "Remember, Power Apps is not specifically designed for fraud detection." |

## QUESTION 5

Answer – A), C), E)

Option A – Dataverse provides secure storage for customer feedback data, ensuring compliance with GDPR.
Option B – Power Automate is useful for automating workflows but does not directly ensure compliance.
Option C – DLP policies protect data privacy and ensure compliance.
Option D – Power BI is useful for conducting audits but is not a complete solution.
Option E – RBAC controls access to customer data, protecting it from unauthorized access.

| EXAM FOCUS | Use Dataverse for secure storage of feedback data and DLP policies to ensure data privacy compliance. |
| --- | --- |
| CAUTION ALERT | Stay cautious, Power Automate for workflows is useful but doesn't ensure full GDPR compliance. |

## QUESTION 6

Answer – B), C), D)

Option A – Dataverse is useful for managing customer data but does not address cost estimation or budgeting.
Option B – Power BI can be used to estimate implementation costs.
Option C – Developing a budget plan for future upgrades ensures preparedness for enhancements.
Option D – Conducting an ROI analysis using Power BI helps in evaluating the long-term benefits.
Option E – Power Automate is useful for automating tasks but does not address cost estimation or ROI analysis directly.

| EXAM FOCUS | *Estimate implementation costs with Power BI and plan for future upgrades and ROI analysis for thorough financial planning.* |
|---|---|
| CAUTION ALERT | *Remember, Dataverse for data management won't address cost estimation or budgeting effectively.* |

## QUESTION 7

Answer – A), C), E)

Option A – Power Apps can be used to create an initial prototype for the student information system.
Option B – Dataverse is useful for storing student data but not directly related to feedback gathering and iteration.
Option C – Conducting user feedback sessions helps gather input from end users.
Option D – Power Automate is useful for streamlining feedback collection but not directly related to incorporating feedback into the prototype.
Option E – Iterating on the design using user feedback ensures continuous improvement.

| EXAM FOCUS | *Create initial prototypes with Power Apps and conduct user feedback sessions for continuous design improvement.* |
|---|---|
| CAUTION ALERT | *Stay cautious, Dataverse is useful for data storage but won't help with feedback gathering and iteration.* |

## QUESTION 8

Answer – A), B), D)

Option A – Azure Logic Apps can manage scalable integration workflows.
Option B – Implementing Azure Functions ensures serverless and scalable integration.
Option C – Dataverse is useful for data management but not a primary action for managing integration dependencies.
Option D – Developing a microservices architecture using Azure Kubernetes Service ensures scalability and manages dependencies.
Option E – Power Virtual Agents can manage queries but not directly related to integration tools and technologies.

| EXAM FOCUS | *Use Azure Logic Apps for workflows, Azure Functions for serverless integration, and microservices with Kubernetes for scalability.* |
|---|---|
| CAUTION ALERT | *Remember, Power Virtual Agents handle queries, not integration dependencies.* |

## QUESTION 9

Answer – A), B), D)

Option A – Using Azure Policy ensures compliance management and alignment with global privacy laws.
Option B – Implementing GDPR compliance using Azure Information Protection ensures data protection measures.
Option C – Power Automate is useful for data processing but not directly related to compliance with

global privacy laws.
Option D – Conducting regular audits ensures ongoing compliance validation.
Option E – Implementing RBAC ensures access control but not directly related to compliance with global privacy laws.

| EXAM FOCUS | Use Azure Policy for compliance, Azure Information Protection for GDPR, and conduct regular audits for validation. |
| --- | --- |
| CAUTION ALERT | Remember, Power Automate is useful for data processing, not directly for compliance management. |

## QUESTION 10

Answer – A), D)

Option A – Developing a comprehensive QA plan ensures effective QA methodologies and metrics.
Option B – Power Apps for defect tracking is useful but not the main focus.
Option C – Power Automate is useful for automation but not specifically for QA.
Option D – Using Power BI for real-time quality monitoring ensures continuous quality control.
Option E – Regular stakeholder meetings are useful but do not directly address the main challenges.

| EXAM FOCUS | Develop a comprehensive QA plan and use Power BI for real-time quality monitoring. |
| --- | --- |
| CAUTION ALERT | Stay cautious, Power Automate is useful for automation but not specifically for QA. |

## QUESTION 11

Answer – A), C), E)

Option A – Implementing ALM practices using Azure DevOps ensures proper lifecycle management.
Option B – Power Automate can help automate processes but is not critical for lifecycle management.
Option C – Developing a detailed migration and end-of-life plan ensures smooth transition.
Option D – Azure Functions can handle integration tasks but are not directly related to lifecycle management.
Option E – Scheduling regular stakeholder reviews ensures continuous updates and improvements through feedback.

| EXAM FOCUS | Implement ALM with Azure DevOps and develop a detailed migration and end-of-life plan. |
| --- | --- |
| CAUTION ALERT | Stay cautious, Power Automate is useful for automating processes but not critical for lifecycle management. |

## QUESTION 12

Answer – A)

Option A – Correct choice as it integrates Power Apps for custom apps, Power Automate for automation, Power BI for analytics, and utilizes SharePoint Online and Teams for collaboration.
Option B – Azure Synapse Analytics is unnecessary for this solution.
Option C – Dynamics 365 Project Service Automation is not needed if the primary requirement is integration with SharePoint and Teams.

Option D – Similar to C, but without direct integration with SharePoint Online.
Option E – Power Apps adds value for custom app development, which is missing in this option.

| EXAM FOCUS | *"Combine Power Apps, Power Automate, Power BI, SharePoint Online, and Teams for a comprehensive solution."* |
|---|---|
| CAUTION ALERT | *"Don't miss the added value of Power Apps for custom app development."* |

## QUESTION 13

Answer – A), B), D)

Option A – Azure DevOps for project tracking and CI/CD is essential for managing agile projects.
Option B – Daily stand-up meetings are a core practice in agile environments.
Option C – Dynamics 365 is useful for CRM but not directly for agile project management.
Option D – Sprint planning and review meetings are essential for adapting to changes in agile environments.
Option E – AI Builder is beneficial for analytics but not directly related to agile methodologies.

| EXAM FOCUS | *Implement Azure DevOps for project tracking and conduct daily stand-up meetings for agile projects.* |
|---|---|
| CAUTION ALERT | *Stay cautious, relying on tools like Dynamics 365 for agile management might miss agile-specific needs.* |

## QUESTION 14

Answer – A), B), D)

Option A – Developing a data governance charter is essential for defining roles and responsibilities.
Option B – Assigning Data Steward roles in Dataverse is crucial for implementing data stewardship.
Option C – Power BI is useful for monitoring but less critical for implementing data governance measures.
Option D – Azure Policy helps enforce data governance standards across the organization.
Option E – Azure Data Factory is useful for data transformation but less critical for defining roles and responsibilities in data stewardship.

| EXAM FOCUS | *Develop a data governance charter and assign Data Steward roles in Dataverse to enhance data quality and compliance.* |
|---|---|
| CAUTION ALERT | *Stay cautious, focusing only on monitoring tools like Power BI without clear responsibilities can lead to compliance issues.* |

## QUESTION 15

Answer – A), C), D)

Option A – Using Power Automate for inventory updates and notifications reduces customization and simplifies maintenance.
Option B – Extensive customization of Dataverse schema increases maintenance complexity and should be minimized.
Option C – Leveraging Power BI for inventory reporting follows best practices and utilizes existing tools.

Option D – Configuring existing Dataverse entities to fit business needs balances flexibility with standardization.
Option E – Implementing custom APIs adds complexity and should be avoided unless necessary.

| EXAM FOCUS | *Please keep in mind, Power Automate simplifies inventory updates and notifications.* |
|---|---|
| CAUTION ALERT | *Stay cautious, extensively customizing Dataverse schema increases maintenance complexity.* |

## QUESTION 16

Answer – A), B), D)

Option A – Correct choice as Power Apps can display data, Power Automate can handle alerts, Power BI for analytics, and Azure IoT Hub for real-time data ingestion.
Option B – Correct choice as Azure Event Hub is also suitable for real-time data ingestion and Power BI for analytics.
Option C – Power Virtual Agents is not needed for this scenario.
Option D – Correct choice as Azure Logic Apps can handle complex integrations and Power BI for analytics.
Option E – Azure Synapse Analytics is powerful but overkill for this scenario.

| EXAM FOCUS | *"Azure IoT Hub and Power Automate ensure real-time data ingestion and automated alerts."* |
|---|---|
| CAUTION ALERT | *"Don't underestimate the need for real-time data handling; Power Virtual Agents is unnecessary here."* |

## QUESTION 17

Answer – A), B), C)

Option A – Utilizing Dataverse helps centralize data management and track compliance.
Option B – Implementing Power Automate to enforce data governance policies ensures ongoing compliance.
Option C – Using Power BI for compliance reporting and auditing provides detailed insights.
Option D – Developing custom connectors adds unnecessary complexity.
Option E – Configuring role-based security in Power Apps is useful but not a primary strategy for governance.

| EXAM FOCUS | *Use Dataverse for centralized data management, enforce policies with Power Automate, and use Power BI for compliance reporting.* |
|---|---|
| CAUTION ALERT | *Custom connectors increase complexity; focus on integrated solutions.* |

## QUESTION 18

Answer – A), B), E)

Option A – Implementing Azure IoT Hub enables real-time equipment monitoring, integrating disruptive technologies.
Option B – Using Power BI provides real-time process analytics, supporting innovative approaches to

solution design.

Option C – Developing custom APIs integrates third-party systems but might add unnecessary complexity.

Option D – Using Power Virtual Agents supports training but might not directly integrate disruptive technologies.

Option E – Implementing Power Automate streamlines workflows and drives continuous improvement in manufacturing processes.

| EXAM FOCUS | *Azure IoT Hub for real-time monitoring; Power BI for analytics; Power Automate for workflows.* |
|---|---|
| CAUTION ALERT | *Custom APIs add complexity; avoid unless necessary.* |

## QUESTION 19

Answer – C), D), E)

Option A – Implementing data encryption at rest using Dataverse ensures data security but is not essential for all primary requirements.

Option B – Using Power Automate to track data access and modifications supports security but is not essential for compliance or ethical handling.

Option C – Enabling RBAC in Power Apps prevents unauthorized data access.

Option D – Developing a clear data privacy policy and sharing it with customers ensures ethical handling of customer data.

Option E – Using Azure AD for secure user authentication ensures compliance with data protection laws.

| EXAM FOCUS | *Enable RBAC in Power Apps and use Azure AD for secure authentication; share clear data privacy policies.* |
|---|---|
| CAUTION ALERT | *Focusing only on data encryption without proper access control can compromise security.* |

## QUESTION 20

Answer – A), C)

Option A – Correct choice as Indexed columns improve query performance.

Option B – Option sets are for picklists, not for performance optimization.

Option C – Correct choice as Alternate keys improve query efficiency and data integrity.

Option D – Hierarchical relationship settings support data structures but do not directly improve performance.

Option E – Business rules enforce validation but do not optimize performance or support data archival.

| EXAM FOCUS | *"Index columns and use Alternate keys to enhance performance and ensure data integrity for large volumes of data."* |
|---|---|
| CAUTION ALERT | *"Option sets and Business rules do not optimize performance or support data archival processes."* |

## QUESTION 21

Answer – A), E)

Option A – Dataverse ensures secure data management, complying with regulatory standards.
Option B – DLP policies are useful for data protection but are not sufficient alone for compliance.
Option C – Azure Functions are useful for custom data processing but do not directly address data protection or compliance.
Option D – Regular security audits using Azure Security Center are important but are not specific technical measures for regulatory compliance.
Option E – RBAC using Azure AD provides secure access control, ensuring compliance.

| EXAM FOCUS | *Implement Dataverse for secure data management and RBAC using Azure AD.* |
|---|---|
| CAUTION ALERT | *DLP policies are useful but not sufficient for strict regulatory compliance.* |

## QUESTION 22

Answer – A), E)

Option A – Dataverse ensures data integrity and quality with managed data storage.
Option B – Azure Data Factory handles ETL processes but does not directly ensure data governance or analytics.
Option C – Power BI is useful for data visualization but not directly for data integrity or governance.
Option D – DLP policies are important for data protection but do not directly ensure data integrity or analytics.
Option E – Azure Synapse Analytics enables big data analytics and supports data governance and lifecycle management.

| EXAM FOCUS | *Dataverse for storage and Azure Synapse Analytics for big data analytics are crucial for global data management.* |
|---|---|
| CAUTION ALERT | *Ensure to avoid components like Power BI that don't directly support data governance or lifecycle management.* |

## QUESTION 23

Answer – B), D)

Option A – Power BI is useful for dashboards but does not directly address user-centered design or accessibility.
Option B – Implementing screen reader compatibility ensures the portal is accessible to users with visual impairments.
Option C – Power Apps for customizable patient forms is useful but not directly related to user-centered design principles.
Option D – Conducting accessibility testing with patients ensures the design meets the needs of all users.
Option E – Power Automate is useful for backend processes but not directly related to UX design.

| EXAM FOCUS | *You should implement screen reader compatibility and conduct accessibility testing with patients for a user-friendly patient portal.* |
|---|---|
| CAUTION ALERT | *Stay cautious about using Power BI for UX design; it doesn't directly address accessibility needs.* |

## QUESTION 24

Answer – B)

Option A – Manual data entry is inefficient and not feasible for real-time integration.
Option B – Developing a custom connector allows for seamless integration of real-time GPS data into Power Apps, improving tracking and efficiency.
Option C – Power BI is used for data visualization, not for integrating real-time data into Power Apps.
Option D – Azure IoT Hub is powerful for IoT solutions but requires additional complexity and is not as straightforward as a custom connector for this use case.
Option E – Dynamics 365 Field Service is beneficial for managing field operations but does not specifically address real-time GPS data integration into Power Apps.

| EXAM FOCUS | "Develop a custom connector for seamless integration of real-time GPS data." |
|---|---|
| CAUTION ALERT | "Manual data entry is inefficient and not feasible for real-time integration." |

## QUESTION 25

Answer – A), B), C)

Option A – Power BI Streaming Datasets enable real-time analytics on production metrics.
Option B – Azure Machine Learning is used for AI predictions, such as predicting equipment failures.
Option C – Power BI Row-Level Security (RLS) ensures secure access to data.
Option D – Power BI Embedded is useful for custom solutions but not directly related to real-time analytics or AI predictions.
Option E – Azure API Management is essential for handling APIs but not directly related to the primary focus of real-time analytics and AI predictions.

| EXAM FOCUS | Use Streaming Datasets, Azure Machine Learning, and RLS in Power BI for real-time analytics, AI predictions, and secure data access. |
|---|---|
| CAUTION ALERT | Don't rely solely on Power BI Embedded for real-time analytics; it's more suited for custom solutions. |

## QUESTION 26

Answer – A), B), E)

Option A – AI Builder can classify customer inquiries automatically.
Option B – Power Virtual Agents can suggest responses based on the classification.
Option C – Azure Cognitive Services is useful but not necessary if AI Builder and Power Virtual Agents are used.
Option D – Dataverse can store data but is not directly involved in response time improvement.
Option E – Azure Policy ensures ethical AI practices.

| EXAM FOCUS | Implement AI Builder, Virtual Agents, and Azure Policy for classifying inquiries, suggesting responses, and ensuring ethical AI. |
|---|---|
| CAUTION ALERT | Be cautious about using Cognitive Services if AI Builder and Virtual Agents meet the needs. |

## QUESTION 27

Answer – B), D), E)

Option A – Power Platform Admin Center is used for policy enforcement but not directly for disaster recovery.
Option B – Azure Backup is necessary for data protection.
Option C – Power BI is useful for creating dashboards but not directly for enforcing compliance.
Option D – Azure Site Recovery is critical for ensuring high availability.
Option E – Azure DevOps helps in testing and validating recovery plans.

| EXAM FOCUS | *Ensure robust disaster recovery with Azure Backup, Azure Site Recovery, and Azure DevOps for data protection, availability, and validation.* |
|---|---|
| CAUTION ALERT | *Be cautious about relying on Power Platform Admin Center alone for disaster recovery; it's for policy enforcement.* |

## QUESTION 28

Answer – B)

Option A – Azure Logic Apps is used for workflow automation but does not directly handle IoT data integration.
Option B – Azure IoT Hub is designed to connect, monitor, and manage IoT devices, making it ideal for integrating real-time equipment health data with Dynamics 365.
Option C – Azure Data Lake is used for storing large volumes of data, not specifically for IoT integration.
Option D – Azure Machine Learning is used for building and deploying machine learning models, not for IoT data integration.
Option E – Azure Cognitive Services provide AI capabilities but are not designed for IoT data integration.

| EXAM FOCUS | "Azure IoT Hub is ideal for integrating real-time equipment health data with Dynamics 365." |
|---|---|
| CAUTION ALERT | "Azure Data Lake and Machine Learning are not designed for direct IoT integration." |

## QUESTION 29

Answer – A), E)

Option A – Correct. Microsoft Compliance Manager automates compliance tasks and reduces manual effort.
Option B – Incorrect. Third-party cloud solutions may not meet the same compliance standards.
Option C – Incorrect. Azure Policy enforces policies but may not cover all compliance needs.
Option D – Incorrect. Power Automate is useful but not primarily designed for compliance automation.
Option E – Correct. Dataverse provides secure data storage and ensures compliance.

| EXAM FOCUS | *Implement Microsoft Compliance Manager and use Dataverse for secure data storage.* |
|---|---|
| CAUTION ALERT | *Third-party cloud solutions may not meet the same compliance standards.* |

## QUESTION 30

Answer – B), C)

Option A – Incorrect. Power BI is useful for visualization but not the first choice for data integration.
Option B – Correct. Azure Data Factory is designed for managing data from multiple sources.
Option C – Correct. Azure Machine Learning is suitable for developing advanced predictive models.
Option D – Incorrect. Storing data in a shared drive is not secure or scalable.
Option E – Incorrect. Custom applications can be costly and complex compared to using integrated Azure services.

| EXAM FOCUS | *Implement Azure Data Factory for data management and Azure Machine Learning for predictive models.* |
|---|---|
| CAUTION ALERT | *Storing data in a shared drive is not secure or scalable for government data.* |

## QUESTION 31

Answer – B), C)

Option A – Incorrect. While useful, Power Automate alone is not sufficient for training and adoption.
Option B – Correct. Regular training sessions and ongoing support are essential for user adoption.
Option C – Correct. A communication plan that includes success stories and benefits promotes acceptance.
Option D – Incorrect. Ignoring user adoption can lead to project failure.
Option E – Incorrect. While useful, measuring success alone does not promote adoption.

| EXAM FOCUS | *Conduct regular training sessions and develop a communication plan highlighting benefits.* |
|---|---|
| CAUTION ALERT | *Focusing solely on technical deployment can hinder user adoption.* |

## QUESTION 32

Answer – B)

Option A – Azure API Management helps in managing APIs but does not provide seamless integration with Dynamics 365.
Option B – Implementing a Custom Connector allows secure, tailored integration with the third-party identity verification system, ensuring compliance with security standards.
Option C – Power Automate with HTTP connector can work but might not meet stringent security standards as effectively as a Custom Connector.
Option D – Azure Logic Apps can integrate services but may be more complex and less tailored than a Custom Connector.
Option E – Microsoft Graph API is not designed for this type of integration.

| EXAM FOCUS | *"Custom Connectors provide secure, tailored integration with third-party systems."* |
|---|---|
| CAUTION ALERT | *"Power Automate HTTP connector may not meet stringent security standards."* |

## QUESTION 33

Answer – A), B)

Option A – Correct. Azure DevOps helps manage version control and continuous integration.
Option B – Correct. Regular code reviews and following best practices ensure maintainable custom code.
Option C – Incorrect. Focusing solely on new features can lead to unmanageable solutions.
Option D – Incorrect. Power Virtual Agents are useful but not the primary tool for managing complexity.
Option E – Incorrect. Avoiding custom connectors can limit solution capabilities.

| EXAM FOCUS | Use Azure DevOps for version control and regular code reviews to ensure maintainability. |
|---|---|
| CAUTION ALERT | Focusing solely on new features can lead to unmanageable solutions. |

## QUESTION 34

Answer – A), B), D)

Option A – Scheduling migration during non-business hours minimizes operational disruption.
Option B – Azure Data Factory efficiently manages and automates the migration process.
Option C – Real-time validation using Power Automate may be complex and less reliable.
Option D – A rollback strategy ensures recovery in case of failures.
Option E – Azure DevOps is useful for monitoring but not directly for minimizing disruption.

| EXAM FOCUS | Schedule migrations during non-business hours and use Azure Data Factory for automation to minimize disruption. |
|---|---|
| CAUTION ALERT | Real-time data validation using Power Automate can be complex; consider simpler validation methods. |

## QUESTION 35

Answer – A), C), D)

Option A – Parallel branches in Power Automate handle concurrent processes efficiently.
Option B – Azure Logic Apps are useful for complex workflows but may not be necessary.
Option C – Optimizing flow design reduces execution time and improves performance.
Option D – Azure Monitor tracks performance metrics, aiding in resource optimization.
Option E – Scheduling workflows during off-peak hours helps but is not a primary load management strategy.

| EXAM FOCUS | Implement parallel branches in Power Automate and use Azure Monitor to optimize workflows and manage high volumes. |
|---|---|
| CAUTION ALERT | Scheduling workflows during off-peak hours alone is not sufficient; optimize design and monitor performance. |

## QUESTION 36

Answer – C), D), E)

Option A – Batch processing might be useful but is less relevant than real-time considerations.
Option B – Licensing is important but not a primary technical requirement.
Option C – Educational data is regulated and must comply with standards.
Option D – The volume of data from course records and grades is significant.
Option E – Timely updates are crucial for academic records and grade synchronization.

| EXAM FOCUS | "Consider regulated, high-volume, and time-sensitive needs for LMS integration with Dynamics 365." |
| --- | --- |
| CAUTION ALERT | "Batch processing might not meet real-time synchronization requirements for academic records." |

## QUESTION 37

Answer – A), B), E)

Option A – Power BI Premium capacity provides dedicated resources for optimal performance.
Option B – Regional Power BI dataflows ensure efficient data processing and compliance.
Option C – A single central database may violate data residency requirements.
Option D – Azure Data Factory is useful for ETL processes but does not directly address data compliance and performance.
Option E – Regional Power BI workspaces help in managing data compliance and providing optimal performance for regional users.

| EXAM FOCUS | Use Power BI Premium capacity and regional dataflows for compliance and performance. |
| --- | --- |
| CAUTION ALERT | Storing all data in a single central database may violate data residency requirements. |

## QUESTION 38

Answer – A), B)

Option A – Role-based views in Model-Driven Apps personalize the interface for different roles.
Option B – Power BI effectively monitors KPIs related to user experience.
Option C – Collecting feedback manually via emails is inefficient and less continuous.
Option D – Static views for all user roles do not cater to personalized needs.
Option E – AI Builder is useful for predicting and recommending improvements but should complement other strategies.

| EXAM FOCUS | Implement role-based views in Model-Driven Apps and use Power BI to monitor user experience KPIs. |
| --- | --- |
| CAUTION ALERT | Avoid collecting feedback manually via emails; it's inefficient and less continuous. |

## QUESTION 39

Answer – A), B), E)

Option A – Dataverse with GCC compliance ensures that the solution meets government data security regulations, which is essential for healthcare agencies. This ensures that the data handling processes are in line with stringent security requirements.
Option B – AES encryption secures data both at rest and in transit, protecting sensitive healthcare

information from unauthorized access and breaches.

Option C – Using public Wi-Fi for data transmission is highly insecure and poses a significant risk to data security, making it an unsuitable choice.

Option D – Regular security and continuity training for all users is beneficial but does not directly implement secure communication or ensure business continuity on its own.

Option E – Azure Backup and Site Recovery provide robust data protection and enable failover capabilities, ensuring that critical data is backed up and systems can be quickly restored in the event of a disruption.

> **EXAM FOCUS** *Use Dataverse with GCC compliance and AES encryption to ensure data security and continuity.*
> **CAUTION ALERT** *Avoid using public Wi-Fi for data transmission; it poses significant security risks.*

## QUESTION 40

Answer – C)

Option A – Create will add new records but won't update existing ones, leading to potential duplicates.

Option B – Update will modify existing records but won't add new records, missing out on new data entries.

Option C – Upsert will either create new records or update existing ones, ensuring no duplicates and keeping all records current.

Option D – Merge is not typically used for real-time data integration scenarios.

Option E – Aggregate is used for summarizing data, not for updating or inserting records.

> **EXAM FOCUS** *"Upsert operation ensures no duplicates and keeps all records current."*
> **CAUTION ALERT** *"Using only Create or Update might result in data duplication or missed updates."*

## QUESTION 41

Answer – A), B), E)

Option A – Azure Kubernetes Service (AKS) provides scalable container orchestration, essential for managing growth and high availability.

Option B – Azure DevOps enables continuous integration and deployment, supporting rapid feature deployment.

Option C – Power Automate is useful for workflow management but does not specifically address scalable architecture or high performance.

Option D – Azure Functions supports serverless tasks but is not sufficient alone for handling large-scale user growth and modular architecture.

Option E – Dataverse offers centralized and scalable data storage, ensuring high performance and availability.

> **EXAM FOCUS** *Use AKS for scalable container orchestration and Dataverse for centralized data storage.*
> **CAUTION ALERT** *Power Automate is useful but not specific to scalable architecture or high performance.*

## QUESTION 42

Answer – B), C), D)

Option A – Power BI is excellent for visualizing data but not specifically for monitoring solution health and performance.
Option B – Azure Monitor tracks solution health and performance metrics, providing continuous monitoring and proactive issue detection.
Option C – Azure Security Center enhances security monitoring, ensuring the solution remains secure and stable.
Option D – Using Azure DevOps pipelines to schedule regular maintenance and updates ensures that the solution stays up-to-date and stable.
Option E – Relying solely on annual manual reviews is inadequate for maintaining long-term solution stability and performance. Continuous monitoring tools are essential.

| EXAM FOCUS | *Use Azure Monitor and Security Center for tracking, and Azure DevOps for updates.* |
|---|---|
| CAUTION ALERT | *Annual manual reviews are inadequate; use continuous monitoring.* |

## QUESTION 43

Answer – A), B), D)

Option A – Power BI can create custom dashboards tailored to the needs of teachers and administrators.
Option B – Implementing data encryption ensures that student information is protected, maintaining data privacy and security.
Option C – Storing data in an unencrypted format compromises security and is not advisable.
Option D – Power Automate can schedule regular data updates, ensuring that the dashboards reflect the latest information.
Option E – Manual reviews of student performance data are not efficient or scalable, especially for large datasets.

| EXAM FOCUS | *Use Power BI for dashboards and implement data encryption.* |
|---|---|
| CAUTION ALERT | *Unencrypted data storage compromises security and privacy.* |

## QUESTION 44

Answer – A), C)

Option A – Correct. Using the Concurrent function allows multiple formulas to run at the same time, speeding up data processing and improving app responsiveness.
Option B – Incorrect. Adding non-delegable functions can actually slow down performance because they process data locally rather than on the server.
Option C – Correct. Reducing the number of controls decreases the load time and increases performance.
Option D – Incorrect. Applying a control dependency could improve manageability but not necessarily performance.
Option E – Incorrect. Increasing data row limits might degrade performance by loading more data than necessary.

| EXAM FOCUS | "You should use the Concurrent function and reduce controls to enhance Power Apps performance." |
| --- | --- |
| CAUTION ALERT | "Non-delegable functions can slow down performance; focus on server-side processing." |

## QUESTION 45

Answer – A), B), C)

Option A – A comprehensive e-learning platform using Power Apps can provide continuous and accessible training resources.
Option B – Power BI can be used to analyze training effectiveness and user feedback, ensuring continuous improvement.
Option C – A support ticketing system integrated with Dynamics 365 can efficiently manage and resolve user issues.
Option D – Email surveys are less efficient and harder to analyze systematically.
Option E – A one-time training workshop is insufficient for long-term user adoption and proficiency.

| EXAM FOCUS | Develop a comprehensive e-learning platform using Power Apps for continuous training. |
| --- | --- |
| CAUTION ALERT | A one-time training workshop is insufficient for long-term user proficiency. |

## QUESTION 46

Answer – A), B), C)

Option A – Using parallel branches in Power Automate can optimize flow performance by running tasks concurrently.
Option B – Implementing Azure Logic Apps for complex workflows provides more robust and scalable workflow management.
Option C – Monitoring flow performance using Power Platform Admin Center allows for proactive performance management and issue resolution.
Option D – Adding more steps to the flow without optimization will degrade performance and efficiency.
Option E – Ignoring resource management will lead to inefficient use of resources and potential performance bottlenecks.

| EXAM FOCUS | "Use parallel branches in Power Automate and monitor using Power Platform Admin Center." |
| --- | --- |
| CAUTION ALERT | "Adding steps without optimization will degrade performance and efficiency." |

## QUESTION 47

Answer – A), D)

Option A – Implementing Power BI's real-time data streaming capabilities ensures timely monitoring of financial data.
Option B – Using Azure Log Analytics provides detailed insights and monitoring capabilities.
Option C – Skipping usage analysis can lead to missed opportunities for improving the solution based on how users interact with it.
Option D – Creating detailed dashboards in Power BI provides comprehensive reporting and insights for decision-making.

Option E – Ignoring user feedback and behavior analytics can result in overlooking critical insights that can improve user experience and solution effectiveness.

| EXAM FOCUS | "Implement Power BI's real-time data streaming for timely monitoring of financial data." |
|---|---|
| CAUTION ALERT | "Skipping usage analysis can lead to missed improvement opportunities based on user interactions." |

## QUESTION 48

Answer – A), E)

Option A – Correct. Evaluating network latency is crucial as it directly impacts the responsiveness of the app, especially noticeable in overseas locations far from the server.
Option B – Incorrect. While important, Dataverse log capacity is less likely to impact international performance issues directly.
Option C – Incorrect. Local data storage could help but does not directly relate to the immediate performance issues experienced globally.
Option D – Incorrect. The service-level agreement (SLA) might dictate performance standards but does not directly contribute to resolving existing performance issues.
Option E – Correct. Assessing network bandwidth is essential as insufficient bandwidth can lead to slower load times and poor app responsiveness, impacting international users.

| EXAM FOCUS | "Evaluate network latency and bandwidth to address international performance issues and ensure a uniform user experience." |
|---|---|
| CAUTION ALERT | "Dataverse log capacity is important but less likely to impact international performance directly." |

## QUESTION 49

Answer – A), B), C)

Option A – Correct. Azure DevOps provides continuous integration/continuous deployment (CI/CD) and version control, essential for managing customizations and ensuring smooth upgrades.
Option B – Correct. Managed solutions help package and deploy customizations efficiently, reducing the risk of upgrade issues.
Option C – Correct. Regularly reviewing and updating customizations ensures they remain compatible with new releases and features.
Option D – Incorrect. While Dataverse is essential for data management, it does not directly address customization lifecycle management.
Option E – Incorrect. Automated testing is beneficial but does not manage the overall lifecycle or balance custom and out-of-the-box features.

| EXAM FOCUS | "Use Azure DevOps for CI/CD and version control to manage customizations efficiently." |
|---|---|
| CAUTION ALERT | "Remember, failing to review customizations regularly can cause upgrade issues." |

## QUESTION 50

Answer – A), B), D)

Option A – Correct. Power BI dataflows can preprocess data efficiently, reducing the overall energy consumption of data processing activities.

Option B – Correct. Incremental data refresh in Power BI helps reduce processing loads, making data processing more energy-efficient.

Option C – Incorrect. While Azure Functions are efficient, they are more suited for serverless computing rather than directly reducing energy consumption of data processing.

Option D – Correct. A Power BI dashboard displaying real-time sustainability metrics can help track and promote sustainability initiatives.

Option E – Incorrect. While a Power Virtual Agents bot can educate employees, it does not directly reduce energy consumption or track sustainability metrics.

| | |
|---|---|
| **EXAM FOCUS** | *"Implement incremental data refresh in Power BI to reduce processing loads."* |
| **CAUTION ALERT** | *"Remember, focusing only on education without tracking real-time metrics can limit effectiveness."* |

# ABOUT THE AUTHOR

Step into the world of Anand, and you're in for a journey beyond just tech and algorithms. While his accolades in the tech realm are numerous, including penning various tech-centric and personal improvement ebooks, there's so much more to this multi-faceted author.

At the heart of Anand lies an AI enthusiast and investor, always on the hunt for the next big thing in artificial intelligence. But turn the page, and you might find him engrossed in a gripping cricket match or passionately cheering for his favorite football team. His weekends? They might be spent experimenting with a new recipe in the kitchen, penning down his latest musings, or crafting a unique design that blends creativity with functionality.

While his professional journey as a Solution Architect and AI Consultant, boasting over a decade of AI/ML expertise, is impressive, it's the fusion of this expertise with his diverse hobbies that makes Anand's writings truly distinctive.

So, as you navigate through his works, expect more than just information. Prepare for stories interwoven with passion, experiences peppered with life's many spices, and wisdom that transcends beyond the tech realm. Dive in and discover Anand, the author, the enthusiast, the chef, the sports lover, and above all, the storyteller.